Democracy's Lawyer

SOUTHERN BIOGRAPHY SERIES

Andrew Burstein, Series Editor

November 7, 2015

To John Bray,

With appreciation for our
shared interest in Tennessee history
and our Middle Tennessee heritage —

Best wishes —

Robert Heller

Democracy's Lawyer

FELIX GRUNDY
OF THE OLD SOUTHWEST

J. RODERICK HELLER III

Louisiana State University Press
Baton Rouge

Published by Louisiana State University Press
Copyright © 2010 by Louisiana State University Press
All rights reserved
Manufactured in the United States of America

Designer: LAURA ROUBIQUE GLEASON
Typeface: GARAMOND PREMIER PRO
Printer: MCNAUGHTON & GUNN
Binder: DEKKER BOOKBINDING

Frontispiece image is from the Library of Congress, Prints
and Photographs Division, LC-USZ62-21283.

Library of Congress Cataloging-in-Publication Data
Heller, J. Roderick (John Roderick), 1937–
 Democracy's lawyer : Felix Grundy of the Old Southwest / J. Roderick Heller III.
  p. cm.
 Includes bibliographical references and index.
 ISBN 978-0-8071-3588-4 (cloth : alk. paper) 1. Grundy, Felix, 1777–1840. 2. Legislators—United States—Biography. 3. United States. Congress. Senate—Biography. 4. Lawyers—Southwest, Old—Biography. 5. Jackson, Andrew, 1767–
1845—Friends and associates. 6. Attorneys general—United States—Biography.
7. Southwest, Old—Biography. 8. Tennessee—Biography. 9. Kentucky—Biography. 10. United States—History—1783–1865—Biography. I. Title.
 E340.G8H45 2010
 328.73092—dc22
 [B]

                         2009030246

ISBN 978-0-8071-4560-9 (pbk. : alk. paper) — ISBN 978-0-8071-3742-0 (pdf)

The paper in this book meets the guidelines for permanence
and durability of the Committee on Production Guidelines
for Book Longevity of the Council on Library Resources. ∞

CONTENTS

ILLUSTRATIONS

ACKNOWLEDGMENTS

*T*his book had its genesis more than forty years ago in a conversation with Professor Charles Sellers at Princeton University. Sellers, well on his way to eminence, was affable and gracious to a college sophomore intrigued by the historian's craft. When I mentioned that my family owned several letters written by Felix Grundy, an ancestor, the professor remarked that Grundy was a significant politician who, despite a biography by Joseph Parks in 1940, awaited a more searching study by someone who had access to more Grundy correspondence than had been available to Parks. I am grateful to Professor Sellers for inspiring this book and for his graciousness many years ago.

Research is one of the great pleasures of writing a book. This is particularly so for a biography, for which the quest for original letters and related documents invariably requires innumerable trips to county courthouses and libraries, large and small, and visits with the many people there who make assisting researchers a priority. I am indebted to those many helpful and interested curators and administrators. I wish particularly to thank the staff members at the Filson Club in Louisville, Kentucky, the Tennessee State Library and Archives in Nashville, the Southern Historical Collection at Chapel Hill, and the Library of Congress. These wonderful repositories contain manuscript and archival material that provided the backbone of this work, and I was the beneficiary of splendid assistance over many years. Darla Brock, Susan Gordon, Marylin Hughes, and Tom Kanon of the Manuscripts section of the Tennessee State Library and Archives provided more assistance than I can fully acknowledge. In Kentucky and Tennessee, Angela Calhoun, Mark Grundy, Robert Hicks, James Redford, Lewis Laska, Justin and Olivia Stelter, Margie Thessin, and Rick Warwick provided enthusiastic support as well as research assistance. I also am particularly grateful to Caitlin Fitts for her detailed research in Tennessee newspapers and to Deborah Cooney for her help in exploring innumerable manuscript collections. Caitlin and Deborah both brought extraordinary care, talent, and diligence to their work.

Although I refer first to research, which was particularly satisfying to me, I do not mean to minimize the assistance of the many others who supported the writing of this book. Dick Moe, Barbara Oberg, and Sean Wilentz provided early encouragement, and Stephen Aron and Richard Ellis offered thoughtful guidance to an unknown but interested student of the period in which they have great knowledge. I am grateful for the comments and constructive suggestions of those who read all or parts of the manuscript, including Karna and Dick Bodman, Bill Cooper, Bob and Jane Geniesse, Howard Hillman, Mike Holt, Tom Kanon, Alan Quinby, Ridley Wills, and Irene and Alan Wurtzel. I am particularly in debt to my dear friend Bill Lilley, who read two drafts and made invaluable suggestions. I also want to thank Marge Mulhall, Dora Macia, and Anna Philpot for their continued good cheer and skill in typing the manuscript; in the computer age I found great satisfaction in writing on a yellow pad.

Illustrations obviously add flavor to a biography, and I appreciate the thoughtfulness and assistance of those who helped locate and assemble the portraits, copies, and other materials included here. Jim Hoobler and Strawberry Luck at the Tennessee State Museum, John Holtzapple and Tom Price at the James K. Polk Museum, Jerry and John Porter and Peggy, Helen, and James Fleming in Columbia, Tennessee, and my brother, Winder, went to great lengths in this respect.

Perhaps most important, I want to thank my family and friends for encouraging the writing of this book and for persevering with me. My daughters, Anne and Lynn, and my son, Rick, and their spouses, Tom Nagorski, Tom Inglesby, and May Heller, read all or parts of the book and could not have been more supportive. Special appreciation and love to my wife, Kay, an excellent historian herself, for her constant encouragement and innovative ideas.

Democracy's Lawyer

INTRODUCTION

*F*elix Grundy "could stand on a street corner and talk the cobble-stones into life." These words from a nineteenth-century Nashvillian echoed contemporaneous assessments of the Old Southwest's greatest criminal lawyer. A well-known Tennessee historian and judge declared that he had listened to Henry Clay and other splendid orators but that Felix Grundy was the greatest advocate he had ever heard. Another judge called Grundy the most lordly man he ever beheld.[1]

Who was this most lordly man, largely forgotten today but widely acclaimed in his lifetime? History has recognized him principally as one of the first radical political reformers in the fledgling United States. Born in Virginia, Grundy lived when America was young, as its institutions and culture were being formed and solidified. Growing up on the frontier, he lost three brothers in Indian wars and became Henry Clay's great rival in early Kentucky, bringing an egalitarian perspective to banking, land, and judicial issues. After serving at thirty-one as the third chief justice of Kentucky, he moved to Tennessee in 1808. Soon elected to Congress, he was so identified with the War of 1812 that a popular slogan attributed the war to "Madison, Grundy and the Devil." A controversial pro-debtor reformer during the Panic of 1819, Grundy became a powerful senator during the presidency of Andrew Jackson, with whom he had a complex relationship for more than thirty years. He served as attorney general and was a close adviser to President Martin Van Buren. After Grundy's death, James K. Polk, his law student and political protégé, became the eleventh president of the United States.

Revolutionary ideals formed the bedrock of Grundy's political philosophy. Grundy grew up and received his education as part of the first post-Revolutionary generation. It was a time when fundamental ideas about government were debated and implemented and when many doubted that the American experiment could succeed. Like almost everyone else in early Kentucky and Tennessee, Grundy accepted the tenets of Jeffersonian Republicanism, believing in liberty and equality, states' rights, minimal government, low or no taxation, and legislative supremacy; he maintained Jeffersonian views throughout his life.

Grundy's dominating belief—equality in access to power—motivated many of his political battles. In his view, aristocratic federalism threatened the principles of the Revolution. His suspicion of privileges for the exclusive few sprang from deep roots. No leveler, Grundy represented and identified with the self-made agrarian entrepreneur; he opposed fetters on freedom of opportunity, whether from government or entrenched economic elites.

Although he was widely known as a politician, Grundy achieved greater fame as a lawyer. He was the first great criminal defense lawyer of the southern frontier—the area known then as the Old Southwest, comprising Kentucky, Tennessee, Alabama, Mississippi, and adjacent areas. No one knows exactly how many defendants charged with first-degree murder he saved from the hangman (the highest reported number is 184), but no one doubted his way with a jury. Criminal trials provided entertainment in early-nineteenth-century America, and Grundy's mere appearance in a courtroom attracted spectators from miles around. "I have heard Felix Grundy speak a hundred times," said one admirer. "If he were alive I would go a thousand miles to hear him again."[2]

A believer in legislative supremacy, Grundy inaugurated a new style of advocacy. The people spoke through the legislature, and he became one of the first lawyers to try to achieve legal aims through legislation, espousing the give and take of bargain and compromise. He chaired committees, wrote and negotiated statutes, counted votes, and looked for the middle ground. Josiah Quincy, a political enemy, described Grundy as a "perfect political jockey," "as good humored as he was cunning." Martin Van Buren, the Little Magician, recognized Grundy's "fondness for the strategical branch of political warfare." More than in Washington, however, Grundy displayed his political skills in the state legislatures of Kentucky, from 1800 to 1805, and Tennessee, from 1819 to 1825, where he led bitterly contested efforts to bring about political reform.[3]

His political and legal reputations were based in part on personal characteristics. Grundy was handsome and impressive, of the "usual" height of five feet eight or five feet nine. Light brown hair with reddish tints crowned a notably high, broad forehead, which, according to Tennessee folklore, marked brainpower. He had a firm, long jaw, a straight nose, and a ruddy complexion. Lively, deep-set blue eyes dominated his face. Self-confident and affable, with a "brilliant intellect," Grundy easily won friends and forged extraordinary rapport with juries.

Grundy's drive and ambition matched his affability, brains, and wit. He worked hard, juggled conflicting demands, and provided leadership in several fields. This youngest son of an immigrant wagon master shared the ambition for wealth and position common to the restless and rough settlers of Kentucky and Tennessee. He bought lots in new towns, acquired farms, and speculated in raw land. He dressed well and built Grundy Place, the first great house in downtown Nashville. Yet he always appeared in good-humored control. He never fought a duel, and if he gambled or raced horses, history has failed to record it.

Grundy's significance, however, rests on more than his activities or his eminence. Born five months after Lexington and Concord, he epitomized the "New American" of the first post-Revolutionary generation. The Revolution brought about a new kind of popular politics and democratic officeholder. Colonial America was hierarchal, and even Jefferson expected political leadership to continue to come from an upper class destined for service. The new order, to the discomfort of the founding fathers, produced feisty and nontraditional leaders. Frequently from what was then the West, and lawyers more often than not, ambitious for wealth and position, they believed in and participated in an entrepreneurial capitalism that dominated early-nineteenth-century America. Grundy and some of his fellow politicians initiated a political system in which birth mattered less, press support counted, and campaigning became the norm. They took a theory and put it into practice.[4]

From Washington in 1812, Grundy reported to his daughter that despite efforts to depict him as a Virginian, he was a westerner. Traditional elitists shuddered. John Randolph, who would describe himself as "an aristocrat; I love liberty, I hate equality," disdained the West as a yahoos' paradise of "Clay, Grundy and Company." Alexander Hanson, of Maryland, referred to Grundy's "lawyer-like dexterity" and "cunning" and sneered at Tennessee as a "high-civilized, polished and refined state." The Jeffersonian Randolph and Federalist Hanson belonged to a passing social and political elite that would not last in the democratic and untidy egalitarianism that characterized the new states of the West. Talented and largely self-made, Grundy represented and derived his political bearings from the people.[5]

Slavery stands out as the unresolved contradiction in Grundy's egalitarian perspective. The issue did not surface as a significant political question until he served as a U.S. senator in the early 1830s. Grundy, a slave owner, took the position then and thereafter that his mentor George Nicholas articulated in 1799: slavery should not have been introduced in America, but it could not be eradicated without unacceptable turmoil and disruption. As the attorney general of the United States, Grundy in 1839, seeking to avoid a legal controversy that would only be resolved in the U.S. Supreme Court in 1841, gave the opinion that the schooner *Amistad* and the Africans who had taken over the ship to escape slavery should be returned to Spain. Grundy's acceptance of human bondage stands in contrast to his otherwise uncompromising libertarian and egalitarian positions.

Grundy's career encompassed the period when the American democratic experiment took hold and slavery became more entrenched. Politicians enthusiastically joined in the push for wealth and power that characterized a country still very much in its formative period. Grundy's life affords a splendid window into this age of exuberance and expansion.

PART I

Frontier Roots

I

THE GREAT ROAD

This combination of poverty and pride set the North Britons
squarely apart.

—David Hackett Fischer

Felix Grundy was born on September 11, 1775, in Berkeley County,
Virginia. Grundy's birth near the Great Road, to enterprising parents
ever questing westward, and five months after the outbreak of the Revolution,
almost perfectly symbolized the enterprise and mobility of this "New American" of the post-Revolutionary generation.

Grundy's frontier heritage had deep roots. His mother, Elizabeth Burkham,
came from yeoman stock and was of the fourth generation in the Chesapeake
colonies. Her great-grandfather, Roger Burkham, arrived in Virginia in 1667
as an indentured servant, probably from southwestern England. In Somerset County, Maryland, by December 1670, within four years of its founding,
Roger planted tobacco on 230 acres near the Nanticoke River, served as under-
sheriff of the county at least in 1687 and 1697, and died in 1702. His son John
and grandson Roger, however, could not maintain this modest status, and by
1725 the namesake grandson had sold the last of the immigrant's holdings.[1]

Attracted by inexpensive land, Roger Burkham, accompanied by his wife,
Catherine, several children, and probably a brother, Joseph, and his family, left
Maryland in approximately 1735 for the expanding frontier—in this case the
Shenandoah Valley, of Virginia. Roger, constable at the organization of Freder-
ick County in 1743, lived at least until 1777 near what is now Berkeley Springs,
West Virginia, north and west of Winchester, the center of the lower Shenan-
doah Valley. The heavily forested county was sparsely populated, with only
2,173 white and 340 black inhabitants in 1755.[2]

Roger Burkham appears to have been a tough man. An enlisted man in
Washington's Virginia Regiment in 1758, he was described as "well-made," five
feet seven and one-half, with a fair complexion and black hair. His name ap-

pears often in Frederick County records, principally in lawsuits against adjoining landowners. All in all, the records suggest an active man at home on the frontier who was quick to protect his rights and not always a pleasant neighbor.[3]

Limited evidence indicates that Roger was a close relation, probably an uncle, of Elizabeth Burkham's and that he raised her after the death of her father, Joseph. Born about 1733 in Maryland, Elizabeth had one sister, Catherine. There are no records or descriptions of her early life; the one reference is with respect to a survey for her and her sister of four hundred acres on the north fork of Sleepy Creek, in Berkeley County, in 1751. Her education was rudimentary at best; a typical product of the frontier, she signed her will and other documents with a mark.[4]

Elizabeth Burkham met and married George Grundy in her early or mid-twenties. A political description of Felix Grundy in 1838, presumably reflecting his input, stated that George Grundy had settled in Virginia "shortly after his emigration from England." The Grundy family hailed from Bury, in Lancashire, in the north of England, and it has been assumed that George Grundy or his father came from that area. Exactly where Grundy, a wagon master, and Elizabeth Burkham met is unknown. It is possible that the British hired George Grundy to haul supplies after Indian hostilities broke out in 1754 and that George and Elizabeth first met along what has been called the Great Road. Originally an Indian trail, the Great Road reached from Philadelphia to Lancaster County, Pennsylvania, in the 1720s, but by 1760 it stretched through the Shenandoah Valley to near Bedford, Virginia, and on to Salisbury, North Carolina. Freight traffic was heavy, and the wagoner was a constant feature of roadway life. Six-horse teams drew heavy German-built Conestoga wagons.[5]

George Grundy settled in the Shenandoah Valley, which owed its eighteenth-century development to the Scots-Irish and, to a much lesser extent, the Germans. The Scots-Irish, who drove the settlement of the entire southern backcountry, fostered a unique environment. Largely Presbyterian, loyal to family and clan and formidably tough, they were characterized by a fierce independence, a commitment to honor, and a strong aversion to governmental control. Descended largely from lowland Scots who had originally moved to the north of Ireland beginning in the late sixteenth century, these hardy immigrants came to the American colonies in family groups to escape both economic and religious discrimination. Their numbers are hard to gauge; the historically accepted figure has been about two hundred thousand from 1717 to the Revolution. They have been grouped with emigrants from the north of England and other northern Britons in a Borderer culture that had a profound influence on American political and social development. "This combination of poverty and pride," writes David Hackett Fischer, "set the North Britons squarely apart from other English speaking people in the American colonies. Border emigrants demanded to be treated with respect even when dressed in rags. Their humble origins did not create the spirit of subordination which others expected of 'lower ranks.' This fierce and stubborn pride would be a cultural fact of high importance in the American region which they came to dominate." Felix Grundy lived most of his life in Kentucky and Tennessee, where Scots-Irish influence predominated. His wife, Ann Rodgers, and her second cousin John C. Calhoun descended from immigrants arriving in 1727 from northern Ireland. The two Tennessee presidents with whom Grundy was so identified, Andrew Jackson and James K. Polk, were Scots-Irish as well. Grundy, presumably of northern Briton stock himself and of the same cultural group as the Scots-Irish, thus grew up and participated in this powerful, if rough-and-tumble, culture of independence and honor.[6]

George Grundy succeeded in colonial America as an energetic frontier farmer and businessman. Like most immigrants, he wanted land. On July 25, 1757, he purchased 159 acres in Bedford County, Virginia, a recently formed county in southern Virginia not far from modern Roanoke. The county stood on the outer reaches of settlement, at the point where the Great Road turned south toward North and South Carolina. George Grundy, whose name appears regularly in the earliest county documents, bought and sold land, ultimately owning 582 acres, and kept cattle, with his mark registered in Bedford County in 1761. He also raised racehorses.[7]

In mid-eighteenth-century Virginia, where almost everyone farmed, George Grundy stood out as an entrepreneur. Family chronicles claim that he owned and operated wagons for hire, and this is supported by the extent of his legal proceedings in counties in which a wagon master would have operated. An active litigant, he appeared as a plaintiff in indebtedness claims in courts in Bedford County and other counties along the Great Road, with one claim brought in the name of "George Grundy and Company." On May 22, 1764, and again on March 24, 1773, he was licensed by Bedford County to keep an ordinary at his house. Taverns and ordinaries, whose importance is reflected in the extent of county regulation, performed a variety of functions on the frontier, serving not only as hotels and restaurants but also as local meeting centers and country stores. George Grundy ran a grinding mill as well. He had apprentices; one complained in July 1766 and successfully requested that he be bound to a new master.[8]

Burgeoning family responsibilities partially motivated Grundy. George and Elizabeth Burkham Grundy had at least ten children who reached adulthood, of whom the first nine were sons. William appears to have been born in 1756, and Joseph, John, and George Jr. between 1758 and 1762. Four more sons arrived while the Grundys still lived in Bedford County—Robert about 1764, Samuel in approximately 1768, Guardum about 1769, and Charles in 1772.[9]

Thus we have a picture of George Grundy—wagon master, miller and innkeeper, owner of 582 acres, and racehorse fancier. Speaking of his early life many years later, Felix Grundy described a family of "affluence" before the loss of his father. Why, then, did George Grundy decide in the early or mid-1770s to pull up stakes and move first to northern Virginia and then to Kentucky?

Western lands and the fortunes to be made from them lured George Washington and many other Virginians in this period. Colonel Richard Callaway, brother of a neighbor of George Grundy's and a leader in Kentucky before his death at Indian hands in 1780, expressed the widespread sentiment that "there is not any better way to make money than by land." A Virginia clergyman in 1775 noted "what a buzzel is this amongst people about kentuck," and John Breckinridge in 1786 put it simply: "Kentucky is the greatest field for speculation, I believe, in the world." Conversation with the Callaways and others about Kentucky could only have been provocative to a man concerned about the future of seven or eight sons—and to some of his sons as well.[10]

Political considerations also made a western move attractive. Several Grundy sons were of military age in 1776. George Grundy was an English-born immigrant who had prospered in the colonies. The absence of any reference to Grundy sons in Revolutionary militia lists is suggestive. They may not have been Tories, but they do not appear to have been ardent patriots either. Whatever the cause, George Grundy left Bedford County about April 1775, after taking title to the four hundred acres on Sleepy Creek originally surveyed for Elizabeth and Catherine Burkham in 1751. He took his family and at least three racehorses to Berkeley County, where Roger Burkham still lived. Berkeley County recognized the Grundys as a family of standing. On December 9, 1776, the Commonwealth of Virginia named George Grundy one of four new justices in Berkeley County.[11]

Felix Grundy was born shortly after the move to Berkeley County, in the same area where his mother grew up and his parents probably met. The actual date, quite surprisingly, is uncertain. Grundy's tombstone lists his birth as September 11, 1777, and biographies refer to that birth date. However, it is clearly recorded in his daughter's Bible that he was born on September 11, 1775; his first obituary, in the December 21, 1840, *Nashville Union,* gives the year of his birth as 1775: and "Leonidas," at the time of Grundy's first electoral bid in Tennessee, in June 1811, wrote that the candidate was then thirty-five years old. The earlier birth date, moreover, is more consistent with all early records relevant to determination of his age. If Grundy was in fact born in 1775, not 1777, why did a birth date of 1777 appear in writings and, more importantly, on his tombstone? The most likely explanation is an uncorrected mistake that was perpetuated thereafter. While this is not wholly satisfactory, the matter almost certainly will never be fully resolved.[12]

Whatever the reason for the discrepancy, it appears clear that Felix Grundy was born in Berkeley County on September 11, 1775. No records survive of his earliest years. Years later, as a member of the U.S. Senate, Grundy visited Berkeley County and his childhood home, finding only a dilapidated stone chimney.[13]

Grundy's background not only shaped his attitudes but also separated him from the colonial elite. The aristocratic culture of the Chesapeake included a disdain for the mores and lifestyle of the frontier and the bumptious individualism of the northern Briton immigrants. No less a personage than George Washington expressed such a view when he traveled in 1748 and 1749 through the area where the Burkhams had settled more than ten years earlier. He described the Shenandoah Valley as "exceeding Rich and Fertile" and the "finest part of Virginia." The early inhabitants, however, fell short: When visiting a justice of the peace in Hedgesville in 1749, Washington dined with "neither a Cloth upon the Table nor a Knife to eat with." Germans were "as ignorant a set of People as the Indians," and the remaining settlers were "a parcel of Barbarian's and an uncouth set of People." The Burkhams, who in 1749 lived twenty-five miles farther west, would almost certainly have been in the group Washington found so distasteful.[14]

Washington's disdainful viewpoint, perpetuated during his lifetime, foreshadowed the changes that would mark the post-Revolutionary world of Felix Grundy. Washington grew up in and would personify a world whose political leaders belonged to the gentry. He would never understand or appreciate the rough-hewn world of the frontier, where individualistic egalitarianism would take deep hold. Felix Grundy would represent a more egalitarian political system than Washington could find acceptable. His frontier upbringing and participation in a Scots-Irish culture of proud independence separated him from the eastern colonial elite.

Grundy's birth date was also symbolically significant. The Battle of Lexington and Concord, in April 1775, had roiled America, and George Washington had joined the American forces outside Boston. Grundy would grow up in a period characterized by change and experimentation and then by celebration of Revolutionary achievement. Much of his early political life would be marked by the question of whether the next generation would be capable of carrying on what the increasingly mythologized forebears of 1776 had created.

2

THE DARK AND BLOODY GROUND

The first indelible impression ... would be the sight of my eldest brother bleeding and dying under the wounds inflicted by the tomahawk and scalping-knife.

—Felix Grundy

The Revolution may have transformed America, but the Grundy family showed little interest in Revolutionary change. In the midst of the war George and Elizabeth Grundy and their nine sons left Berkeley County and moved deeper into the Virginia frontier.

Despite his designation as a justice by the Commonwealth of Virginia, there is no evidence that George Grundy performed any services as such. By June 1778 the Grundys, with young Felix in tow, had moved to Augusta County, Virginia, where George Grundy purchased a four-hundred-acre farm at Simpson's Creek, near present-day Bridgeport, West Virginia. The Virginia frontier of the 1770s was not for the fainthearted. Border warfare intensified as the Revolutionary War accelerated, and Ohio-based Shawnees, aligned with the British, conducted raiding parties in 1777 and 1778. In mid-June 1778 Indians attacked William Grundy and two friends as they were returning home. The two friends escaped, but William did not, dying of wounds from tomahawk and scalping knife.[1]

The Grundy family remained at Simpson's Creek until 1779. Felix's only sister, Mary, was born there on August 29, 1778. When young Felix was four and one-half years old, in 1780, the Grundy family traveled down the Ohio River to Kentucky, among the first settlers of Virginia's western outpost. It is unclear whether this move was attributable to the death of William, a predetermined plan, or passage of the Virginia Land Act in 1779.[2]

Kentucky was the promised land by 1780. Early visitors rhapsodized about the beauty of the landscape, the luxuriant growth of cane and trees, and the abundance of wildlife. Speculators from contending North Carolina and Virginia groups trumpeted the undeniable attraction of these beautiful and uninhabited lands. When Virginia successfully asserted its control, well-connected Virginians received grants for valuable lands. Virginia made Kentucky a county and then enacted the Land Act of 1779. The complicated act provided 400 acres for each person who could prove settlement on land in Kentucky before January 1, 1778, plus preemption and purchase rights for an additional 1,000 acres. Settlers during 1778 were entitled to a 400-acre preemption at a price of forty pounds, in depreciated currency, per 100 acres. Those arriving in 1779 and after could only purchase land through Virginia land offices or, if they were soldiers with proven service, through bounty warrants. Brisk trade in treasury and military warrants ensued, with purchases by both settlers and land speculators.[3]

Acquisition of fertile acreage in Kentucky was only for the courageous and persistent or the well connected. More people talked of going to distant Kentucky than actually went, and Tories, with their own reasons to flee the Revolution, represented a significant percentage of immigrants. The continuing Indian menace required constant vigilance. While Indians did not inhabit Kentucky, they knew it as a hunting ground of great bounty and opposed its settlement.[4]

Two main routes led to Kentucky from the East, both difficult. The Appalachian Mountains, rising to more than three thousand feet in elevation, were largely unbroken by gaps suitable for travel. The sole land route to Kentucky traversed the famous Cumberland Gap, which was only wide enough for a packhorse. Travelers took the Great Road to Fort Chiswell, near what is now Wytheville, Virginia, and then continued through an extension of the road through the Gap. The trip was long, taking at least thirty-five to forty days, and dangerous, with Indians a preoccupation. To reach Kentucky before the growing season, settlers traveled for the most part in winter, enduring cold, snow, rain, and other difficulties.[5]

The other route took settlers down the Ohio River. Easier and shorter, this route was more expensive and to some extent open only to the more well-to-do. It too involved great risk. River disasters could lead to the loss of all possessions, but as on the overland route, Indians constituted the real danger. One pioneer remembered a keelboat floating down the Ohio River with every person on it dead. On October 3, 1779, Indians near the Little Miami River killed Colonel David Rogers, who was traveling to New Orleans with military supplies, and most of his fifty men.[6]

Notwithstanding the dangers, in 1780 the Grundys embarked on the river route from the Monongahela River. The winter of 1779–80 was severe, called the "Hard Winter," and the Grundys remained icebound until at least March

1780. They almost certainly traveled to Kentucky with other family members and friends, including Elizabeth Grundy's sister, Catherine Allen, and her husband, William. The year 1780 saw a large-scale influx of settlers, with almost three hundred large boats carrying families arriving at the Falls of the Ohio by early May.[7]

The trip down the Ohio engendered nervousness and fear. Although Grundy left no record, his trip would have been similar to that of his close friend John Rowan, who traveled with five other families to the Falls in 1782, when he was nine years old. The river passed through an unbroken wilderness inhabited only by hostile Indians. The crude flat-bottomed boats had been constructed with "sides higher than a man's head, of plank too thick to be perforated by a rifle ball, and with port holes for defensive operations in case of attack." While the Rowans arrived safely, three families traveling with them were less fortunate: soon after disembarking at Limestone Creek (Maysville) they were massacred.[8]

The Falls of the Ohio, where the Grundys arrived, became the base of operations for George Rogers Clark, the most significant figure in early Kentucky. In 1778 Clark, an ambitious military leader and land speculator, built a stockade on Corn Island, which, moved to the south side of the river and enlarged, became Louisville. The Grundys, who were among the earliest settlers, stayed at a station on Beargrass Creek in Jefferson County, one of three counties into which Virginia divided Kentucky in May 1780. They lived in an isolated and hostile world. John Floyd, an early surveyor and the first militia chief in Jefferson County, advised Governor Thomas Jefferson in January 1781 that he had only about four hundred men able to bear arms in the county. A tiny group, indeed, in what today comprises most of western Kentucky.[9]

Conditions were primitive. We have no description of the Grundys' station, but it must have been like Harrodsburg four years earlier, "a poor town ... row or two of smoky cabins, dirty women, men with their britch clouts, greasy hunting shirts, leggings and Moccasins. I there ate some of the first corn raised in the country, but little of it, as they had a very poor way to make it into meal; we learnt to eat wild meat, without bread or salt." Settlers built small, one-story log cabins with no windows and a single door and chimney.[10]

Security concerns dominated. What little governmental authority existed could not provide protection against the continuing Indian menace. In 1780, the year of the Grundys' arrival, John Floyd wrote Jefferson that "hardly one wek pass without some one being scalped between this [place] and the Falls and I almost got too cowardly to travell about the woods without company." In

April 1781 Floyd reported that all settlers were forced to live in forts and that notwithstanding all precautions, forty had been killed or taken, and a number wounded, since January. In 1781 many settlers returned to Virginia and other eastern states, and 1782 became known as the year of blood. Floyd himself died at Indian hands in 1783.[11]

The lack of adequate security cost Virginia support, but a deeper hostility to the Richmond government also emerged. Newcomers learned how much land well-connected Virginians had claimed. Aside from the extent of acreage taken up, a relatively small number of individuals obtained large tracts, with eight of them receiving more than two hundred thousand acres each. The inequitable land system gave rise to resentment, protests, and a "new state" movement, with little result. George, John, and Joseph Grundy signed two revealing petitions to the Continental Congress in the spring of 1780. The first, dated May 15, 1780, reflected strong animosity toward Virginia and called for a separate state. The second, dated May 1780, is particularly telling. The signers had ventured into the wilds "in daily jeopardy of being inhumanly murdered," only to find that almost the "Whole of the lands . . . are Engrossed into the hands of a few . . . the greater part of which live at ease in the internal parts of Virginia." The signers would gladly have returned to the East, but having expended "the greater part of their fortunes," they could not. Now "drove to the Extremity," they only had three choices: remain in Virginia and "become Slaves to the Engrossers of Lands and to the Court of Virginia"; travel down the Ohio and settle on lands owned by Spain; or cross the Ohio River and settle on Indian lands. The signers requested permission to take possession of the Indian side of the Ohio and to govern themselves, "subject to the United States at large and no other State or power whatsoever." The Continental Congress never responded.[12]

We do not know how fully George, John, and Joseph Grundy subscribed to these anti-Virginia sentiments or the extent to which they expressed their outrage to young Felix. George Grundy, however, a strong man in an environment demanding toughness, came from a different background than the well-connected Virginia landholders, and it is likely that he and his sons regularly voiced their anger. Felix Grundy consistently displayed strong opposition to any favoritism in governmental policy for the well-positioned few, whether in access to land, banking credit, or tariff protection. We have no direct evidence, but his family's experience almost certainly had a formative effect on Felix Grundy's strong opposition to preferential treatment.

The recently arrived Grundys learned all too soon how anguishing life in early Kentucky could be. The British and Indians struck at relatively defenseless

Kentucky. After taking several stations and almost 350 prisoners while George Rogers Clark was in the Illinois country, British Captain Henry Bird retreated toward Detroit. Clark returned and by the end of July had assembled a force of approximately 1,000 men to pursue the largely Indian force. On August 8, 1780, Clark's force reached the Shawnee village of Pechuwe (Piqua), where it engaged in a hard-fought battle of three hours against approximately 300 warriors, the largest Revolutionary War battle west of the Appalachians. Indians more than held their own until Clark's small cannon and superior numbers prevailed. Clark lost 14 men killed and 13 wounded, compared with an Indian loss supposedly three times greater. The dead included "Joseph Grundey."[13]

Despite the magnate-weighted land system and the loss of a second son, the entrepreneurial George Grundy rose to the opportunities in Kentucky. First, in the spring of 1781, he received a license to operate an ordinary and leased four hundred acres at Dowdall's Station, on the Salt River. Since his lease carried the right to work the ferry on the Salt River, George operated a ferry and ordinary on the Wilderness Road, the main overland route west to Louisville from the Cumberland Gap.[14]

Second, George and his sons began their land acquisitions, focusing on an area sometimes called the "Outer Bluegrass." They bought astutely. In a coordinated series of entries, George Grundy and his son John filed for land along Beech Fork and Cartwright Creek between present-day Springfield and Bardstown, Kentucky. The Grundys purchased land on or not far from the Wilderness Road, facilitating the operation of taverns and positioning the family to ship agricultural commodities south by water and livestock east by road. Beech Fork and Cartwright Creek, although not insulated from attacks, were south and west of principal areas of Indian activity.[15]

The Cartwright Creek properties are located approximately twelve miles east of Bardstown, Kentucky, along what is today Grundy Home Road. The land is gently rolling, with prime farming land located between low-lying ridges and the creek, reputedly navigable by flatboat coming off the Salt River. Glenannie, one of five Grundy homes named in 1979 as part of a historical district on the National Register of Historic Places, reportedly dates from 1785. Although this Federal-style brick home could only have been constructed much later, several solidly built outbuildings with logs up to fifty inches thick may be original cabins from the 1780s.

Felix Grundy was a young boy when his family was establishing its base in Kentucky and when he lost his father. George Grundy executed his will on Felix's eighth birthday, September 11, 1783, and died within six months, less than four years after arriving in Kentucky. The first will recorded in Jefferson County, the testament provided that except for a horse, a cow, and a calf to each minor child upon coming of age, Elizabeth Grundy would have full use of all her husband's property for the remainder of her life unless she remarried. John, George Jr., and Elizabeth Grundy were named executors.[16]

It is impossible to assess how much of Felix Grundy's later drive and makeup can be attributed to his father's influence, but it appears clear that Felix's support for an entrepreneurial world of agrarian capitalism received its earliest impetus from the example of George Grundy. An immigrant who achieved success in four outlying areas of Virginia, George did not limit himself to self-sustaining agriculture; he operated taverns and gristmills, kept racehorses, and appears to have run a successful transport business (George Grundy & Company) on one of the great highways of colonial America. He participated fully in the nascent commercial activity of the frontier, foreshadowing his sons' participation in the expanding market economy that soon took hold in Kentucky.

The decade following George Grundy's death in 1784 saw extraordinary changes in Kentucky. Although Indian attacks remained a worry until the Battle of Fallen Timbers in 1794, frontier settlers wrested farms from the forests and canebrakes while political leaders developed governmental, educational, and business institutions. Growth fueled changes. When John Filson proclaimed the virtues of Kentucky in 1784, he assessed the population at 30,000. By 1790, however, the first federal census set the population at 73,577, of whom 61,133 were whites and 12,430 were blacks.[17]

The land of Nelson County, formed from part of Jefferson County in 1785, with Bardstown as the county seat, attracted various families that would be important to Felix Grundy. Local historians claim that Abraham Lincoln, a Revolutionary War captain and grandfather of the future president, was killed in 1784 in the region: a historian of the bicentennial notes that "had he lived his economic standing would have matched that of the Grundys but an Indian murderer quashed those dreams." Regardless, his family, including sons Mordecai and Thomas, planted themselves at Lincoln's Run on Beech Fork, about six miles northeast of the Grundys. Nearby too lived the Berry family and their niece, Nancy Hanks, the mother of the future president. Catholic immigrants from Maryland also settled near the Grundys, and in 1787 the Reverend Charles Whelan, the first Catholic priest in Kentucky, arrived in Nelson County.[18]

The disruption of his early years—major family moves and the deaths of two brothers and his father before he was nine—do not appear to have had adverse effects on Felix Grundy. He enjoyed the continuing presence and backing of a large family and the support of his enterprising mother. Elizabeth Grundy obtained the first Nelson County license for an ordinary on June 28, 1785, and thereafter appears to have continually operated a well-known inn. With some of his older brothers establishing their own households, Felix, Polly, and those of his older brothers who remained at home did much of the work at Widow Grundy's Tavern. Working with family slaves, the young Grundys handled the tasks involved in running an inn and tavern, from tending horses to serving at the bar and table. Exposure to the travelers of the day, with their diverse backgrounds and wealth, helped provide young Grundy with the ease and effectiveness that so famously marked his adult relationships. His affability, quick wit, and perceptive understanding of people must have been in part attributable to the years he worked at "the Widow Grundy's."

Felix grew up in a vital and driving time on the rowdy frontier. While he left little record of his boyhood, we can glimpse his early activities. First, frontier life centered on the backbreaking labor of clearing fields and establishing farms. In addition to operating an inn, the Grundys farmed. The widely separated farms gave rise to rugged self-reliance. Few towns existed in Kentucky, with Lexington, the largest, having ninety to one hundred houses in 1786. The Grundys' area of Nelson County was fertile but sparsely settled. Travelers, including one who stayed at the Widow Grundy's, described beautiful wooded land, a "Lonesome road," and few settlers. Dress reflected frontier needs, with the hunting shirt worn universally and a weapon kept nearby to guard against unexpected Indian attacks. While Felix does not appear in the skimpy militia records until 1806, when he was a captain in Nelson County, there are numerous references to his brothers in the Washington County records.[19]

Second, the frontier attracted tough men seeking a better life and often not particular as to method. The Grundys' location on the Wilderness Road meant that they saw a constant flow of travelers. Settlers worked hard but made the most of their social occasions. Monthly court days played an important role. "Everybody came to court, and the day was spent drinking, fighting and jollifying just 'for fun.'" Social events regularly got out of hand. Fistfights were common, yet "if a pugilist had dared to raise a stick or draw a knife, he would have fared badly."[20]

Liquor abounded and fueled much of the frontier's roughness. Bishop Francis Asbury, the indomitable circuit rider of Methodism, who crossed the Appalachian Mountains an estimated sixty times, understood and appreciated the culture of the West. For him, whiskey constituted the prime curse of the United States. In the early nineteenth century Americans drank more alcohol than they ever would again; in 1830 alcohol consumption averaged more than five gallons per person. In Kentucky, where bourbon became a principal product of Nelson and Washington counties no later than 1785, good product abounded. Liquor played a major role in Kentucky elections, with Humphrey Marshall reporting that the "way to men's hearts was down their throats."[21]

Felix Grundy described himself as the "last and favorite" of Elizabeth Grundy's sons, and it is reasonably clear that she launched her youngest son on his career path. When George Grundy died in 1784, Elizabeth, aged fifty-one, began widowhood with land on Cartwright Creek, at least two slaves, and a significant number of livestock. By 1795, in Springfield, Kentucky, she owned 232 acres on Cartwright Creek, lots in Springfield valued at thirty-six pounds, and seven slaves. In addition to operating a farm and an ordinary, Elizabeth and her family continued the Virginia tradition of breeding horses. In 1793, for example, she advertised that the "famous horse Belmount" would spend half the season at the Widow Grundy's and half with Robert Grundy.[22]

Elizabeth Grundy's strength and independence produced an unusual result: a lawsuit against her by her children. On March 2, 1793, she and John, as executors of George Grundy's will, were sued in Washington County by all of her other children, including seventeen-year-old Felix. The claimants apparently despaired of ever receiving more than one horse, one cow, and a calf from their father's estate. The complaint describes an activist widow who engaged in a variety of transactions, including the purchase of four hundred acres of land, paid for partially by livestock belonging to the estate. In asking for a detailed estate accounting, the plaintiffs claimed that the widow Grundy was converting estate assets into land, Negroes, and other property and asserting that such property was her own, subject solely to her disposition. We do not know what prompted the suit, which was settled on unknown terms on October 3, 1794.[23]

Felix had significant support from others as well. John Grundy, who was eighteen years older than his youngest brother, possessed the initiative and energy manifest in his father. A successful farmer in southern Washington County, he played an influential role in both county and state government. Jefferson County appointed John Grundy deputy sheriff on April 7, 1784, and Nelson County continued John in the same role in 1785. The oldest Grundy also served as a member of the eighth and ninth "preliminary" conventions to the Kentucky constitutional convention of 1792; in the ninth, and last, convention he voted with the majority in the 24–18 vote favoring Kentucky statehood. Significantly for Felix's future, John pressed for formation of Washington County from Nelson County in 1792 and became the first sheriff of that county, a presidential elector, and a justice. In brief, John became a leading member of the county oligopoly.[24]

Matthew Walton, the political father of Washington County and one of the largest landowners in Kentucky, also backed Felix Grundy. Walton, who arrived in Kentucky in 1784, opposed adoption of the U.S. Constitution at the Virginia convention in 1788 and served as a member of the Kentucky constitutional convention in 1792. The forty-five thousand acres he held in Washington County in 1792 abutted Grundy lands. Samuel, the most successful of Felix's brothers, lived in Walton's household in 1788, probably as a surveyor. John Grundy and Matthew Walton, who were about the same age, bought land together and collaborated on governmental matters.[25]

Felix Grundy, a member of the first generation of state leaders to grow up in Kentucky, never forgot the Indian threats of his childhood, when hatred of the Shawnees unified the dispersed settlers. In a much-quoted speech delivered in the U.S. Senate over the course of two days, February 28 and March 1, 1830, he emphasized pioneer travails, describing certain "honored men" in Congress as the remnant of large families lost in the settlement of the West. He concluded this segment of his speech with deeply personal remembrances:

> I can remember when death was in almost every bush, and every thicket concealed an ambuscade. If I am asked to trace my memory back, and name the first indelible impression it received, it would be the sight of my eldest brother bleeding and dying under the wounds inflicted by the tomahawk and scalping-knife. . . . I have seen a widowed mother plundered of her whole property in a single night; from affluence and ease reduced to poverty in a moment, and thereby compelled to labor with her own hands to educate her last and favorite son.[26]

The struggle against the Indians indirectly cost Felix yet another brother, the one closest to him in age. Charles Grundy, born in 1772, perhaps attended Salem Academy with Felix. On October 6, 1793, Charles, sergeant of a cavalry regiment, executed his will, in which he referred to the uncertainty of life as he set "out on an expedition among the Indians." He left most of his property to his mother and his clothes to Felix. Charles did die soon thereafter, but not by Indian hands: on December 10, 1793, he succumbed to smallpox.[27]

3

EDUCATION ON THE FRONTIER

*[Priestley viewed the] indolent and trifling with displeasure and often
with indignation.*

—"G" [Grundy]

elix Grundy regarded himself as a self-made man. His mother,
however, deserves credit for the education of her youngest son. She made
possible an outstanding education for Felix, particularly under the tutelage of
James Priestley and George Nicholas, the leading scholars of early Kentucky.

The earliest evidence of Felix's education dates from 1785, when John Moore
provided to the Grundys, for 8 pounds, 8 shillings, three-quarters of a year's
schooling for seven children. Since by this time Elizabeth Grundy's oldest
sons were no longer minors, the seven children may have included two or more
neighbor children, along with Charles, Felix, and Polly. We know nothing of
Moore, but it is reasonable to assume that, common to the period, he taught
reading, writing, geography, and arithmetic, which could include geometry,
trigonometry, and algebra.[1]

Felix's talent was evident early, for he went to Lexington at age thirteen
for advanced education at Transylvania Seminary. Presbyterians had persuaded the Virginia General Assembly to charter the seminary in 1780, to be
supported by donations, tuition, and four thousand acres of land formerly belonging to Tories. Indian strife claimed the lives of six trustees, and the fledgling institution suffered from financial problems. Nevertheless, after moving
from Danville, the seminary opened in Lexington on June 1, 1789, at the public schoolhouse. The thirteen students included Felix Grundy. The all-day commencement, featuring elegant speeches by the students and the performance of
both a tragedy and a farce, took place on April 10, 1790. One can only imagine
what must have been Felix's first reported performance.[2]

Grundy spent only one year at Transylvania, entering Salem Academy in
Bardstown in the fall of 1790. Bardstown, on the Wilderness Road and less

than fifteen miles from the Grundy homestead, boasted a population of 216 in 1790. It was the seat of Nelson County, the second largest county in Kentucky, with a population of 11,315, including 1,248 slaves.[3]

Salem showcased James Priestley. A Scots-Irish Presbyterian minister born in Ireland in 1757, he immigrated to Virginia as a child and attended Liberty Hall, the predecessor of Washington and Lee University. Priestley announced on November 22, 1788, in the *Kentucky Gazette* that he would conduct the Salem Academy and teach "the Latin, Greek and English languages, with the several arts and sciences commonly studied at Academies and Colleges in this country." Tuition would be five pounds a year ($16.65), with twenty shillings in cash and the remainder in cattle and country products at market prices. Priestley led Salem Academy and taught a remarkable number of future Kentucky leaders until his departure in 1792. A classicist, he set high standards, reflected deep learning, and displayed an irascible and imperious temper. An illuminating obituary probably written by Grundy intoned that Priestley viewed the "indolent and trifling with displeasure and often with indignation."[4]

Grundy attended Salem Academy from 1790 to 1792. While there is no real evidence of his academic performance, an account in 1838 suggests that he and John Rowan developed a keen rivalry in their studies of Greek and Latin. A political commentator noted in 1806 that Grundy was skilled in the learning of the Greeks and Romans, and Supreme Court Justice Catron, a good friend of Grundy's, wrote years later that Priestley had excelled in teaching the "dead languages." Grundy deeply admired Priestley, naming his third son James Priestley Grundy in 1807. Later, as a trustee of Cumberland College, in Nashville, Grundy championed Priestley's selection as president of the institution and sent one of his sons to study there. Sharing Grundy's respect for Priestley, Rowan enrolled two of his sons at Cumberland.[5]

Grundy formed strong friendships at Salem, some with men who would be lifelong political allies. Most important was the relationship with John Rowan, known today principally as the builder in Bardstown of Federal Hill, immortalized by Stephen Foster in his song "My Old Kentucky Home." Rowan (1773–1843) was in his time a colorful and politically powerful lawyer. Of Scots-Irish origin, he moved with his family to Kentucky in 1782 and to Bardstown in 1790. Grundy and Rowan, educated and admitted to the bar together, participated in the constitutional convention of 1799. Rowan served various terms in the Kentucky executive and legislative branches, as the U.S. congressman from Nelson County (1807–9), and as a U.S. senator (1825–31).[6]

Another close friend, John Pope (1770–1845), Kentucky senator and a territorial governor of Arkansas, later characterized their earliest days together as "small boys" amidst "savage warfare." One-armed as a result of a childhood accident, handsome, and popular, Pope included among his wives a sister of Mrs. John Quincy Adams and Frances Walton, the wealthy widow of Grundy's mentor Matthew Walton. Grundy and Pope often worked together, although Pope periodically changed his political allegiances.[7]

Grundy decided to become a lawyer during his last years at Salem Academy. In 1838 we find a succinct statement of Grundy's career choice: "The first intention of Mr. Grundy's mother was that he should be educated for the medical profession, but a talent for debate, evidenced when at school, and his own subsequent wishes, ultimately led to the selection of the law." Grundy had some experience with law, since both of his parents were active entrepreneurs, his brothers John and Samuel had served as county sheriff, and he and his siblings had been plaintiffs in the action against his mother. Moreover, having grown up in the land-crazy environment of the 1780s, Felix Grundy certainly recognized the confusion and complexity of land law. Law would be a natural career choice for an intelligent, educated young man who wanted to make his mark.[8]

Kentuckians viewed lawyers with ambivalence. Attorneys had stature in their communities, and their cases were followed with interest, but they also engendered suspicion and dislike. "Salamander" exclaimed in the *Kentucky Gazette* on December 24, 1791, that "the fewer lawyers and pick pockets there are in a county, the better the chance honest people have to keep their own." Acting on the often expressed view that lawyers should be excluded from the legislature in order to keep laws simple and clear, voters chose only two lawyers— George Nicholas and Benjamin Sebastian—among the forty-five delegates elected to the convention that wrote Kentucky's constitution of 1792.

Much of the animosity toward lawyers reflected the traditional countryman's concern that better-educated folk would deprive honest men of their land and labors through complicated laws and processes. In Kentucky, implementation of the Virginia Land Law of 1779 exacerbated that fear. No systematic surveying of land was carried out in Kentucky, and overlapping claims bedeviled landholders for generations. Countless Kentuckians lost all or part of their land. Kentucky's surveyor general summarized the problem in 1797: more than 24 million acres had been granted, but "all the Counties contain but 12,476,116 Acres, so that some persons will fall short." Moreover, as reflected in one of the Kentucky petitions of 1780 to the Continental Congress, well-connected Virginians such as Matthew Walton claimed many large tracts of land early in the process. In 1790 probably fewer than half of Kentucky's males were landowners.[9]

The lawyers subject to such ire in Kentucky were largely Virginia born and trained. John Brown, Kentucky's first U.S. senator, arrived in 1783, and George Nicholas and John Breckinridge, leaders in the first and second Kentucky constitutional conventions, respectively, reached Kentucky in 1789 and 1793. In a fast-growing region these lawyers did well, although Breckinridge wrote upon his arrival that "there is a large docket and a large number of lawyers." Only with Felix Grundy, John Rowan, John Pope, and others in the late 1790s did Kentucky begin to have locally trained lawyers.[10]

George Nicholas (1743–99), under whom Grundy read law in Lexington from 1792 or possibly 1793 to 1795, laid the foundation for the indigenous Kentucky bar. From a prominent Virginia family, Nicholas served in the Continental army, in the Virginia legislature, and in the Virginia constitutional convention in 1788. After settling in Danville in 1789, he quickly became Kentucky's most successful lawyer. By 1795 he was Mercer County's wealthiest citizen by far, with more than ninety-four thousand acres of land, forty-eight slaves, and the only four-wheeled carriage in the county. He dominated the constitutional convention of 1792 and became Kentucky's first attorney general, and he served briefly as the first professor of law at Transylvania University.[11]

No one forgot George Nicholas. Plump, short, and almost bald, with wisps of blond hair, he was described as "a plum pudding with legs to it." With "large glowing blue eyes," a big head for his stature, and exceptional charm, Nicholas inspired devotion among his friends and students. He had an incisive mind and a self-assurance that his students must have hoped to emulate.[12]

Nicholas taught many of Kentucky's nineteenth-century leaders. During Grundy's apprenticeship, fellow students included John Rowan and John Pope from Salem Academy, Joseph Hamilton Daveiss, Isham Talbot, Jesse Bledsoe, and William Garrard. Nicholas's tutelage of his law students featured moot courts and debating societies, as well as study and service as legal assistants. General Robert McAfee wrote of his apprenticeship with John Breckinridge from January 1800 until September 1801, which would have been similar to study under Nicholas seven years earlier. (Both Nicholas and Breckinridge had studied at William and Mary under George Wythe, who supplemented Blackstone with his own lectures and with moot courts and debating societies.) Breckinridge offered free instruction and the use of his books, particularly Blackstone and Vertot's history of the Roman Republic. Eight to ten students met weekly for moot courts or debates and submitted papers and took examinations on a regular basis.[13]

Grundy honed his speaking skills in debates and moot court. His close relationships with Rowan and Pope deepened, while he formed a strong friendship with Joseph H. Daveiss, the academic leader of Nicholas's students. Daveiss (1774–1811), from Bedford County, Virginia, moved with his family to Kentucky in 1779. He practiced law in Danville from 1795 to 1799, served as Nicholas's executor, and became Kentucky's U.S. attorney in 1799. Notably, he became a Federalist in a Republican state.[14]

Grundy lived in Lexington during his year at Transylvania Seminary. In the same town in his late teens, however, he experienced a more sophisticated environment—and a more commercial one. The burgeoning town became the heart of western America, with a population of about 1,500 and several hundred log houses in 1795. Initially a trading center, it developed tanning and rope-manufacturing plants. The 1800 census emphasized Lexington's leadership, disclosing a population of 1,797 people, compared with 628 in Frankfort, 345 in Nashville, and 1,565 in Pittsburgh. City fathers passed a variety of ordinances to control the rowdy and striving society, including a ban on horse racing in town streets in 1793. The *Kentucky Gazette,* the state's most influential paper, began publishing in Lexington in 1787. Travelers attested to schools of music, French, and dancing.[15]

Living in Lexington increased Grundy's exposure to criminal law. Kentucky's criminal laws, based on English practice, prescribed the death penalty for more than twenty offenses. At least two hangings took place in Lexington while Grundy was a student there. On June 10, 1794, a counterfeiter met his death before his wife and children as well as an estimated eight thousand to ten thousand spectators. In 1795 Lexington witnessed the hanging of a convicted horse thief. Reform loomed, however. In 1797, under the active leadership of John Breckinridge, Kentucky reformed its criminal laws, revoking the death penalty except for first-degree murder.[16]

Grundy absorbed more than law during his years in Lexington. Robert McAfee recalled that when he was a law student in 1800 he "formed my Political opinion, as all the questions of that eventful Period were discussed in our Society and moot court." Grundy had much the same experience, but with George Nicholas as political savant. The early 1790s were heady times for students of government and politics. Political and philosophical debate in Kentucky arose not only from reflections on government by Nicholas and James Madison, who freely gave his views to early Kentuckians, but also from the conflict and sectionalism in the state.[17]

Division marked early Kentucky. Virginia, to its credit, provided county government and representation, but settlers of varied ethnic backgrounds and attitudes differed with respect to slavery, religion, and governmental structure.

Virginians may have constituted a slight majority, but that hardly assuaged Pennsylvanians and others unaccustomed to the Virginia form of government by the elite. Even among Virginians, "tuckyahoes," Anglican and from the older settled areas, often opposed "cohees," typically from the frontier. Unlike in Virginia, where they settled largely in the backcountry, the Scots-Irish, an estimated 25–30 percent of the population, constituted a significant and influential element everywhere in Kentucky. The Grundys, who were not Scots-Irish but from a similar Borderer cultural background, would certainly have been considered Cohees.[18]

The longest-enduring division centered on the Bluegrass. For many, the Bluegrass, particularly the so-called Inner Bluegrass, near Lexington, re-created the landholding and social structure of Tidewater Virginia. Lexington and the Bluegrass attracted the early lawyers, the government, even though it had been located at nearby Frankfort, and commercial capital. Almost inevitably, the Bluegrass also attracted the ire and envy of Kentuckians in other counties, who believed Virginia land speculators had acquired the best land, who detested lawyers, who disliked traveling to Bluegrass legal centers, and who feared the wealth and influence of the elitist Virginians dominating the Bluegrass. The opposition to Lexington and the Bluegrass leadership initially came from smaller landholders within the Bluegrass and elsewhere, but by the late 1790s it had shifted to leaders from newer counties, particularly in the Southside, the area south and west of the Kentucky River.

Political alignments mirrored the divisions in Kentucky. Nicholas, Breckinridge, and others similarly positioned formed the power elite in Kentucky—the so-called court party in Lexington and Frankfort—and favored rule by their own kind. They believed in republican government but feared unchecked majority rule. They accordingly supported a bicameral legislature, an independent judiciary, and a bill of rights that could protect a minority. As lawyers, they saw the advantages of a legal system that would provide the order and uniformity required for effective governance and economic development and, importantly, one that they would administer. A more radical and rural group, including some in the Bluegrass, favored a minimal government directly responsive to the voter. They preferred a unicameral legislature, annual election of almost all state and local officials, and a judiciary that would offer cheap, speedy, local justice with more emphasis on farmers and plain common sense than on established legal norms.

The divisions in Kentucky became apparent in the election for the first constitutional convention of Kentucky in 1792. Harry Innes, Kentucky's first federal judge, wrote on August 27, 1791, that "the people of Kentucky are all turned Politicians . . . the Peasantry are perfectly mad—extraordinary prejudices and without foundation have arisen against the present Officers of Government—the Lawyers and the Men of Fortune—they say *plain honest Farmers*—are the only men who ought to be elected to form our Constitution." Will Wisp, in a letter to the *Kentucky Gazette* published on October 13, 1791, put it more succinctly: "Let everyone who is for the good of the country keep up the cry against Judges, Lawyers, Generals, Colonels and all other designing men, and the day will be ours."[19]

Despite the divisions in Kentucky, the Nicholas moderates generally prevailed in the elections for the constitutional convention. The Kentucky Constitution, drafted only five years after the U.S. Constitution, provided for three branches of government but gave little power to the executive. It called for free white male suffrage without property qualifications; a separate judiciary, with the supreme court having original jurisdiction in land cases; significant legislative authority; and a bicameral legislature with representatives allocated based on population.[20]

Slavery was the most contentious issue for the constitutional convention. The well-known Presbyterian David Rice and other ministers failed, 26–16, in the only recorded vote of the convention, to overcome the arguments of Nicholas and other proslavery adherents. Kentucky, which was the fifteenth state admitted to the Union and the first west of the Appalachians, became the first state to provide constitutional protection for slavery, prohibiting the legislature from passing laws for emancipation without owner consent or fair cash compensation. Article 9 also prohibited the legislature from preventing immigrants from importing their own slaves but did stipulate legislative power to bar slaves' being brought into Kentucky for sale.

Nicholas and the new Kentucky Constitution also carefully allocated power between the state government and the counties, particularly the county courts, and, as a corollary, between the Bluegrass, with Lexington at its core, and the rest of the state. Both the governor and the senate would be chosen by electors rather than by direct suffrage, thus providing a check on the powerful legislature. Even more important, a centralized judiciary would control the fragmentation inherent in the proliferation of county courts. Nicholas and his fellows clothed their arguments in democratic parlance, but their position ensured continued dominance by Lexington and the Bluegrass, in which Nicholas was the most formidable presence.

Grundy could see and hear firsthand how the conflicts and strains under

Kentucky's constitution played out in practice. More broadly, Nicholas taught, thought, and corresponded about the role and structure of government during a period of extraordinary ferment and intellectual vitality. As if this were not enough, Grundy studied under Nicholas just as national political parties were forming in the 1790s. Kentucky identified fully with the Republicanism of Jefferson and Madison, both good friends of Nicholas. Humphrey Marshall, a cantankerous Federalist, acknowledged sadly that all Kentuckians were Republicans. The core tenets of Jeffersonianism—agrarian values, minimal government, strict construction of the Constitution, states' rights, low taxation, no military establishment, peace—resonated with the striving, land-hungry farmers of early Kentucky. Nicholas and John Breckinridge, and soon Henry Clay, became vocal proponents of Jefferson, but the principles of the emerging Republican Party took deepest root outside the Bluegrass, where localism and agrarianism reigned. For Felix Grundy, from Washington County, these became bedrock principles.[21]

Jefferson, Madison, and Nicholas deeply believed in states' rights, and Grundy probably had his first in-depth exposure to this issue from Nicholas. Nicholas, along with John Breckinridge, led Kentucky's opposition to the Alien and Sedition Acts and set forth in 1798 a classic statement of the states' rights view of the U.S. Constitution. Nicholas provided balance, however, as reflected in a statement of his views:

> The laws which we complain of may be divided into two classes—those which we admit to be constitutional, but consider as impolitic; and those which we believe to be unconstitutional, and therefore do not trouble ourselves to enquire as to their policy; because we consider them as absolute nullities. . . .
>
> As to the second class, or the unconstitutional laws, although we consider them as dead letters, and therefore that we might legally use force in opposition to any attempts to execute them; yet we contemplate no means of opposition, even to these unconstitutional acts, but an appeal to the real laws of our country.[22]

Grundy became close to his mentor Nicholas. A magazine article in 1838 stated that similarity of opinion on public matters cemented a personal friendship and "warmest affections." Many of Grundy's later views reflected his teacher's precepts, including states' rights, nullification, and a strong opposition to dueling. Yet although Grundy deeply admired Nicholas and was undoubtedly much influenced by him, Grundy was to show by 1799 that he was his own man, particularly with respect to the state's judicial structure.[23]

The Kentucky Constitution gave original jurisdiction in land cases to the court of appeals, Kentucky's highest court. Nicholas hoped by this approach to help clarify titles and break the logjam of cases. This centralized judicial system, however, detracted from the power traditionally exercised by the county courts and gave significant advantages to the Bluegrass bar and land speculators. Unhappiness with the structure and some decisions by the court of appeals led to changes in the judicial system created by the constitution. In 1795 the legislature terminated original jurisdiction for the court of appeals and vested criminal and land jurisdiction in six new district courts. The quarter-sessions courts—comprising the county justices of the peace—were given concurrent jurisdiction with the district courts in all but criminal cases.

These jurisdictional issues appear arcane today, but they were bitterly fought over while Grundy studied under Nicholas. They dealt with by far the most important issue in early Kentucky, namely, who controlled entitlement to land. They also reflected deep-seated political and cultural differences, most manifest in the split between the Bluegrass and the Southside. Traditional elites, represented by George Nicholas and John Breckinridge, sought to perpetuate their legal and financial control; they were opposed by emerging political leaders imbued by more egalitarian ideals. These differences did not originate in, and were not restricted to, Kentucky (neighboring Ohio and Tennessee confronted similar questions), but were given specific form and nuance by Kentucky's geography, settler origins, and economy.

The judicial compromise in 1795 satisfied few, and the adherents of a decentralized judicial system vowed further efforts. Grundy would fight for circuit court reform only four years later.

PART II

Kentucky

4

FELIX GRUNDY, ESQUIRE

Horses and lawsuits comprise [the] usual topic of conversation.
—François Michaux

*F*elix Grundy completed his legal studies in the spring of 1795. There being no minimum age for the practice of law, he began his career at age nineteen. On August 6, 1795, the judges of the court of quarter sessions in Washington County admitted to practice Grundy, John Rowan, and John Allen. Grundy received similar approval from other county and district courts in 1795, including those in Mercer, Fayette, Hardin, and Green counties. He began law practice much better prepared than most of his contemporaries. Since no formal training was required, most attorneys spent a year clerking in the office of a leading attorney before joining the bar, in contrast to the two or three years Grundy studied under Nicholas.

Washington County—the first new county established by the state of Kentucky—would be a propitious base for Felix Grundy. Matthew Walton created a new town, Springfield, as the county seat, and Elizabeth Grundy moved there in the spring of 1795, giving up her hostelry near Cartwright Creek but receiving a tavern license from the new town on June 4, 1795.[1]

As important as his mother may have been, Felix's brothers furnished the real nourishment for his career. John Grundy relinquished his duties as sheriff to his brother, Deputy Sheriff Samuel Grundy, in 1795 but continued to be a major figure in the oligarchy controlling Washington County. By 1797 John, then a justice, owned almost four thousand acres of land and thirteen slaves. John Grundy also strengthened his family's ties to the prominent Catholic community in Washington County by his third marriage, in August 1794, to Jean Speaks. He and other large landowners wanted outlets for their farm products, preservation of rights to land acquired under the Virginia land laws, and continued control of their counties.[2]

Felix's other brothers also flourished in Washington County. All farmed, although Guardum Grundy obtained a license in 1793 to operate an ordinary at his home, nine miles northwest of Springfield. Samuel Grundy, according to the 1797 tax lists, owned 800 acres and 13 slaves, while Robert Grundy held 400 acres on Rolling Fork and 5 slaves. George Grundy owned 450 acres, and Guardum Grundy owned 200 acres. The brothers all married neighbors and thus constituted, with their in-laws and extended families, a formidable voting group.[3]

Felix Grundy's decision to return to Washington County in 1795 reflected personal and professional preferences. He had been in Bardstown and Lexington for the past six years. Returning home to family and friends as a young lawyer, with studies under the celebrated George Nicholas, could only have been satisfying. The decision, however, also revealed hardheaded realism. Numerous lawyers, almost all older than Felix, practiced in Lexington, and Grundy enjoyed few advantages in attracting business. The most successful lawyers, George Nicholas and John Breckinridge, came from Virginia, with established reputations and, more usefully, the representation of eastern speculators. Grundy surely recognized that southwestern Kentucky was growing rapidly and that he would be in an ideal position to build his practice base in that region.

Even though the first portrait of Felix Grundy was not painted until much later, we have a reasonable picture of what Grundy looked like as he began law practice. Of medium height, Grundy had light brown hair and a firm, square jaw. Slender and animated, he possessed a ready wit, a quick imagination, and strong self-confidence. His self-assurance is hardly surprising. He enjoyed not only his mother's favor but also the admiration and support of his brothers, one of whom, George, had already named his second son Felix. Contrary to the suggestions of some Clay biographers, Grundy was not an unsophisticated agrarian. As a student in Lexington and Bardstown for three or four years before spending at least two years with Nicholas in Lexington, he had absorbed some of the manners and dress of those larger towns. His interest in debate and the ease with which he soon projected himself on the Kentucky scene suggest, too, that he was fully accustomed to the verbal jousting and humor central to the fellowship of early lawyers in Kentucky.

Grundy spread his legal wings in a dynamic and growing state. In 1793 James Madison received a letter saying that "Improvement in this Country is almost beyond conception" and that "I shall behold the happiest and richest Country in the world" if the Indians were at peace, the Mississippi open, and the title to lands clarified. By 1798 the Indian troubles were largely over and the Mississippi open; even if land titles remained a jumble, that constituted good news for an ambitious young lawyer.[4]

Conviviality and hospitality also marked the fast-growing state. A traveler received a glass of whiskey as a matter of course, good manners then requiring "a man of breeding and standing always to get out the bottle of whiskey or brandy." François Michaux, who made a famous trip through Kentucky in 1802, commented that "horses and lawsuits" comprised the usual topic of conversation among Kentuckians. Henry Clay and John Rowan, inveterate gamesters, exemplified a culture of card playing and gambling. Horse racing had already taken hold, and Springfield mounted an annual October event, almost certainly fostered by some of the horse-breeding Grundys. Cockfighting was another favorite sport.[5]

Grundy established himself quickly in his profession; he was the first lawyer in Springfield. On November 5, 1795, three months after his admission to the court of quarter sessions, he was admitted to practice before the county court of Washington County. He opened an office at lot 2, adjacent to his mother's tavern at lots 3, 4, and 5. Grundy's plans took greater shape, however, on April 7, 1796, when he purchased fifteen acres in Springfield from Matthew Walton for eleven pounds, four shillings, and soon built a house. The young lawyer also became active in town affairs. Trustees administered Springfield, which in 1800 was the tenth largest town in Kentucky, with a population of 163 people. Grundy joined that group in February 1797 and became president of the Springfield trustees in 1802.[6]

Washington County rewarded its young attorney. In 1796 the county court appointed Grundy county attorney, paying him 18 pounds, 24 pounds, and 30 pounds, respectively, for that service for 1796, 1797, and 1798. The court made other payments to him, including 4 pounds, 10 shillings, on July 7, 1796, for finding a house "for the court to sit in" and 5 pounds, 10 shillings, on December 2, 1796, for the use of his house as a courthouse. He received more compensation than other officials; the 18 pounds he received in 1796 greatly exceeded the 7 pounds, 15 shillings, paid Samuel Grundy as sheriff and the 5 pounds, 4 shillings, paid John Reed as clerk. The greater payments to Felix Grundy appear unusual, since the sheriff was typically the most powerful official in the county. The amount and pattern of the compensation suggest that the leaders of Washington County, including his brothers and Matthew Walton, were promoting the career of a promising protégé.[7]

Law in early Kentucky was rough and ready. County actions and suits necessarily involved more commonsense accommodation than application of Blackstone. They also provided immediacy. The county court constituted the citizen's principal, often only contact with government. The court was made up of justices of the peace sitting together, usually monthly. Self-perpetuating and typically comprised of the wealthy, it was hardly democratic. Yet this local oligopoly carried out all local responsibilities, from road maintenance to judicial functions. It met its obligations by dividing all its costs by the number of "tithables," males over twenty-one and slaves over sixteen years of age. This pay-as-you-go system meant a direct correlation between governmental functions and citizen tax payments.[8]

Building on his base as county attorney, Grundy developed his law practice in the next several years. Grundy's success came quickly. In May 1799, when the twenty-three-year-old's holdings were assessed for tax purposes, Grundy owned seven town lots in Springfield, valued at fifty-two pounds, 51 acres on the waters of Cartwright Creek, and two horses. He also held title to 242 acres, with seven slaves, on the Green River in Green County.

Grundy's income derived from a diverse practice. In addition to serving as Washington County prosecutor, Grundy represented plaintiffs in private criminal proceedings. Most of Grundy's practice involved land litigation, however, because of the complexity of Kentucky's system and the money to be made in this field. Grundy represented Mordecai Lincoln, an uncle of the future president, in a 1797 suit in Nelson County against heirs of John Reed. Lincoln claimed all or at least half of 2,268.5 acres to which his father, Abraham Lincoln, was entitled under land warrant but thereafter had been held by John Reed as Lincoln's surveyor. Although the suit dragged on until it was discontinued in 1813, it was characteristic of the work done by Grundy. The young lawyer also testified as an expert witness on the value of land.[9]

The itinerant practice of law then characteristic of Kentucky suited Grundy's outgoing personality. Particularly after circuit court reform in 1802, lawyers traveled from courthouse to courthouse, usually with the judges. Travel was difficult, on horseback in good and bad weather, sleeping two or three to a bed and putting up with whatever meals the local tavern supplied. But it featured good fellowship and nightly rituals of food and drink, both at supper and in the rooms of judges or other attorneys. The lawyers knew one another well and dueled with wit and logic, fueled by local bourbon. An observer writing nostalgically of a slightly later period remembered that although libraries were small, one learned to beware of men with few books but great ability, for all were well grounded in basic principles.[10]

Unlike many of his contemporaries, Grundy continued the itinerant life of the circuit lawyer throughout his career. Henry Clay, Ninian Edwards, and others in the early Kentucky bar turned increasingly to farming or the civil litigation that took place in commercial centers. Grundy's later success as a criminal lawyer in Tennessee, however, necessitated his travel throughout the Old Southwest, occasionally by stage but usually on horseback. This meant not only lengthy absences from family but continuing stays at inns or homes of friends, constant fellowship, and, most important, unceasing exposure to political and social crosscurrents. Almost every observer of Grundy commented on his political sensitivity and intuitive understanding of jurors, much of which surely must be attributed to the almost daily interchange he had with the innkeepers, lawyers, travelers, and other countrymen encountered in his unending rounds of travel and trials.

Grundy's legal career received a boost when his friend and mentor Matthew Walton retained the twenty-one-year-old in 1797 for a suit in the Bardstown district court against Gilbert Imlay and General Henry Lee, a cousin of General Henry "Light Horse Harry" Lee. Imlay, a New Jersey–born adventurer, popularized the advantages of Kentucky but is more famous for his romances in Europe. In Paris in 1792 he met the noted feminist Mary Wollstonecraft, still a virgin at thirty-four. She gave her love and virginity to Imlay, had a daughter, and attempted suicide when Imlay took another mistress. She died in 1797 giving birth to her other daughter, Mary Shelley, author of *Frankenstein* and wife of the poet Percy Bysshe Shelley.[11]

The suit brought by Walton arose from his sale, on August 3, 1783, of significant acreage to Imlay and Lee. Since Walton received only a small part of the consideration, and Imlay left the United States in 1788, Lee on February 15, 1794, gave Walton a bond signed by John May for twenty thousand acres of land and conveyed back to Walton one-half of all lands subject to the agreement of 1783 but not yet reflected in grants from the state. May, however, had already paid the bond, as allegedly known by Lee. Moreover, on August 12, 1796, Lee had assigned all the lands under the agreement of 1783 to Henry Banks, a Philadelphia speculator, who was obtaining patents for the land. The suit asked for an injunction against issuance of patents by the Register of Land and for mandatory reassignment of all the original lands to Walton.

Banks answered that he had paid Lee in excess of twenty thousand dollars and that despite extensive dialogue with Walton's agent subsequently, Walton "never uttered a Word . . . to [lead one to] expect that he should contest the Titles." Banks denied all fraud or collusion with Lee or Imlay and argued that he was a bona fide purchaser of the land. The case was settled, with Revolutionary general Thomas Posey negotiating with Grundy on Lee's behalf. Walton received U.S. Treasury warrants for three thousand acres of land and certain assurances.

Grundy engaged in little criminal defense work while in Kentucky, which is surprising given his later focus and reputation. His Scots-Irish friend John Rowan did, however, establish a reputation as a criminal lawyer, based in Bardstown. Tall and fearsome, Rowan personified the dominant culture of honor. Fond of both cards and the bottle, he and a young doctor, James Chambers, quarreled in a Bardstown tavern in January 1801, allegedly over which of them was the finest scholar of Greek and Latin. They exchanged blows, Chambers issued a challenge, and in the resultant duel Rowan mortally wounded his opponent. Various studies state that Grundy resigned as commonwealth attorney rather than prosecute his friend for Chambers's death. This is a good story and conceivably true, although no evidence has been found to bear it out. Also, there seems to be some confusion over Grundy's role as commonwealth attorney for Washington County, the county adjacent to Nelson County, where the duel occurred. Even if the story is inaccurate, however, it points to a larger truth: Grundy's loyalty to his friends and to the culture in which he lived.[12]

By far the most momentous event of these years for Grundy occurred on May 11, 1797, when he married Ann Phillips Rodgers, a pretty, oval-faced brunette then seventeen years old, commonly called "Nancy." Nancy Rodgers was the third daughter and fifth child in a family of five daughters and four sons who had moved with their father, John Rodgers, and members of his extended family to the Danville, Kentucky, area in 1781. John Rodgers farmed and raised livestock with modest landholdings, two slaves, twelve horses, and twenty-nine cattle in 1795.[13]

Grundy did not benefit financially from his marriage, unlike his famous contemporaries Henry Clay, who married the daughter of one of Lexington's wealthiest men, and John C. Calhoun, whose wedding to a cousin brought land and affluence. What Nancy Rodgers lacked in money, however, she made up for in staunch Scots-Irish roots. Her father was a cousin of John Rodgers, one of the great ministers of the eighteenth century, and her grandmother Margaret Rodgers (1720–1800) was the only daughter of John Caldwell, the founder of the Cub Creek settlement in frontier Virginia, a focal point for the spread of Presbyterianism. Grundy enhanced his political ties by personal linkages to his wife's relatives. John Rodgers's first cousin Robert Caldwell (1762–1837) presided at the adoption of the Kentucky Resolutions of 1798, and another of his first cousins, General John Caldwell (1757–1804), served as lieutenant governor of Kentucky and was a political ally of Grundy's. Subsequently, Grundy forged a strong friendship with his wife's second cousin John C. Calhoun.[14]

Nancy Rodgers brought not only Scots-Irish Presbyterianism to her husband but also a similar frontier heritage. Her mother's background was the stuff of fable. Shawnees captured Margaret Ann Dougherty (1748–1808) when she was a young child. Less than a decade later, her father and other Virginians found a number of captive girls in an Ohio Valley village. Since the girls looked and dressed like Indians and followed Indian customs, Thomas Dougherty could not readily identify his daughter. Dougherty then sang a household hymn, and one of the girls joined in. Thus, Margaret, or someone of similar background, rejoined her family and subsequently married John Rodgers.[15]

We do not know how Nancy Rodgers and Grundy met, but they married in Green County, where John Rodgers then lived and operated a mill. Samuel Grundy and Nancy's sister Polly witnessed the consent of John Rodgers on April 19, 1797; and John Reed, the clerk of Washington County, Moses Rice, and Grundy signed the marriage bond. Nancy and Felix Grundy returned to Springfield, where their first child, Louisa Caroline, was born on February 10, 1798. Thereafter, children would arrive with some regularity, assuring the young lawyer a rich family life and ongoing financial responsibilities.

5

POLITICAL BEGINNINGS

Now be honest in all your purposes, and never deceive the people.
—George Nicholas

$\mathcal{F}$elix Grundy achieved wealth and recognition in his first decade of legal practice. But in early Kentucky, success generally meant politics, and it was in the political realm that Grundy first received statewide notice. In May 1799 Grundy was elected to the second Kentucky constitutional convention, participating in the convention at Frankfort in July and August 1799 of that year.

From the outset, many Kentuckians vigorously opposed the constitution of 1792, understandable given the conflict between the centralizing features of the constitution and the centrifugal forces arising from Kentucky's expansion. Between the first two censuses, Kentucky's population increased by approximately 200 percent, from 73,677 in 1790 to 220,955 in 1800, compared with the 35 percent increase for the United States as a whole. The percent increase in the slave population during the same period, from 12,430 in 1790 to 40,343 in 1800, an increase of almost 225 percent, exceeded that of the settler population. Slaveholding was widespread. In 1800 approximately 25 percent of all households owned slaves, with an average of 4.39 slaves per household. In Washington County, where Grundy resided, 24.3 percent of households owned slaves, with an average holding of about 4 slaves.[1]

The expansion of Kentucky led to increased localism. Kentuckians wanted easily available land, an increased supply of slave labor, and more counties, both to provide convenient government and to satisfy individual ambitions for office. The Kentucky General Assembly responded to constituent pressures and added counties, increasing the number from the original nine at statehood in 1792 to forty-one in 1800. The large number of counties, each with its own courts, ambitious leadership, and local issues, both satisfied and created desires for accessible government.[2]

The Kentucky Constitution reflected George Nicholas's objective of counteracting local pressures with institutions that were more centralized and thus less susceptible to popular control. The Bluegrass elite could be expected to dominate the court of appeals, with its original jurisdiction over land, and the governorship and the senate, chosen by electors. These institutions would protect large landholdings, provide for a tax system to support a state road system and nascent manufacturing, and minimize the fragmentation of power to county courts and local justices. Nicholas's system failed, partially because of some self-inflicted wounds, such as unpopular judicial decisions, but also because of widespread opposition to its aristocratic features: the senate, for example, was soon viewed as "self-created Kentucky nobility." Only a constitutional provision for a new constitutional convention to be held in 1799 forestalled earlier efforts to change Nicholas's handiwork.

The Alien and Sedition Acts, in the summer of 1798, diverted the impetus for constitutional change. County meetings provided the principal means of expressing outrage at the "aristocratical and tyrannical federal government." Humphrey Marshall, Chief Justice Marshall's cousin, unhappily conceded that Kentuckians unanimously opposed the acts. The unrest in Kentucky had important consequences. It provided the vehicle for Henry Clay's first public success, a fiery speech in Lexington before a partisan crowd of four thousand to five thousand people. It enabled some opposed to change in the constitution, such as John Breckinridge, to regain some of their lost popularity. Finally, it resulted in the Kentucky Resolutions, ostensibly authored by Breckinridge but largely the work of Thomas Jefferson, which set forth a far-reaching theory of states' rights. Each state retained its sovereignty, relinquishing to the federal authority only specified powers. Under the Constitution, each state had the power to determine whether a federal law should be applied. Although Breckinridge toned down Jefferson's resolutions—omitting, for example, the reference in Jefferson's original draft to a state's power to nullify a federal law—the final resolutions were less restrained than the companion Virginia Resolutions, the work of James Madison.[3]

Despite Bluegrass opposition, the Kentucky legislature enacted a statute calling for a constitutional convention in July 1799, with delegates elected in May. Nicholas, adhering to a pledge never to hold public office again, worked behind the scenes and masterminded Bluegrass positions to minimize adverse change. On January 26, 1799, at Bryan's Station, outside Lexington in Fayette County, a meeting arranged by Nicholas adopted a five-point platform, including a bicameral legislature, with the senate elected directly by the people; representation in the house of representatives by number, not by county; an independent judiciary; continuation of the compact with Virginia (under which Kentucky landholdings granted under Virginia laws would be protected); and no emancipation of slaves without consent of the owners or full cash compensation.[4]

Nicholas and Breckinridge also organized county slates committed to the Bryan's Station principles and mounted a public campaign focusing on slavery. If emancipationists could take away property in the form of slaves, other forms of property would also be endangered. The emancipators, centered in Lexington, obliged their opponents by also stressing that emancipation was the core issue of the convention election. The emancipators, as Henry Clay recalled, did not favor immediate abolition; rather they advocated gradual emancipation, as in Pennsylvania, where all slaves born after a specified date would be free at age twenty-eight. The election resulted in a decisive defeat for the emancipators: Kentuckians chose only four delegates favoring emancipation in any form.[5]

There are no newspaper or other accounts of Grundy in this period, and there is no evidence of controversy in Washington County, where voters favored the convention. Washington County, solidly agrarian, was the fifth most populous county in the state in 1800, with 9,050 inhabitants—7,611 whites, 1,422 slaves, and 17 free blacks.

Felix Grundy's election to the convention in May 1799 points to a selected slate and deference to establishment candidates reminiscent of the Virginia tradition. Washington County chose John Grundy and a prominent Catholic leader, John Lawrence, as delegates to the house of representatives and Felix Grundy and Robert Abell, another Catholic leader and one of the original justices for Washington County in 1792, as the two delegates to the convention. Among the more distinctive delegates, Abell was the only Catholic, and Grundy, two months shy of his twenty-fourth birthday, was the youngest.[6]

Kentucky's second constitutional convention took place in Frankfort from July 22 until August 17, 1799. Frankfort was a river town of 628 located below imposing bluffs. Its early population consisted of warehouse owners, pilots, and itinerant rivermen running corn and whiskey down the Kentucky River to the Mississippi. Streets were of mud or plank-covered logs laid across the roadbed. Moses Austin described a village of sixty houses, eight of which were "Brick and Stone"; he found the capital building to be "a good Convient [*sic*] Hous but not Elegant" and "Other Publick Buildings . . . not worth Notice." After Frankfort was chosen as the state capital in 1792, its innkeepers enjoyed a regular legislative clientele, who took over the two leading inns when the General Assembly was in session. The innkeeper Turnstall used his upper story as a dormitory, where guests occasionally slept four or five to a bed. One large dining room, measuring forty-two feet by seventy-two feet, served as the site for legislative negotiations and conviviality. During the convention summer the fifty-eight delegates dominated the little town. The routine of two sessions a day, one in the morning and one in the late afternoon, afforded ample time for luncheon and dinner debate and discussion in taverns and private residences.[7]

This must have been a stimulating time for young Grundy, who was making his initial foray on the state political scene. But there were emotional overtones as well. Nancy gave birth to the second Grundy daughter, Elizabeth Burkham, on August 24, 1799, just one week after the convention ended. In addition, George Nicholas was very ill. According to a later account presumably furnished by Grundy, during the convention Nicholas took his former student aside and said, "MR GRUNDY, you have commenced political life. Now be honest in all your purposes, and never deceive the people, and your success is certain." Grundy took this advice to heart, later speaking with pride of this guidance and obviously seeing himself as having been loyal to his teacher's precepts. On July 25, 1799, soon after the meeting, Nicholas died.[8]

Contrary to their prevalence today, lawyers did not dominate the convention, at least not numerically. There were only nine lawyers among the fifty-eight delegates. Five represented the core Bluegrass establishment—Breckinridge and four judges, Caleb Wallace of the court of appeals, the federal district judge Harry Innes, and the state district judges John Allen and Buckner Thruston. The other four lawyers reflected the coming of age of a Kentucky-educated bar, with Grundy, John Rowan, and William Logan having studied under Nicholas. Eight of the nine lawyers, including Grundy, joined the important drafting committee. All but one delegate owned slaves, with twenty-eight delegates owning more than ten slaves, and thirty-six had served as county justices. Somewhat surprisingly, only ten members had participated in the first constitutional convention, seven years earlier, one being the redoubtable and respected Benjamin Logan. Three ministers served, compared with seven in the first convention.[9]

The convention itself was a straightforward affair, with relative order and marked dispatch, particularly in view of the changes effected. The election results had removed the emancipation issue from the agenda and brought to the convention a pragmatic group of delegates with a variety of legislative interests. The Bryan's Station party, headed by Breckinridge and Caleb Wallace, reflected the views of the most powerful—and most conservative—bloc of delegates. Opposing them, Samuel Taylor and John Bailey, an emancipator of 1792, now from frontier Logan County, presented a fairly consistent democratic position and displayed considerable hostility to the Breckinridge group. The veteran assembly leaders Alexander Bullitt, Robert Johnson, and Philemon Thomas led the wealthy planters, who generally supported legislative supremacy. The four young lawyers, while not a bloc, tended to vote together.

These principal groups within the convention reached broadly acceptable compromises. The delegates eliminated the electoral college and decided that voters would elect the governor and the senators. They also established the office of lieutenant governor, modeled loosely upon the vice presidency in the U.S. Constitution. The court of appeals, the highest court in the state, was limited to appellate jurisdiction, and the legislature was authorized to establish subordinate courts. Delegates retained the slavery provisions of the constitution of 1792 and the compact with Virginia. They also made amendment of the constitution extremely difficult.

We can judge Grundy's record at the convention only through the abbreviated record and some later references. The official journal provides a straightforward account of actions taken in the relatively brief, twenty-six-day session, but it does not include debates, which were not recorded. In contrast to the constitutional convention of 1792, which had only one recorded vote, there were twenty-six roll-call votes in the 1799 convention. John Breckinridge kept notes on the first half of the convention, apparently as an aid in preparing his own positions, and his notes, now at the Library of Congress, provide some flavor.

When Grundy incurred the ire of the Lexington establishment in 1805–6, his adversaries noted that he had first become known for his advocacy of the circuit court system at the convention. John Breckinridge reported Grundy's advocacy of circuit courts but also disclosed Grundy's first legislative initiative, a proposal to reduce the minimum age of representatives in the house of representatives from twenty-four to twenty-one. It is a measure of Grundy's confidence that he made this readily defeated proposal even though he had not attained the age of twenty-four, specified for delegates by the existing constitution.[10]

Advocates promoted a circuit court system to make justice more convenient in an agrarian society. The issue arose through a proposal to end the district court system and limit lower-court jurisdiction to the county. Samuel Taylor, a leading proponent, pointed out that a localized circuit court system would be more convenient and save money. Green Clay, a wealthy landowner whose erratic convention views nettled Breckinridge, suggested that there be a court in each county, comprising one circuit judge and two resident assistant judges. Cases would be tried in the county where the defendant resided, where the real estate at issue was located, or where the crime had been committed.[11]

Grundy, who became one of the principal spokesmen for circuit courts, comes alive in Breckinridge's notes with respect to this issue. Setting forth the basic principle that justice should be available with minimum delay and expense, Grundy stated that the circuit courts would facilitate attendance and minimize the inconvenience and injustice of witnesses' having to travel long distances. Young Felix appears, however, to have sought revision of the court system for reasons that went deeper than convenience and cost. Echoing his father and brothers, he opposed a judicial system imposed by Virginia that gave access and control to the landholding elite of the state, represented by Bluegrass lawyers.

Breckinridge spoke directly to Grundy's position, generally accepting broad principles but disagreeing with Grundy's conclusion. He conceded that a few states did have a county court system, but he argued that the existing system could be modified to accommodate concerns and produce a more consistent and coherent system of law. Ultimately, however, Breckinridge suggested that the creation of subordinate courts be left to future legislatures. The convention accepted Breckinridge's position on August 7, 1799, after first rejecting, by a vote of 29–23, Green Clay's suggestion that the circuit court system be tried for a few years.[12]

The vote on circuit courts revealed one of the major divisions at the convention. Almost all the delegates from the Bluegrass opposed the circuit court system, while most of the representatives of the newer counties supported the change. Not surprisingly, the five senior lawyers, beneficiaries of the existing system, voted no, and all of the younger lawyers—Grundy, Rowan, Logan, and Bledsoe—favored trying the new approach.[13]

Breckinridge noted only one other occasion on which Grundy spoke. Grundy expressed concern that in an election with five or six candidates for state office, a person could win only if he had a plurality. Grundy suggested that the legislature decide the election if none of the candidates received a majority. Although the proposal was defeated, it reveals Grundy's support for leg-islative power, a position reflecting his Jeffersonian fear of a strong executive and one that he would maintain for much of his career.[14]

The twenty-six roll-call votes illuminate Grundy's emerging political views more clearly than do Breckinridge's notes. Grundy joined most of the "demo-cratic" group in a successful initiative to reject property qualifications for the post of state senator and in losing efforts to preserve the vote for free blacks and Indians, to preserve a future option of secret ballots in voting, and to set aside the Virginia compact with respect to land rents. Grundy, moreover, un-successfully favored the election of the sheriff and lower-ranking militia offi-cers. Grundy also shared the widespread desire to diminish the power of the judiciary. He joined the majority in allowing judges to be removed for official acts or judicial opinions and permitting diminution of judicial compensation while judges were in office.[15]

On the issue of slavery, the maneuvering before the election assured that there would be no fundamental change with respect to emancipation. In the only significant vote affecting slavery, Grundy joined the majority in voting down, 37–14, a provision allowing the legislature to ban future importation of slaves into Kentucky. One admirer of Grundy's, writing in the 1840s, attrib-uted to him and Breckinridge the slavery provisions of the 1799 constitution. This, however, appears to be an overstatement in light of the preconvention votes, and as far as Grundy is concerned, it probably reflects his prominence and political power in the years after the convention.[16]

An anecdote reveals Grundy's good-humored toughness. At the convention, Grundy roomed with the Catholic Robert Abell and a former minister turned lawyer, almost certainly William Bledsoe, who had been a Baptist preacher. Bledsoe told his roommates that he intended to propose that no Catholic be el-igible for office in Kentucky. Upon hearing this, Grundy immediately assured Bledsoe that he would propose that "no broken-down Presbyterian preacher" could hold office either if Bledsoe presented such a provision.[17]

Grundy's role in the constitutional convention of 1799 was important in three respects. First, it marked his emergence as a spokesman for Kentuckians outside the Bluegrass and as a promising political figure. He represented a new generation in Kentucky politics, raised and educated in the state. Second, the available record suggests that Grundy already had formed egalitarian political views. He favored legislative supremacy, no property qualifications for voting, enfranchisement of free blacks and Indians, direct election of the sheriff and some militia officers, and control of the judiciary. Only with respect to preservation of the constitutional protection of slavery did he adhere to the more traditional position.

Third, Grundy's recorded votes at the convention make clear the extent to which Grundy differed from Breckinridge and what remained of the court party that had long dominated Kentucky. This youngest member of the convention in fact opposed John Breckinridge more than almost all other members. Grundy's willingness to take on the Kentucky establishment reflects his self-assurance and his commitment to his emerging political views.[18]

Although Grundy has become known to historians as the principal opponent of the "Bluegrass System" because of his later opposition to the banking provisions of the Kentucky Insurance Company, he did not emerge suddenly and full blown as an oppositionist. His stances in 1799 foreshadowed his role in 1804. At the constitutional convention he adopted positions different from those of John Breckinridge and other Bluegrass spokesmen. Grundy's later allies were drawn from the same ranks as those who largely voted with him in 1799, and his opponents tended to be from the Breckinridge supporters.

6

CIRCUIT COURT REFORM

The cunning and intriguing conduct of Mr. Grundy and others.

—Achilles Sneed

*G*rundy's participation in the constitutional convention of 1799 led to service in the Kentucky legislature. He was elected to the house of representatives in May 1800, after his brother John stepped down in 1799. Reelected for the two succeeding sessions, Grundy became one of the most powerful Kentucky legislators. He led the Green River settlers in seeking debt relief, a recurring, contentious issue. In an environment of conflict between the Bluegrass and the Southside, and building on the ambitions of like-minded young lawyers, Grundy succeeded in 1802 in effecting circuit court reform along the lines originally proposed in the constitutional convention.

Legislative sessions in early Kentucky were relatively uneventful, featuring only a few initiatives of any importance. The legislature met in Frankfort for six or seven weeks in November and December, during the lull in the agricultural cycle, and spent much of its time on elections and salaries, divorce petitions and private bills of varying types. One veteran legislator commented with respect to the 1801 session that out of sixty-eight acts, only five or six were of a general nature, and even those were "short laws." Legislators like Grundy, however, began to recognize the legislature's potential to bring about fundamental change.[1]

The split between the Bluegrass, north of the Kentucky River, and the Southside dominated Kentucky politics during Grundy's political years in the state. The isolation of the Southside meant that self-sufficient farmers cared little about government, which rarely intruded in their lives. Two issues mattered most and could be all-important: entitlement to land and access to courts. Unsurprisingly, questions surrounding land and the judiciary engendered bitter controversy.

The Green River country, the heart of the Southside, nurtured tough egal-itarianism and Jeffersonian Republicans. No less a personage than the future king of France, Louis-Philippe, gave an unvarnished, if biased, account of life there in 1797. He found provisions scarce, but what made the trip "absolutely unbearable" was "the quality of the new settlers . . . the most villainous breed of men I have ever come across. . . . the scum of Ireland and America, . . . They are crude, lazy and inhospitable to an extreme." In the Barrens, twenty-two miles above the Green River, "everybody railed to his hearts content. They claim to be overwhelmed by taxes, although there may be no civilized people who pay any-where near as little." They said that it was useless "even to pay for the support of the local government of Kentucky," and they "complain, with the same angry acerbity, of government by rich eastern businessmen." Louis-Philippe, who dis-dained such "paltry Jacobin commonplaces," wrote that the settlers carped that "the rich are not happy merely selling land at exorbitant prices but find various ways to extort what little money the settlers make."[2]

Grundy emerged as the leader of the Southside, and particularly of the Green River settlers. Populous Washington County, in the Outer Bluegrass, not only provided a strong political base for Grundy but also was located near the Green River region. Grundy's marriage into a Scots-Irish family in Green County increased his political network. His law practice extended to the newer counties, which was particularly important in a region that had not yet devel-oped strong elites. Grundy's outgoing affability and good humor also served him well in the highly personalized campaigning that marked rural Kentucky. Most significantly, Grundy's votes in the 1799 convention revealed an egalitar-ian and democratic perspective well suited to the political views of the farmers of the Southside. Indeed, Grundy would exhibit initiative and unwavering sup-port of Southside issues—the little guy's desire for access to land, debt relief, and the courts—throughout his variegated career, at both the federal and state levels. From start to finish, Grundy was egalitarian, a "Southsider."

The issue of debt extension for lands originally in the Green River military district highlighted the differences between Bluegrass and Southside. Known as the Barrens because of their lack of forest, the military district lands had been set aside by Virginia in 1779 to satisfy Revolutionary military warrants. In 1795 Kentucky ended the soldiers' exclusive claimant rights but could not agree on how to dispose of the increasingly valuable land. Bluegrass leaders, who hoped to sell the Green River lands for the benefit of the state treasury, opposed low land prices and easy credit. Concerned about population flow to these squatter lands, they feared a changing political dynamic in the legislature. They had good reason: twenty-one of the thirty-five counties created between 1792 and 1801 lay south of the Kentucky River. A class ethic contributed to these concerns. The Bluegrass leaders feared that the Green River lands would be populated by settlers who did not have established wealth and who would show little deference to the educated elite around Lexington. In words reminiscent of George Washington in 1749, John Breckinridge wrote that the Green River area would be a place where "wretchedness, poverty and sickness will always reign."[3]

Unable to resolve differences, the legislature temporized. In 1795 it provided relief for the growing number of squatters in the military district, authorizing a preemption right of two hundred acres per settler at thirty cents per acre. In 1797 the general assembly extended the preemption right to anyone moving into the Barrens before July 1798, for up to two hundred acres at slightly higher average prices. Significantly, the legislators did not require payment for a year, and those who had not yet paid for lands provided under the 1795 act could also pay later, at 5 percent interest. When extension arose in 1798, John Breckinridge led an unsuccessful effort to restrict the extension only to poor and permanent settlers, and not speculators. Unsurprisingly, the cheap Green River lands drew settlers. The Houston family, from North Carolina, for example, in 1805 passed up land near Louisville at six dollars per acre and bought land on the Green River at fifty cents per acre. The prices and financial terms led to some of the highest rates of landownership in Kentucky. In Logan County, 67 percent of free adult males owned land in 1800, with rates not far behind in such counties as Christian, Barren, and Green. Smaller farms predominated, with half the farms in Muhlenberg County in 1811 comprising no more than two hundred acres.[4]

The Green River settlers wanted debt relief. The son of David Purviance, a political leader from Bourbon County, wrote in 1848 that Grundy from the beginning espoused the Southside cause, whereas Breckinridge opposed debt relief. The Green River champion generally succeeded in obtaining favorable terms. In the 1800 session, concessions to Green River settlers included a further lowering of the price of land, to twenty cents per acre for settlers occupying up to four hundred acres. More significantly, the legislature made major adjustments in the debt payment terms. By a vote of 37–17 in the house, with Grundy voting with the majority, the legislature divided the amounts due the state into nine installments, with the first not due for two years.[5]

Grundy showed an early interest in the details of the legislative process. He also proved persistent and imaginative, ready for negotiation and compromise, but he did not like to lose. After a legislative setback on debt relief in 1800, Grundy visited Governor James Garrard, who asked why he was in a bad humor, noting, "I thought that you dreaded no member of the house but Breckinridge." Grundy replied that he dreaded no man but that Purviance had bested him. With the governor's support, Grundy soon negotiated a compromise with Purviance, achieved after artful maneuvering.[6]

Grundy augmented his political strength in the Green River district—and the Southside generally—by his battle for circuit court reform. Yet again, the legal establishment in the Bluegrass opposed Grundy and the ambitious young lawyers in other areas of the state. Agrarian democrats may have railed against lawyers, but they elected attorneys to the legislature in increasing numbers. As Kentucky-trained lawyers established practices throughout the state, they often turned to politics, just as Grundy, Rowan, and William Logan had participated in the constitutional convention of 1799. In November 1802 William Russell, a prominent Fayette County planter, wrote John Breckinridge, "We have a large number of attorneys in the lower house; therefore at no loss for speakers."[7]

The legal establishment, centered in Lexington and Frankfort, featured lawyers appearing before Kentucky's court of appeals and the U.S. district court, both in Frankfort. The Bluegrass bar, headed by the Federalist U.S. attorney Joseph Hamilton Daveiss, believed that the existing system of six state district courts and the court of appeals, anchored by the U.S. district court, facilitated the development of an integrated body of law for Kentucky. They were mindful, however, of the system's advantages to them.[8]

Lawyers in the Southside, on the other hand, mainly practiced before county courts. A circuit court system, which would eliminate the district courts and enhance the authority of county courts, would be to the advantage of Southside lawyers, who both resented and aspired to the success of the Bluegrass bar. The circuit courts would require judges and circuit attorneys, who would be paid in cash—a scarce commodity. Grundy became identified with circuit court reform and was the unquestioned leader, but John Pope, Ninian Edwards, and Allen Wakefield also strongly advocated change. Benjamin Logan, the grand old man of Kentucky politics, provided stalwart support.

Ninian Edwards (1775–1833) exemplified the energy and ambition of the young lawyers behind Grundy. Born in Montgomery County, Maryland, and educated at what is now Dickinson College, in Carlisle, Pennsylvania, he moved in 1794 to Nelson County, Kentucky, and joined Grundy and other young lawyers traveling together in the county court system in the Outer Bluegrass. In 1798 Edwards relocated to Logan County, where he became a land speculator, leader of the bar in Russellville, the business center of southwestern Kentucky, and part of the politically controlling Ewing faction. A natural ally of Grundy's, he followed him to the Kentucky Court of Appeals before being appointed by President Madison as governor of the Illinois Territory in 1809.[9]

The arguments for and against the circuit court system first appeared in the constitutional convention in 1799. Repeating the same themes, Grundy in 1800 proposed to abolish the district and quarter-sessions courts and establish circuit courts to meet three times a year for six-day terms. This measure, pushed by Grundy as the representative of a committee dealing with judicial matters, passed the house by a vote of 36–22 but was defeated in the senate through the efforts of John Breckinridge. The assembly's activities in 1800 did not win plaudits in the Bluegrass. Henry Clay wrote Breckinridge that the legislature had "attempted much and done little," thereby providing evidence of their wisdom.[10]

Grundy, undaunted, strengthened his position by helping to remove a rival. In 1800 a senate seat became available, and Breckinridge, hoping to join his newly elected friend Jefferson in Washington, decided to run. Although John Adair was generally Grundy's ally, Grundy played a major role in Breckinridge's 68–13 win over Adair, garnering Green River support for Lexington's leading lawyer. There is no written evidence regarding why Grundy supported Breckinridge, but it is hard to avoid the conclusion that the astute Southsider saw the advantages of having the Northern Champion distant in Washington.[11]

Grundy returned to the circuit court issue when the legislature convened in 1801. He decided to offer a more radical suggestion, going back to Green Clay's suggestion in the convention of 1799: each county would have its own circuit court (although some of lesser population would share), with a traveling circuit judge trained in the law, and two assistants in each court, who would not be required to have legal training. The *Frankfort Palladium* of November 20, 1801, reported Grundy's proposal, summarizing its pros and cons. Debate in the legislature lasted four days. Grundy's opening statements set forth unobjectionable principles. The well-being of the people—the basic purpose of government—could be achieved only if advantages and privileges were equally and conveniently available to all citizens. The present system provided benefits only to some, working mainly to the advantage of the wealthy and some lawyers, but not the small farmer. The elimination of district courts would reduce the cost and inconvenience now imposed on principals and witnesses forced to travel long distances from their home counties. In addition, at the quarter-sessions court talented lawyers took advantage of the judges' lack of legal knowledge;

this would be remedied by a circuit court system in which lay judges could be supported by a judge trained as a lawyer. Grundy also asserted that the new system would save six thousand dollars annually.

Opponents objected to much of Grundy's presentation, including his cost assessments. They principally argued that the district court system produced uniformity in decisions, particularly in land disputes. They also argued that a circuit court system would mean even greater judicial subservience to the legislature. Just as the convention of 1799 had authorized reducing judicial compensation, the assembly, by constant changes to the judicial structure, would reduce the authority and stature of judges. Thomas Todd, a Bluegrass judge of the court of appeals, wrote Breckinridge that Grundy proposed to abolish the Paris district court as the first step in dismantling the entire system. After heated arguments, Grundy's measure failed by eleven votes. Nathaniel Hart, an astute vote counter, believed that the legislature would satisfy the young lawyers by establishing two or three more district courts. Circuit court adversaries did suggest additional district courts in the Southside, but Grundy rejected the compromise.[12]

Samuel Hopkins attributed the impetus for circuit court reform to the Southside. The regional differences were also evident in an unsuccessful initiative to move the capital from Frankfort to Bardstown. North-south issues emerged in a more novel way. Tennessee's governor, Archibald Roane, proposed that Kentucky cede to Tennessee a portion of Green River County, as the residents allegedly desired. Although the unanimous house report rejected any cession, Samuel McDowell surmised that the Green River debt had triggered the desire for separation and suggested that, as Breckinridge had predicted, Kentucky would lose the debt or the people.[13]

Any conservative hopes that the circuit court proposal would not be revived were dashed in 1802. The indefatigable Grundy pushed his plan for the fourth successive year and succeeded in securing its adoption, assisted by political jostling arising from selection of the newly authorized congressional representatives and conservative unwillingness to compromise in any way.[14]

Kentucky's population in the 1800 census entitled the state to six representatives to the U.S. Congress. Some delegates favored statewide selection for all congressmen, but the legislature opted for districts, carving up the state to suit particular members. Correspondents informed Breckinridge of the latest rumors and explained that the process had taken time, intrigue, and cunning because of the need to satisfy ambitious men.[15]

Many delegates assumed that Grundy would be a candidate for Congress, and given his ambition, he certainly wanted the post. But there was a rub. Matthew Walton, the leading citizen of Washington County and a consistent supporter of Grundy's, apparently also desired the seat. Robert Breckinridge wrote on December 2 that Walton or Grundy would contest one district, but on December 27 Christopher Greenup advised John Breckinridge that only Walton and Robert Wickliffe would be candidates. Whether Grundy withdrew when Walton expressed an interest or whether the two reached an accommodation is not known, but Grundy did not offer himself for Congress.[16]

In the midst of the congressional maneuvering, John Pope, Grundy's classmate and a young lawyer in Shelbyville, reintroduced the circuit court proposal. After this measure failed, Grundy produced a bill extending the district courts that was similar to the measure defeated the year before. To the consternation of Thomas Todd, adherents of the status quo rejected any significant change, either misreading votes or being foolishly stubborn. They failed to recognize that many assembly members wanted more convenient justice even if they had previously opposed more radical measures. After the defeat of the district court proposal, Grundy brought forth his familiar circuit court bill, which now passed with thirty-four votes in the house and fifteen in the senate. Governor Garrard objected to the bill on both policy and technical grounds, but the legislature overrode his veto by a majority in each house, the first such action in the state's history.[17]

Grundy's success brought predictable reactions. Angry members of the Kentucky elite inundated Breckinridge with letters. Harry Innes described the bill as crude and charged that it had been adopted by tampering and bribery. James Brown, a talented but haughty stalwart of the Bluegrass bar, wrote that he was moving to New Orleans, in part because of the instability of the judiciary system. Achilles Sneed blamed the legislation on "the cunning and intriguing conduct of Mr. Grundy and others."[18]

The new law took effect on passage, with nine circuit court judges, each to be paid $750 per year, and two assistants for each county, to be paid $2 per day. Grundy rewarded his allies. Ninian Edwards, Allen Wakefield, and Christopher Greenup became circuit court judges, joining the six on the district court bench.[19]

Judge Harry Innes's intemperate reaction led to a tantalizing exchange. Innes plaintively wrote Breckinridge on June 19, 1803, that he had learned that the contents of his earlier letter had been leaked and that he was worried about Grundy's reaction. Breckinridge gave Innes little comfort, recalling that Innes had said that improper practices had been used, "even bribery itself," and volunteering that he had heard repeatedly of corruption in the circuit court vote. He also disclosed that the source of the leak could only have been Joseph Hamilton Daveiss, the U.S. attorney and Grundy's good friend. Regrettably, no evidence exists as to whether Grundy and Innes met on this matter, and there is no suggestion beyond these letters of any corruption.[20]

Grundy had achieved his first significant legislative triumph. He did not initiate the circuit court proposal, which had originally been put forward by Green Clay in the constitutional convention of 1799 and was similar to one adopted in Ohio at about the same time. Nor was he the only lawyer to see that providing a more localized judicial system would enhance professional opportunities. But Grundy persevered and prevailed. His persistence and determination over four legislative sessions resulted in a dramatic change in the system, one that was upsetting to many. Grundy used a newly established leadership base and shrewd management of the legislative process to achieve his goal. Perhaps most important, he had the self-confidence and courage to take on the Bluegrass leadership.[21]

The circuit court system, in modified form, remains the Kentucky approach. Even though the use of two lay assistants was criticized from its inception, did not work well in practice, and was eliminated in 1816, there is little doubt that this approach was consistent with the popular view that judicial decisions should be heavily interlaced with common sense. Moreover, it is doubtful that a system based on county courts having more than one judge could have been created otherwise, since there simply were not enough trained lawyers outside the major legal centers at the time. Yet today one can only be sympathetic to the Bluegrass argument that development of a coherent legal system for Kentucky would be impeded and delayed by a county-based system relying on lay assistants and only nine judges. The extension of the district court system would have been a more sensible and less radical solution.

7

GRUNDY AND CLAY

Exclusive privileges shall not be granted.
—William Littell

fter his legislative success in 1802, Grundy did not stand for re-election to the Kentucky General Assembly. Instead he moved to Bardstown in early 1803. His legal—and political—base increasingly centered in the burgeoning Green River country. Bardstown, more conveniently located, featured a larger legal and social community. In addition, the passage of the circuit court legislation gave more weight to Bardstown and Nelson County, the center of one of the judgeships. Grundy also may have decided that a change of community would be desirable for his family, since his first son, George Seay Grundy, born on May 26, 1801, had died on September 11, 1802, Felix's twenty-seventh birthday.

Bardstown differed little in appearance from when Grundy had attended Salem Academy. Louis-Philippe described Bardstown in 1797 as large for a Kentucky town, with perhaps 150 houses on a plateau surrounded by dense forest. The population included merchants, innkeepers, and laborers. When Grundy moved to Bardstown in January 1803, he rented a house next to Banes Tavern, on Arch Street. On April 15, 1803, he purchased ten acres adjacent to Market Street, on the western side of Bardstown, for two hundred dollars, and he apparently built a house there.[1]

The move to Bardstown did not result in major change. Bardstown was only twelve miles away from the Grundy family homestead on Cartwright Creek, and Grundy maintained his base in Springfield. He continued to serve as the Washington County attorney until April 7, 1806, although he stepped down as a trustee of Springfield at the end of 1802. Residence in Bardstown did place him in more regular contact with other lawyers, and it allowed him to participate in the Bardstown Pleiades, a social and debating society.[2]

Grundy's practice flourished in Bardstown. Not surprisingly, he became the attorney for Nelson's newly established circuit court, receiving an allowance of one hundred dollars per year. His office soon included young lawyers seeking training, just as he had studied under Nicholas. One of the first, Benjamin Hardin Jr. (1784–1852), subsequently a five-term U.S. congressman and famous trial lawyer, read law with Grundy for a year, beginning on April 1, 1805. Hardin's biographer, who included an admiring portrait of Grundy, reported that he had a valuable practice and spreading fame.[3]

Grundy continued to add to his family responsibilities. John Rodgers Grundy joined his two older sisters on December 7, 1803. Two more children arrived in Bardstown: Margaret Ann Camron, born on October 6, 1805, and James Priestley Harrison, born on October 2, 1807. Thus, shortly after Felix's thirty-second birthday, he and Nancy had five living children.

Significantly in light of her heritage, Nancy Grundy joined the local Presbyterian church in 1803. Felix, however, did not become a member and was seemingly unaffected by the religious revivals sweeping Kentucky. Robert McAfee, who was studying law with John Breckinridge in 1800–1801, wrote that "it was firmly imposed on my mind that a person could not be religious and a Lawyer at the same time" and that the only lawyer in the state who professed religion endured jeers and derision. Early Kentuckians were relatively unchurched, and Grundy's brothers took wives from varying denominations. George and Guardum Grundy both married Baptists, Robert Grundy wed a Presbyterian, and John Grundy's third wife was Catholic. Felix Grundy's noted tolerance started at home.[4]

Like other aspiring politicians, Grundy welcomed civic responsibilities. In 1801 he joined the Masons, a secret order that was then expanding dramatically. Originally an apprentice in the Lexington chapter, he became a member of the lodge in Bardstown, and he continued to be an active Mason throughout his life. In an important symbol of acceptance, the trustees of Transylvania University elected their former student to the board in October 1802. Political developments remained of paramount interest to Grundy, however. He visited Frankfort during the assembly sessions in December 1803 and did not conceal his ambitions. Benjamin Howard advised Breckinridge that Grundy intended to run for the U.S. Senate. Grundy's focus changed, however. He returned to the Kentucky house of representatives in 1804 and engaged in an epic struggle with Henry Clay for leadership of the assembly and the future direction of Kentucky. At issue were banking privileges for the Kentucky Insurance Company.[5]

*   *   *

Jefferson's dream of agrarian self-sufficiency was never achieved in Kentucky, which from its earliest days participated in a market economy and exported its products down the Mississippi. The difficulties of land transport in the pre-steamboat West meant that hemp and other manufactured products from Lexington, as well as salt, tobacco, and whiskey from throughout the state, were shipped by river to New Orleans. Exports accelerated as the Napoleonic Wars in Europe created demand, just after the Treaty of San Lorenzo in 1795 permitted full American navigation of the Mississippi. The Lexingtonians, who dominated trade in early Kentucky, typically imported manufactured goods on credit and then sold the goods in return for ownership of agricultural products exported to New Orleans, with sales proceeds remitted to eastern creditors. Hard money, eastern bank notes, and letters of credit customarily drained back to the Atlantic states in payment for the manufactured goods.

As a result, early Kentucky fell chronically short of gold or silver coin, or specie. Barter predominated. Parties expressed contractual obligations in both dollars and British pounds even twenty-five years after the Revolution. Personal notes, often of one or more third parties, traded at discounts. When Grundy bought an interest in Greenville Springs, at Harrodsburg, he expressed his investment in both dollars and pounds, with payments to be made in a farm to be purchased, his notes, and obligations to make certain expenditures. The system worked reasonably well in an agrarian economy, but its complexity in payment and valuation limited its usefulness in a more sophisticated society.[6]

The merchants of the early Ohio Valley took the lead in trying to address some of these problems. Pittsburgh and Cincinnati innovators in 1802 and 1803 established commercial export corporations. Lexington merchants answered with the Kentucky Insurance Company, organized in early 1802. In its first months the company engaged principally in insurance and operated without a state charter. In December 1802, however, the organizers submitted to the Kentucky General Assembly a charter with two important provisions, under which the Kentucky Insurance Company could issue negotiable notes with interest. The charter was approved with little review, and the insurance company became the Lexington Bank, complete with a new bank building and fifty thousand dollars in quickly raised capital. The well-managed institution soon paid an annual dividend of more than 15 percent.[7]

Banking operations like those conducted by the Kentucky Insurance Company appeared simple but required disciplined management for long-term success. A bank made loans by issuing its own notes, which stipulated that the bank would pay on demand or at a specified time a designated amount in specie. The notes became a medium of circulation, usually trading at discounts based on interest rate, distance from the bank, and confidence in the bank's ability to redeem its notes. Since notes were not usually redeemed, the bank could become very profitable by making more loans, usually at multiples of specie reserves. This proliferation of credit could have a devastating effect if there were a loss of confidence and notes were called for redemption in amounts exceeding the specie available for payment. Few banks over the long term would be able to gauge and maintain a proper balance between notes and specie in the vault.

The operations and success of the Kentucky Insurance Company attracted attention and became the centerpiece of the legislative battles of 1804. Should the insurance company be allowed to exercise the banking privilege of issuing negotiable notes with interest, anathema to true Jeffersonians? Opponents argued that legislators from Lexington had slipped the provision under the noses of distracted legislators in 1802 and should now be denied banking privileges.

Henry Clay led the defense of the Kentucky Insurance Company. Clay, elected to the house in 1803 as a delegate from Fayette County, first attracted public attention as an antislavery voice during the maneuvering before the 1799 convention and as a forceful and eloquent opponent of the Alien and Sedition Acts. A Jeffersonian Republican, he adhered to the more conservative principles of the dominant Bluegrass gentry almost from the day of his wedding in 1799 to Lucretia Hart, the daughter of Colonel Thomas Hart, a leading Lexington merchant and manufacturer. Clay's oratory, common sense, and charm gave him quick success as a lawyer. The death of George Nicholas in 1799, the accession of John Breckinridge to the U.S. Senate in 1800, and Clay's brother-in-law James Brown's acceptance of a position in Louisiana in 1803 made Clay preeminent at the Bluegrass bar.[8]

In Clay's first legislative session, in 1803, the legislature again postponed payments due on the Green River lands and defeated an effort to eliminate the banking provisions of the Kentucky Insurance Company Act. The Southside opposed Lexington interests, yet in Grundy's absence the "thinking members from the Blue Grass were not unduly alarmed." Grundy rejoined the house in August 1804, as a delegate from Nelson County, setting the stage for his battle with Clay. His election even as a county newcomer surprised no one. The acknowledged leader of the Southside, he had been campaigning throughout the region against the Kentucky Insurance Company. Moreover, his family had

long been prominent in the region, and Grundy had attended school in Bardstown, provided leadership in a neighboring county, and had close ties with John
Rowan and other Nelson County leaders.[9]

The clash between Clay and Grundy in 1804 and 1805 made great theater.
Historians have delighted in drawing sharp contrasts, even with respect to their
physical appearance, between Grundy as a rough-and-ready spokesman for the
frontier and Clay as a more sophisticated and suave representative of a cultivated Lexington. Aside from the inaccuracies, these characterizations obscure
the similarities between Clay and Grundy and simplify a more nuanced political struggle.

Grundy and Clay were both born in Virginia, with Grundy being the older
by a little more than one and one-half years. Each had numerous older brothers, Grundy the youngest of nine sons and Clay the seventh of nine children,
and each suffered the death of his father at an early age, Grundy at eight and
Clay at four. Each family enjoyed modest status. Grundy, however, grew up on
the frontier, while Clay had only left eastern Virginia in 1797. Grundy's years at
Salem Academy had provided him with the frontier version of a classical education, which Clay lacked, but both had benefited from the tutelage of a distinguished lawyer, George Nicholas and George Wythe, respectively. Clay clearly
had the advantage of years in the sophisticated society of Williamsburg and
Richmond, but Grundy was no rube, having spent several formative years in
Lexington. Both had married at twenty-two, to wives that widened their political reach, although Clay's marriage to Lucretia Hart had brought more immediate social and financial benefit.[10]

Clay and Grundy both benefited from an outgoing and attractive personality. Their early success was principally due to their wit, common sense, and
ability to assess human character. Contemporary descriptions of them are surprisingly similar, although Clay comes across as more engaging and more of a
partygoer, with a liking for cards, wine, and pretty women. Full of enthusiasm,
vigor, and ambition, they entered happily into the political life of early Kentucky.

Notwithstanding their similarities, Grundy and Clay differed in core respects. Part of Clay's charm rested on his impetuosity and his willingness to
take risks at long odds, demonstrated later in famous gambling sessions in
Washington. He was a master of repartee whose satiric wit left wounds and enemies. Grundy, by contrast, always appeared in control, and as a Senate eulogy
by Silas Wright, of New York, later attested, "calm, cool and collected." Affa-

bility and warmth did not fully mask his shrewdness, or as some would say, calculation. He leavened his quick wit with humor and kindness and made few
enemies on the legislative floor, whether in 1804–5 or later.[11]

Politically, both Grundy and Clay followed Jeffersonian ideals, although the
next few years would foreshadow the divisions that would ultimately lead Clay
to support the Whig Party. Grundy, shaped by familial opposition to Bluegrass
and Virginia-style exclusionary leadership, was definitely more egalitarian than
Clay, who was already the voice of the business-oriented class favoring governmental support of commerce.

Although Grundy and Clay were young men when they began their political rivalry in 1804, aged twenty-nine and twenty-seven, respectively, both
had already attained leadership status. Clay continued the tradition of George
Nicholas and John Breckinridge in representing the interests of Lexington and
the Bluegrass. Grundy's more diverse followers of the Southside ranged from
the egalitarian small farmers to county oligopolists, such as Grundy's own family in Washington County, but all shared agrarian interests. William Littell,
a lawyer and legislative reporter, amusingly presented the background of the
conflict to come:

> And there was in the South Country, a certain man named Felix, who was
> one of the chiefs of the people. Moreover, this man Felix was a mighty man
> of words, and was skilled in all the learning of the Greeks and Romans, and
> was expert in all the laws and ordinances of the realm of Kentucky, and with
> mighty arguments convinced he the people. . . .
>
> And . . . when the merchants of the city of Lexington heard that the wrath
> of Felix was kindled against them, they were sore afraid. . . .
>
> Then all the people looked on Henry. . . . Now Henry was an exceeding
> learned counselor, the spirit of discretion and eloquence was in him; and
> when he spoke, all the people marveled at his wisdom.[12]

In an atmosphere of animosity the legislature convened on November 5,
1804. The election had produced important newcomers, such as Richard M.
Johnson, twenty-four years old, who would become a lifelong friend and ally of
Grundy's. The assembly chose another close Grundy friend, William Logan, as
speaker. Battle lines first emerged over the selection of a U.S. senator. The Bluegrass, which had furnished all of Kentucky's senators since statehood, were divided over the candidacies of John Brown, of Frankfort, who was up for reelection, and Judge Buckner Thruston, of Lexington. The Southside—and

Grundy—enthusiastically supported John Adair, a Revolutionary War veteran and successful planter from Harrodsburg with whom Grundy had collaborated in the constitutional convention of 1799. Nervous legislators wrote Breckinridge about the activities and effectiveness of Grundy. One effort failed. Grundy spoke with his friend Jo Daveiss, stalwart in his claim that John Brown had been part of a treasonable conspiracy involving Spain in 1788. Grundy, according to a disappointed Daveiss, went "all over town and told it; but—don't be startled—Brown did not loose [*sic*] one Vote by it nor was I even called on."[13]

In a tight contest the legislature selected Thruston. The Clay forces exalted, with Clay proving "entirely too hard for Grundy in all the pinches." The vote tended to harden positions. Clay and his followers had denied the Southside a senator, yet since Brown's success had been expected, the Southside's strength was an ominous foreboding for the friends of the Kentucky Bank. As a follow-up to the election, a correspondent warned Breckinridge that Adair would likely be a candidate at the next election for the U.S. Senate, and failing that, the "indefatigable Felix will oppose you." Breckinridge may have been heartened by the writer's view that he had nothing to fear from Adair or Grundy, but as subsequent events were to show, he at least took Grundy's potential candidacy seriously.[14]

The larger struggle over the Kentucky Insurance Company played out over most of the legislative session ending on December 17, 1804. The first week of December featured impassioned oratory extending into the evening, with Grundy leading the charge against the bank and Henry Clay defending the charter before galleries crowded with spectators. The judges closed the court of appeals for a day in order to hear the arguments. The *Kentucky Gazette* reported an animated debate, the warmest since the 1802 circuit court bill. Harry Innes, a fierce Bluegrass defender, characterized the discussion as violent.[15]

Grundy drew on diverse viewpoints and concerns as he assembled his antibank coalition. In contrast to the circuit court battle, which involved a straightforward effort to move judicial control from established Bluegrass centers, the 1804 arguments were more nuanced. Grundy needed to woo two camps of potential antibank votes. At a time of strong allegiance to Jeffersonian principles of minimalist government, one group of representatives opposed banks in principle, as a threat to republican values. This group even included a Bluegrass oligarch, William Russell, of Fayette County. There is a suggestion that John Breckinridge, distant in Washington, may have been in this camp.[16]

A second group was made up of representatives from the Southside who feared Bluegrass commercial dominance. They may have shared Jeffersonian concerns about banks in general, but they were pragmatic and willing to accept accommodation and regulation. Grundy geared his emphasis on exclusivity to the second group.

Grundy launched a far-reaching attack on the bank, silently supported by representatives who sat "like staring statues, too ignorant to comprehend one word that fell from their leader, and too wise to utter a single sentence themselves." He claimed that the original authorization to issue notes at interest had been obtained by fraud and subterfuge or had slipped by an unsuspecting legislature through the wiles of clever Bluegrass lawyers. (The statute omitted specific mention of a bank, even though it otherwise used language common to American bank charters.) This argument has been given more attention than it deserves. Although most historians have suggested that the insurance company took advantage of the legislature, a Clay biographer attributed responsibility to Grundy, arguing that he must have been aware of the banking powers granted in 1802, when he dominated the assembly and pushed through his circuit court bill. A less nefarious interpretation appears more likely. Focused on congressional apportionment and the circuit court bill in 1802, Grundy simply did not pay close attention to the specific enabling legislation. Once banking operations began and opposition swelled, Grundy necessarily excused his and the legislature's failures by emphasizing Bluegrass deviousness. That this approach dovetailed with a broader argument against a moneyed aristocracy only added to its appeal.[17]

Fundamentally, Grundy based his argument on exclusivity, the traditional agrarian position that commercial centers were being given opportunities denied to more rural areas. Focusing on geographical concerns in its opposition to the privileges of the wealthy, commercially oriented Bluegrass and on social concerns in its suggestion that further strengthening the commercial class would accentuate a trend toward aristocratic leadership that was already too evident, his argument spoke to traditional Southside themes. William Littell certainly viewed exclusivity as Grundy's concern, asking, "Was it not written of all time, that no man should make money out of rags? And is it not a law with the wise men and the chiefs of the people, that exclusive privileges shall not be granted?" Years later, George Bibb brought Grundy's words to life when he wrote, "You once said on the floor of representatives of this state, that, you saw the tall figure of Aristocracy, with opened mouth wide extended, hollow eyes and lantern jaws, stalking over the principles of the Constitution and trampling under foot equal rights, cheating the people of their birth right, maintaining the doctrine of exclusive privileges and establishing dangerous precedents."[18]

Grundy built on traditional themes, such as the rural distrust of lawyers and commercial wealth that Kentucky's hero, Thomas Jefferson, had used against Alexander Hamilton and the despised Federalists. He played more narrowly on the distrust of paper money, widespread in rural areas, and argued that bank operations would lead to the concentration of specie in Lexington, initially to the real disadvantage of the Southside. He also asserted that the act creating the insurance company was unconstitutional, both because it had been obtained by fraud and because it conferred rights on some but not all.

Grundy stressed his lack of financial knowledge, but more as an oratorical tool than as a factual statement. He pointed out that the sixty- and ninety-day loans provided by the Kentucky Insurance Company did not meet the longer-term financial requirements of farmers for crop loans or land acquisition. He argued, too, that the bank could misuse its powers: notes not based on specie were inherently dangerous, and no limit had been placed upon the total bank notes that could be issued. Finally, and importantly, he stressed that banks favored commercial transactions based on the purchase and sale of goods, and not real-estate loans. There would thus be little benefit to his constituents but much to residents of Lexington, which was closer to eastern financial interests.[19]

Clay's position contained no surprises. The operations of the Kentucky Insurance Company would benefit not only the merchant class but also the farmer. At any rate, Kentucky and the West in general needed to move beyond barter and primitive ways of doing business and establish a system more suitable for commercial expansion. More fundamentally, Clay argued that the bank had been legally formed and that repeal would be unconstitutional, violating rights of the corporation created by the state. Clay's emphasis on the sanctity of the contract resonated particularly with those seeking a positive governmental role in promoting business development.[20]

Wonderful theater that it may have been, the clash of Clay and Grundy did not change the result prefigured by the Senate election; the Southside simply did not have the votes. The climax occurred on December 12, 1804, when Grundy's motion to repeal the two bank-enabling provisions of the 1802 act was defeated by a vote of 29–28. Most of the Southside and eastern counties voted for repeal, as did several delegates from Jefferson, Henry, and Shelby counties, which usually adhered to the Bluegrass position. One historian attributed the one-vote margin to bargaining by Clay for the votes from Henderson and Muhlenberg counties. Following the vote, two regulatory measures competed for consideration. Friends of the bank, attempting to counter Grundy criticisms, proposed to eliminate the insurance company's monopoly, limit notes to the value of the bank's assets, and make officers and directors personally liable for notes exceeding that amount. Grundy countered with his own regulatory measure, which would hold all stockholders liable, and for the full amount of notes issued, not only for the amount of the overissue. His bill also included an important mechanism providing for enforcement by the courts and fines for violations. The regulatory bill proposed by the bank's friends passed in the house, 30–28, the same margin by which Grundy's proposal failed. A last-ditch effort by Grundy to establish a commission to investigate the insurance company's activities and report back at the next session also failed, 35–23. The bank regulatory bill then passed in the senate and was signed into law by the governor.[21]

The compromise in 1804 constituted a setback for Grundy. While he could claim that he had ended the monopoly and placed limits on bank operations, the bank still stood. Clay wrote that opposition to the bank would now subside. He also received plaudits from the bank's supporters, including praise from his brother-in-law James Brown, in New Orleans, for resisting "that unprincipled demagogue Grundy."[22]

Other bank advocates did not share Clay's optimism. Almost immediately opponents and advocates launched a press war premised on resumption of the bank battle in 1805. In a series of nine messages to the *Kentucky Gazette,* "A Poor Farmer" pilloried Grundy with the sharp vituperation of the period, ascribing Grundy's actions to ambition for a seat in Congress and suggesting that he had fallen prey to King Mob and ignorance. He was "a young man of some talents, but no learning, or experience; profoundly skilled in the arts of intrigue; exceedingly *personal* in his political motives, and whose easy dissimulation, in playing upon ignorance, prejudice and credulity, is the most prominent feature in his parliamentary character." Grundy's supporters joined the fray, as reflected in letters in the *Kentucky Gazette* responding to "A Poor Farmer." Grundy addressed the "People of Kentucky" in the *Bardstown Western American.* A revealing paragraph reflects democratic concerns:

> Whenever you put it in the power of any set of men, to become affluent without *Labour,* you give them an ascendancy in society which is dangerous to liberty, you give them license to devise, and influence to execute plans hostile to our welfare; you permit them to acquire an interest distinct and variant from

that of the community, and owing to the power which is inseparable from wealth, whenever your interest and their's shall conflict, your's must yield— By means of this institution, the monied men of the whole state will become united, having one interest; they can have but one will, and it can easily be discovered, that as their interest is different from that of the people at large the latter will be prostrated to the former.

Grundy also actively campaigned for house members who would oppose the bank, particularly in the Southside.[23]

Grundy may have become a veteran of the political wars by this time, but the abuse bothered him. In a letter to Clay dated February 4, 1805, Grundy expressed unhappiness about inaccurate statements attributed to him and asked that Clay provide a certificate stating what Grundy had actually said. There is no evidence that Clay responded. Grundy developed a thicker skin over time, and he appears not to have been unduly troubled thereafter by personal attacks.[24]

One job opportunity apparently tempted Grundy to leave the state; it is unclear, however, whether the proponents of the initiative sought to take him from the Kentucky Insurance fight. On February 28, 1805, the Kentucky delegation in the U.S. House of Representatives recommended to President Jefferson that Felix Grundy be appointed a commissioner to ascertain the titles and claims to land in upper Louisiana. Subsequently, Matthew Walton, Grundy's longtime friend and mentor, wrote the president from Springfield, Kentucky, that, doubting that any other signatories would discuss the matter with Grundy, he had done so himself and found Grundy willing to serve if appointed, unless his inability to understand French would be disqualifying. Walton added that Jefferson could not make an appointment that would "give more satisfaction" and that Grundy was a "Lawyer of a high standing as any in this state, and a man of profound education." John Breckinridge, perhaps mindful of Grundy's potential interest in the Senate, also joined in the effort, proposing to President Jefferson on April 24, 1805, that Grundy be appointed a commissioner.[25]

The commissioner's post had already been filled by the time Breckinridge's recommendation reached Secretary of the Treasury Albert Gallatin, but Gallatin proposed a remunerative post as land agent, which Grundy declined. The letters of recommendation make clear that Kentuckians in Washington, not Grundy, initiated the proposed appointment. His willingness to accept the appointment at a time when the debate over the Kentucky Insurance Company would continue in the legislature, however, is suggestive. Grundy's ambition and the compensation and opportunities that his appointment as commissioner would bring perhaps outweighed his belief in a more egalitarian banking system.

The state elections of 1805 provided a referendum on the Kentucky Insurance fight and strengthened Grundy's position in the legislature. Bank opponents ousted eleven bank supporters, and six probank members, including the wavering William Russell, became antibank. With the loss of only three antibank members, the election resulted in a net gain of fourteen antibank voters.[26]

Bank supporters reacted in dismay. Reflecting their fears, some Lexingtonians made a direct appeal to Grundy in the *Kentucky Gazette* on September 17, 1805. Noting that John Breckinridge had accepted the position of attorney general of the United States in August 1805, the unsigned communication stated that the U.S. Senate seat was open and that John Brown and Felix Grundy had been mentioned as worthy candidates. Grundy, subject to scurrilous attacks by "A Poor Farmer" and others in the *Gazette,* could only have felt satisfaction when the paper then stated:

> Should Mr. Brown, however, not offer his services . . . the people should, without hesitation, turn their attention to Mr. Grundy, provided he becomes a candidate. Young, and ardent in the pursuit of knowledge, possessed of good natural abilities, and sufficiently acquainted with parliamentary proceedings to assume a dignified attitude on the floor of the Senate, Mr. Grundy in a short time may be equally distinguished for his patriotism and usefulness—It is to such *improvable capacities* that an enlightened people should delegate [*sic*] their confidence.

Alas for the *Gazette,* Felix Grundy did not respond to this rather blatant overture.

The Kentucky General Assembly convened on November 4, 1805, and soon elected John Adair to complete Breckinridge's unexpired term in the U.S. Senate. Grundy did not become a candidate, perhaps because of an obligation to Adair or perhaps because he believed his commitment to the insurance-company issue precluded his resigning from the general assembly. Adair's 45–35 win over John Pope, the Bluegrass candidate, gave the Southside its first U.S. senator, showing the degree of change since the rejection of Adair the previous year.

On November 4, the first day of the session, Grundy introduced a bill to repeal the Kentucky Insurance Company's banking privileges. Grundy renewed the previous year's attacks on the company, stressing that banks were enemies of a free government because they tended to move wealth out of the hands of the people and that the law was unconstitutional because it conveyed exclusive privileges. The heated debates between Grundy and Clay lasted two weeks, even though few new arguments emerged. This year Grundy had the votes, and his repeal legislation passed handily in both houses, 37–19 in the house on November 21 and 15–8 in the senate on November 23. The Southside was nearly unanimous in its opposition, although representatives of three counties abstained. Even in the Bluegrass, delegates defected to Grundy, with Jessamine County representatives voting for repeal and William Russell in Fayette County doing the same, accepting the ire of his Lexington constituents.[27]

To the surprise of many, Governor Christopher Greenup vetoed the bill, accepting Clay's arguments and emphasizing that any change in the act would be an unconstitutional violation of contract. Other acts of incorporation could be undermined by a vote nullifying created rights. The house, disturbed by this unusual assertion of gubernatorial authority, overrode the veto on the same day, 40–18, with four bank supporters joining the antibank group.[28]

At this point, with the senate expected to override the veto as well, the political maneuvering became intense. First, facing likely passage of the repeal act, Lexington merchants prepared and made public a petition to the Bank of the United States requesting that a branch be established in Lexington. The petition, to be presented only when repeal was final, was intended to pressure the legislature to maintain a small local bank rather than lose all control to eastern financial interests.

Second, and far more effectively, Henry Clay went back to the well of the Green River debt. Early in the legislative session, Clay submitted a resolution to coerce payment of the longstanding debt of the Green River settlers. Both Clay and Grundy knew that the votes of the so-called Green River Band were annually held hostage to this debt and that in 1801 opponents less skilled than Clay had used the threat of required debt payment to defeat Grundy's circuit court bill. Now, after the first reading of the senate override bill, Clay, on the floor and in private, attacked the Green River bartering of votes as a public scandal and panicked those seeking extension of the Green River debt. Harry Innes reported "great warmth" and that the "Debt has become enormous, and the great burden is on speculators." Clay mustered enough votes from various interest groups potentially to derail Grundy's repeal bill and made clear that probank members would oppose coercion only if the Green River Band went along with the governor's veto.[29]

Into this legislative maneuvering stepped Green Clay, who had so nettled

Breckinridge at the 1799 constitutional convention. On December 11 he proposed the establishment of a state bank with capital of six hundred thousand
dollars divided equally between private investors and the state. The bill deftly
met most of Grundy's concerns—branches throughout the state, limitations
on notes issued, with personal liability for violations, and an annual review
by the general assembly of the bank's books and records—and solved the coercion problem by appropriating the Green River debt to the purchase of the
bank stock. Grundy, in danger of losing his Green River support, promptly
and smoothly moved to support Green Clay's initiative. One bemused observer
wrote, "Grundy, the enemy to Banks, strange to tell, became the leader for preparing it, and his party was so strong that he new-modeled the whole Bill."[30]

The battle now shifted totally. Instead of being opposed to a bank, Grundy
became a proponent. Once again, Clay and Grundy battled, this time largely
over the terms under which the state would be involved. Grundy argued that
the bank notes should be backed solely by the credit of the state, while Clay
now adopted Grundy's earlier position that the notes must be supported by
bank assets. Green Clay's state bank bill lost, 37–20, with the defeat attributable to the rush to adjournment and the unwillingness of legislators to pass
complicated provisions that they did not fully understand. Grundy unaccount-
ably joined Clay in opposing the bill, probably to preserve publicly his antibank
credentials.[31]

The failure of the state bank bill led to the senate vote on the override of
the governor's veto. The override effort failed, 12–10, with five senators changing their votes. The five included Philemon Waters, from Grundy's Washington County, and two senators from central Kentucky, all allegedly under the
influence of Green River speculators.[32]

The great legislative struggle of 1804 and 1805 over the Kentucky Insurance
Company's banking privileges thus ended. Henry Clay, by preventing repeal of
the company's banking privileges, enjoyed his first significant triumph in Kentucky politics. Grundy had put together a formidable antibank coalition by
vigorous oratory and newspaper controversy and had forced legislators to take
a public stand on the banking issues. He fought the Bluegrass to a standstill for
two years but ultimately failed in his specific objective. Each man had demonstrated to a statewide—and regional—audience that he possessed exceptional
leadership talent, and each would be rewarded. The vehemence of the attacks
against Grundy certainly revealed what a force he had become in the state.

Even though Grundy antagonized many Bluegrass leaders in the circuit
court and banking fights, he seems not to have made many lasting enemies. His

good humor and wit spared him deep-seated animosity. Years later, the Frankfort paper *Kentucky Commonwealth* looked back to the debates of 1804 and 1805 and recalled that Grundy, with a sparkling wit, had caused his opponents to join in the laughter even though his intent had been to render them ridiculous.[33]

Bluegrass leaders attacked Grundy for allegedly putting aside his talent and position in the interests of political notoriety—and to obtain a seat in Congress. The absence of his correspondence on the Kentucky Insurance issue makes it difficult to assess how much of his stance was principled and how much was political opportunism. Although his earlier advocacy of circuit courts increased career possibilities for young lawyers, it was motivated by familial and regional concerns of distance from Bluegrass power and a desire to localize some judicial authority. He initially failed to grasp the full dimensions of the banking provisions in the 1802 act, but once alerted, he quickly mobilized his anti-Bluegrass forces. The struggle over the bank was a contest for Kentucky's future direction and the extent to which the Southside would participate in the control of the state. Grundy's agrarian constituency feared the power of banks and did not believe it needed the more sophisticated financial systems favored by Lexington. Grundy himself was flexible and pragmatic and primarily opposed Bluegrass arrogation of privileges not available to the Southside. His willingness to support a state bank, in which the Bluegrass would be less dominant, revealingly demonstrates his core interest and practical acceptance of compromise.

The great banking controversy of 1804 and 1805 ended with a whimper in the legislative session of 1806. In less than two weeks in December 1806 the legislature approved the establishment of a new bank with $1 million in capital, twenty times that of the original Kentucky Insurance Company. The new Bank of Kentucky was modeled after the proposal in Green Clay's bill of 1805. The legislation encouraged branches and provided more flexible limitations on note issuance than in the 1805 bill. Payment of the Green River debt would be made in twelve annual installments, with debt payments allocated exclusively to the purchase of bank stock. Grundy and most of the Southside joined Clay and the Bluegrass in voting for the bill, with votes on December 26, 1806, of 28–20 in the house and 16–5 in the Senate. Only the eastern counties remained solidly opposed.[34]

Not everyone was happy with the outcome. Jeffersonians, who opposed banks on principle, particularly complained. William Russell had spoken out against the banking provisions and now privately forecast Kentucky's fall from Republican grace. When Henry Clay wrote a circular to his Fayette constituents implicitly criticizing Russell and others who opposed the bank, Russell, forced to reply, acknowledged that in writing his defense he was "at a great loss for the want of Grundy and his talents."[35]

The debates over the banking privileges of the Kentucky Insurance Company prefigured similar struggles for Grundy throughout his career, with the same issues arising in different factual guises. In Tennessee, as the leading proponent of a state bank following the Panic of 1819, and nationally, as Jackson's ally in the battle against the Second Bank of the United States, Grundy opposed the concentration of the financial power of privately owned banks. For Grundy, the fear of untrammeled power by an "aristocratic" few resonated above all else.

The recurrence of the issue of access to capital had two implications for Grundy. First, he and other, similarly inclined frontier egalitarians sought continuing availability of capital for the purchase of land and slaves. In difficult times they would seek to ease the plight of agricultural debtors, particularly overextended entrepreneurs. These approaches would tend to pit Grundy against entrenched financial interests. Grundy's position came naturally enough to someone from a family of entrepreneurs, resentful of distant control of access to land and money. His stance also reflected a political calculus. Grundy, who constantly referred to the "voice of the people," represented in Kentucky and Tennessee the farmers and merchants who needed capital for acquisition and expansion. Belief and opportunity came together.

Second, and perhaps more seriously, Grundy confronted a continuing dilemma. Unlike William Russell and later Andrew Jackson, Grundy did not oppose banks in general and did not believe that a hard-money approach could work in the specie-short West. He appreciated the importance of credit in an expanding economy and sought a balance between the need for a sound credit system and his fear of centralized control by the few. In 1804–5 and thereafter he often tried to reach a middle ground. Finding the proper balance would prove difficult, however, and Grundy and the country would lurch inconsistently between a controlled national banking system that tended to restrict capital in difficult times and a looser system in which there was a proliferation of state-chartered banks and unreliable paper credit.

8

CHIEF JUSTICE

His fame was forensic rather than judicial.
—John Doolan

The Kentucky insurance fight enhanced the careers of both Felix
Grundy and Henry Clay. Grundy, who was reelected to the house in August 1806, continued to serve on major committees and direct affairs. He also
considered the U.S. Senate. John Adair had been elected in 1805 to complete
Breckinridge's term, but in 1806 the legislature had to choose a U.S. senator for
the full term beginning in 1807. The house nominated Adair and four others,
including Grundy and his old friend John Pope. After three ballots, the house
narrowed the selection to the two highest vote-getters, Pope and Adair. Pope
won, and Adair, piqued, immediately resigned from the Senate.[1]

Henry Clay's career further accelerated in 1806, when he successfully defended Aaron Burr in grand-jury proceedings brought by Joseph Daveiss related to claims that Burr was treasonously seeking to create a separate state in
the West. Clay ran in November 1806 for the few months remaining for the
Senate seat just relinquished by Adair. Clay defeated George Bibb by a vote of
68–10, with Grundy supporting Clay.

Kentuckians focused, however, not on elections but on Aaron Burr and his
designs on the West and on the continued unraveling of an alleged conspiracy two decades earlier, when Spain had made payments to prominent Kentuckians. John Pope chaired, and Grundy joined, a committee investigating
the Spanish payments. When Benjamin Sebastian, a judge of the court of appeals since Kentucky's statehood in 1792, resigned after the committee determined that he had been the recipient of a Spanish pension, Grundy persuaded
the house to take no further action, suggesting that Sebastian's resignation ob-
viated the need for other punishment.

After his bruising battles with respect to circuit court reform and the Kentucky Insurance Company, Grundy appears to have been less involved in the legislative session of 1806. His interest had turned to a new job. Shortly after the assembly opened, the *Kentucky Gazette,* on November 17, 1806, announced that Felix Grundy would be a candidate for lieutenant governor and that he was permitting his name to be presented only because of the nomination of other candidates. This notice and his inclusion on the house list for U.S. senator demonstrated his ambition. Grundy enjoyed a powerful political base and a reputation as an exceptionally talented leader, but he remained controversial, particularly in the Bluegrass, as his failure to obtain a U.S. Senate seat suggests.

Despite Grundy's interest in the lieutenant governorship, he soon accepted a different opportunity. On December 6 Governor Greenup nominated Grundy to succeed Sebastian on the four-man court of appeals. Although the senate promptly and unanimously approved the nomination, Grundy's commission on the court as second judge came too late for him to participate in cases in the fall session of 1806. Before the spring term of 1807 Grundy was the chief justice, succeeding Thomas Todd, newly appointed to the U.S. Supreme Court.

Grundy succeeded Todd as chief justice on April 11, 1807. Service on the court of appeals was prestigious but also onerous, time-consuming, and unremunerative. The court held spring and fall terms in Frankfort, with opinions typically issued the same term as the cases were argued. Its increasingly burdensome caseload reflected the growth of the state. In 1805 there were 19 decisions in the spring term and 8 in the fall; in 1806, 13 cases in the spring term and 9 in the fall. In 1807, however, when Grundy was chief justice, the court decided 41 cases, 23 in the spring and 18 in the fall. The following year, after Grundy's resignation, the gates opened, with 111 decisions in the spring term alone.[2]

Poor compensation was the principal drawback of service on the court of appeals. Early commentators and historians bewail how the legislature, anxious to preserve its primacy, limited court salaries. In 1801 the legislature restricted service on the court of appeals to two terms but added a fourth judge and increased judges' compensation to $833 per year, which was still inadequate since lawyers in private practice could earn ten times that amount. In 1804 Governor Greenup advised the legislature that better salaries must be paid in order to attract enlightened, virtuous, and independent men to the judiciary. The legislature failed to respond, making it difficult to retain qualified judges. Given Grundy's leadership in the house during these years, it appears ironic that he accepted service on a court rendered less attractive because of his own inaction on judicial compensation.[3]

Grundy served as chief justice in the spring and fall terms of 1807, too brief a period to warrant any meaningful evaluation, although a leading student concluded that Grundy was a brilliant man but that "his fame was forensic rather than judicial." Grundy announced no decisions of particular significance. Most cases dealt with questions of procedure; of the twenty-three cases in the spring term of 1807, for example, fifteen had to do with procedural matters, and seven resolved land disputes. Cases were decided by opinions of the court, with the chief justice speaking for the court in the relatively few attributed opinions. Grundy wrote five opinions during his tenure, three in the spring term and two in the fall.[4]

Only one case, *Cunningham v. Caldwell,* argued in February 1807, has attracted attention, but only because Grundy and all four counsel later served as U.S. senators. Isham Talbot and Jesse Bledsoe appeared for the successful appellant, and Henry Clay and John Rowan represented the appellee. The case and the others for which counsel are identified emphasizes the close-knit and distinguished character of the early Kentucky bar. These lawyers, who knew each other well, could argue cases and serve as opposing counsel with fierce vigor and then have drinks together afterwards. These ambitious young men were building Kentucky and their own reputations with hard work and conviviality.

Grundy resigned from the post of chief justice on January 5, 1808, in order to move to Nashville. That he served as chief justice for less than a year suggests that he quickly concluded that a judicial career was not for him. Grundy was outgoing, vital, and quick-witted, with a mind that responded to the stimulus of debate; he was used to influencing others through his charm and power of argument. The more reflective and scholarly approach of a judge could not appeal to him in the long run. Moreover, Grundy, who had not inherited wealth, had to support a wife and five young children. As a legislator, with only a single session in the fall, from early November to mid- or late December, he had ample opportunity to earn the legal fees that came with his growing reputation. As chief justice, by contrast, he presided over a growing judicial docket for long months in the spring and fall, away from his family, and received an inadequate fixed compensation.[5]

Grundy also knew that opportunities for an ambitious lawyer lay outside his home state. Even though he led the bar in Bardstown, practice in a small rural community proved limiting. And in the state of Kentucky Grundy had burned at least some of his bridges with the commercial and manufacturing establishment. Even if the Bluegrass elite grudgingly conceded Grundy's talent, they hardly would prefer the Southside leader to Henry Clay and other Lexington lawyers.

Nashville, by contrast, offered opportunity. Jo Daveiss, a close friend, found Tennessee legal work "very considerable" and profitable to the bar, and Kentucky's federal judge, in assessing judicial candidates, found a lack of legal ability in Tennessee, with only G. W. Campbell and Jenkin Whiteside singled out as belonging to the first rank. Moreover, West Tennessee (as Middle Tennessee was then called), with Nashville at its core, enjoyed bright economic prospects and a climate, topography, and fertility much like those of the Bluegrass. A number of Grundy's friends and acquaintances, including R. C. Foster, had previously moved to the Nashville area, less than 150 miles south of Bardstown.[6]

Whatever the interactions of motivation, Grundy decided to move to Nashville, Tennessee, in late 1807. His resignation from the chief justiceship occurred only three days before the announcement of his move appeared in the Nashville papers. Putting a capstone on the decision, he sold his 15 acres of land in Springfield on August 12, 1809, for sixty pounds, although he retained 1,680 acres of land in Green County and 550 acres in Nelson County. Grundy maintained his ties to family and friends in Kentucky and frequently returned to the state. Despite the brevity of his tenure, Grundy clearly was proud of his service as chief justice of the Kentucky Court of Appeals. Regardless of later titles, he always preferred to be called Judge Grundy.[7]

Grundy's resignation and move to Nashville appear surprising to twenty-first-century Americans. It seems odd that Grundy, successful and established in his chosen career, stepped down from the highest judicial position in his home state to move elsewhere. Yet his decision is emblematic of America in the early nineteenth century. Americans were on the move, especially on the western frontier. Grundy's Tennessee move appears unusual only because of his prominence. His choice testifies to his ambition and self-confidence and to the openness of frontier society and the fluidity of leadership and status. Success, however, was not preordained. That Grundy later became a major leader in Tennessee and the nation does not minimize his courage in giving up the security of Kentucky for the uncertainties of Nashville.

9

GREENVILLE SPRINGS

There was a GREAT collection of people at the Springs in 1807 and 1808.
—Henry Speed

The frontier fostered an entrepreneurial culture of opportunity and risk. Fortunes could be quickly won and quickly lost. Both of Grundy's parents displayed ambition and drive, and their youngest son inherited a heady dose of the same spirit. Much of the entrepreneurial economy originated in land, either in outright speculation or in the more sober assessment that the continued flow of settlers ensured appreciation. Felix Grundy never lost his interest in making money through real estate, and he invested in land throughout his career, with political activity typically followed by entrepreneurial initiatives. Unlike many of his contemporaries, however, Grundy did not focus on large-scale speculation until late in life; instead he engaged primarily in what would now be called development.

Grundy's real-estate investments began early, as he was establishing his legal practice at age twenty. In addition to purchases for a home and an office, Grundy bought lot 31 in the new town of Springfield and built a house, which he leased in August 1797 for three years at 30 pounds annually. He also bought a lot in Greensburg, in Green County, on April 5, 1798, and recorded a grant of 495 acres on Pleasant Creek in Nelson County. Subsequently, on October 23, 1800, Grundy made one of his first major acquisitions: 1,480 acres on Meadow Creek, in Green County, adjacent to Rodgers Mill, where his father-in-law lived, for 518 pounds. In three separate transactions he also acquired approximately 540 acres on Buffalo Creek in Nelson County, including 300 acres of a 400-acre tract originally purchased by his father almost twenty years earlier. In acquiring land during his early years of practice, Grundy followed a pattern regularly repeated in the antebellum South, where successful lawyers became the single most influential class.[1]

A much more significant real-estate investment occurred in Harrodsburg, Kentucky, in 1807, shortly after Grundy became chief justice of the court of appeals. Natural springs, long known to the Indians, attracted rich and poor alike for their healing benefits. Grundy had been impressed by the success of a retreat for the Bluegrass gentry some forty miles north of Lexington, purchased and improved by Colonel Thomas Hart, Henry Clay's entrepreneurial father-in-law. By 1805 the Olympian Springs included cabins, lodges, and a dining room that seated one hundred. The salubrious waters drew some, but most visitors came for social purposes, with the resort given to cards, billiards, and horse racing. When Grundy learned of springs at Harrodsburg, thirty-five miles southeast of Lexington, he became the driving force behind one of the first real-estate developments west of the Allegheny Mountains, a resort to compete with Olympian Springs.[2]

The Reverend Jesse Head, of Springfield, served as the broker for this initiative. Head, a Baltimore-born cabinetmaker, migrated to Kentucky in 1796, where he was a close friend of Grundy's. He became a Methodist minister and succeeded Grundy as chairman of the board of trustees of Springfield. While visiting Harrodsburg in 1806, Head saw his health improve dramatically when he took the iron and saline waters on the 228-acre farm of Captain Lucas Van Arsdal, immediately south of the town. Head soon extolled the potential of the springs to his friend Grundy, living in Bardstown.[3]

At about the same time, Head unknowingly ensured his place in history. On June 12, 1806, at the farm of the bride's uncle, some eight miles north of Springfield, Head married twenty-three-year-old Nancy Hanks and twenty-eight-year-old Thomas Lincoln, the younger brother of Grundy's client Mordecai Lincoln. While it is almost certain that the thirty-year-old Grundy knew Thomas Lincoln, we can only speculate as to whether he attended the wedding of Abraham Lincoln's parents.

One year later, on June 12, 1807, Grundy acted on the enthusiastic reports of Jesse Head, purchasing a one-half interest in the Van Arsdal farm, including the springs. According to the agreement between Grundy and Van Arsdal, never recorded and apparently superseding an earlier document signed at Frankfort on May 26, 1807, Grundy was to pay 750 pounds for half of the farm, 600 pounds of which was to be in the form of another good farm in Mercer County. Grundy further agreed that if he had not found such a farm by Christmas 1807, he would give Van Arsdal his own house and sixty acres of cleared land, rent free, and pay all moving expenses from Mercer County. In return he would be entitled to one-half of all profits from the farm, including

receipts from pasturage and use of the waters. Van Arsdal would retain possession of the farm until Christmas 1807, when Grundy was to take over control
and management of the facilities and business. All expenses would be divided
equally.[4]

Grundy's purchase of the one-half interest in the Van Arsdal farm led
to the development of a new minerals resort, felicitously called Greenville
Springs. The four springs on the farm were situated on rolling, wooded land
with beautiful glades. Although he was not yet entitled to control and management, Grundy began to build cottages and otherwise develop the resort at
the time of his purchase. More importantly, the two owners persuaded Daniel
Jennings, the proprietor of a successful tavern in Springfield and a competitor
of the Widow Grundy's, to move to Harrodsburg. By a partnership agreement
written by Head intended to be effective in June 1807, Van Arsdal and Grundy
leased the farm to Jennings for five years. Jennings would establish and operate
a tavern and inn, and Van Arsdal and Grundy would bear the expense of new
cabins and a new dining room. Van Arsdal, Grundy, and Jennings would share
certain other expenses and divide all profits equally. A clerk would be hired to
maintain financial records.

The resort soon included twenty-one guest cottages and a large frame inn,
which cost between $700 and $900. The new springs flourished. Henry Speed,
a Danville banker who offered to buy a one-half interest, testified in later litigation that "there was a GREAT collection of people at the Springs in 1807 and
1808." Speed gave full credit for the development to Grundy and estimated that
the improvements cost $1,500.[5]

Grundy's ownership of Greenville Springs lasted only seven months. When
he decided to move to Tennessee, he sold his one-half interest in the farm and
springs to Daniel Jennings on December 20, 1807, apparently for $2,500. He
also loaned the new partnership of Van Arsdal and Jennings a total of $1,916.67,
of which $500 was promptly repaid. The balance of $1,461.67, although acknowledged as due, became involved in litigation between the new partners.
Jennings apparently paid his share of the obligation, but Grundy sued Van Arsdal in the Mercer County Court in 1810 for $450 still owed.

It is impossible to determine whether Grundy made any money on his investment. The early termination of his ownership interest on December 20,
1807, required revision of the original purchase agreement, since various provisions were not even to take effect until Christmas 1807. The effects of those
changes, as well as basic financial information, are sketchily presented in the
available documents. There are, moreover, inconsistencies in the various ac-

counts as to the original purchase price and the forms of payment. What is clear, however, is that Grundy did not pay close attention to financial or other details. Land agreements were not recorded, and some agreements were not signed, apparently because the young chief justice was not available. No one kept adequate books. Grundy's investment seems to have been the catalyst for the initial success of Greenville Springs, but because of commitments in Frankfort and his decision to move to Tennessee, he did not provide sustained management or focus.

Greenville Springs enjoyed great success until 1827, when it was purchased by a competitor and closed. Grundy apparently visited the resort from time to time. We do not know how he evaluated this investment, but his activities in Tennessee were to include real-estate development on a larger scale.[6]

PART III

Tennessee

10

TENNESSEE AND CONGRESS

I have uniformly entertained the same political sentiments I now profess.
—Felix Grundy

On January 7, 1808, the *Impartial Review and Cumberland Repository,* a weekly newspaper in Nashville, announced: "FELIX GRUNDY has settled in Nashville, and will practice law in the following Courts (to wit:) the Superior Courts of West Tennessee, the Federal Courts holden in Nashville, the County Courts of Davidson, Sumner, Williamson and Rutherford."

Grundy's new hometown was founded in 1780, about the same time that George Grundy took his family to Kentucky. Sited at the French Lick, a salt lick and sulfur spring adjacent to a limestone bluff some sixty feet above the Cumberland River, the town owed its origin to North Carolina–based pioneers led by James Robertson and John Donelson. Despite Indian attacks, West Tennessee expanded rapidly. By 1800 Davidson County, with Nashville as the county seat, claimed approximately 9,600 residents. Tennessee as a whole had a population of 105,000, with 91,700 white inhabitants and almost 14,000 slaves. Although most land-hungry settlers lived on farms, Nashville grew as well, with almost 350 residents in 1800 and 1,100 in 1810.

François Michaux visited Tennessee in 1802. He found Nashville to be a town of about 120 houses distributed over twenty-five to thirty acres of largely bare rock. The houses were of wood, except for seven or eight built of brick. Even though Nashville lacked manufacturing or public buildings, it proudly pointed to a printing office with a weekly newspaper, a newly established college with seven or eight students and one professor, and fifteen to twenty shops. Merchandise from Philadelphia and Baltimore cost more and was of lesser quality than articles sold in Lexington. The inhabitants were "very engaging in their manners, and use but little ceremony."[1]

Nashville was a commercial town. Its early history was dominated by merchants buying and selling goods in the West Tennessee interior. Some 200 rugged miles from Tennessee's capital at Knoxville, it was the first stop of boatmen returning from taking export products down the Mississippi to New Orleans, 1,240 river miles away. The little town had lofty pretensions. One Tennessean wrote in May 1805 that Nashville was becoming a "place of considerable consequence. We have now two companies of play actors exhibiting two or three times a week—We have also Profile Cutters—and others sailing thro' the air in balloons—all for money, of which they collect fountains."[2]

When Grundy arrived in 1808, Nashville, bustling and no longer in its infancy, sported a new brick courthouse, perhaps two hundred houses, and three newspapers, the *Democratic Clarion and Tennessee Gazette,* the *Impartial Review and Cumberland Repository,* and the *Whig.* Grundy initially rented a newly constructed frame house on the corner of Cherry and Broad streets. When it was offered for sale in September 1808, it was described as a comfortable but hardly luxurious dwelling of four rooms, two below stairs and two above, with numerous outbuildings. In 1809 Grundy and his family moved to a 100-acre farm in Davidson County, where they remained until 1812, when they relocated to a farm six miles north of Nashville on Mill Creek. Continuing his major land acquisitions, Grundy purchased 1,120 acres for less than one dollar per acre on the South Harpeth River in Williamson County in February 1810.[3]

Grundy's family was growing. Mary Malvina Chenault was born on August 22, 1810. Importantly for the future, Grundy also acquired a Nashville brother-in-law, Randal McGavock, part of a family described by Tennessee's distinguished historian Alfred Leland Crabb as "for a century . . . perhaps the section's leading family." Settling on the Virginia frontier, the Scots-Irish immigrant James McGavock (1728–1812) directed his sons in extensive land purchases in Kentucky and Tennessee. David McGavock (1763–1838), a surveyor, began making annual visits to Tennessee in 1786 and settled permanently in Nashville in 1795. He drew up the first map of Nashville, served as register of lands from 1806 until his death, and, with his father, purchased 2,240 acres in Davidson and Williamson counties, including much of what became North Nashville.[4]

David's youngest brother, Randal McGavock (1768–1843), graduated in 1794 from what is now Dickinson College in Carlisle, Pennsylvania, where he debated and became a lifelong friend of Roger B. Taney, class of 1795. Originally a deputy to his brother in the Land Office, Randal served as clerk of the circuit court of Davidson County from 1810 to 1834 and mayor of Nashville in

1824–25. Although by the mid-nineteenth century the Tennessee McGavocks would be identified as rich, social, and gregarious, David and Randal, in early Nashville, operated quietly in offices of great bureaucratic power. Content to stay in the political background, they amassed land, wealth, and the power that comes with information. After the Grundys arrived in Nashville, Randal met Sarah Dougherty Rodgers (1786–1854), Nancy Grundy's sister, and married her on February 28, 1811.

Grundy quickly established himself professionally. He came with recognized stature, as the former chief justice of an adjacent state and a well-known politician. Tennessee papers had reported on Grundy's activities, particularly his battle against the Kentucky Insurance Company. Years later, Thomas Hart Benton recalled the welcome afforded the distinguished newcomer.[5]

Grundy soon acquired a lucrative law practice. As in Kentucky, he initially focused on land law. David McGavock wrote in 1805 that Tennessee's land laws were "in confusion" and likely to continue so for some time. Jenkin Whiteside (1782–1822) led the bar before Grundy's arrival, but from 1808 to 1811 he and Grundy competed and collaborated as the most successful of an expanding group of lawyers. Grundy took cases where he could find them, throughout Tennessee. As in Kentucky, he quickly became a member of the bar in each county where he expected to practice. For example, Grundy, Andrew Jackson, and Thomas Hart Benton presented their credentials at the first meeting of the court of Bedford County, three miles north of Lynchburg, in December 1807.[6]

Although Grundy handled civil disputes, he increasingly represented criminal defendants. Significantly, his first case in Tennessee involved a criminal matter, and Andrew Jackson was his client. In 1807 Jackson's political career was in eclipse owing to financial difficulties and a duel in which he killed Charles Dickinson, a popular young doctor. Importantly, however, Jackson commanded Tennessee's militia, and Tennessee was a state that revered the military. Proud, sensitive to the point of paranoia, and prone to violence, Jackson engaged in a series of feuds and altercations. On May 15, 1807, a Davidson County grand jury indicted Andrew Jackson for assault with intent to kill Samuel Jackson, a distant cousin. On November 9, 1807, a jury found Jackson not guilty. When the confrontation between the Jacksons became an issue in Andrew Jackson's presidential campaign in 1828, Grundy gave his account in a letter to Tennessee's secretary of state in May of that year. Grundy recalled that while deciding whether to move to Tennessee, he assisted Judge Stewart and Colonel Joseph H. Daveiss in representing General Jackson. After a heated argument, Samuel Jackson threw a stone at General Jackson, and he was throwing another one when General Jackson wounded him in the side with a cane spear. Counsel successfully defended Jackson on the basis of his "justifiable . . . course" of conduct.[7]

This case probably was the occasion of Grundy's initial meeting with Andrew Jackson, with whom he would have an uneven, continuing relationship for thirty-two years. We do not know how Daveiss and Grundy, then Kentuckians, joined Stewart in defending Jackson. It is likely that Daveiss, knowing Jackson from the Burr controversy and considering his own move to Tennessee, was asked to assist Stewart and in turn arranged for Grundy's representation.

The first case to bring Grundy great fame as a criminal lawyer in Tennessee took place in November 1810. Andrew Jackson was again involved, but this time as a character witness for the prosecution. On October 24, 1810, Patton Anderson, the brother of the state surveyor, William Preston Anderson, and a "sporting" man of "uncontrollable passion," quarreled with David Magness in the courthouse square in Shelbyville. Patton Anderson purportedly drew a dirk but was restrained by his friends. Sometime later, Magness shot Anderson through the heart, under disputed circumstances. Magness's trial for murder took place in Franklin, in Williamson County, after a venue change requested by Grundy.[8]

Andrew Jackson had a long history with Patton Anderson. Jackson and the Anderson brothers ran a cockpit and racecourse at Clover Bottom, near Jackson's store. Many of Jackson's well-known feuds arose from the sporting events and attendant betting, conducted by them. Jackson raged at the homicide, which he and other friends regarded as a calculated assassination by one of three brothers with whom Anderson had quarreled.

The town of Franklin focused on little else during the trial, held from November 16 to November 24, 1810, less than a month after the homicide. One tavern housed adherents of the defendant and his brothers, the other Jackson and other Anderson friends. Alfred Balch, a Princeton graduate, led the prosecution, assisted by John Haywood, a prominent lawyer and scholar recently arrived from North Carolina, and Thomas Hart Benton, a young Williamson County lawyer recently elected to the state senate. Counsel for the defense included Felix Grundy, Jenkin Whiteside, and Stockley Donaldson Hays, although most accounts note only Grundy's role. Jackson appeared periodically; an early Jackson biographer reported that an inebriated Jackson harangued the crowd with fearful vehemence.[9]

The trial featured a large number of witnesses, and it was the first instance in which Grundy was accused of packing the jury. William Preston Anderson wrote that he did not like the jury and that "Grundy and Hays was guilty of a most ungentleman like and in fact rascally act in packing some of them." Jackson's reply to a Grundy question is the best-known legacy of the case. When requested by Grundy to give his opinion on Anderson's reputation for peaceableness, Jackson confronted a dilemma, since the deceased was known to have a violent temper. Jackson replied instantly, "Sir, my friend, Patton Anderson, was the NATURAL ENEMY OF SCOUNDRELS."[10]

Grundy took advantage of this statement. He opened his jury summation by eulogizing Jackson, stressing his directness and honesty. Never before, however, had Jackson spoken so ambiguously. Jackson clearly did not want to speak against his friend, and yet he did not want to lie either. Grundy would leave to the jury the assessment of Jackson's ambiguous and evasive response. An angry Jackson heard Grundy's speech to the jury and complained to Benton: "That is not fair play. . . . When you come to sum-up for the prosecution, I want you to skin Grundy alive on this point." "I'm afraid, General," Benton replied, "[that he has] got us down on this point—flat on our backs. I reckon we had better let it alone."[11]

The jury convicted Magness only of manslaughter, and he was sentenced to eleven months' imprisonment. This result, in light of the charge of first-degree murder, the known facts, and Jackson's belligerent stance, could only be viewed as a victory for the defense, and so it proved. Grundy's talents had been much in evidence, including his selection of the jury, probing of witnesses, and summation. The verdict solidified his emerging position as the leading lawyer in Tennessee.

Two months after the trial, on January 25, 1811, the *Democratic Clarion and Tennessee Gazette* announced the candidacy of Felix Grundy for Congress. By 1811 Grundy was well known in West Tennessee, the largest of Tennessee's three congressional districts. His travels as a lawyer had taken him to most of the county seats, and his quick success at the bar had accorded him status and renown. Grundy also had taken a leadership role in civic and political affairs, participating as a speaker in the dinners that marked public life. When Lieutenant Colonel Hardy Murfree, a hero of the Revolution, died in April 1809, Grundy gave the funeral oration for his fellow Mason, which was sufficiently noteworthy to be printed in full in the *Democratic Clarion and Tennessee Gazette*. Thereafter it was a rare public event in Nashville when Grundy did not provide the oration. Education was particularly important to Grundy. In 1809 he became a trustee of Cumberland College, originally Davidson Academy, founded in 1785, and he remained a trustee until his death.[12]

Grundy clearly wanted the congressional seat. Even though he did not formally announce his intention to run for Congress until January 1811, prescient observers had no doubt of Grundy's plans at an earlier time. Thomas Hart Benton wrote Henry Clay on September 18, 1810, that he had learned that Clay was going to the House of Representatives and that he would soon be joined by Grundy. Grundy appears to have carefully assessed his probable opposition and tried to dissuade all those who might run against him, as soon would be revealed.[13]

Grundy sought to discourage possible opponents because he was running without the backing of the factions that controlled Tennessee's political life. In the personalized and fluid political and economic environment of Tennessee, surveyors and speculators dominated, with almost everyone focused on land and even bitter enemies sharing economic interests. Yet with due allowance for nuance, it appears appropriate to characterize as factions the groups of leaders in Tennessee before the rise of political parties in the 1830s.

Unquestionably the most powerful leader in early Tennessee was William Blount. One of Tennessee's first two U.S. senators, Blount used his political roots in North Carolina to lead the effort for Tennessee statehood and, more importantly, to amass land claims in Tennessee on a gargantuan scale— Charles Sellers called it "the most fabulous land grab in American history." Although he died in 1800, his capable nephew Willie Blount, who was governor from 1809 to 1818, carried on the family policies of protecting North Carolina–based land claims and minimizing taxation. Pleasant Miller and Hugh Lawson White in East Tennessee and John Overton and Andrew Jackson in West Tennessee provided powerful support. John Sevier, who fought Indians and charmed Tennesseans equally well, had forestalled total Blount political domination by occupying the governor's seat from 1803 to 1809, but he proved unable or unwilling to develop and nurture a political faction not dependent on him. In 1811 Sevier and John Rhea, a member of the Blount faction, were set for Congress, but West Tennessee lacked a candidate.[14]

When Grundy announced his intentions, he did not expect serious opposition. Jeffersonianism dominated Tennessee, and Grundy sported undeniable Republican credentials, as he emphasized in proclaiming his candidacy on June 17, adding, "I have uniformly entertained the same political sentiments I now profess." Moreover, Grundy had taken a strong nationalist stance in his public positions as Tennessee had become increasingly hostile to British interference with American interests. Tennessee suffered from widespread dissatisfaction with the same issues that earlier had embroiled Kentucky—access to courts and credit—and the legislature had enacted judicial reform in 1809. Grundy's leadership on these issues in Kentucky gave him credibility with reformers in Tennessee.[15]

Grundy's candidacy did produce a reaction, however: a public meeting in Nashville on June 27, which recommended General James Winchester for Congress instead. This effort to block Grundy only five weeks before the election was largely the work of friends of Andrew Jackson—Colonel Barclay Martin, William Preston Anderson, and John Coffee, who was a former business partner of Jackson's, a friend of Patton Anderson's, and subsequently a hero of the Battle of New Orleans. Winchester's reputation, his residence in Summer County, and his absence at the time of the public meeting made him appear a plausible candidate.

Grundy, anxious to nip this effort in the bud, immediately attacked in the press, pointing out that of five hundred men in Nashville the day of the meeting, a bare majority of only twenty men had approved the proceeding. He characterized his opponents as speculators fearful of his independence or men wounded by his successes in the courtroom. He also charged that the opposition had arisen because he would pursue only the interest of the people of West Tennessee and would "not permit myself to be dictated to by a *junto* or *faction*." Grundy also wrote that Winchester, now out of the state and known to be a friend, had agreed not to offer himself as a candidate and would indeed support Grundy. Grundy then annexed a statement from Stephen Winchester and William Cage, business partners of General Winchester, affirming Grundy's stance.[16]

Barclay Martin responded to Grundy one week later, rejecting charges by Grundy and asserting that Grundy had usurped democratic principles by securing advance agreements from prospective opponents, including Winchester, not to run. Two weeks later "Leonidas," presumably Grundy, presented lengthy statements rebutting what appear to be sham arguments—that Grundy should be rejected because he was a lawyer and a newcomer to Tennessee. Winchester, after his return to the state, said nothing, and the press revealed that an alleged list of his supporters included apprentices, underage boys, and fictitious names. "Leonidas" argued that an aristocratic cabal opposed Grundy, and others asserted that Yazoo speculators supported Martin.[17]

In the anti-Grundy effort, Barclay Martin took the public role in the press, but Anderson and Coffee worked hard behind the scenes, arranging for publication and distribution of anti-Grundy circulars. Anderson wrote Coffee from Nashville on July 30, 1811, that Nashville was in "considerable bustle" over an anti-Grundy piece but that it was difficult to move articles quickly: "The printers are all under the influence of Grundy and can hardly be got to do anything." Anderson arranged for the circulars to be sent to surrounding towns, and Coffee, in addition to personal distribution, solicited friends to vote against Grundy. John Doak, in Lebanon, Tennessee, replied on August 2 that Winchester would take a majority of votes in Wilson County. Another correspondent wrote that he was pleased by publication of the truth "against the little villain" but could only say that Grundy would not receive the majority initially expected in Bedford County.[18]

The most interesting question about this opposition to Grundy is the degree of Andrew Jackson's involvement. I have found no direct evidence of participation by Jackson, yet some of Jackson's closest associates led the anti-Grundy initiative. Moreover, Jackson had been a leader of the Blount faction and could not have been enthusiastic about Grundy, an upstart outside of faction control. Most importantly, the Magness trial had taken place only nine months earlier. Jackson's denunciation of Grundy at the trial, his volatile and passionate nature, and his close ties to Patton Anderson make it probable that he was involved in the effort to undermine Grundy.

Despite their prominence, the anti-Grundy group offered too little too late. A "Voter from Robertson County" reported on June 29 that Grundy had the "most friends, if not so noisy and boisterous," and that he held a commanding majority in Davidson County. Election returns published in the *Democratic Clarion and Tennessee Gazette* on August 6, 1811, showed Grundy with an overwhelming lead in Davidson County, 1,164 votes to 233 for Roberts and 142 for Winchester, offsetting his second-place position in other counties. On September 17, 1811, the Tennessee legislature proclaimed Felix Grundy a member of Congress. He garnered 7,878 votes in the Third District, compared with 2,465 votes for John Rhea in the First District and 4,331 for Sevier in the Second.[19]

II

WAR HAWK

War or Honorable Peace.
—Felix Grundy

*T*he historic Twelfth Congress opened in Washington on November 4, 1811. The 152 members, with 63 newcomers, included the group thereafter known as the War Hawks, the most prominent of whom were Henry Clay, of Kentucky; William Lowndes, Langdon Cheves, and John C. Calhoun, of South Carolina; Peter B. Porter, of New York; and Felix Grundy, of Tennessee. Determined to restore national honor, the War Hawks brought new vigor to a fractured Congress and a hesitant presidency. When Britain did not meet the conditions demanded for peace, they enthusiastically supported a declaration of war.

The rise of the War Hawks came against a backdrop of years of mounting anger and a sense of national humiliation. In the European struggle of the early nineteenth century the fledgling United States was only an afterthought, and it—and other neutrals—benefited and suffered from the changing dynamics of the European war. The warring powers' demands for American foodstuffs and other products initially led to dramatically increased U.S. exports at greater prices and expansion of the carrying trade by an augmented U.S. merchant fleet. But the European conflict intensified in Jefferson's second term, and infringements of American rights, particularly impressments of alleged deserters by British naval captains, increased.

Although both Britain and France imposed controls affecting American interests, the British trade restrictions on Napoleonic Europe bit most deeply, and the United States watched helplessly. The American military enjoyed little respect, in part because Jeffersonian principles of minimal government had reduced funding for the army and the navy. A policy of neutrality, and avoidance of war and a military establishment, had been central to the beliefs of many

Republicans. By 1810, however, the strategy looked misplaced. The West, whose agricultural exports through New Orleans were in thrall to British policy, in particular voiced its outrage about national passivity. The agrarian Republicans of Tennessee suffered mightily after the closing of foreign markets. Depending on the product, prices in New Orleans fell by 20–50 percent from 1805 to 1811. The British, enemies during the Revolution and regularly characterized as instigators of Indian attacks, now held the economic prosperity of Kentucky and Tennessee hostage. The slogan "Free Trade or War" aptly summarized popular feeling.[1]

Grundy shared the increasingly nationalistic attitudes of the West. His constituents in Kentucky and now Tennessee depended on outlets for their agricultural products, and the British thwarted western commercial expansion. Grundy officiated and spoke at public meetings decrying the constraints imposed on the United States. He also continued to speak out against the Federalists, considering them Tories of the Revolution in modern guise, linked by trade and cultural affinities to the British and doing little to grapple with western issues.[2]

The supine reaction of the United States to British and to a lesser extent French provocations brought to the fore the more intangible concept of national honor. Honor meant a great deal on the tough, individualistic frontier, and the prevalence of dueling at the individual level mirrored a larger concern about national honor and self-respect. The celebration of the Revolution and the establishment of new governments in Kentucky and Tennessee emphasized the uniqueness and fragility of the American experiment. Politicians trumpeted that only a citizenry worthy of the Revolutionary generation could carry forward the ideals and independence proclaimed in 1776. That all this gave rise to self-doubt is hardly surprising, particularly in an immature and new nation lacking settled traditions and confidence. Grundy reflected this position in a message for the press from Washington dated November 5, 1811, stating that he hoped to see a manly attitude adopted and pursued until foreign nations respected American rights. "The situation of our country is truly embarrassing—something however must be done, or we shall lose our respectability abroad, and even cease to respect ourselves." Grundy described the generational responsibility in a letter to Jackson in December: "Our Fathers fought for and bequeathed liberty & Independence to *us* their children—shall they perish in our hands? No, a firm and manly effort now, will enable us to transmit to *our children* the rich inheritance unimpaired."[3]

Grundy's first view of Washington in November 1811, raw and desolate, could not have been inviting but reflected the national mood. Washington would retain its unfinished look for decades. The relatively few buildings were strewn over swamps and open fields, and partridge could be raised within three hundred yards of the Capitol. Even a meeting at the White House could necessitate travel by horseback, since carriages from Capitol Hill would get bogged down in deep mud during rainy periods. Washington was larger than Georgetown, but it only had 8,208 residents, of whom 1,437 were slaves and 867 were free blacks. Federal employment reflected the Jeffersonian belief in minimal government. The payroll carried fewer than four hundred employees, of whom almost half held seats in Congress.[4]

When Grundy arrived to speak for western interests, he quickly made clear that he brought a different perspective; although he was claimed as a Virginian, he said, he was a "Western man altogether." Grundy in fact represented the most western of all congressional districts. As far as we know, his journey to Washington was his first trip as an adult outside Kentucky and Tennessee, and few of his fellows in Congress could match his experience growing up on the frontier. In legislative experience Grundy had few rivals. His years in Kentucky had given him a zest for debate and at least a local reputation perhaps excelled only by Clay's. The War Hawks are generally characterized as young men, but Grundy, at thirty-six, was almost two years older than Henry Clay, seven years older than Calhoun and William Lowndes, and one year older than Langdon Cheves.

Congressmen lived in boardinghouses, usually on Capitol Hill and almost always with housemates from the same party or faction. Historians have reported that Grundy was part of the famous War Mess at a house where Clay and Bibb, of Kentucky, lived with Matthew Clay, of Virginia, and Cheves, Calhoun, and Lowndes, of South Carolina. It is a nice story but untrue with respect to Grundy. He took up quarters at Claxton's, one of the larger houses on Capitol Hill. His thirteen housemates largely shared his Republican views, but only Anthony New and Stephen Ormsby, of Kentucky, also represented western districts. Grundy and his colleagues had diversions, mainly dinner, gambling, and occasional shows. John Sevier kept a diary, in which he noted dinners with Grundy and balls and parties in Georgetown. In general, however, politics dominated. It was intrinsically interesting, and also the only game in town.[5]

Grundy, like most legislators, went to Washington without his family.

Nancy Grundy stayed at home with the children. She also was pregnant again: Martha A. F. Grundy was born on June 25, 1812, while her father was still in Washington.

The political game began quickly in 1811. On November 5, the first day of the session, the House elected the war-minded nationalist Henry Clay as Speaker in a 75–38 vote over William Bibb, of Georgia, foreshadowing a 79–49 vote to declare war seven months later. This unprecedented election of a first-time member as Speaker reflected the cohesive power of the new Republican congressmen. On November 12 Clay appointed nine members of the House's Select Committee on Foreign Relations: Peter Porter, of New York, as chair and John C. Calhoun, Grundy, John Smilie, of Pennsylvania, John Randolph, of Virginia, John A. Harper, of New Hampshire, Phillip B. Key, of Maryland, Joseph Desha, of Kentucky, and Ebenezer Seaver, of Massachusetts. Porter, Calhoun, Grundy, Harper, Desha, and Seaver generally adhered to Clay's standard of war or honor, but Key was a Middle Atlantic Federalist, and Randolph was almost a party unto himself, with his acid wit particularly directed at those Jeffersonians who had deserted his view of Republican principles.

In light of their past and future political struggles, it is ironic that Felix Grundy owed his political opportunity in Washington to Henry Clay. The choice of Grundy as a member of the powerful Committee on Foreign Relations in a session to be devoted to issues of war obviously reflected Clay's calculus of Grundy's position: he had little doubt that he and Grundy shared western interests. Clay knew Grundy's talents for debate, and the House, more active than the Senate, was the forum where oratory was prized and spectators thronged galleries to admire and be admired. Moreover, Grundy had been more than willing to take on the business establishment in Kentucky and could be expected to treat the varied factions in Congress with wit and aplomb. In short, Grundy would be an eloquent and forthright spokesman for the West. Clay was right. Grundy, largely unknown outside Kentucky and Tennessee upon his arrival, achieved national recognition within months.[6]

Tennessee wanted a "speaking" congressman, and Grundy quickly demonstrated that the western district had elected the right man, taking the floor as a freshman congressman on November 15 and arguing that U.S. jurisdiction extended to crimes committed on Indian territory. He also took an active role on a special House committee dealing with congressional apportionment and raising delicate North-South issues.[7]

But the main issue was war. The divisions that marked previous Congresses continued in the twelfth. The thirty-seven Federalists in the House, most from

New England, generally followed a policy of remaining silent in the debates of 1811–12. John Randolph and his antiwar Republicans opposed war on Jeffersonian grounds of opposition to military establishments and foreign entanglements. Moderate Republicans, including Grundy's Kentucky friend John Pope, now a senator, doubted the wisdom of confronting Great Britain, particularly given the dismal state of America's military preparedness. The War Hawks, including at their core the six congressmen from Kentucky and three from Tennessee, comprised perhaps a third of the House. More properly categorized as a loose grouping rather than cohesive faction, they differed widely in how to implement their views but were united in their desire for an end to the temporizing of the last four years. In addition, a more or less cohesive minority tends to carry its position among fragmented parties, and the War Hawks unrelentingly pushed their views. Ironically, the drumbeats for war came from the frontier, a natural market for British products and a source for British imports and without a merchant fleet, while opposition to war fever came from New England, with its seagoing interests and potential as a serious competitor to British trading superiority.[8]

Historians have assessed Grundy as one of the leading players in the uncertain drama culminating in the declaration of the War of 1812. But most have been content to provide conclusions, often following the political judgments of the time. Contemporaries viewed him with animosity or admiration. John Gardner, an outspoken antiwar minister in Boston, may have originated the slogan that the war was due to "Madison, Grundy and the Devil," but he only reflected a widespread view among Federalists of the Tennessean's significant and malevolent involvement. John Randolph disparaged "Clay, Grundy and Company." Congressman Alexander Hanson, of Maryland, in congressional debates in 1813 described Grundy as "the fiery, furious gentleman, who, during the war session, went about beating up to arms and enlisting recruits, crying out, follow me ye of stout hearts, let the faint-hearted now leave us." From his constituents, and from westerners generally, however, he received enthusiastic praise and support. Grundy himself in 1829 described the war as one that he had been in some degree instrumental in producing. Although characterizations abound of Grundy as "reckless" or "impetuous" or as the leader of "a party seeking immediate war," Tom Kanon, in an impressive review, has concluded that Grundy was not the warmonger he and his supporters have been made out to be.[9]

The evidence suggests that Grundy's leadership role was complex and nuanced. A summary overview helps put Grundy's position in perspective:

- Grundy saw himself as a spokesman for the West, which had articulated interests and a strong conception of national honor.
- Grundy became a symbol of the West and the War Hawks. The press contributed significantly to Grundy's identification with the war. He had a gift for the memorable comment, and his phrase "the Rubicon is passed" captured the movement to decisive action. But Grundy's political skills also played a major role in his rise. Josiah Quincy, a Federalist from Boston, wrote that Grundy "is a perfect political jockey, and as good humored as he is cunning." Even though Grundy's votes did not dramatically differ from those of his fellows from the West, his advocate's personality and his oratorical skills matched the demands of the moment and gave him recognition.[10]
- Grundy did not favor immediate war. He sought instead an honorable resolution. His writings are replete with his straightforward position "War or Honorable Peace."
- Grundy doubted Madison's leadership. He vigorously opposed temporization and pushed Madison and Congress generally to a decision rather than continued vacillation. Overoptimistic about the country's capacity to wage war promptly, Grundy never hesitated in pushing an internal buildup of the military.
- Grundy maintained a fine line between "War or Honorable Peace" and his Republican principles. He supported expansion of the military and the necessary imposition of hated taxation but upheld legislative prerogatives against attempts to expand executive power, opposed development of a navy, and rejected federalization of the state militia.

The unfolding of the Twelfth Congress's move to war began with Madison's message to Congress on November 5. The president did not ask for a declaration of war but played to the enhanced militancy expected from the House. Madison proposed the expansion of U.S. military forces and other more warlike measures to put the United States "into an armor and attitude demanded by the crisis." As the Committee on Foreign Relations was preparing its response to the president's message, Washington learned that William Henry Harrison and a mix of army regulars and militia had achieved a costly victory over the Prophet, Tecumseh's brother, at Tippecanoe on November 7. Among the 179 Americans killed was Jo Daveiss, Grundy's good friend and the commander of the Kentucky cavalry.[11]

Grundy's position of "War or Honorable Peace" did not mandate war.

Grundy believed that the time for accepting humiliation had passed, that national honor, the elimination of the Indian threat, and the opening of the European continent to U.S. exports demanded decisive action. He saw two necessary tasks. Congress had to prepare for war, both to demonstrate American
resolve to wavering countrymen and the warring European powers and to carry
out war if required. The second, more difficult task was to prod Madison to implement the authority provided and move to war or a diplomatic solution.

The preparations for war fell largely to Porter's Committee on Foreign Relations. Grundy took a clear stance. Writing to Andrew Jackson on November 28, he said that if the committee's position were to prevail, "the Rubicon is
passed—with a full determination to report in favor of actual war at a given period, we for the present, shall recommend" a variety of preparatory measures.
He went on to say that "I as one member wanted a pledge as to the application
of the force before I could heartily join in raising—and still, I could not think
of War until I knew something like the means provided—Rely on one thing—
we have War or Honorable peace before we adjourn or certain great personages
have produced a state of things which will bring them down from their high
places." His fellow westerners agreed. One had written Jackson in October that
if the choice were between war and a perpetual embargo, a little bloodletting
would relieve the system.[12]

Peter Porter presented the report of the Committee on Foreign Relations
on November 29. Acknowledging that many people wanted an immediate declaration of war, Porter reported that the committee had decided to build on
Madison's recommendations. It called for expansion of the army by the addition of ten thousand regular troops and fifty thousand volunteers and completion of warships already under construction. In recognition of the likely role of
privateers, the committee urged the arming of merchant ships. Porter, moreover, candidly stated that the committee itself wanted an open war and that
the United States would destroy British fisheries and British commerce with
America and the West Indies and conquer Canada. Although the committee
took the lead, the executive helped shape the committee's program. Grundy acknowledged in his letter to Jackson on November 28 that the president had
approved the preparatory measures and that indeed the "cooperation of that
department in ulterior measures was promised, before a Majority of the Committee could be brought to so mild a Course."[13]

In the ensuing debates, Grundy spoke first for the committee, responding to
a jibe from Randolph about the committee's constitutional basis. He took the
floor on December 9 as the House considered the second committee resolution,

calling for additional regular troops, what Grundy called the vital part of the report. Grundy addressed his remarks to the Republican members, referring to the choices required and asking whether the country's institutions and liberties could stand the shock of war. He reached out to his fellow Republicans in part because of the party's historical animosities toward war, taxation, and military preparedness. In 1798 the Republican Party had opposed Federalist proposals on armaments and the military; now, just thirteen years later, Grundy had to justify bellicose views. He argued for a fundamental change in Republican ideology, distinguishing between 1798 and 1811 on the basis of the greater threat now perceived from the British and the loss of national honor. Whether or not his argument was persuasive, he became, as Henry Adams would later write, the true spokesman of the committee.[14]

Grundy's speech straightforwardly assessed the causes for war. In his view, "the true question in controversy . . . is the right of exporting the productions of our own soil and industry to foreign markets." Just as the West in the 1780s and 1790s had demanded unrestricted access to New Orleans for its exports, it now sought rescission of the British orders in council denying European markets for those same products. Rejecting any suggestion of foreign regulation, Grundy emphatically declared that he preferred war to submission.[15]

Grundy decried impressments but called Indian incursions an even greater justification for war. The Indian threat carried emotional overtones, and few Westerners doubted that as in the Revolution, the British were inciting the tribes. Grundy had lost two brothers in 1778 and 1780, and the Indians had just taken the lives of other valiant westerners, including Jo Daveiss. Grundy proclaimed that war in fact had begun, intoning, "I pledge myself for my people—they will avenge the death of their brethen."[16]

After concluding that the United States had too long submitted to British demands, Grundy pointed out that war would have its advantages. Going well beyond the committee's report, which contained no such reference, he stated that war would include U.S. acquisition of Canada. Annexation of Canada would be beneficial to the North and would offset the southern objective of obtaining Spanish Florida. This geographical theme had political implications of the first order, with Republican Party leaders seeking to preserve the unity of the party's southern and northern wings. Yet it is important to recognize that Grundy cited the acquisition of Canada only as an advantage deriving from the conduct of the war, not as a war objective. Westerners, accustomed to military, not naval, operations against British-led Indians, would almost necessarily envision that the army would move against the enemy's territory.[17]

Grundy's oration was answered the next day by the colorful, acidic Virginian John Randolph, a Jeffersonian without Jefferson. Randolph asked for proof of British support of Indian uprisings, blaming Indian actions on the American thirst for territory. He also suggested that western constituents, as hemp growers, would benefit from a war with England because of the increased prices it would bring; he raised the possibility of slave insurrections if the British invaded; and he argued that American citizens would not submit to the taxation that would be required to support a war of conquest and dominion. Randolph aimed a personal insult at Grundy: "If we must have an exposition of the doctrines of Republicanism, we should receive it from the fathers of the church, and not from the junior apprentices of the law."[18]

John C. Calhoun came to Grundy's defense, ably answering Randolph's barbed response. Randolph's attacks reflected not only the singularity of his personality but also the extent of the gulf between westerners and the aristocratic Randolph and some of his fellow Republican Quids, not unlike the gap between elitist Virginians and frontier settlers reflected in George Washington's comments in 1749. Westerners, who at this stage were almost entirely Republican, supported many of the same principles as Randolph—primacy in agriculture, economy in government, and states' rights. They differed, however, in the rough-and-ready reaction of the West to issues of national honor, the Indian threat, and the British position on Western exports. The real difference, however, was more personally rooted. Grundy and his fellows parted company with Randolph in two critical areas: western particularism and egalitarianism. Randolph despised the West of "Clay, Grundy and Co.," that Yahoo's paradise, where a common immigrant from Europe "can get dead drunk for the hundredth part of a dollar." Randolph too could say, "I am an aristocrat; I love liberty, I hate equality," a point of view not likely to be well received by the egalitarian Grundy. Randolph's personal attacks on Grundy, and on Clay as well, stemmed from this long-nosed perspective, which was increasingly out of touch with the raucous democracy of Kentucky and Tennessee.[19]

Despite Randolph's attacks, all the resolutions of the Committee on Foreign Relations had passed by December 19, 1811, with impressive margins. The army bill, which called for raising twenty-five thousand troops (proposed by Madison opponents to embarrass him: he and the committee had requested only ten thousand) passed on January 9, 1812, by a vote of 94–34, leading the *Niles Register* to declare on January 11 that indeed the "Rubicon is passed." Although Lowndes believed that few approved of the bill, the vote was considered a test of support for the war.[20]

The War Hawks may have been relatively cohesive in pressing for war or an honorable peace, but they were sharply divided on how the war should be fought. Most western War Hawks, especially Grundy, could not be persuaded to depart from traditional Republican approaches unless absolutely required, and passage of war measures now forced adherents to measure traditional Jeffersonian principles of minimal government against the dictates of military preparedness. A seminal issue involved the power of the executive. In the debate on the army bill, an amendment proposed delegating to the president sole power to raise the troops. Grundy stood in opposition, stating that it was up to Congress to declare war. In discussing allocation of powers, he said that if he had any objection to "our excellent Constitution, it was on account of the very great powers placed in the Executive." Grundy carried the day, the amendment being defeated 66–57, with Grundy, Rhea, Sevier, Porter, and most Federalists opposed but Calhoun and most of the Kentucky congressmen in favor.[21]

A related issue concerned state powers over deployment of militia, the most available resource for the conduct of war. At issue in the debate over the Volunteer Bill was whether the president, in the absence of explicit constitutional authority, could dispatch the militia against Canada. Clay and Langdon Cheves took the nationalist high ground, asserting that a declaration of war necessarily carried with it the right to use the militia for such a purpose. Peter Porter and Grundy both objected to any such broad construction, denying federal power to nationalize state militia. This issue had significant historical precedents, such as Shays' Rebellion and the Whiskey Rebellion, raising again the question whether the federal government could call on state troops to suppress domestic unrest. Grundy was in the minority, voting to restrict militia use to the United States. The Volunteer Bill ultimately passed but left unsettled whether the president could call upon the militia for foreign service.[22]

The question of federal power arose in a more sharply focused context when Cheves and Lowndes proposed to add twelve ships of the line and twenty frigates to the small navy. Expansion of the navy made sense for South Carolinians, which had mercantile interests, but western War Hawks expected the war to be fought on the ground. In the view of Grundy and most of his western colleagues, a navy would only lead to taxes and the government establishment decried by Jeffersonians. The bill to add frigates went down to defeat on January 27 by a vote of 62–59, with most Federalists in favor. All of the congressmen from Kentucky and Tennessee except Speaker Clay voted against the bill. As a leading biographer of Clay stressed, "The shift of two votes—of a Grundy, so suspicious of Madison's sincerity for war, and a Johnson, so loudly concerned about impressed sailors . . . would have spelled victory."[23]

If Grundy in particular and fellow westerners generally feared federal power, then taxation would certainly put their support for war preparedness to its sternest test. Ezekiel Bacon, chairman of the Ways and Means Committee, visited Grundy in his room on February 12 to discuss war financing. They differed in prioritization, Grundy opposing an early decision on taxation. He argued that the appetite for war would be affected by the imposition of taxes and that a system of taxation could become permanent. Bacon went forward anyway, and on February 17 the Ways and Means Committee called for a heavy increase in import duties, taxes on salt and stills, and apportionment of a direct tax among the states, to be effective only upon a declaration of war. Grundy spoke vigorously and successfully against imposition of an excise tax on whiskey but acquiesced in overall taxation measures. He wrote a constituent that taxation would be a necessary consequence of war, and he declared publicly that nothing but war could induce him to vote for taxes. Thereafter Grundy consistently supported measures to provide funds for the war, including both taxes and the loans on which the government increasingly relied.[24]

Despite War Hawk bellicosity, the measures enacted in 1811–12 reflected the deep divisions within Congress and the ambivalence to war among Republicans. The only two changes of military importance, the addition to the regular army of twenty-five thousand men for five years and the calling to service of fifty thousand state militia, had to be balanced against the failure to enact a naval bill and tax measures to be effective only in the event of war. Yet, even these limited measures could only be implemented by the executive, and Grundy and others questioned Madison's capacity and desire: would the president bring an end to indecision?

Madison's role in the prewar political maneuverings has been the subject of extensive analyses and debate. His best-known biographer has suggested that Madison, not the passive and indecisive figure usually portrayed, agreed with the War Hawks that there should be war if Great Britain adhered to its orders in council but thought that the decision should be postponed until May to allow time for an agreement. William Lowndes, who wrote on December 7, 1811, that unless England repealed its orders in council, war would be declared before the close of the session, believed that Madison supported the War Hawk position. But Grundy doubted the president's resolve. Grundy's uncertainties about Madison, reflected in his letter to Jackson on November 28, 1811, surfaced in another letter to Jackson on Christmas Eve. After describing the status of congressional deliberations, Grundy concluded that Great Britain must recede or Congress would declare war, but "if war is not resorted to, . . . this nation or rather their representatives will be disgraced." Samuel Taggart, a portly Federalist from Massachusetts, considered Grundy the "most dangerous man" for the administration and concluded that "no man defies them more." Taggart believed Grundy was trying to kick Madison into war and reported that Grundy had told him that the executive "should either fight or quit talking about it, or he would expose them in their true colors."[25]

The drive for war or an honorable peace lagged during the first several months of 1812. Grundy reflected his frustration in a letter to Jackson on February 12, pointing out that the bill for raising twenty-five thousand men had been in effect for six weeks, and only Commander in Chief Henry Dearborn had been appointed. "Is there nothing rotten in Denmark?" he asked? "Shall we have War? That is the question you want answered—So do I—I thought some time ago, there was no doubt." But the administration dawdled. Some, certainly including the president, recognized that since the regular army could not be quickly raised and the volunteer militia could not be deployed outside the United States, Congress had not yet given the president a single soldier. But the War Hawks wanted executive action, and their unhappiness did not go unnoticed. Taggart wrote Jackson, "I am apprehensive that Cheves, Grundy and a few others will in the end prove enemies more dangerous to the administration than all the Federal opposition could be. They are men of too much talent, honour and independence to keep up this system of political juggling."[26]

Grundy, perhaps no longer playing to Jackson's bellicosity, took a restrained tact in a letter to a friend in Tennessee dated February 22, 1812, just ten days after his letter to Jackson. Grundy reiterated that he had been, and would be, for war unless Great Britain receded, but he justified the national delay because intelligence from Europe could avoid the calamities of war. He referred to the novelty of the situation, in which for the first time the nation was trying to exert its energies while reconciling great diversity of opinion.[27]

Great differences did indeed exist. Congress and the executive branch contended with widely varying perspectives on war, preparedness, and the roles of Great Britain and France. But at least one other consideration influenced the deliberations: the president's reelection prospects. Grundy had informed Jackson on February 12 that intrigue surrounded the presidency and that Madison's position was delicate. The Republican nominee for president would be chosen by congressional caucus, in which the War Hawks would be a vocal bloc.[28]

The extent to which Madison adapted his policies to meet the demands of the powerful young Republicans of his party has been extensively debated. Samuel Taggart believed Madison had succumbed to the pressure of the War Hawks by spring. More directly, Senator Worthington, of Ohio, recorded in his diary that Clay and other War Hawks had met with the president on April 12 or 13, 1812, and advised him that the congressional caucus would withhold support for his nomination unless he recommended war. During the war debates, Federalists made the same charge. On June 18, 1813, Congressman Hanson, in responding to Grundy with respect to conduct of the war, referred to a self-created committee of congressman who had called on the president and given him the electoral ultimatum. "Mr. H. inveighed in strong terms against . . . a Presidential election . . . made to depend upon a recommendation of war." I have found no evidence with respect to Grundy that would add to the arguments concerning whether Clay and the War Hawks used a threat of withholding renomination support to coerce Madison into war. The degree of coercion is probably irrelevant. The War Hawks, cohesive and insistent on war or an honorable peace, kept constant pressure on the president. Madison, cautious, perhaps not actively opposed to war and concerned about his reelection, ultimately took the position advocated by the War Hawks.[29]

Events in Washington moved toward war in late March and April, after the long and tedious months of laborious debate and indecision on the part of the executive branch. On April 1, Madison recommended a sixty-day embargo, which was quickly approved by the House, 70–41, after Grundy and then Clay pronounced it a war measure. Extended to ninety days by the Senate, the Embargo Act went into effect on April 4. The pace quickened further in late April. The Senate, much less militant than the House, rejected by a vote of 15–8 an effort to repeal the Non-Importation Act and place France and England on equal footing, with Pope, of Kentucky, on the losing side. In May the House rejected, 57–31, a proposal to repeal the embargo; Grundy's "impassioned words [against repeal] . . . exerted the most influence." On May 18 the nominating caucus took place, with 82 of the 83 congressmen present voting for Madison's renomination as the Republican choice for president. Few doubted now that Madison would push for war, and that doubt was eliminated on May 22 when the ship *Hornet* brought news of England's rejection again of any change in its orders in council.[30]

Madison presented his war message to Congress on June 1, 1812. Two days later the Committee on Foreign Relations released its "Report on the Causes and Reasons for War." Although historians have long debated the authorship of the House report, it probably was written largely by John C. Calhoun with some input from Grundy. A review of the actual manuscript of the report suggests that Grundy wrote at least the final paragraph.[31]

The war measure moved forward despite continuing fulminations in the Federalist press. The House conducted its final sessions in secret, apparently to minimize opposing voices. (Calhoun wrote much later that he and Clay had wanted the war question to be discussed in public session, but others, including Grundy, had not. Clay, Grundy, and Calhoun then met with the president, and Madison sided with Grundy.) Assuming the accuracy of Calhoun's recollection, Grundy and President Madison appear to have been more concerned about the adverse effects of open dissent than was warranted. At any event, little discussion took place in the lower chamber, given the extensive debate that had already occurred. The House passed the war bill on June 4 by a vote of 79–49. Needless to say, Grundy and all other representatives from Tennessee and Kentucky voted for war. Grundy wrote Andrew Jackson one day later, "I am proud, that I am a member of the House of Representatives."[32]

The Senate took longer. Of the temporizing alternatives proposed in the upper house, one that would have changed the House action from a declaration of war to issuance of letters of marque and reprisal almost succeeded, with a vote of 16–16. According to Lowndes, Madison's cabinet generally favored this last-ditch effort to prevent war, and Grundy was brought over by its advocates. This seems curious in light of Grundy's consistent position for war or honorable peace, but it cannot be dismissed out of hand. Grundy and John Pope, who proposed various alternatives, had worked together since they were students, and it is likely that Grundy did have concerns about war preparedness. In any event, Lowndes wrote that many senators and representatives rejected the idea, determined to do nothing or "have a War in common form." Ultimately, the war bill passed in the Senate on June 17 by a vote of 19–13, with Pope opposed. On June 18, 1812, President Madison signed the bill declaring a state of war between the United States and Great Britain.[33]

12

CONGRESS AT WAR

This is not time for temporizing: he who is not for us, is against us.

—Felix Grundy

*T*ennesseans enthusiastically supported the war, and Grundy threw himself behind its prosecution. By 1813 Grundy had overcome his earlier skepticism regarding Madison, becoming the de facto leader of the administration in the House. His defense of the war effort aroused intense hostility, however, and contributed to his defeat when he ran for the post of Speaker of the House in 1814. His nationalistic ardor remained undimmed even as he resigned from Congress in July 1814 due to his wife's illness.

Andrew Jackson captured the mood of Tennessee on March 7, 1812, calling for volunteers with the ringing declaration, "The hour of national vengeance is now at hand." Grundy himself exhorted his constituents to show themselves worthy of the Revolutionary generation. In a call to arms dated June 25, 1812, he summarized the causes of war as annihilation of commerce, impressments of almost seven thousand Americans, and British instigation of the Indians. He asked rhetorically whether the "mighty spirit of our fathers is in us" and invoked biblical injunctions: "Your country is in arms, rise in your strength, put on your armor, be terrible in battle: This is not time for temporizing: he who is not for us, is against us. And now it may be said in the language of old 'cursed be he that doeth the work of the Lord deceitfully, and cursed be he that holdeth back his sword from blood.'"[1]

Congress, as well as Grundy, directed its attention during the war years to financing and import-export matters and left the actual conduct of the war to the executive branch. That was just as well for Thomas Jefferson, who wrote to Madison, "That a body containing 100 lawyers in it, should direct the measures of a war, is, I fear, impossible." Reflecting the spirit of his constituents, Grundy became an unequivocal advocate for forceful pursuit of the war.[2]

As Grundy assumed a leadership role in Congress from 1812 to 1814, two core elements of his character became more evident: his advocate's mentality and his good humor. From his earliest legislative days in Kentucky, Grundy showed not only self-assurance but also combativeness, a willingness to take on the status quo. As Grundy's experience increased both at the bar and in legislative halls, his advocate's approach became more marked. Yet at the same time, Grundy's affability and good humor manifested themselves. His wit leavened almost every speech, and he refused to treat his judicial or legislative adversaries as enemies.

It is with this background that Grundy must be viewed during the War of 1812. After war was declared, Grundy became a leading spokesman for the administration rather than a skeptic and attacked war opponents with vigor and caustic jibes. Federalists responded by villainizing Grundy, not Clay or Calhoun, as the personification of the bellicose War Hawk.

Grundy demonstrated his resolve when Congress reconvened in the late fall of 1812. The U.S. Treasury held $18 million in bonds and $5 million in duties from the seizure of goods sent to the United States after Great Britain terminated its orders in council on June 23, 1812. The goods had been shipped based upon Congress's determination in 1811 that the Non-Importation Act would be repealed upon revocation of the orders, but unfortunately for the merchants, war was declared before the goods were sent. Grundy supported Secretary of the Treasury Gallatin in arguing that the government should use its share of the seized goods to finance the war, pointing out that American merchants had directly contravened the purposes of the Non-Importation Act by buying the goods in Great Britain. Langdon Cheves, chairman of the Ways and Means Committee, opposed Grundy, claiming that imposing penalties on the merchants would cost the confidence of the only class that could finance the war. Congress ultimately remitted all capital and profits on goods shipped from England before September 15, 1812, the date on which news of the war declaration ostensibly reached England.[3]

Grundy further raised his profile in debates with Josiah Quincy on army needs. The Massachusetts Federalist strongly opposed the war but, as one biographer noted, provided little leadership, essentially speaking for himself. In December 1812, while the House debated whether to raise an additional twenty thousand soldiers for one year, Quincy bitterly attacked war supporters, calling eastern Republicans "toads or reptiles which spread their slime in the drawing room" and a campaign to invade Canada too absurd for serious examination. Grundy fired back, strongly criticizing Quincy for his desire to halt fighting and negotiate. Treasonous talk and division in Congress only contributed to the failure of U.S. forces, he said. Grundy also denied that repeal of the orders in council should lead to cessation of hostilities. Repeal may have been a major war objective, but obtaining redress for unjust "spoliations" of American property and ending the impressments of American seamen had been, and remained, prominent causes of war. He urged Quincy to show less pity for the Canadians and instead consider the impressed American seamen and the westerners exposed to Indian outrages.[4]

Grundy deftly used the impressment issue to divide the Federalists. Building on a proposal by Secretary of State James Monroe, the Committee on Foreign Relations on January 29, 1813, proposed that British and other foreign seamen be prohibited from serving on American naval or merchant ships, thereby removing the ostensible British reason for halting American merchant ships. Grundy, speaking for the committee, stressed that American honor would be preserved, yet passage would send a signal that Congress wanted to minimize disharmony with Britain. Exclusion of non-Americans from naval service would also stabilize the labor force and reduce the likelihood of future wars. Grundy, reported by a Maryland Federalist to be almost the only zealous patron of the bill, gleefully wrote that the bill for excluding foreign seamen had puzzled the Federalists inordinately and forced a split in that party. The bill with which Grundy was so pleased passed the House on February 12, 1813, by a vote of 89–33, with Republicans and some Federalists in support, and became law on March 3.[5]

In his advocate's partisanship, Grundy targeted the Federalists, depicting Josiah Quincy as a symbol of near-treasonous conduct. Quincy, however, recorded a conversation with Grundy on February 15, 1813:

[Grundy] said to me yesterday: Quincy, I thought I had abused you enough, but I find it will not do.

Q. Why, what is the matter now? I do not mean to speak again
G. No matter; by heavens, I must give you another thrashing
Q. Why so?
G. Whey, the truth is a d——d fellow has set up against me in my district—a perfect Jacobin, as much worse than I as worse can be. Now except Tom Pickering, there is not a man in the United States so perfectly hated by the people of my district as yourself. You must therefore excuse me. By G——, I must abuse you, or I shall never get reelected. I will do it, however, gently. *I will not do it as that d——d fool of a Clay did it—strike so hard as to hurt*

myself. But abuse you I must. You understand, I mean to be friends not-withstanding. By G——, I mean to be in Congress again, and must use the means.[6]

Quincy's comments, written shortly after Grundy's attacks on him on the new army bill, bring the political Grundy to life. The mild profanity, the ambition, and the good humor are evident. What stands out is Grundy's confidence in his own charm and in his appearance of guileless simplicity—that he can remain friends with a principled opponent because, after all, they are actors in a polit-ical game in which words and actions are not always what they seem. Grundy the advocate made clear that he would do what it took to accomplish his objec-tive. Yet at the same time he intended to be "friends." Grundy never doubted that candor, friendship, and good humor could win over adversaries.

The election referred to by Quincy pitted Grundy against Newton Can-non, a thirty-one-year-old planter and state senator from Williamson County. Grundy need not have been too concerned about his reelection. Tennessee ap-preciated his advocacy and national recognition, and he benefited from wide-spread support, including from John Sevier and James Robertson, vaunted figures in Tennessee. The *Democratic Clarion and Tennessee Gazette* and the *Nashville Whig* endorsed Grundy on March 2, 1813, and February 17, 1813, re-spectively. Both Grundy and Cannon conducted the campaign with civility, with the only unusual feature being Cannon's subsequently withdrawn asser-tion that Grundy might not be a candidate because of his acceptance of ap-pointment as governor of the Indiana Territory. The electorate voted over-whelming for Grundy, 3,277 votes to 757, with the incumbent carrying all five counties.[7]

Congress reconvened for its special session on May 24, 1813, with Grundy second in command to Calhoun on the Committee on Foreign Relations. By now the Federalist press regularly demonized him. In a noteworthy example, the *Boston Patriot* reported that the Reverend S. J. Gardner from the pulpit had referred to southerners as possessed of all the evil qualities of which human na-ture is capable and stated that by separating from the Union, "you have noth-ing to loose but Thomas Jefferson, James Madison, Albert Gallatin and Felix Grundy." Congressional correspondence reflected Grundy's prominence. John Randolph, defeated in his bid for reelection, put the best face on his loss in a let-ter to Quincy on June 20, writing that he would rather be at home than under the "discipline and order of the Calhouns, Grundys and Seavers." Daniel Web-ster on January 6, 1814, wrote that Secretary of War Armstrong was likely to go, the only thing preventing it being "the influence of Clay, Grundy and the other lights of the West, who are supposed to be for More War, and for Armstrong."[8]

Grundy's speeches and letters to the press during this period reflect firm determination with respect to prosecution of the war. Private letters to his oldest daughters in December 1812 and June 1813 show the same resolve but are more revealing in their fatherly homilies and their more emotional political assessments. On December 19, 1812, in a letter to his oldest daughter, Louisa, he declared that disgracefully, all army efforts had failed and that "I can never agree to make peace with Great Britain while things remain in this state. It was a maxim with the old Romans never to treat or sue for peace in times of adversity, as I say now—give us victory, and honorable terms, and I am for peace, not otherwise."[9]

Grundy enhanced his national reputation by his role in two controversies that dominated the first session of the new Congress. The first arose from an effort led by Daniel Webster to embarrass President Madison for allegedly withholding information about the repeal in 1811 of certain French decrees. The British government on April 21, 1812, had stated that it would repeal the orders in council when the French, through an authorized public statement, repealed the Berlin and Milan decrees. In what would have been comic were it not treated so seriously, the House debated what would have happened in 1812 had the president disclosed in a timely manner that the United States had allegedly been advised both in 1811 and on May 1, 1812, that the French had repealed the Berlin and Milan decrees on April 28, 1811, even though the repeal had not been published. If Madison had revealed receipt of the information, so the argument went, the war could have been averted. Since Madison had disclosed the information in March 1813, only after a House request, most observers concluded that the president had withheld information. Daniel Webster, a newcomer making his mark, presented resolutions on June 10, 1813, intended to force the facts from Madison and cast the administration in an unfavorable light. Grundy defended the administration and argued forcefully on June 18, 1813, in a speech lasting one hour, that not only had the French not issued a public statement but the repeal would have applied only to the United States, and not all neutral trade as demanded by Great Britain.[10]

Holding a weak hand in light of Madison's failure of disclosure, Grundy went on the attack and spoke of "moral treason," a phrase that he thus made famous. He noted initially that he had been careful never to charge any member of the opposition with responsibility for the war's disasters, and he acknowledged that many war opponents had been governed by honest motives and stayed within constitutional boundaries. But he now accused those who stayed at home and aided the British of moral treason, making them even more heinous than those who deserted to the enemy. The Federalists who refused to support the war effort with loans were particular targets: "I accuse him who sets himself to work systematically to weaken the arm of this Government . . . who has used his exertion to defeat the loan and to prevent the young men . . . from going forth to fight their country's battles."[11]

Grundy's speech struck a Federalist nerve, and the debates on Webster's resolutions centered thereafter as much on Grundy and his new doctrine as on Madison's failure of disclosure. Congressman Shepherd mildly noted that Grundy did not distinguish very accurately between moral obligations, in which individuals make their own determination, and legal obligations, to which all are subject. Others argued that Grundy failed to recognize critical constitutional rights of dissent and free speech. Much of the attack, however, was directed against Grundy himself, as a cunning lawyer from the backwoods, as a mouthpiece for Calhoun, and as an apologist for France. Alexander Hanson, of Maryland, "exhausted himself" in his attack on Grundy, referring sarcastically to "the lawyer-like dexterity, and a characteristic skill and cunning, for which he understood the member stood unrivaled and pre-eminent in the high-civilized, polished and refined state which honored the House with his presence here."[12]

Grundy's statement on "moral treason" became his best-known legacy of congressional service during the War of 1812. When publishers issued a lithograph of Grundy as attorney general, the caption included his language of June 18, 1813. Grundy never retreated from his position, although he modified it, most sharply on January 6, 1814, when he acknowledged constitutional rights of dissent even while reiterating his stance.[13]

The second significant controversy revived the question whether to impose an embargo. Indignation concerning the Federalists' lack of support for the war mounted among war advocates. Many Americans, particularly in New England, continued to supply goods to the enemy, seeing no reason why their livelihoods should be impaired by a foolish war. Even though an embargo had proved ineffectual in 1807 and 1808, angry War Hawks resolved to take whatever steps were necessary to stop trading with the enemy. On July 20, 1813, Madison recommended an immediate prohibition of exports. The bill was referred to the Committee on Foreign Relations, which opposed the initiative.

Calhoun, the chairman of the committee, preferred to remove all restrictions on imports, even from Britain, and then pay for the war with import duties, an approach previously presented by Cheves. Unfazed by Calhoun's opposition, Clay and Grundy secured a resolution providing for appointment of a special committee with Grundy as chairman. The committee promptly reported out a bill imposing an embargo on all ships and vessels in U.S. harbors, with Grundy writing Andrew Jackson that an embargo offered the only way to prevent Americans from supplying the British. Although the House passed the bill, 80–50, with Calhoun and Lowndes opposed, the Senate did not, and the special session ended in late July with no embargo.[14]

Conditions did not improve, and American military fortunes reached a near nadir in late 1813. President Madison resubmitted the embargo proposal at the regular session of the Thirteenth Congress, which began on December 6. Grundy, for the Committee on Foreign Relations, presented the bill, and this time both the House and the Senate passed an embargo that covered both coastal and foreign trade. Grundy wrote the editors of the *Nashville Whig* on December 20, 1813, that he hoped now to determine whether "we have not *honest* men enough in this nation to prevent *traitors* from feeding our enemies."[15]

In a somewhat poisoned atmosphere, Grundy soon faced a different election. After British prime minister Castlereagh opened the possibility of negotiations with the United States, President Madison proposed a commission made up of John Q. Adams, James Bayard, Henry Clay, and Jonathan Russell to treat with the British. On January 19, 1814, Henry Clay resigned as Speaker of the House. Grundy's strong stance in support of the war effort and the increasing distance between the president and the South Carolina trio of Calhoun, Cheves, and Lowndes made Grundy the natural administration candidate to be Clay's successor. On the day of Clay's resignation, the House selected a new Speaker, with Langdon Cheves and Felix Grundy the principal candidates. Cheves received 94 votes to Grundy's 59, with 12 votes scattered among other, unidentified candidates. There is no breakdown of votes, but it is reasonable to surmise that Federalists and Republicans opposed to commercial restrictions united behind Cheves, while westerners and other strong proponents of the war and the restrictive system supported Grundy. Francis Scott Key, soon to achieve star-spangled immortality, wrote John Randolph from Georgetown of Cheves's election, describing it favorably and as a defeat for the administration. "Whig," writing in the *Daily National Intelligencer* on February 1, 1814, noted the extent to which the Federalist press had been rejoicing at the election of Cheves and said that they did so not because of political principles but because of gratification at his success over Mr. Grundy, always a thorn in the side of Federalists, who viewed Grundy with a "peculiar dread."[16]

Grundy's loss of the Speakership did not lessen his ardor. When the House considered a $25 million war loan, Grundy declared that the United States must continue to pursue the sword if negotiations failed, and he expressed confidence that the American people would subscribe the necessary funds. He pointed out that those who complained most about the defenseless state of the country were the very men who refused to grant men and money for its defense.[17]

His passion notwithstanding, Grundy was less active in Congress following his defeat for the Speakership, partly because, as he wrote John Overton on March 6, "We are doing very little business here." Upon the embargo's repeal on April 14, following the president's recommendation, Grundy said nothing. He did, however, speak up with respect to war financing. The struggle against Britain was largely being paid for through borrowings, and New England, the only section with significant specie, was reluctant, to say the least, to lend money to the government. A writer in the *Boston Gazette,* a paper that was continually unfriendly to Grundy, captured the northeast mood in April: "Any *Federalist* who lends money to the government, must go and shake hands with *James Madison,* and claim fellowship with *Felix Grundy.* Let him no more call himself a *Federalist,* and a friend of his country."[18]

Grundy and others proposed a national bank to help provide funds for the war effort. After several New Yorkers petitioned for a bank to facilitate borrowing and help straighten out government finances, in January 1814 the House Ways and Means Committee reported its view that Congress had no power to create a national bank, without the consent of the states. Calhoun suggested sidestepping the constitutional issue by establishing a bank within the District of Columbia, but this idea only deferred the question, since bank branches outside the district that were required to raise loan funds would raise the constitutional issue anew. After this back and forth for several months, Grundy, perceived as acting for the administration, on April 2 proposed that a committee be appointed to determine the desirability of a national bank. Grundy, who stated that he had "reflected much," wished to see a bank established as a "national object" and entertained no constitutional scruples. After passage of the resolution, 76–69, Grundy became chairman of the special committee; however, confronting likely defeat in the House, he moved to dissolve the committee on April 8.[19]

Grundy's career in the House of Representatives came to a close in the summer of 1814. He resigned with one session left in the Thirteenth Congress. On July 19 the *Clarion and Tennessee State Gazette* announced his resignation with regret, attributing his action to a long illness within his family. Years later, when political opponents charged that he had resigned to defend a client on a charge of murder in Mississippi, Grundy provided an explanation for his resignation, stating that his wife had been ill since 1812, that he had been away from home ten or eleven months during the session in which war was declared, and that during this tenure he had been present for all votes raising money for the war by loan or taxation. He also pointed out that the killing in Mississippi occurred after August 1, 1814, when the governor issued a proclamation for the election of Grundy's successor. Revealingly, after disclosing considerable detail about the continuing suggestions of friends and family that he resign in 1813 and 1814, Grundy stated, "I could not abandon the public service, until I saw some prospect of the termination of the war which I had been in some degree instrumental in producing." Only in 1814, when Napoleon had been defeated in Europe and peace negotiations had commenced, did he feel that he could resign. His enlightening letter may have been self-serving, but it does suggest that even when his wife was quite ill he refused to abandon his congressional obligations. One can only speculate whether Grundy would have resigned if he had been elected Speaker in January 1814.[20]

The press reacted predictably to Grundy's resignation. The Federalist papers excoriated him and happily reported his departure. The *Daily National Intelligencer* reflected a different perspective when, on August 6, 1814, it noted with much concern that Grundy was resigning on account of his wife's ill health: "In the absence of Mr. Grundy's commanding talents and elevated patriotism, the national councils will sustain a loss not easily repaired, and which is, at this interesting period of our political affairs, a cause of deep regret." The press reaction revealed the extent to which Grundy, virtually unknown in 1811, enjoyed national recognition in 1814. He would return to Nashville, his residence for only six years, with stature and potential.

13

RETURN TO NASHVILLE

The house ... was an amazing thing for the frontier of Tennessee.
—Donald Macdonald Millar

*G*rundy spent the five years from 1814 to 1819 in private pursuits in Nashville; it was the longest period in his adult life without significant political activity. As he continued to build his legal reputation and engaged in real-estate development, he also constructed Grundy Place, a splendid downtown home symbolizing the stature and prominence he now enjoyed. The house—the town's finest—also reflected the maturation of Nashville, which was rapidly assuming a preeminent role in the Southwest.

Jackson's victory over the British at New Orleans in January 1815 provided westerners the perfect ending to the War of 1812. The battle, following American naval victories on the Great Lakes, allowed Tennesseans to forget the largely unsuccessful military effort during the war and even the humiliation of the burning of Washington in August 1814. War Hawks from Kentucky and Tennessee had led the charge to restore national honor, and Kentuckians and Tennesseans had demonstrated in Congress and on the battlefield what a new generation of Americans could do. Nashville celebrated Jackson's return in May 1815, and as usual Grundy delivered the welcome speech.[1]

Nashville shared in the boom that followed. Tennessee's population, which by census figures increased from 261,727 in 1810 to 422,813 in 1820, including 45,535 and 80,107 slaves, respectively, mirrored the growth in Davidson County. In 1810 Davidson County had 15,608 inhabitants, including 6,305 slaves, compared with 20,154 inhabitants, including 7,899 slaves, in 1820. This population increase, together with postwar optimism and easy credit, meant accelerated purchases of land and slaves as well as imported goods. Jacob McGavock wrote in January 1816 that there were fifty dry-good stores in Nashville. Property that had been worth from $450 to $550 now sold for $800. A North Carolina physician in 1818 reported surprise at the town's size and elegance, with its three long streets, a spacious square, and large brick houses. Tennessee homes still fell short of this North Carolinian's standards, however, lacking carpets and handsome fences or gates.[2]

The event displaying the most tangible evidence of the changes affecting Nashville occurred on March 11, 1819, when almost the entire town watched as the first steamboat, the *Andrew Jackson,* arrived in Nashville. Nashville's market economy had long been oriented westward, and the new steamboat, fittingly owned by the entrepreneur and military leader William Carroll, accentuated Nashville's expanding commercial links, particularly to the Mississippi. In 1826 Nashville had its first coach line, to Lexington, and by 1834 large stages able to accommodate from twenty-five to thirty passengers would take them from Louisville at 5:00 AM to Nashville by 5:00 PM the next day for sixteen dollars. The changes in transportation and communication that would so transform America, and that are so convincingly celebrated in Daniel Walker Howe's *What Hath God Wrought,* were opening up Nashville.[3]

While Grundy participated in the euphoria accompanying the conclusion of a war he helped bring about, he focused his attention and considerable energy outside politics. Announcing his return to the practice of law in July 1814, he engaged in criminal defense work almost immediately. His reputation as a criminal lawyer grew dramatically. Marcus Winchester wrote his father, General James Winchester, that a defendant indicted for felony and almost certainly guilty was acquitted because of Grundy's art. After praising Grundy's eloquence and management, the younger Winchester reported that "Grundy in true military style rather attacked than defended, anticipating every ground the prosecution would take, and it may be said he beat them from it before they were able to fortify the vacant post."[4]

Law constituted only a part of Grundy's multifaceted life following his return from Congress. He threw himself wholeheartedly into the main sport of Middle Tennesseans, making money from land. The large-scale speculation that dominated early Kentucky and Tennessee had now moved westward and to the south. Jackson's victory over the Creeks resulted in one-sided acquisition of huge parts of Alabama and Georgia. Speculators also bought acreage in areas of Tennessee still held by Indians, and new arrivals bid up land prices in West Tennessee for cotton production.

Grundy engaged in a variety of transactions, including larger-scale ventures outside Tennessee and Kentucky. In early 1815 he and a partner acquired 2,500 acres on Forked Creek in the Indian Territory. In a purchase he was later to rue, Grundy on July 3, 1818, bought 950 acres on the Homochito River in Mississippi for $20,000, paying $2,000 up front and the balance in yearly installments of $2,000. Randal McGavock reviewed the land, and George Poindexter, the Mississippi territorial representative in Congress during the War of 1812, acted as Grundy's agent.[5]

The former War Hawk, however, mainly made investments closer to home, in downtown Nashville. The town's growth meant opportunity. Grundy purchased four lots in 1810 and then, from March 3, 1815, until June 15, 1822, he bought an additional eleven lots. His purchase price for all fifteen lots totaled slightly more than $16,500. Grundy sold only a few of these lots before 1827, and those lots that he did sell brought significant gains. For example, he bought lot 40 on College Street for $300 in June 1817 and sold a portion of that lot for $3,500 in June 1820. Grundy's commitment to Nashville meant that he was taxed in 1816 as the single largest holder of property in the town, with 255 acres and nine lots.[6]

Grundy's purchases in downtown Nashville followed a pattern. Rather than participating principally in large-acreage land speculation, he saw promise in urban real estate. In Kentucky he had acquired lots in Springfield and Greensburg and then decided to develop Greenville Springs. In Tennessee the influx of new residents and growing wealth suggested that development of towns would be profitable. Thus on July 28, 1814, Grundy purchased 375 acres of land, at $15 per acre, on the southwest side of Gallatin, a small town approximately twenty miles north of Nashville. In 1819, as a step in the first large-scale real-estate promotion in Gallatin, he sold 50 acres of this tract to an investment partnership of thirteen men from Gallatin and Nashville, including himself and his fellow defense counsel O. B. Hayes. The partnership planned to subdivide the tract into residential and commercial lots and sell them at auction on May 18, 1819, the second day of the circuit court.[7]

Grundy took the same approach in Franklin, the small county seat twenty miles south of Nashville where he had defended Magness in the Patton Anderson case. Grundy, his brother-in-law Randal McGavock, James Trimble, Alfred Balch, and James Irwin bought ninety acres of land, suitable for sixty lots, from Hinchlua Petway on the southwest side of Franklin. The lots were sold at public auction on February 6, 1819, with the principal paid over three years and security furnished to the Franklin Bank. Grundy bought one of the first twenty-six lots sold, and McGavock, two. Like the one in Gallatin, this venture was the first real-estate development effort in the town. The Panic of 1819 interrupted the project, but "Hincheyville" proved ultimately successful, with Grundy selling his one-fifth interest to Randal McGavock for three thousand dollars on November 13, 1824.[8]

Not surprisingly, Nashville's leading attorney participated in a variety of civic activities. Institutions were being developed, and Nashville gradually evolved into a more settled community, with many voluntary associations. As early as 1810 Grundy and Randal McGavock joined a committee to construct a church building. Grundy was supportive, and his wife more so, when Nashville's first Presbyterian church was founded in 1813. Grundy continued his Masonic activities in Tennessee. He joined the Hiram Lodge in Franklin, served as the deputy grand master pro tem, for the "Annual Communication" in October 1814, and was the principal speaker at many Masonic meetings. Grundy and other Nashvillians founded the Tennessee Antiquarian Society on July 1, 1820.[9]

On a lighter note, Grundy supported the formation of an amateur theatrical company in July 1818. *Dramatic Life as I Found It,* written by the impresario of this venture, N. M. Ludlow, provides an entertaining account of theatrical development in the Mississippi River valley in the nineteenth century. Ludlow, who found Nashville to be a well-built city of about three thousand inhabitants but the "hottest place I ever was in," had previously staged the first performance in Nashville of a regularly organized dramatic company on July 10, 1817. Sam Houston and John Eaton took leading roles in the company, and Jackson and Grundy agreed to serve as honorary members. Ludlow reported that the audience at a performance of the comedy *Speed the Plough* laughed when a character referring to a rural oracle not seen in the play asked, "What will Mrs. Grundy say?" A Nashvillian explained to the dumbfounded actors that Nancy Grundy, who was "highly respected," belonged to a church that prohibited its members from attending theaters.[10]

Grundy concentrated on areas of particular concern. Education remained his primary interest, as evidenced by his ongoing membership on the board of trustees of Cumberland College. A promoter of education for girls, he supported Mrs. Keets's female academy, established on February 8, 1813, which his daughter Louisa Caroline attended. In 1816 he and most of the city's leaders founded the Nashville Female Academy, a boarding school for girls at the corner of McLemore and Church streets (now Ninth Avenue and Church Street), which was destined to be one of the South's leading educational institutions. Grundy served as one of the academy's five trustees when it commenced operations in August 1817.[11]

Nancy Grundy too made memorable contributions, although obviously not to the theater. Whatever her illness in 1813 and 1814, and Grundy later wrote that she had been confined for almost two years with a severe disease in her side, Nancy actively engaged in community activities. She helped found and manage the Female Bible and Charitable Society of Nashville, established in May 1817, to provide relief for the poor. The first welfare organization in Nashville, the society solicited charitable donations and distributed goods and Bibles to needy citizens. Nancy Grundy conceived of a Sunday school, and in July 1820 she and a Methodist minister from Kentucky, Samuel Ament, opened Nashville's first, with fifteen students. Local churches fiercely opposed the initiative and denounced the teachers as Sabbath breakers. The school, which operated every Sunday at 8:00 AM in a small, run-down building, used the New Testament and a Webster speller. Tennessee lacked public schools, and Sunday schools served a broader purpose than religious education, becoming a primary vehicle for educating poor children. The churches eventually relented, and by November 1822 one housed the Sunday school.[12]

Nothing the Grundys did in Nashville in this period, however, had the effect of their construction of a new house. As part of his purchase of lots, Felix acquired the entire city block bounded by Union and Church streets and Vine and Spruce streets (now 7th and 8th avenues). On this high point in downtown Nashville, he constructed a splendid house from 1818 to 1821 called Grundy Place. A scholar who found the original plans at the Library of Congress described the house as "an amazing thing for the frontier" and unlike anything else in Tennessee for design and size. The imposing home, which measured seventy-five feet wide, had a cedar shingle roof and stone steps and window sills. Dark green window shutters contrasted with white trim and red brick in Flemish bond. The house and its extensive grounds, certainly Nashville's finest, testified to Grundy's financial and social prominence.[13]

Grundy Place was largely built by slave labor. Some Nashville slaves possessed valued skills and enjoyed considerable autonomy, with their services occasionally leased for varying periods. On June 1, 1821, presumably after the house was completed, Grundy sold Jerry, a bricklayer, and Jim, a brick mason, each about thirty years old, to Ephraim H. Foster.[14]

Family developments partially triggered Grundy's decision to build an impressive residence. In mid-1814 he and Nancy had seven living children, three of them teenagers, and an eighth child, and sixth daughter, Maria, joined her siblings on October 7, 1815. Grundy also turned forty in September 1815, and in addition to his wife's illness, other intimations of mortality must have affected him. In the spring of 1814 John Grundy, a dominant influence in his youngest brother's life, had passed away in Kentucky at approximately fifty-six years of age. Less than a year later, in February 1815, George Grundy, another successful role model, died at age fifty-three. The deaths of these two brothers, at comparatively young ages, meant that only three of Grundy's original eight brothers remained alive by the spring of 1815. Another brother, Robert, died between 1818 and 1823.[15]

It was not long after Grundy returned to Nashville that he had to deal with a teenage daughter. Grundy's second daughter, Eliza, married Ramsey Mayson on November 18, 1816, when she was seventeen years old, without her father's consent. Knowing little about Mayson, Grundy wrote John C. Calhoun asking for his assistance in finding out about Mayson's family in South Carolina. In his reply Calhoun expressed his sympathy and reported that Mayson's connections appeared to be respectable.[16]

Grundy's eldest daughter married only a few years later but on a very different basis. Louisa Caroline, attractive and vivacious, had known Jacob McGavock, the nephew of her aunt Sally's husband, Randal McGavock, for some time. Jacob had moved to Nashville in 1807 from his native Virginia with the encouragement of his Tennessee uncles. Wounded in the Creek War at Enotochopco on January 24, 1814, he had become the clerk of the circuit court of Davidson County in 1816. Parental consent posed no problem when Jacob wed twenty-one-year-old Louisa Caroline at Grundy Place on May 11, 1819. One of the bridesmaids, Sarah Childress, would marry James K. Polk a few years later.[17]

These births and deaths presumably influenced Grundy when he joined the Presbyterian Church by baptism in April 1821. There is no record of why he joined the church many years after Nancy's commitment. Times, however, had changed, and deism no longer characterized the Old Southwest. As society matured, religious institutions took hold, and some of Grundy's closest friends, such as Colonel Robert C. Foster, became quite devout. Grundy had been elected a vice president of the North American Bible Society in 1816, and he followed his wife's lead in encouraging Sunday schools throughout the country. But there is little evidence that Grundy became "born again," as his enemy Patrick Darby stated, and nothing to suggest that his religious commitment approached the devotion or intensity of his wife's. His identification with the Presbyterian Church did not lessen Grundy's tolerant acceptance of other denominations. Catholics viewed him as "liberal-minded . . . and always friendly" to their faith. Bishop Spalding, of Kentucky, gratefully mentioned the Grundys' hospitality on a visit he made to Nashville in 1821, and Grundy supported the establishment of a Catholic church in the town. Unusually for a Tennessee politician of this era, he also had a niece who became a nun. His brother John's daughter Esther took vows and became Sister Theresa in 1815.[18]

14

CRIMINAL LAWYER

I have heard Felix Grundy speak a hundred times. If he were alive I would
go a thousand miles to hear him again.

—Josephus Conn Guild

*C*riminal trials have always attracted great attention, and in early-
nineteenth-century America they offered wonderful spectacles. With few
diversions from the labor and routine of rural life, farmers and townspeople
alike flocked to county courthouses for the drama and excitement of a murder
trial. In an age when huge crowds listened to political figures debate for hours
on end, a murder trial provided a focused stage, with lawyers sparring over fact
and law and a man's life at stake.

Grundy achieved his greatest success and reputation in these trials. Contemporaries accorded him a near-unrivaled status as lawyer and orator. At his death
a Whig paper, no friend politically but wishing to pay tribute to "his genius,"
concluded that as an advocate at the bar "he had few rivals and, perhaps, no superior in the West." The leading student of Tennessee's bar stated in 1898 that
Grundy was easily the ablest and most successful criminal lawyer of his time
in the Southwest. The journalist Henry Watterson described Henry Clay and
Felix Grundy as at the pinnacle of a unique group of "stump orators," marked
men who never failed to captivate their audiences.[1]

Josephus Conn Guild, the author of *Old Times in Tennessee,* the most acclaimed study of early Tennessee, wrote that he decided to become a lawyer
after observing Grundy in court. He described the effect as follows:

It was a great intellectual feast to hear Booth in his Richard the Third, For-
rest in his Macbeth or King Lear, Miss Cushman as Lady Macbeth, or Jo. Jefferson in his Rip van Winkle, but to hear Felix Grundy in a closely contested
case of homicide, when all his fires were burning, his passions aroused; to
see his actions, the flash of his gray eyes, the vivid flashes of lightning burst-

ing from his lips; at times to witness his scathing sarcasm, and then his sparkling wit; take it all in all, it was the grandest exhibition that any Tennessean ever witnessed. He found himself carried away by a storm of eloquence that was irresistible. He felt that he was aroused by the same feeling and passion that moved the godlike advocate. I have heard Felix Grundy speak a hundred times. If he were alive I would go a thousand miles to hear him again.[2]

It is difficult to re-create or even fully assess Grundy as courtroom advocate, when so much of the atmosphere and inflection of the time has been lost. Guild wrote that Grundy's genius could not be fairly written down, and the *Daily National Intelligencer* reported that his eloquence in Congress "was entirely sui generis" and lost on paper much of the attraction it had in delivery. Yet his success can be measured by his record and the recollections of others. In 1858 a distinguished orator of the day, John Bright, said that of 165 persons Grundy defended for capital offenses, only 1 was finally condemned and hanged. (Bright did not tell us, and we do not know, how many defendants were acquitted and how many received lesser verdicts, such as manslaughter.) Other commentators have given other numbers, ranging from 105 to 185, but all with the same result: only a single criminal executed.[3]

Grundy's remarkable record must be considered in a broader context. American penal reformers in the late eighteenth century expressed continuing dissatisfaction with the English system of criminal justice, which was still in place in many states, and began pushing for change. Not long after his authorship of the Declaration of Independence, Thomas Jefferson wrote Edmund Pendleton about plans to reform Virginia's criminal justice system. England's system had up to two hundred capital offenses but relied on the use of pardons to offset the effects of the statutes. Jefferson favored less severe laws more uniformly applied, thereby increasing the deterrent effect. The reform of the criminal laws in Kentucky in 1797 and in other southern states reduced the number of crimes for which death could be demanded, principally murder, but also minimized judicial discretion. Grundy thus came of age at the time when American states were adopting their own criminal codes and when there was increasing awareness of the relationship between deterrence and mercy in criminal law.[4]

During much of the time that Grundy practiced law, Tennessee suffered under an outmoded approach to criminal justice. Its laws comprised an incongruous mass of statutes and common law and the "barbarous act of 1807," which, as in pre-reform Kentucky, called for the death penalty in a wide range of circumstances. Second offenders could be executed for a theft of more than ten dollars, horse stealing, forgery, or burning a house or warehouse. For first offenses, the law prescribed the pillory, the whipping post, and the branding iron, including thirty-nine licks on the bare back. The state had no penitentiary, so imprisonment was in the county jail, where first-time offenders were required to pay for their keep.

Reformers ultimately succeeded in effecting change. Grundy suggested construction of a penitentiary and criminal law reform in 1819 but focused primarily on financial matters. On October 1, 1821, Governor William Carroll, a social reformer, proposed abolition of the death penalty for all crimes except first-degree murder. A penitentiary would be built in the state, and those convicted of such crimes as arson, robbery, larceny, and horse stealing would be incarcerated there for one- to ten-year terms. The failure of West and East Tennessee to agree on the penitentiary's location resulted in the bill's defeat. Finally, in 1829, the same legislative session in which Grundy was first elected to the Senate, Tennessee authorized construction of a penitentiary and soon thereafter amended its penal code to eliminate the death penalty for all crimes except first-degree murder.[5]

Aside from statutory changes, Tennessee criminal defendants benefited from respect for the rights of the accused. Anticipating twentieth-century jurisprudence, in a case in 1826 in which Grundy represented George Nelson, the arresting officer cautioned the suspect not to say anything until he had retained a lawyer. Judges dealing with the messy realities of capital cases frequently decided criminal appeals to ensure a fair result and claimed that they were duty bound to protect accused persons.[6]

Respect for the defendant's circumstances and rights reflected cultural mores. There is extensive literature on the violence and culture of honor widespread in the South; many southerners, sensitive to their position, were quick to seek redress for perceived slights. The Scots-Irish origin of many early Tennesseans affected perspectives on crime and related social issues. Clannish, fiercely egalitarian, individualistic, and resistant to central authority, they protected their "honor" with fist, blade, or, when occasion demanded, the dueling pistol. Heavy drinking exacerbated the tendency to unbridled response. Grundy famously estimated that 80 percent of the criminal cases he defended involved the use of alcohol. A jury of adult white men understood all too well the mixture of liquor and anger that led to homicides and accordingly were reluctant to sentence to death by hanging someone they knew or whose family they knew.

The case of Charles L. Bennett sheds unusual light on Tennessee attitudes toward murder. This was probably the case that became a byword for Grundy's career as a criminal defense counsel, the only one in which a defendant he represented was hanged. As is true for all criminal cases in early Tennessee, we have no trial transcript, and information can only be gleaned from appellate records and sketchy newspaper accounts. Mr. Bennett allegedly murdered W. T. Hay in Wilson County, was tried and convicted in Bedford County, and then was imprisoned for several years in Nashville while the court of error and appeal considered his case. The appeal was denied, and the state hanged Bennett in Franklin, in Williamson County, on November 20, 1819. The homicide was brutal, and Bennett may have confessed after the trial. Nevertheless, his case led the *Clarion and Tennessee State Gazette* to suggest an end to capital punishment, asserting that his conduct in jail showed that Bennett could become a useful member of society. The editorial stance is not what we might expect; it suggests that while the culture may have been violent and driving, it was also sympathetic to redemption.[7]

Grundy's tactics as a criminal defense counsel become much more comprehensible in light of this environment. First, Grundy sought a jury that would be sympathetic to his client's plight. As noted earlier, William P. Anderson wrote that in the celebrated Magness case, in 1810, Grundy was guilty of a rascally act in packing the jury. Similarly, in a case in Edwardsville, Illinois, in 1825, Grundy made sure that the young Tennessean being charged would be tried by a jury consisting only of Tennesseans. As late as 1840 Henry Clay described Grundy as a jury-packing lawyer.[8]

Grundy also used witnesses in nontraditional ways. He typically called a large number of witnesses, far more than the prosecution, and used them to uphold the character and credibility of the accused. The testimony, from witnesses who would know or be known to many jurors, would bring home that a life was at stake and, perhaps more important, give weighty evidence of community feeling. In a trial in 1827 for the murder of Peyton Randolph, Grundy produced eighty-seven witnesses, to the state's thirty-two, in the presentation and rebuttal phases.

Moreover, Grundy provided the proper background and atmosphere for his defendants. He stage-managed trials and positioned family members and prominent personalities as he deemed appropriate. In 1825, for example, Grundy arranged for Ninian Edwards, the first governor of the Illinois Territory, to be prominently seated with the defendant's family in the front row. Placement of the defendant's supporters at a trial is an elementary tactic today, but it was a significant innovation in the early nineteenth century, and again it emphasized the jury's moral responsibility in taking a life. Micah Taul, the father of a homicide victim, attributed a more controversial tactic to Grundy. Taul, bitter at the acquittal of his son's killer, charged that Grundy had demonized the victim.[9]

In law as in politics, Grundy presented a compromise position to the jury. He sought a middle ground, positioning his stance as the most reasonable among extreme alternatives. Before a jury reluctant to send a man to death, Grundy's capacity to place the homicide in an understandable context and perhaps to show that the defendant otherwise enjoyed a fine reputation did not always mean acquittal, but he customarily avoided the death penalty.

Grundy's remarkable success, however, cannot be attributed solely to the environment, which would have influenced all trials, or his defense tactics, which, once employed, could be used by others at the criminal bar. His personal talents and characteristics played their role. Grundy's appearance favorably predisposed the jury. Grundy's personal appearance was uniformly described as "pleasing, commanding and impressive," and his figure, "strikingly graceful and commanding." Grundy's voice was attractive, not harsh and disagreeable like Thomas Hart Benton's, for example. He could use his voice to convey any emotion. Grundy possessed a brilliant intellect, a characteristic almost always applied to him in nineteenth-century accounts but less recognized by more recent historians. Samuel Laughlin, who knew him extremely well, referred to his splendid imagination and the excellence of his memory. One early Tennessee historian referred to Grundy as having "the most noted memory on record."[10]

Grundy's humor and stories were legendary, and he continually used anecdotes to illustrate a point or evoke a favorable reaction from listeners. Again and again, we read that his quick wit enabled him to turn the tables on an opponent. He regularly employed anaphora, the repetition of a word or phrase in successive sentences. Grundy was self-deprecating, suggesting to his audience that he was one of them. Perhaps most unusual to a modern reader, he used tears extensively. Crying was an accepted lawyer's technique, so much so that the Tennessee Supreme Court in 1897, rejecting the argument that a lawyer should not display such emotion, stated that a lawyer who was able to do so might have a professional obligation to shed tears on appropriate occasions.[11]

It is also important to stress what Grundy was not. Our popular image of the nineteenth-century lawyer is a florid figure of big words and notable pomposity. Grundy was the opposite, speaking in a conversational tone and in language his audience understood. One scholar concluded that Grundy always behaved in a composed and dignified manner. He did not engage in "boisterous or vehement declamation" or "forced and extravagant figures of speech." The

Washington correspondent for a Richmond paper commented on Grundy's down-to-earth style and the flow of his logic in totally comprehensible language.[12]

Two qualities of Grundy's were regarded as determinative by contemporaries. First was his judgment. Samuel H. Laughlin, echoing comments in obituaries, said, "The great contracting faculty of his mind was his profound and clear judgment. He was imbued with a greater share . . . of common sense than any man I ever was acquainted with. The man nearest to him in this respect, whom I have known, is his favorite pupil and friend, James K. Polk, the present President of the United States." John C. Calhoun wrote to Grundy in 1816 that "from long and intimate personal acquaintance, I have been taught to pay great respect to the soundness of your judgment."[13]

Second was Grundy's assessment of human nature and his capacity to speak to what really mattered to his audience. "He understood men at first sight, as if by intuition, better than any man I have ever known," wrote Laughlin. John Haywood's biographer recounted a conversation with an early judge who discounted any similarity between Haywood, a logical lawyer, and Grundy: "Grundy let them decide cases for him because they wanted to and regarded the privilege as a boon. Grundy knew every man on the jury, not by name perhaps, but he knew the man and the stuff he was made of; he could penetrate to his heart and to his brain; he knew what would move him and how to apply it, and when he was done with him the juror was ready to decide for him, facts or no facts, law or no law." Grundy understood the heritage, background, and core beliefs of his audience, and jurors identified with him.[14]

Grundy's success led to criticism and envy. The Tennessee historian James Phelan in the late nineteenth century wrote warmly of Grundy, saying that the Southwest had never produced a lawyer of equal fame. His graceful and commanding figure, his open, refined face, and his disposition of great affability, joined to a mellow flow of words, gave him unvarying success. But Phelan voiced the view of some opposing lawyers that Grundy was "full of stratagems and wiles" and not overscrupulous in the tactics he used to save a client, a view that other nineteenth-century historians rejected. A more frequent charge was that Grundy did not explore legal matters in depth. Even Guild, who described Grundy as someone who "will always rank among the greatest men this country has produced," stated that Grundy was not a "book man or a case lawyer" and referred to an ejectment case in 1821. William L. Brown and Grundy, colleagues in resolving the Kentucky border dispute in 1820, together represented a client. Grundy expected to make the closing speech and had not examined the details of the case or the law, anticipating that he would rely on Brown's opening presentation. For whatever reason, Brown did not open, and Grundy, compelled to speak first, failed completely. Guild concluded that Grundy relied more for his success "upon his knowledge of men, his brilliant wit, and his un-rivalled eloquence, than upon the dry details of the law."[15]

Grundy does appear to have been less attentive to detail and less of a legal scholar than some contemporaries. A brilliant extemporaneous speaker, many of his arguments appear to have been presented with little preparation. Yet Samuel H. Laughlin reveals a different picture, based on the more than one hundred nights he shared a room with Grundy over the course of fifteen or six-teen years of court attendance. While acknowledging that Grundy read men more than books, Laughlin wrote that Grundy engaged in detailed analysis known only to a handful of his most intimate friends. Grundy would take but few notes in a case and then join in "cheerful conversation, telling anecdotes which he did inimitably, and in hearing and joining the heartiest laughs at those told by others." He went to bed early and fell asleep in two or three min-utes. He slept soundly until about 1:00 AM and only then began intense study and case preparation, arranging the main points for his speeches. He even pre-pared his "splendid sentences" and quotations in advance and committed them to memory, and "nothing committed to his memory was ever lost or forgot-ten."[16]

These descriptions and assessments, however illuminating, do not convey any real sense of how Grundy conducted courtroom defenses, how he prepared for a trial. One reminiscence, however, provides some insight. John Catron, who became a justice of the U.S. Supreme Court in 1837, wrote a biographical letter in 1851. In it he recounted that early in his career he had asked "a really great advocate,"

"Why, Mr. G., how in the world do you intend to get along in this dread-ful case of murder; you have not even a law brief prepared?" "Well," said he, "what book is Mr. Attorney-General going to rely on to prove it murder?" "Mainly on Espinasse, Bacon, and Hawkins, I think," said I. "Ah, yes," was the reply, "I'll find enough, just above or just below, for my purpose, I warrant you." And so he did; and acquitted his client, who ought, undoubtedly, to have been hanged. This was one of the very best drilled circuit lawyers I ever knew. He first studied and comprehended all the facts and motives involved in his case, and then thought over how society appreciated them; and lastly, searched for law to sustain the case his facts made.[17]

The approach Catron described did not apply only to defendants in murder cases. Scarce state or local resources, as well as anger or desire for vengeance, often led families or the government to hire counsel to assist in the prosecution of alleged killers. In Courtland, Alabama, an early merchant, Noble Ladd, killed a Doctor Mitchell in the square. The slaying divided the town, and the friends of Doctor Mitchell hired Grundy to prosecute Ladd. While Grundy failed in convicting Mr. Ladd, his eloquence was such that many children in the county were named for him.[18]

Grundy handled a variety of trials besides murder. Two of the earliest cases reported in the Nashville press demonstrate the range of Grundy's criminal practice. In 1820 the state charged a Mrs. Pig and several sons for the attempted poisoning of their neighbors, the Saunders, by mixing a potion in their coffee and for hiring an elderly woman to administer love potions to Miss Saunders to induce marriage or seduction. John Catron, Sam Houston, and John Overton assisted the prosecution, and Grundy and two other lawyers represented the defendants. During the three-day trial Grundy explored the properties of the drugs and brought out that the families were respectable and close neighbors. The jury acquitted the defendants. The circuit court of Bedford County tried a very different case in 1821. Richard Hooper, indicted for mayhem, had hired Joseph McBride as his storekeeper. Hooper learned of an affair between McBride and Hooper's wife and, after feigning a journey, caught McBride entering his wife's bedchamber. When McBride fled the house, Hooper pursued him for half a mile, knocked him down, and then castrated him. The state showed that Hooper had previously consulted a physician about the effects of castration. Grundy defended Hooper. The unfavorable facts certainly suggested premeditation, but Grundy convinced the jury after two hours to return a verdict of not guilty.[19]

Grundy dominated the criminal bar in Tennessee. As a result, he traveled extensively, juggling many clients. In June 1822 Grundy wrote Andrew Jackson that he had been so engaged in professional pursuits that he had not attended to political matters. A letter to Ninian Edwards in 1825 makes clear the demands of his legal practice. Grundy wrote on February 20 that he had returned home the night before and was about to set out for a distant court. He would then leave the following Friday for Illinois. Nancy Grundy emphasized the same thing in a letter to her sister. Regretting her inability to visit, she wrote that

> my Husband keeps but two horses—and he has just been sent for to go Up-
> land for a Criminal, in the eastern part of this state. His trial comes on the
> 20th of this month, so he has to start in four days from this. The Hardin's trial
> is now on hand, and has been for twelve days. I hope they may get through to-
> morrow, my husband has not been at home but one day since you left here and
> unless he gets [*sic*] from Murfreesboro on Sunday, he will not be at home until
> the first of next month (I have a pain in my heart); tell Maria the lawyers are
> such runabouts. I think she had better marry a Farmer.[20]

These references emphasize how hard Grundy worked, particularly when compared with lawyers who engaged in civil litigation in hometown courts. In demand, constantly traveling and balancing legal responsibilities, political interests, and civic commitments, Grundy maintained a schedule for most of his
adult life that left him little time for leisure.

Grundy's cases took him far from Nashville, with known trials in Kentucky,
Illinois, Mississippi, and Alabama, as well as throughout Tennessee. Although
his reputation derived from trial work, he managed a significant appellate
practice as well, occasionally appearing before the U.S. Supreme Court. Francis Scott Key and Grundy collaborated as counsel in *Smith v. Bell*, 31 U.S. 68
(1832), a will-interpretation case decided by Chief Justice John Marshall, while
Grundy was sole counsel for the plaintiff in error in *Green v. Lessee of Neal*, 31
U.S. 291 (1832).[21]

The lack of surviving records makes it difficult to gauge Grundy's financial
success. Owing to the lack of specie in the West, lawyers often received payment in kind and would insist on retainers as security to ensure payment of
fees. The earliest evidence of Grundy's fee is from 1808, when he received $10
for handling an estate. Grundy could command large fees in criminal trials. In
one Maury County case, when he obtained acquittal of a young man accused
of murdering his grandfather, Grundy purportedly was paid $5,000 for the de-
fense and an additional $3,000 to handle the will and certain litigation with re-
spect to the deceased. Grundy left us only one account of his fees. In July 1830,
upon returning to Nashville from his first session as a U.S. senator, he wrote a
warm letter to Senator Levi Woodbury, of New Hampshire, commenting that
when he arrived the circuit court was in session, and he "took a hand with the
boys," receiving fees "upwards of $1000—this is better at least more profitable

than playing Senator." Grundy's earnings at the peak of his career, however, almost certainly never attained the level of William L. Brown and Ephraim Foster, who purportedly earned $40,000 to $50,000 per year, largely from land contests and collection matters for eastern businessmen.[22]

Grundy practiced in partnership with other lawyers. His partner in the early 1820s was James C. Trimble, born in 1781 of Scots-Irish descent, a gentle, courteous man and Sam Houston's legal mentor. They practiced as Grundy and Trimble from July 1, 1822, until Trimble's death. Beginning in December 1824 Grundy associated with James Rucks (1791–1862) in a large practice that was expanded in 1826 to include William E. Anderson, a talented, six-feet-eight lawyer noted for his sociability. After this partnership dissolved in 1828, Grundy practiced law principally with his sons. On May 2, 1828, Grundy announced his association with Edwin Wallace and John R. Grundy. On September 15, 1830, Grundy formed a partnership with James Dozier and his son James P. H. Grundy.[23]

Grundy served as a legal mentor to many aspiring lawyers, charging up to several hundred dollars for a full course. William S. Fulton studied under Grundy in 1816–17. He settled in Arkansas and represented that state in the U.S. Senate from 1836 until his death in 1844, serving part of that time with his teacher. Milton Brown, later a Whig congressman, trained under Grundy and first gained fame in 1834 for his defense of the well-known criminal John Murrell. Francis Fogg, a studious New Englander, and James K. Polk, Grundy's most renowned protégé, read law with Grundy at the same time. After Grundy was elected to the legislature in 1819, Polk learned from Fogg that the position of clerk of the state senate was vacant and that Fogg had declined Grundy's offer to arrange the job for him. Polk told Fogg and then Grundy that he would like to be considered instead. Grundy obtained the position for the aspiring lawyer and politician, thus launching Polk's political career.[24]

The relationship with Polk was one of the most important in Grundy's life. Polk and Grundy became close politically and, more importantly, warm personal friends. One of Polk's earliest biographers, writing in 1850, shortly after Polk's death, described Grundy as not only a legal preceptor but also a wise and experienced "Nestor." He wrote that Polk had cherished his friendship with Grundy, which had stood the test of years and changes in circumstance.[25]

Ann Phillips Rodgers Grundy, wife of Felix Grundy. Painting by Ralph E. W. Earl (1785–1838).

Felix Grundy, 1834. Painting by Washington B. Cooper.

Courtesy Tennessee State Museum.

James Priestley, frontier educator. Painting by Ralph E. W. Earl.
Courtesy of the Tennessee State Museum

Earliest known representation of Nashville, ca. 1825
Courtesy James Hoobler

Grundy Place, 1840s, Nashville, Tennessee. Watercolor by Felix Grundy McGavock.
Courtesy of the Tennessee State Museum

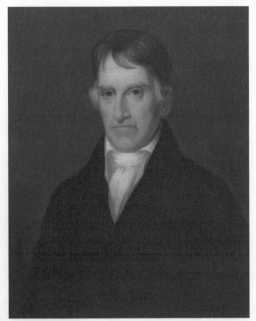

Randal McGavock, brother-in-law of Felix Grundy and early civic leader of Nashville. Painting by Ralph E. W. Earl.

Courtesy of Winder McGavock Heller

Sarah Dougherty Rodgers McGavock, wife of Randal McGavock and sister of Ann Rodgers Grundy. Painting by Ralph E. W. Earl.

Courtesy of Winder McGavock Heller

Carnton (back view), Franklin, Tennessee, ca. 1905

Courtesy Carnton Plantation

Sam Houston, Nashville lawyer and political leader in the 1820s. Painting by Washington B. Cooper.

Courtesy of the Tennessee State Museum

Entrepreneur and military leader William Carroll. Painting by Washington B. Cooper.

Courtesy of the Tennessee State Museum

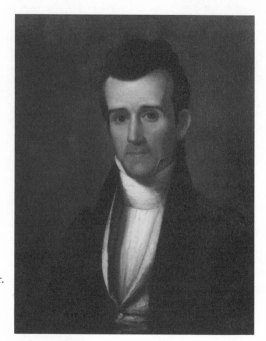

James K. Polk as a young lawyer.
Painting by Ralph E. W. Earl.
*Courtesy of Polk House, Columbia,
Tennessee*

Sarah Childress Polk, wife of
James K. Polk. Painting by Ralph
E. W. Earl.
*Courtesy of Polk House, Columbia,
Tennessee*

Earliest known photograph of a United States president and his wife: President and Mrs.
James K. Polk

Courtesy of Polk House, Columbia, Tennessee

Andrew Jackson, 1837. Painting
by Ralph E. W. Earl.
*Courtesy of the Tennessee State
Museum*

Martin Van Buren. Painting by
Washington B. Cooper.
*Courtesy of the Tennessee State
Museum*

15

THE PANIC OF 1819

He is solicitous of popularity.

—John H. Eaton

The postwar Era of Good Feelings came to an abrupt end with the Panic of 1819. Economic distress led to a dizzying series of initiatives to minimize financial distress. Grundy, at the forefront of the political awakening in 1819, dominated the Tennessee state legislature until the end of his term in 1825. Grundy's mastery gave him a reputation for legislative wizardry and management and provided an invaluable lesson for his protégé James K. Polk.

Factional divisions over banking marked Grundy's legislative reemergence in 1819, emphasizing again the centrality of access to land and capital in early-nineteenth-century politics. Judge John Overton, cagey, wealthy, and Jackson's oldest and closest friend, now led what we still call the Blount faction. John H. Eaton and William B. Lewis, Jackson favorites, assisted Overton in West Tennessee, and Hugh Lawson White, Overton's brother-in-law, and Pleasant M. Miller, Blount's son-in-law, provided powerful support in East Tennessee. Although Andrew Jackson no longer played the active role of earlier days, he maintained close relationships with the Blount leaders.

Andrew Erwin, of Bedford County, another land speculator, by 1819 headed the leading opposition group, whose members were generally united by their hostility to Jackson. Erwin and Jackson had a history of bitter enmity, and the merchant John P. Erwin continued the family's quarrel from Nashville. The Williams brothers, from East Tennessee, John a U.S. senator and Thomas a state senator, supported Erwin, as did Congressman Newton Cannon, from Middle Tennessee. In an essentially one-party state, where all followed Jeffersonian Republicanism and their own self-interest, factions coalesced behind particular individuals, and personal loyalties and relationships were determinative.

In 1815 the Blount faction controlled Tennessee's two banks. Stephen Cantrell, an ally of John Overton's, led the Nashville Bank, chartered in 1807. Hugh Lawson White, in Knoxville, founded the Bank of the State of Tennessee in 1811, and Overton served as president of the Nashville branch. Although small, these banks assumed importance when the infusion of federal dollars for equipping troops in the War of 1812 and the expansion of cotton lands called attention to their financing capacity.[1]

The Blount faction's control of the two state-chartered banks irked many, particularly in Nashville, a merchant's town. The mercantile community saw an expanding need for credit, as the fast-growing population wanted to purchase more land and slaves, as well as luxury goods. Accordingly, after Congress chartered the Second Bank of the United States for twenty years in 1816, Nashvillians petitioned for a branch in Nashville. The application, submitted in 1817, included the signatures of sixty influential citizens, headed by Felix Grundy and William Carroll. Grundy and Carroll introduced new elements to the struggles of the Blount and Erwin factions. Neither was identified with any political group, but both lived in Nashville, knew the various faction players, and had significant popularity. Grundy had emerged as the eloquent voice of the West during the War of 1812. Carroll, who had arrived in Nashville in 1810 at the age of twenty-two, operated a successful hardware store and nail factory. Carroll took over as commander of the Tennessee militia upon Jackson's promotion to the Regular Army, and after New Orleans he enjoyed a military reputation second only to that of the Hero. Grundy had a professional relationship with Jackson but definitely was not a Jackson intimate; many in the Blount group regarded him with suspicion. Carroll had quarreled with the New Orleans victor.[2]

The Blount faction effectively opposed the branch bank. After his election to the state legislature, Hugh Lawson White persuaded his colleagues to assess a fifty-thousand-dollar annual tax on any bank in Tennessee not chartered by the state. To achieve this result, he agreed to the chartering of ten new banks in small towns. Since these institutions could become branches of the older banks, and quickly did so, the legislation increased both the capital and the political influence of the old banks and laid the groundwork for a powerful, unified state banking interest.[3]

Grundy and Carroll fumed. At a public meeting on January 31, 1818, Grundy presented the benefits of having a branch in Nashville, after which attendees adopted resolutions to that effect and declared the taxation law "impolitic and unconstitutional." A committee made up of Grundy, O. B. Hayes, John P.

Erwin, George Gibbs, Jenkin Whiteside, Alfred Balch, and Andrew Hynes petitioned for the immediate establishment of the branch. Grundy supplemented the formal submission with a private letter to the president of the Second Bank, William Jones, in which he referred to the puerile attempts of the legislature and suggested thirteen citizens to whom management of the branch could be entrusted. Despite such efforts, the branch-bank initiative failed, engendering increased hostility to the existing bankers.[4]

Inadequacies in the banking system became apparent in the period leading to the Panic of 1819, America's first great depression. The War of 1812 had wrought great changes in the American economy, including the growth of domestic manufacturing, extensive government borrowing, the increase in the number of banks, and inflation. After the war, imports and exports increased, but so did the desire for credit. The Second Bank of the United States and the proliferating state banks issued bank notes almost without limitation. Credit expansion led to a boom in real-estate prices, speculation in public lands, and rapidly growing indebtedness on the part of farmers and merchants.[5]

The boom created by credit expansion inevitably had to end, and it did, with dramatic effect. The Second Bank of the United States, confronted with foreign demand for specie, initiated a painful series of deflationary actions in 1818. The restrictions tightened in early 1819, when new directors ousted William Jones and replaced him with Grundy's War Hawk colleague Langdon Cheves. The whole network of paper credit came tumbling down. Non-Tennessee banks called their loans to Tennessee banks, and Tennessee banks in turn demanded payment from debtors. Debts immediately due shot up, particularly from the planters and yeoman farmers who had financed the planting of crops and the purchases of more land and slaves. Suddenly, almost as a capstone, world commodity prices collapsed in the spring of 1819. One index for prices of U.S. exports fell from 169 in August 1818 to 77 in June 1819.[6]

Banks now confronted the snowballing consequences of a credit system based on notes redeemable in specie and collapsing commodity prices. Tennessee banks, lacking sufficient gold and silver, could not cover almost $5 million in obligations. To safeguard assets, all the banks in Nashville suspended payments in specie in the latter half of June 1819. West Tennessee, which had large-scale cotton farms and rampant speculation, was more adversely affected than East Tennessee, the hilly region of smaller farms.[7]

Grundy was elected to the Tennessee legislature in the summer of 1819. Why he chose to run has been the subject of speculation, with Charles Sellers asserting that Grundy, "whose sensitivity to public opinion made him the Tennessee prototype of the new-style politician of the emerging democratic era," did so when he recognized the political possibilities of the relief question. Contrary to the view of Sellers, however, Grundy did not run for the legislature in response to the Panic. He announced his candidacy on April 3, 1819, four months before the election. Grundy must have recognized the extent of the deterioration of economic conditions, but the cotton markets had not yet collapsed. A more plausible explanation than that given by Sellers is that Grundy, who liked the give and take of political life and consistently opposed monopolistic banking, continued to be angry that the legislature had prevented the establishment of a Nashville branch of the Second Bank, and ran for a two-year term on the first occasion he could do so. Given the circumstances of his resignation from Congress in 1814, national political life still seemed out of the question, but the state legislature provided a theater for his talents. Grundy said of himself, perhaps somewhat facetiously, that he had been born a legislator; service in his home state several months a year only added spice to his career. Once the Panic accelerated, the supremely self-confident Grundy responded to the challenge, taking exactly the leadership role referred to by Sellers and other historians.[8]

Regardless of his motivation for running, Grundy participated in a public meeting on July 19 to discuss relief measures and was elected to the legislature soon thereafter, although he was not the top vote-getter. "Unquestionably the ablest member of the House of Representatives," he assumed leadership when the legislature convened at Murfreesboro on September 20, 1819. He joined legislators of variegated backgrounds. While statistics for 1819 are not available, a study in 1825 reported that the sixty members of the Tennessee General Assembly included thirty-eight farmers or nonprofessional men, five physicians, five merchants, and twelve lawyers, suggesting that lawyers, while becoming more important, did not yet dominate the legislature.[9]

Grundy promptly took control of relief initiatives. He introduced a series of resolutions calling, among other things, for an investigation of the condition of banks, limitations on the rights of banks under their existing notes, and prohibition of imprisonment for debt under specified circumstances. These resolutions set the stage for dealing with the suspension of specie. Suspension in June had helped the banks avoid ruin. Suspension arguably also helped debtors, since banks, relieved of the pressure to pay specie, should be more willing, at least in theory, to delay calling or otherwise enforcing loans. But suspension did nothing with respect to the core issue for debtors, the loss of circulating gold and silver, the only legal tender. Debtors whose loans were called lacked hard money, and few purchasers had ready cash to acquire the properties that were increasingly being offered for sale at a time of plummeting prices. Debtors wanted either a stay law to delay debt collection or a property law that required creditors to accept property in lieu of specie.[10]

Over the next several months the legislators debated various plans to provide relief and in the end adopted several measures to help the planters and merchants of Tennessee. Grundy, omnipresent, became the spokesman for the relief effort and thus the Tennessee debtor. His principal opponent, Pleasant M. Miller, a criminal lawyer characterized by Grundy as one of the most skillful men he had ever confronted, represented an East Tennessee district. Miller regarded specie suspension as a mistake and proposed that banks pay 8 percent on all notes they were unable to redeem. Grundy and Miller squared off in a closely watched debate, with the *Nashville Gazette* on October 27, 1819, reporting warm discussion. This legislation, which infuriated both West Tennessee bankers and forces of relief, did not pass, largely because of Grundy's efforts.[11]

Grundy sought major debt relief. Although East Tennesseans staved off more dramatic inflationary bills, they could not prevent passage of several measures. One, introduced by Grundy and passed in October 1819 by strong majorities in the house and the senate, stayed the execution of all judgments for two years unless creditors accepted notes of the Tennessee banks at par. A related bill, introduced by Grundy's corepresentative from Nashville, William Williams (later an opponent of relief), was, after revision and passage, generally regarded as Grundy's work. It stipulated that a bank was prohibited from executing on any judgment obtained against a debtor for two years unless it made clear that its own notes, presumably heavily depreciated, would be accepted as payment at par.[12]

Two other significant issues came up in the 1819–20 legislative session. The first related to settlements in former Indian lands. By treaties in 1817 and 1819 the Cherokees ceded to the United States most of their land in East Tennessee, and in 1816 and 1818 the Chickasaw transferred lands in what is now western Tennessee. The North Carolina cession agreement required Tennessee to accept Revolutionary War warrants given to North Carolina soldiers. As in Kentucky twenty years earlier, the principal issue concerned the rights accorded squatters. Grundy and Miller collaborated on terms of settlement for former Cherokee lands, with no preference given to squatters, but opposed each other vigorously with respect to Chickasaw lands in western Tennessee. Grundy, arguing for the holders of North Carolina warrants, lost, and the final bill permitted squatters to claim 160 acres each.[13]

Grundy's espousal of the claims of speculators in western Tennessee warrants departed from his support in Kentucky of the settlers in the Green River district. Grundy, who had acquired at least one certificate for land in western Tennessee himself, now represented constituents in Nashville, many of whom were large-scale buyers of warrants. In one important matter, however, Grundy opposed speculators and collaborated with Miller on far-reaching legislation with respect to the statute of limitations. North Carolina statutes of 1715 and 1796 provided that a person holding land for seven years under a grant or under a deed founded on a grant would be protected against other claimants. Judges were divided, however, as to whether a grant under which possession was held had to be connected by a regular chain of title to the original grantee. The problem became acute when Patrick Henry Darby (1783–1829), a talented but unscrupulous lawyer who arrived in Nashville in 1815, contracted with heirs of original grantees and sought to eject those holding possession without linkage to the original holders. Darby and Grundy had had differences with respect to Darby's purchase of land claims as early as 1816, and Grundy may have tried to have Darby disbarred.[14]

Since little attention had been given to the preservation of deeds or their registration or to the tracing of titles in early Tennessee, almost half of the population of West Tennessee could potentially lose their lands as a result of Darby's initiative. The problem was compounded by the fact that North Carolina's warrants to its Revolutionary War soldiers often conflicted with Tennessee's grants based on entries, resulting in the interminable litigation that made early Tennessee such a splendid place for lawyers. In very popular legislation, Grundy led the successful effort in 1819 to enact a measure that ensured title to claimants who had had undisputed possession of lands for seven years under either North Carolina or Tennessee grants, with no need to connect the titles. The legislation laid the groundwork for future trouble, however, since it did not apply retroactively.[15]

Grundy demonstrated further reform interests. As the state's leading criminal lawyer, he fittingly introduced a bill calling for a state penitentiary, paralleling initiatives in other states. He called for the revision of the state criminal laws but, given the primacy of the banking and land issues, did not make it a priority. He sought the transfer of the state capital to Nashville; in 1822 Grundy obtained sixteen votes for the move, as opposed to twenty-one against. He emphasized his reformist views clearly with respect to the abolition of imprisonment for debt. "This idea could have only prevailed on the ground that money ought to be more highly esteemed than liberty. This mode of thinking . . . has long since been entirely exploded in the land of freedom." While he was initially unsuccessful, Grundy introduced legislative issues that were finally enacted under William Carroll.[16]

Grundy interrupted his leadership of the relief effort to deal with another major issue, the border with Kentucky. The location of the state line between Kentucky and Tennessee had long been in dispute. The northern border for North Carolina had legally been established since 1665 at latitude 36°30' N. Difficulties abounded, however, in fixing this boundary between North Carolina and Virginia, and later between the spun-off states of Tennessee and Kentucky, over hundreds of miles of forested and often mountainous terrain to the Mississippi River. Expansion westward led North Carolina and Virginia in 1779 to authorize Judge Richard Henderson, of North Carolina, and Doctor Thomas Walker, of Virginia, to undertake a survey. The commissioners could not even agree on the proper starting point, and ultimately each commissioner pursued his own line, although only Walker carried his survey as far as the Tennessee River. As a result of poor measurements, both lines went north of the agreed latitude, with the least inaccurate, Walker's, being some twelve miles north, at the Tennessee River. Since it took some time for its inaccuracies to be recognized, the Walker line served as the boundary between Kentucky and Tennessee for a number of years.[17]

Kentucky would not accept as its southern border the "grossly unscientific" Walker line and as early as 1801 fruitlessly authorized commissioners to run a line with Tennessee. As a Kentuckian, Grundy had been on a select committee to examine this issue in 1804. After desultory initiatives by both states over the years, in 1818 the exasperated Kentucky legislature repealed all prior laws on the boundary, declared latitude 36°30' N as its southern border, and again appealed to Congress. Finally, in February 1819, faced with continuing inaction, Kentucky appointed commissioners, requested that Tennessee do the same, and stipulated that its commissioners, Robert Alexander and Luke Munsell, would run the line unilaterally at latitude 36°30' N if Tennessee failed to act. Tennessee did not act, and Alexander and Munsell conducted their survey.[18]

Tennessee had not been totally inert. Governor Joseph McMinn engaged in discussions with Henry Clay and other Kentucky members in Washington in January 1819. The governor apparently asserted that Tennessee was prepared to present its case for the Walker line before the Supreme Court. More significantly, Grundy and William L. Brown, presumably representing the governor, went to Frankfort for unsuccessful discussions in early January 1819.[19]

After Kentucky acted, Tennessee finally realized that it must deal with the problem, particularly because if the Alexander and Munsell line was followed, significant parts of Tennessee, including the city of Clarksville, would go to Kentucky. Accordingly, in November 1819, while grappling with the relief question, the legislature authorized two commissioners to negotiate a settlement and pledged to ratify any settlement that was reached. Tennessee selected Grundy and Brown as commissioners, giving them plenipotentiary power.[20]

Grundy and Brown dutifully went again to Kentucky, meeting with the two Kentucky commissioners, John J. Crittenden and John Rowan. Grundy had ties to both commissioners. Rowan had been his schoolmate and close friend, while Crittenden, eleven years Grundy's junior and already well launched in his successful career, had studied law under George Bibb. The Kentucky press gleefully emphasized Grundy's roots and expressed the hope that he had not forsaken his Kentucky views. Grundy appears to have been troubled by the attitude of the press but also, to Governor McMinn's astonishment, confident of a solution.[21]

The four negotiators took their work seriously, although Crittenden, notifying Richard M. Johnson of his appointment, wrote humorously that Tennessee's John Eaton might be "converted into a Kentucky Senator" because "Nashville is my object." After preliminary negotiations, Grundy and Brown provided their final proposition: the boundary would extend from the Walker line to the Tennessee River, from the Tennessee River to the Alexander and Munsell line, and from that line to the Mississippi. Importantly, given the deep interest of land speculators, North Carolina grants north of the Alexander and Munsell line would be treated as valid unless they conflicted with Virginia claims, as would Virginia claims south of the Walker line unless they conflicted with North Carolina claims.[22]

The Kentucky commissioners split, with Crittenden being willing to accept the Tennessee proposals with some modifications, and Rowan, to whom 36°30′ N was inviolate, refusing to do so. After the Tennesseans rejected arbitration, the two Kentucky commissioners submitted separate reports to their legislature.

With negotiations at an impasse, Grundy and Brown sought congressional authorization for the U.S. Supreme Court to intercede. But Crittenden's view—that the Walker line had been accepted by parent states and that it would be difficult to force Tennesseans into Kentucky—ultimately prevailed in the Kentucky legislature. Rowan resigned and was replaced by Robert Trimble, and negotiations resumed. Both parties proved flexible and reached agreement rather quickly. In essence, Grundy and Brown brooked no compromise on the Walker or Alexander and Munsell line, refused to give any compensation, and made modest adjustments along the Tennessee River. Significantly for speculators, however, they made major concessions on land claims, one being that all North Carolina claims north of the Alexander and Munsell line would be void. The Kentucky legislature promptly ratified the agreement, and the Tennessee legislature did so in a later session.[23]

Grundy and Brown did a good job for Tennessee. Although Tennessee had the better argument—a fact Crittenden recognized—the Tennesseans made the most of their position and achieved a relatively straightforward and decisive agreement. Their acceptance of the Alexander and Munsell line (rather than carrying the Walker line to the Mississippi) and their decision to give up North Carolina land claims reflected statesmanship.

Not everyone applauded. Tennesseans in the most directly affected areas enthusiastically supported the settlement, the *Clarksville Gazette* calling it a "happy" result. The speculator press, however, criticized the accord. The *Clarion and Tennessee Gazette,* the organ of the Erwin faction, believed that the settlement of private claims was "very objectionable," and Tennessee's secretary of state, Daniel Graham, wrote Governor McMinn that he thought Grundy and Brown were "politically defunct."[24]

Perhaps the best measure of the reaction of the land speculators came from Senator John H. Eaton, an important member of the Blount faction. Eaton wrote to John Overton on April 3, 1820, that he regretted Grundy's diplomatic failure, saying, "He is solicitous of popularity." By failing to pursue a course sensitive to the "opinions of the virtuos [*sic*] and good, whose favorable opinions are alone worth possessing," Grundy had slowed his progress to the Senate seat, which Eaton believed was his goal. Eaton modified his elitist perspective, however, by a fair-minded assessment that nothing in the treaty deserved censure.[25]

A Davidson County grand jury echoed Eaton's grudging conclusion. In urging a special legislative session to deal fairly with holders of warrants for an estimated eighty thousand acres north of the Alexander and Munsell line, the grand jury simply stated that the unhappy dispute had been honorably settled by mutual concessions. Such also has been the judgment of history.[26]

16

LEGISLATIVE LEADERSHIP

They want Mr. Grundy out of the way.
—*Clarion and Tennessee Gazette*

The Panic of 1819 brought economic distress that engulfed the nation over the next several years. Baltimore's leading commercial house, Smith & Buchanan, collapsed and took down more than one hundred merchants. The leader of the Republican Party in Virginia, George Nicholas's brother Wilson Cary, also failed, exacerbating the financial problems of Thomas Jefferson, who had cosigned notes. In Tennessee, Davidson County recorded the filing of an estimated five hundred debt suits in the first six months of 1819, and William Carroll reportedly lost $66,500. Readers poured over newspapers to see whose farm would be next to fall for delinquent taxes. A grand jury called for a special session of the legislature to protect citizens against the "evils of a deficient, decreasing and defective currency." Merchants and farmers, who were most adversely affected, blamed bankers and land speculators. The *Murfreesboro Courier,* more thoughtful than some papers, attributed the calamity to the fall of foreign markets and the lack of circulating specie and dolefully reported that owners of property being sold to pay off debts would probably only realize about one-fifth of the property's alleged real value.[1]

Grundy, who had been required to resign his seat when he took on the Kentucky-Tennessee border dispute, ran for the Tennessee legislature again, announcing his candidacy by May 23, 1820. He and other relief leaders called for a special legislative session to address the crisis. His endorsement law failing to satisfy the popular temper, Grundy now proposed a state loan office, which would issue paper notes. The Blount faction and its paper, the *Nashville Whig,* opposed Grundy, while the Erwin group and its paper, the *Clarion and Tennessee Gazette,* notwithstanding its unhappiness with the resolution of the border dispute, vigorously supported him. The Blount interests feared that a state loan office would end their banking monopoly and that any government issuance of paper would further devalue bank notes. The *Clarion and Tennessee Gazette* referred to Grundy's genius and eloquence and charged that opposition came only from land speculators, moneyed aristocrats, and East Tennesseans: "They want Mr. Grundy out of the way." When the polls closed, it was obvious that there were not enough land speculators or moneyed aristocrats; Grundy had a comfortable majority of 883 votes to 644 for his opponent, Colonel Thomas Williamson.[2]

At the special session at Murfreesboro on June 26, Governor McMinn, acting in concert with Grundy, proposed a state loan office that would issue treasury certificates and a stay law that would postpone judgments for two years unless the loan office certificates were accepted at par. This approach, a refinement of Grundy's election proposal, was referred to a special joint committee proposed by Grundy, of which he was a member. After political jostling, four additional members joined the committee, Grundy became chairman, and the committee reported the bill on July 4. In the extensive debate that followed, Pleasant Miller raised a variety of objections, including the unconstitutionality of the measures. An initial version passed the house, 26–13, and then was revised by Grundy in a joint committee of the senate and the house. The final bill, passed by the legislature on July 26, created the Bank of the State of Tennessee, with capital of $1 million, a headquarters bank at Nashville, and a branch at Knoxville. The bank was authorized to issue notes up to five hundred dollars to individuals at 6 percent, with funds allocated among counties based on tax payments and population. The legislation provided that revenues of the state not otherwise appropriated and receipts from sale of certain Indian lands would be pledged as security. The notes would be legal tender and could be used to pay off debts and thereby relieve economic suffering in the state.[3]

The bill passed with a significant, if unintended, assist from Andrew Jackson. Jackson, by 1820 an advocate of hard money, visited Murfreesboro to oppose the state loan office. In typical fashion, he became incensed and at a tavern in Murfreesboro called all those who had voted for the bank "d——d perjured sons of b——s." Jackson's efforts to drum up opposition backfired, with some legislators objecting to his remonstrance as dictatorial and intemperate. William B. Lewis wrote Jackson that he considered the loan-office bill a dangerous experiment but that most people in his vicinity favored it. He also apparently accepted Grundy's agreement on constitutionality—that if the loan office was unconstitutional, so were state chartered banks—and took Jackson to task for his behavior at Murfreesboro.[4]

The new state bank, widely known as the "Saddle-Bags Bank," was then and thereafter recognized as Grundy's creation. Supporters hailed, and critics assailed, its novelty and extension of government power. Not surprisingly, opponents variously charged that it went too far or, from a debtor perspective, did not go far enough. A Tennessee correspondent advised Calhoun that Grundy and his state bank were in "full tide of successful experiment" and that Grundy "will share its fate." In Knoxville, opponents charged that Tennessee, in no difficulty, was risking its public credit to pay private debts. They contrasted classical governments, in which an individual's interest or life could be sacrificed for the state, with modern legislation, under which public funds would be provided to needy individuals, thereby making the "government support the people instead of the people maintaining the government."[5]

The *Knoxville Register* assessment reflects the magnitude of Grundy's legislative accomplishment. The state-bank legislation was radical, particularly in its provisions for direct loans to individuals. It stretched the role of government dramatically and evoked protests of unconstitutional action from not only excitable leaders like Jackson but also thoughtful members of the judiciary. Its passage not only reflected the severity of the crisis but also emphasized the willingness of worried legislators to put their trust in an innovative and untested plan. Grundy incurred the wrath of the banking and financial elite, just as he earned the praise of those he sought to help. Grundy's stance on the loan office, even more than his earlier battle with respect to the Kentucky Insurance Company, marked him as a populist leader of the first rank.

Conservative elements took control of the new state bank soon after it was organized on July 29, 1820. Three directors initially chosen—Nathan Ewing, David McGavock, and John Catron—objected to serving and were replaced by M. Barrow, W. L. Brown, and John H. Eaton. The evidence is not conclusive but suggests that Grundy supported those who declined to serve, who were close friends and political allies.[6]

Operation of the state bank began smoothly enough, although many proponents considered the 6 percent interest rate too high. After initially refusing, the private banks acceded to public opinion and honored the new bank's notes. Pleasant Miller wrote on January 1821 that the state bank's paper was accepted. More than a year and a half later, Alfred Balch, a Nashville lawyer and Grundy ally, stated that the directors were cautiously managing the bank and sustaining its credit but had forgotten why the bank was created.[7]

The state bank, a creation of the legislature, encountered challenges from both the judicial and the executive branches. First, the Supreme Court of Tennessee in 1821 declared unconstitutional both the endorsement law of 1819 and the stay provision of the state bank law on several grounds, including impairment of contracts. In a special legislative session in 1822 Grundy provided a simple response: the Tennessee judiciary had no power to declare an act of the legislature unconstitutional. The members of the House promptly agreed, voting unanimously against repeal of the law the court had declared unconstitutional. Needless to say, this brought about a storm, with papers in East Tennessee particularly upset by what they viewed as flagrant disregard of the court.[8]

The second, more serious challenge arose in the executive branch. Demonstrating again that labels should be used with circumspection, Joseph McMinn, governor of Tennessee from 1815 to 1821 and part of the Blount faction, sympathized with debtors and reform efforts in 1819 and 1820. He had taken up Grundy's proposals, and in his outgoing message in 1821 he urged that creditors be required to accept property of debtors at some proportion of real worth—a minimum appraisal law. Grundy thought that went too far, violating contract rights, and emphasized in a house report a familiar theme of opposition to executive power: that the legislature alone had the power to regulate indebtedness and judgments. Grundy also reiterated that imprisonment for debt should be ended except in cases where debtors tried to conceal their property.[9]

William Carroll, who succeeded McMinn in 1821, did not share McMinn's views. The candidate of the Erwin group, Carroll had gained an easy victory, winning by a vote of 31,290 to 7,294 over Andrew Jackson's neighbor and friend, the wealthy Edward Ward. Carroll, who attributed his financial woes in part to the banking machinations of the Blount faction, accepted the need for banks but opposed paper credit, believing that banks should be required to redeem their notes in specie. Ward could not overcome his association with the bankers, whose severity toward debtors and attempts to destroy Grundy's state bank at the same time that they continued to pay dividends had made them few friends.[10]

In his message to the legislature the new governor was unsympathetic toward the problems of debtors, suggesting the "cultivation of industrious habits and the practice of rigid economy." This reflected Carroll's broader approach of reducing government spending and enacting forward-looking social measures. More specifically, Carroll favored prompt resumption of specie payment by banks. Grundy, however, raised three objections when a bill to such effect was brought forward. First, if they were forced to resume specie payments, banks would necessarily have to call in loans, increasing distress rather than relieving it. Second, the new state bank would be included in the legislative scope, and Grundy doubted that the sale of lands in a period of acute distress would be strong enough or occur soon enough to provide funds to the bank for redemption of its notes. The new bank accordingly would have inadequate time to launch its operations. Third, Tennessee banks probably would not be able to redeem their notes in specie and would fail, thereby leaving Tennessee without needed credit. Grundy fought artfully and achieved various important amendments, including postponement of the commencement date from November 1823 to April 1824, but ultimately his forces capitulated. Specie resumption would be required of the banks the first Monday in April 1824.[11]

No one doubted that specie resumption would cause hardship, and in 1823 Grundy proposed a complicated amendment to give the banks more time. The ensuing debate marked the emergence of James K. Polk. Grundy's law student, elected to the house in 1823 after serving as senate clerk since 1819, instantly took on his friend and benefactor and urged that Grundy's proposal be stopped at the threshold even though he knew the bill was "the favorite child of the Gentleman from Davidson." Polk feared further destruction of economic confidence if the house allowed continued use of depreciated notes by the banks. Grundy, using the same arguments of earlier sessions, softened the bill but had to agree to full resumption by July 1826.[12]

The legislative relief won by Grundy proved insufficient to save the banks. Specie resumption began as required in 1826, but the Nashville Bank suspended payments shortly thereafter and went out of business, and the Knoxville Bank followed in 1827. Grundy's state bank limped along until 1829, when Carroll asked the legislature to shut its doors. The loss of Tennessee's banks would bring another chapter in Tennessee's financial system and political alignments, as Nashville's merchants would again seek a branch of the Second Bank of the United States.

Grundy's state bank never realized the aspirations of its proponents. Grundy himself attributed the bank's failure to the "faithlessness" of some in its management. Conservative interests did manage the bank cautiously. Fundamentally, however, the bank could not overcome the opposition of hard-money adherents like Jackson and Carroll, who did not accept the need for a sophisticated paper credit system. In addition, although the state loan office may have been more conceptually egalitarian than privately owned banks, it suffered from the same defects in difficult times.[13]

Historians have always been puzzled by the fact that Grundy, a wealthy lawyer in Tennessee's banking center, led the relief effort. Joseph Parks confessed uncertainty whether opportunism or a desire to put his abilities to work motivated Grundy. Charles Sellers, James K. Polk's leading biographer, championed Grundy's political sensitivity but viewed him as a poor boy susceptible to the market's rewards and as "an able politician without any consistent aims but his own advancement, who with marvelous adeptness pursued an independent course" between the fiercely antagonistic Blount and Erwin factions.[14]

A fuller review suggests a different and less opportunistic interpretation. First, the characterization of Grundy as a poor boy is inaccurate. Although they lived on the frontier, his family achieved success and affluence in Virginia and Kentucky and Grundy, who was comparatively well educated, appears always to have been a believer in the market's rewards. Second, Grundy took on Tennessee banking interests less than eighteen months after he and William Carroll opposed the same interests in their effort to secure a Nashville branch of the Second Bank of the United States. The exclusionary banking policies of the Blount group clearly angered Grundy and may well have triggered his decision to run for the legislature. At any rate, Grundy had little sympathy for these selfsame banks when the Panic of 1819 began, particularly when their quasi-monopolistic position derived from the same type of legislative privilege enjoyed by the Kentucky Insurance Company sixteen years earlier.

Third, it is possible, perhaps probable, that Grundy led the relief effort because of his own financial exposure. As noted, the paucity of financial records makes it difficult to appraise his wealth. He earned a great deal of money, but he lived well and supported a large family. Grundy also had entered fully into the land boom preceding the Panic, with his lot purchases in Nashville, his development programs in Franklin and Gallatin, his speculative acquisitions of 2,500 acres in Indian Territory and 950 acres in Mississippi, and his continued ownership of other lands. Moreover, he had begun construction of Grundy Place. Personal interest thus may have given Grundy more reason to address the crisis than historians have assumed. Supporting this view, an observer in 1821 wrote that Grundy, head of the debtor party, was himself a debtor.[15]

Fourth, Grundy's experience in Kentucky both induced and prepared him for his leadership in Tennessee. There are obvious parallels between Grundy's opposition to the banking provisions of the Kentucky Insurance Company and the relief effort in Tennessee. In both cases Grundy opposed state-chartered financial institutions owned by a commercial "aristocratic" elite. In both states Grundy represented constituents excluded from banking ownership, the Southside farmers in Kentucky and the planters, merchants, and yeoman farmers suffering from the Panic of 1819 in Tennessee. In each state he took on the banking establishment, the Kentucky Insurance Company in Lexington and the Blount faction in Tennessee. In Kentucky Grundy supported, and in Tennessee he initiated, a state-owned bank as the solution. In Kentucky in 1804 and 1805 and Tennessee in 1820 Grundy used the legislature to deal with economic issues and restrict private financial interests.

Lastly, Charles Sellers's suggestion that Grundy ensured that his state bank would be operated in the interest of the banking monopoly simply does not square with what we know of Grundy. It is difficult to credit that he would strive to create a state bank, for which he knew he would have great and continuing opposition from banking interests, and then sabotage his own objectives shortly thereafter by ensuring that a conservative board would manage the institution inconsistently with that bank's visionary objectives. Grundy's own previous experience with the state legislature in Kentucky and in Congress during the War of 1812 demonstrates that he was not afraid to take on the most powerful vested interests; indeed, he appears to have relished the stage on which he exasperated—and demolished the arguments of—his opponents. He fought and supported banking interests from 1819 on because he favored continuation of a commercial system in which his friends and constituents participated as bankers and borrowers. Different approaches had to be tried in a deepening crisis. At times his solutions coincided with the interests of the bankers, and at times they differed.

It is also important to put Grundy's relief initiatives in a broader context. Murray Rothbard, in his magisterial survey of the Panic of 1819, concluded that debt relief, in the form of stay laws, minimum appraisal laws, and inconvertible paper through state banks, constituted the relief platform throughout the United States, with eight states adopting stay laws, four adopting minimum appraisal laws, and four (Illinois, Missouri, Kentucky, and Tennessee) establishing state banks. Grundy is correctly viewed by Rothbard and others as being at the forefront of relief initiatives in the United States, but his solutions and approaches were not unique.[16]

Moreover, in a judgment that Rothbard also drew for states other than Tennessee, the relief measures that Grundy championed were not for the poor and needy. A Summer County grand jury charged in 1820 that the banking crisis could be attributed to the moneyed class and that a state bank would only delay the day of reckoning for speculators, a conclusion echoed by East Tennesseans, who were opposed to all relief and had no doubt that the "broken" traders of Nashville were responsible for the outcry. Our modern usage of the word *relief* misleads us when we examine the banking crisis of 1819. While the depreciation of paper currency caused widespread distress, those who needed relief from the banks were those who either had borrowed too much or had too much to be ignored by their political leaders.[17]

Finally, Grundy's banking efforts from 1819 to 1824 reflected a trial-and-error approach. He viewed the legislature—the voice of the people—as the vehicle for economic change and experimentation. In words that must have infuriated Andrew Jackson, Grundy stated that laws on the execution of legal judgments reflected "a law making power, and . . . the legislature alone has the constitutional right to declare" such laws. Within the legislature, as the representative of the mercantile interests in Nashville, he recognized the utility of banking and sought to find an approach that would work in unprecedented times. Grundy's banking positions from 1819 on fit the pattern of a legislator trying to find a solution. His first effort, the endorsement law, was an artful compromise. It provided relief for debtors and maintained the currency of bank notes, thereby trying to assure stability within the existing system. When that failed to provide relief, and bankers continued to declare themselves handsome dividends, Grundy turned to the remedy initiated in Kentucky sixteen years earlier, a state bank. His efforts thereafter to prevent premature resumption of specie payment, including by his own state bank, were intended to forestall collapse of the banks and assure a credit system that did not rely solely on specie. That all banks foundered when specie payment finally resumed testifies to the accuracy of his perception. In the uncertain times of America's first great panic no one had the answers, and Grundy, in Tennessee as in Kentucky, shifted ground to try to find a solution to unprecedented difficulties.

Grundy's state bank dramatically expanded the role of state government in a period of financial crisis. At the same time, in a different but also innovative way Grundy used his old tools of land entitlement and legislative bargaining to achieve a different purpose: the financial stability of Tennessee colleges. Over the long term, Grundy's maneuvering in laying the financial foundations for three important educational institutions may have been far more influential than his role in banking.

Shortly after moving to Tennessee, Grundy became a trustee of Cumberland College and initiated the unanimous selection in 1809 of his old teacher James Priestley as president. The college shut down operations in 1816, but even as the Panic of 1819 spread, the trustees resolved to reopen in December 1820. Priestley died on February 6, 1821, however, and on March 28 the *Nashville Clarion* reported bleak news: the trustees were seeking a replacement for Priestley, but efforts to raise money from the public had failed, and legislative aid was out of the question. East Tennessee College confronted similarly dire circumstances. The plight of these institutions set the stage for a secret bargain that put both Cumberland College, subsequently the University of Nashville and now the George Peabody College of Vanderbilt University, and East Tennessee College, now the University of Tennessee, as well as the University of North Carolina, on a firmer financial footing.[18]

The catalyst for these legislative gyrations—North Carolina land claims—originated in the cession of Tennessee to the United States. In its deed of cession North Carolina reserved the right to satisfy its Revolutionary War warrants from the ceded land and at the same time passed a law assigning to the University of North Carolina the claims of soldiers who died without heirs. After Tennessee opened the so-called Congressional Reservation in Tennessee for warrant holders in 1819, the university submitted its claims. The stakes were high, the *Nashville Whig* asserting that the university could own from two hundred thousand to three hundred thousand acres of the best land in Tennessee.[19]

Grundy intervened, sponsoring a resolution passed by the legislature on November 16, 1821, that stayed issuance of grants to the University of North Carolina until the legislature had decided on the appropriate approach. Before that bill passed its second reading, Grundy changed course and proposed that a two-member commission decide ownership of the land warrants. The bill passed the house but failed in the state senate because of opposition from University of North Carolina alumni. Grundy's position, popular in most of Tennessee, outraged friends of the university, who feared that a two-member commission would only follow the popular will. They believed, however, that Grundy was amenable to some sort of deal. Indeed, Daniel Graham wrote that Grundy would be willing to help the university if a sweetener could be given, not to the negotiator, but "to the people."[20]

Into this situation stepped Archibald Murphey (1777–1832), appointed by the university along with General Joseph Bryan to negotiate with the Tennesseans. Murphey had been a successful state senator, lawyer, historian, and professor of languages. In financial straits in 1822, Murphey agreed to serve as the university negotiator, for which he would receive a commission in Tennessee lands. His letters to North Carolina and related correspondence provide unusual insight into Grundy's legislative maneuvering.[21]

When Murphey reached Nashville, he contacted John C. McLemore, a knowledgeable land speculator. McLemore, surveyor general of the military district, had been a subagent for Thomas Henderson, who as the university's agent had located 295,706 acres of escheated lands. Entitled to share in Henderson's commission, McLemore reported great excitement about the warrants but believed that a compromise could be effected. Murphey took his soundings and concurred.[22]

Murphey moved smoothly. He appointed McLemore as his primary agent, and he gained the support of Senator John Eaton, a former University of North Carolina student, who believed that the university lands were worth at least five dollars per acre. Murphey then prepared a memorial for the general assembly, under which he laid the grounds for a compromise by suggesting that Tennessee take some of the North Carolina lands in return for giving the University of North Carolina some exemption from taxation. Murphey also separately commented on the "Rich Spoil" in lands in Tennessee that had been secretly divided among a very few—he named Colonel Polk and John McLemore, among others.[23]

Murphey went to Murfreesboro for a special session of the legislature in August 1822. "Intrigue and Bargaining (they call it Log-Rolling here) are at the Bottom of everything," he would report. This was the environment in which Grundy flourished and dominated. In a remarkably candid letter Murphey spelled out the details, marveling at the process:

> Every thing of importance is here carried by management, when Public Feeling or Opinion is against it, but never have the People been more deceived than in the business of the Trustees. We have carried our Point against a dead Majority in one branch of the Legislature, against the weight of all the Presses in this Place [Nashville] and in Knoxville, and against a popular Feeling that several of our Friends in the General Assembly were afraid to disregard: and We have carried it by the very Man who first stirred up the Assembly against us.[24]

Grundy and Murphey met in Grundy's hotel room and made a deal in less than an hour. Grundy explained that he wished to provide for the Tennessee colleges. Grundy's plan, which required complete secrecy, called for resurrection of his earlier bill. Two commissioners would be appointed to investigate the claims: Judge James Trimble, Grundy's law partner, and Jenkin Whiteside, both well-known and able lawyers. If the commissioners accepted the claims, Cumberland College would receive forty thousand acres, East Tennessee University would receive twenty-thousand acres, and the University of North Carolina lands would be exempt from taxation until 1850. Since the commissioners would have to be appointed by the governor, Grundy met with Carroll, who readily accepted the plan and agreed to appoint Trimble and Whiteside if an appropriate bill could be passed.

Only passage of the bill remained. Murphey and Jenkin Whiteside drew it up, and the main actors went through a well-oiled masquerade. Grundy delivered a long and animated attack on the claims but suggested appointment of the commissioners. General Bryan did his part, expressing ignorance and surprise but ultimately accepting an investigation. Thereafter everything went as planned; the bill was passed, the commissioners appointed, and the agreement struck, with sixty thousand acres of warrants to be transferred by the University of North Carolina and the North Carolina lands to be exempt from taxation until January 1, 1850. Murphey exulted that the "Fortune of the University is made," estimating the present value of the lands at two hundred thousand dollars and judging that it would likely be five hundred thousand when they were sold. He emphasized that everything was otherwise above board, with nothing dishonorable even hinted at by either party.[25]

Grundy's approach in the legislature had immediate benefits for Grundy's favorite educational institution, Cumberland College. Cumberland quickly gained title to its new lands and sold them. The trustees also launched a fundraising campaign, which by 1824 had pledges of more than seven thousand dollars. This improved financial position enabled Cumberland in 1824 to recruit to its presidency Phillip Lindsley, of Princeton, who would become the most eminent educator in the history of Nashville. In 1826 Lindsley and the trustees persuaded the state assembly to award a charter for a new institution, the University of Nashville, which would gradually subsume Cumberland.[26]

Grundy could not have envisioned all of the changes for Cumberland that followed his legislative success. Yet he probably had some in mind, for this episode epitomizes Grundy's widely discussed cleverness, as well as his willingness to engage in questionable tactics. Grundy largely manufactured the opposition against the University of North Carolina claims, as Murphey recognized. Had Grundy already thought of the plan by which Tennessee's colleges would benefit? Certainly Grundy's actions in late November 1821 are linked in time to the pronounced weakness of Cumberland College. Similarly, upon the second reading of the bill he had proposed in 1821, he changed it to a very different measure, calling for two commissioners to investigate the claims. Had he decided that the use of commissioners would facilitate a plan he had already formed? Finally, when Murphey was advised upon his arrival that a compromise could be effected and subsequently prepared a memorial for the general assembly setting forth the basic agreement, was he presenting the terms that Grundy had already conceived and passed on through intermediaries? Given the subtlety of Grundy's mind, as well as his cleverness, these questions are more suggestive than fanciful.

Murphey's account of these events in 1822 leaves us with one more evaluation—of Felix Grundy himself. In the margin of a letter to the state treasurer, John Haywood, Murphey wrote: "Mr. Grundy is no very great lawyer: he does not make high pretensions in that way. He is a profound Judge of Mankind, cool and dispassionate, entirely free from malignity. In these respects, and in his Talent for Plot and Management, he resembles the Cardinal De Retz, more than any Man I ever saw."[27]

PART IV

Jacksonian

17

ANDREW JACKSON FOR PRESIDENT

He has more influence than any other person in our Legislature; and when
he brings forward any measure . . . he supports it fearlessly, and most generally succeeds.

—William Carroll

*P*residential politics preoccupied Tennessee politicians from 1822 to
1825, the last years in which Grundy served in the general assembly. In
1822 John Quincy Adams, President Monroe's secretary of state, appeared to be
the leading candidate for the 1824 presidential race, but he faced a talented field
of challengers that included Henry Clay, John C. Calhoun, and William H.
Crawford. Some enthusiastic Tennesseans put out feelers for Andrew Jackson, who, while well known, was considered lacking in the political experience
deemed essential for the presidency. Yet by 1825 Jackson had won the popular
vote but lost the presidency in the House of Representatives to Adams by virtue
of what Jackson decried as a corrupt bargain between Adams and Clay. Also by
1825, Grundy had become a Jackson partisan, and for the remainder of his life
he would be identified as a Jacksonian. How and why had Grundy, whose ties
to Jackson had previously been professional at best, come to be a public proponent of Jackson for president?

Grundy's prominence in the Tennessee General Assembly in these years of
decision made him a natural target of those maneuvering for their presidential
candidate. Writing to Henry Clay on February 1, 1823, Governor William Carroll observed that Grundy expressed his sentiments cautiously. This assessment
seems squarely on the mark; the former War Hawk was a master politician who
kept his cards close to his chest. Yet Carroll also wrote that "it is equally true,
that he has more influence than any other person in our Legislature; and when
he brings forward any measure in that body, he supports it fearlessly, and most
generally succeeds." Grundy's independence from factions, his popularity, and
his adept maneuvering gave him credibility as a power broker.[1]

Henry Clay naturally looked to his former colleague for support. Grundy and Clay had known each other for almost twenty-five years, and they had worked together closely in Washington from 1811 to 1814. For many Jacksonians, such as John H. Eaton, Clay was Grundy's "old friend," and Carroll had suggested that Clay write Grundy, noting that "you know him . . . better than I do." Clay occasionally asked Grundy to assist in debt-collection matters in Tennessee and had retained him in the settlement of his father-in-law's estate. Apparently, on February 16, 1818, Clay suggested humorously that Grundy consider a return to the U.S. Senate. Significantly, too, in July 1822 Clay asked Grundy to serve as a Kentucky commissioner in a dispute with Virginia. John C. Calhoun also may have expected Grundy's endorsement. Calhoun and Nancy Grundy were second cousins, and Grundy and Calhoun had been warm friends since their War Hawk days in Washington. As would later become clear, they shared many political views, including strong views on states' rights.[2]

By contrast, Grundy did not initially have a warm relationship with Jackson. Joseph Parks concluded that while Grundy and Jackson were never enemies, they were only political friends. This judgment, however, fails to take into account the complexity of their association. It appears reasonably clear that their ties evolved over time from cool respect to real friendship, particularly after the establishment of the Whig Party created fault lines among Jackson's partisans.[3]

Grundy and Jackson had met by 1807, and they became more fully acquainted after Grundy moved to Tennessee. He sold two slaves to Jackson in 1810, and at least one letter reflects financial dealings in 1811. Whatever their social and business relationship, however, Grundy's defense of Magness in the killing of Patton Anderson put the two at odds. The enmity between Jackson and Newton Cannon apparently began when Cannon served as a juror in the trial of the third Magness brother in 1812, and given Jackson's temperament, it is highly unlikely that Jackson lightly cast aside his view that Grundy should be "skinned alive." Jackson's friends initiated and led the effort to deny Grundy a House seat in 1811 and to a lesser degree in 1813.[4]

The surface cordiality between Grundy and Jackson during the War of 1812 and Grundy's service as orator when Jackson returned from the Creek battles in 1813 and New Orleans in 1815 masked an uneasy relationship. Grundy, confident of his persuasive charm, did not like to make or have enemies and appears to have made a special effort to soften any Jackson hostility. He kept the Tennessee militia leader apprised of political developments and the maneuvering leading to war. His letters to Jackson are respectful and almost deferential. He also arranged meetings and appointments for Jackson's friends and relatives.

However, Grundy acknowledged strains. In a letter to Jackson dated December 14, 1811, he alludes to their relationship and says that "in no instance shall private feelings influence my conduct and on all occasions I shall pay that regard to your opinions which is due to superior military information."[5]

Jackson, for his part, recognized Grundy's eloquence and his role in bringing about the war. He also sought Grundy's aid from time to time, and Grundy felt free to offer Jackson advice. In 1819 Grundy counseled Jackson, now "near the close of an illustrious life," to go to Washington to defend himself against Speaker of the House Henry Clay, Secretary of the Treasury William H. Crawford, and others who had criticized his invasion of Florida and his actions there.[6]

Grundy maintained his independent course among the factions in Tennessee politics. He did, however, defend an avowed Jackson enemy, Judge William Cocke, in an impeachment trial in 1811 and 1812. Cocke, an experienced Indian fighter and frontiersman, was one of Tennessee's first two senators. He was impeached on November 11, 1811, by the Tennessee house on three articles, the third alleging that Cocke had refused to issue certain writs because of bias. The state senate, as the high court of impeachment, acquitted Cocke on the first two articles but convicted him on the third. Cocke was then removed from office, the first Tennessee jurist so treated.[7]

Jackson and Grundy necessarily encountered each other in the small community of Nashville. No special significance should be attached to the choice of Grundy as speaker for Jackson's triumphal returns; the War Hawk appears to have been the speaker of choice at Nashville public events at this time, and he would have been expected to be fulsome in praise in 1815 for the Hero of New Orleans. But Grundy seems to have included among his good friends various avowed enemies of Jackson. Perhaps not too much should be made of this, since Nashville and Tennessee were still small and Jackson made enemies quickly and tended to keep them, while Grundy, in contrast, sought to maintain friendly relationships with everyone.[8]

Few ties of background or personality linked Grundy and Jackson. Jackson, forced to fend for himself at an early age, could accurately describe himself as a self-made man. Grundy, by contrast, had been raised in a large, supportive family with a strong mother, still alive in 1822, who treated her favorite son with special care and with brothers who stood in for the father he had lost at age eight. Jackson had relatively little formal schooling, while Grundy, "skilled in the knowledge of Greeks and Romans," had received a comparatively good education, certainly the best obtainable in frontier Kentucky. Jackson's military experience had given him a national reputation, while Grundy's service had been limited to the militia. Personality counted even more, however, than background. Jackson was passionate, impetuous, prone to sudden anger, particularly when drunk, and touchy, a person for whom most differences became personal. A man of action and decision, he inspired fierce loyalty. Grundy, witty and affable, projected an aura of serenity and "non-malignity." His supreme self-confidence and command of language and emotion did not always mask the shrewdness and cunning with which he dealt with men and problems.

In contrast with Jackson, for whom his biographer Parton in 1860 estimated one hundred serious quarrels, Grundy tried to maintain friendships and, as Martin Van Buren later observed, had almost no enemies. Grundy accepted disagreements as part of the political process. As far as we know, he never fought a duel or even came close. It is hard to imagine the affable lawyer engaged in the brawls and feuds that so enlivened and scarred Jackson's life. Grundy inspired friendship and affection, not the awe or enmity that followed Jackson. The caution and indirection that sometimes characterized Grundy were alien to Jackson. Indeed, Jackson, who could be eloquent but saw himself otherwise, seems to have distrusted Grundy's oratorical skills, smooth manners, and subtlety. Perhaps the greatest difference, however, involved Grundy's defining characteristic, his capacity to relate with others. Grundy's speaking skills ultimately rested on an intuitive capacity to reach and understand men, which made him uniquely successful with juries. By contrast, Jackson understood only one position—his own.

In important respects, however, Grundy and Jackson were similar. Jackson's unrelenting pursuit of his goals is well known. Grundy too approached his goals "fearlessly," to use Governor Carroll's word, whether it was circuit court reform, war or honorable peace, or a Tennessee state bank. He was "indefatigable Felix" in Kentucky for good reason. Both Grundy and Jackson displayed strong loyalty to friends and ideas. Raised on the frontier, they both believed in the virtues of agrarian life and entrepreneurship and considered themselves Jeffersonian Republicans.[9]

The coolness between Grundy and Jackson was highlighted in the years just before Jackson's presidential bid. Jackson's strong opposition to Grundy's state bank was widely noted, and even later it was the subject of the national press. (The *Daily National Journal* on April 21, 1830, for example, referred with amusement to the fact that Grundy and Jackson were now on terms of "affectionate intercourse," in contrast to Jackson's anger over the passage of the bill creating the state bank.) Jackson also opposed Grundy's view of legislative power. In 1822 he advised his nephew not to study with "quacks" in Nashville. He should study law, not politics, and particularly not "the absurd doctrine that the Legislature is the people."[10]

The historical record is sparse with respect to the machinations behind the movement to nominate Jackson for president. Charles Sellers argues that the Blount faction developed Jackson's candidacy as a means of regaining control of Tennessee but that the candidacy soon took on a life of its own, surprising and overwhelming those who had provided the original impetus. Despite the meager evidence, I find Sellers's thesis persuasive, except that he minimizes the extent to which Grundy, seeking to continue his pivotal role in the legislature, had to be wooed by Jackson before he fully committed to the future president.[11]

Grundy's role in 1822 can only be understood in light of his independence of the two major factions in Tennessee, both of whose major interests continued to be land and banking. Grundy's leadership role in the Panic of 1819 ran directly afoul of the Blount faction's control of both major Tennessee banks. Grundy had fewer direct conflicts with the anti-Blount, anti-Jackson group led by Andrew Erwin and Senator John Williams, and Erwin's paper, the *Clarion and Tennessee Gazette,* supported him in his quest for the legislature in 1821. The election of Governor William Carroll, the Erwin candidate, over Jackson's neighbor Edward Ward dealt a major blow to the Blount faction and to Grundy, since Carroll did not support the state bank, Grundy's signature issue.

Pleasant Miller, with an eye on a Senate seat in 1823, proposed to John Overton a gambit that might restore the Blount faction's primacy. On January 27, 1822, Miller enumerated for Overton the benefits that would accrue if the popular Jackson should become governor. A Jackson victory over Carroll would facilitate the defeat of Senator Williams in 1823 and enable the Blount group to achieve legislative objectives, including relocation of the state capital and the penitentiary and changes in the judiciary and land laws. As part of his presentation, Miller reported that he had received a "private letter from the west stating that Grundy had abandoned the head of department of Nashville [Carroll] and said that he would stick to me.—This I believe in part." We do not know how many, if any, of these arguments Miller or Overton conveyed to Grundy, but several would have appealed to him. Grundy favored locating the capital at Nashville, and he had proposed a penitentiary, which in turn would facilitate revision of the criminal laws, and was collaborating with Miller on land questions.[12]

Miller's plan to advance Jackson for governor came to naught but metamorphosed into a campaign to nominate Jackson for president. Although William Lewis and others have taken or been given credit for initiating Jackson's candidacy, John Overton played an important role. Overton described his participation as follows: "Previously to the setting of the Legislature of Tennessee in 1821 it forcibly struck me, that J. ought to be our next president. . . . —To prepare the public mind pieces were thrown into Wilson's paper [the *Nashville Gazette,* founded by George Wilson in 1819]. . . . The Legislature met and then I communicated to a leading member, Mr. Miller, my views, which he gave into—communicated then with Grundy, who at first seemed a little surprised, but came into the measure of recommending him, by our legislature."[13]

Grundy's support for Jackson could hardly have been taken for granted. Miller believed that Grundy intended to back Clay, and the Kentuckian's allies certainly thought so. Yet Grundy decided to take the lead in recommending the Hero. On June 27, 1822, he wrote Jackson asking whether there was any good reason why his name should not be presented as a candidate for president. The general assembly would meet on July 22, 1822, in a special session, and he believed Jackson could be nominated unanimously. Grundy stressed one point of pride: that such a nomination would refute a "Slander" that Jackson was not popular at home. Jackson did not respond, but Grundy moved forward. On July 27 the members of the general assembly unanimously nominated Jackson for president, and the Senate concurred on August 3.[14]

Thomas Hart Benton, in Nashville en route to Missouri, learned what was afoot and wrote Clay on July 12, 1822. He reported that Grundy would manage Jackson's nomination, which would surprise Clay, that Governor Carroll would be "active and efficient" for Clay, and that Blount forces would oppose John Williams for the Senate and support General Sam Houston for Congress over Newton Cannon.[15]

Clay did not know how seriously to take Tennessee's caucus nomination of Jackson. He attributed it, first, as an effort by other candidates to suggest a division in the West between Clay and Jackson; second, as an effort to affect the local elections of Jackson critics John Williams, General John Cocke, and Colonel Newton Cannon; and third, as a compliment from his own state to Jackson. Clay proposed that other states manifest public sentiment for his own candidacy, thereby ending any suggestions of division in the West, adding that there was reason to believe that Tennessee, even if it was serious in recommending Jackson, would not persist in "a vain and hopeless object."[16]

These few elliptical references provide little help in determining why Grundy chose to take the lead in the nomination of Jackson. Political considerations certainly dominated. First, personality drove Tennessee elections. Almost all Tennesseans voted Republican, and friendships and business ties tended to govern political decisions. Jackson had many enemies, but as the national hero, he enjoyed great popularity with the rank-and-file voter. Grundy had little to lose by supporting a fellow Nashvillian, particularly as compared with the distant Clay. Second, Grundy substantively had much to gain by improving his ties to the Blount faction. He and that group both opposed some of Governor Carroll's initiatives, and Grundy and Miller regularly collaborated on land and judiciary issues. Third, and most difficult to assess, is how seriously Jackson's candidacy was viewed. No one knew whether Jackson would even run. If he did, Grundy as a Tennessean might wind up supporting the state's favorite son anyway; if he did not, Grundy would have gained by linking his political name with the state's military hero. Grundy, like many, probably thought that a successful Jackson candidacy was implausible and that support for Jackson would entail few costs, allowing later support for Clay.

It is inappropriate, however, to carry this search for motive too far. No one could have known the full implications of a Jackson candidacy, and political decisions had to be made with the usual levels of uncertainty and nuance. Henry Clay, an astute politician with good sources of information, did not know how seriously to take the Jackson initiative, and it is reasonably likely that Grundy was in the same position. Benton reported as late as July 1823 that hardly anyone in Tennessee thought Jackson had a chance. Grundy kept his lines to Clay open, making clear that his support for Jackson did not preclude a subsequent turn to his old friend if Jackson should falter. On February 1, 1823, Governor Carroll, in the same letter in which he stressed Grundy's influence in the legislature, said that Clay could rely on Tennessee if "Jackson should cease to be a competition" and that Grundy had "assured me, that if the prospects of General Jackson became hopeless, he would be for you, and that he would endeavor to have you nominated at the next meeting of our Legislature."[17]

Jackson's candidacy caught fire, but not before further political machinations in Tennessee created additional strains in the relationship between Grundy and Jackson. Nashville, which had twenty-three lawyers in 1822, was a relatively small arena, in which large ambitions regularly clashed. Grundy's bad relationship with the land speculator Patrick Darby spilled over into Jackson's presidential bid. Although Darby appears to have acknowledged Grundy's talent and respectability, he saw Grundy as an enemy who had generated much of the ill feeling toward him in Nashville. The enmity between the two—and there is no other word for what appears to have been the exception to the rule of Grundy's good relationships with others—became manifest when Darby threatened to horsewhip Grundy.[18]

This bad blood affected politics because of the still unsettled state of Tennessee land laws. As earlier noted, Grundy in 1819 had sponsored a bill providing secure title to anyone who had undisputed possession of land by grant from either North Carolina or Tennessee for seven years. This was not retroactive, however, and the Tennessee Supreme Court opened the door wide for speculators like Darby when it reversed earlier law and held, with Judge Haywood dissenting, that an occupant's claim was invalid unless it was connected, without any break in title, to the original grant. This was anathema to Grundy, because it cast doubt on the landholdings of so many Tennesseans. In 1821 Miller and Grundy together succeeded in persuading the legislature to enact a bill against champerty, making it illegal to purchase titles to lands whose occupants claimed adverse possession. The next year, aided by Haywood, they collaborated on legislation that added a judge to the Tennessee Supreme Court. Ultimately, a new majority reversed the decision on adverse possession, "which drove Darby out of the state and gave repose to the people and the country."[19]

Strangely enough, Jackson linked himself with Darby. Jackson had hired Darby in April 1821 to lead a major lawsuit against Andrew Erwin. In 1823 Darby engaged an Overton protégé, Stephen Cantrell, in a bitter newspaper war over Cantrell's charge that Darby had defrauded Cantrell's father and Darby's countercharge that Cantrell had corruptly administered federal pensions. Jackson appears to have sided with Darby in this matter against Overton, Cantrell, Miller, and Grundy, even when Darby accused Overton and Miller of conspiring to pack the Tennessee Supreme Court. In his attacks on Grundy as part of the alleged cabal, Darby tried to link himself directly to Jackson. He accused Grundy of taking his enmity to Darby to the legislature by joining with Andrew Erwin, Jackson's foe.[20]

Grundy's relationship with Darby became even more publicly strained after Darby announced his candidacy for one of the two Davidson seats in the state legislature, in opposition to Grundy. Then on April 14, 1823, Secretary of War John C. Calhoun appointed Grundy and Robert C. Armstrong as a court of inquiry to investigate Darby's charges that Cantrell, the pension agent at Nashville, had "corruptly" received U.S. notes or specie and paid pensioners in depreciated Tennessee and Kentucky bank notes. Darby, through his paper, the *Constitutional Advocate,* cried foul, stating that Grundy would be so biased that he could not evaluate the charges fairly. Jackson sympathized with Darby and thought it unfortunate for Grundy that he was involved. To modern eyes,

Grundy's acceptance of an inquiry role seems extraordinary. Yet, in the event, the court of inquiry issued a report that led to the dismissal of Cantrell, suggesting that Grundy was more objective than Darby believed. Grundy also easily won reelection over Darby, receiving 1,134 votes, although he trailed the leading vote-getter.[21]

Against this backdrop of strained relations with important backers, Jackson confronted the Tennessee senatorial election in 1823. John Williams was running for reelection, supported by the Jacksonian Hugh Lawson White, his brother-in-law, and Erwin faction members. Pleasant Miller and John Rhea, both in the Blount faction, wanted the seat. Many believed that a victory for Williams, a critic, would significantly damage Jackson's credibility as a presidential candidate.

Grundy's role in the senate election of 1823 is unclear and fraught with suggestive implications. Charles Sellers asserts that Overton and Grundy worked for a Williams victory and that the Williams forces viewed Overton, White's brother-in-law, as an ally. Grundy led the fight to bring about a prompt election, and on September 18 he proposed resolutions instructing Tennessee senators to try to prevent a nomination by congressional caucus, the traditional means of choosing a president. The *Nashville Whig* reported on September 22, 1823, that Grundy had said in debate that he was ready to give his vote, since John Williams had fully and satisfactorily resolved his only difficulty. These various moves were interpreted as favorable to Williams, since the instruction with respect to the caucus and the newspaper report appeared to eliminate the most serious objection to Williams, that he would support Crawford in the caucus. Legislators wrote Jackson that Grundy was backing Williams. Jackson responded that he was aware of the "schemers of the opposition with Mr. G. as their head and spokesman."[22]

Taking place in the midst of the senatorial election, the settlement of Jackson's long-standing lawsuit against Andrew Erwin on September 19, 1823, the day after Grundy's introduction of the caucus resolution, assumes an interesting dimension. Patrick Darby, who handled the lawsuit, disagreed with the settlement. Several years later, in 1827, Darby claimed that Jackson had entered into a "combination" with his enemies under which "Darby would be sacrificed to secure Felix Grundy's support for Jackson's Senate bid."[23]

The Williams candidacy proved formidable, and neither John Rhea nor Pleasant Miller could garner the needed votes. Efforts on October 1 to postpone the election until October 3 passed in the senate but failed in the house; under the circumstances, John H. Eaton and William B. Lewis, who were monitoring the election, saw no alternative but to bring Jackson forward as a candidate. The Hero was nominated on October 1, 1823, and elected by a vote of 35–25. Unfortunately, there is no breakdown of member voting in the house journal or press reports and no other evidence beyond Darby's assertion as to whether Grundy supported Jackson over Williams. After 1823, however, Grundy was publicly a Jackson man.[24]

The relationship between Jackson and Grundy changed over time, and Grundy became one of Jackson's chief lieutenants in the U.S. Senate. Whatever their earlier differences, Jackson mellowed toward Grundy. Grundy, however, made the greater accommodation and was identified as a strong Jacksonian at least by 1827. His allegiance came at a considerable cost, however. Grundy had followed an independent course from his earliest political days, certainly in Kentucky but also during the War of 1812 and in the Tennessee General Assembly from 1819 to 1825. After Jackson won the popular vote for the presidency in 1824, he dominated the Tennessee political scene. A politician was either for or against him. Grundy, who had been nobody's disciple, was now a Jackson lieutenant, and his political positions followed those of the Hero. Of course this choice may have been inevitable, given the explosive force of Jackson on both the national and the local scene. Grundy certainly benefited from national office as a Jacksonian, but he paid the price of the loss of his earlier independence and political fearlessness.

18

ELECTION TO THE SENATE

He has been so long accustomed to manageing men and has so deep a
knowledge of the human character that I scarcely know a man who would
make a better counsellor than Grundy.

—James Campbell

*A*fter stepping down from the legislature, Grundy devoted the next
several years to private pursuits. He chose not to run for Congress in
1825, to Sam Houston's relief, but did run in 1827 with Andrew Jackson's support, unexpectedly losing to John Bell. When he was elected to the U.S. Senate
in 1829, Grundy began a tenure of service at the national level that only ended
with his death in 1840.

As discussed earlier, the Panic of 1819 and its aftermath did not leave Grundy
unscathed, although the precise effects are hard to measure. He did not transfer an unusual number of his lots in Nashville in the early 1820s, but he did dispose of land elsewhere, selling 945 acres from June 1819 to 1822. More significantly, Grundy confronted a major financial problem that was only resolved in
the U.S. Supreme Court: his obligation for Mississippi land.[1]

Grundy's purchase in 1818 of 950 acres in Mississippi for twenty thousand
dollars included the provision that he pay two thousand dollars up front, followed by yearly installments of two thousand. When he did not pay installments due in January 1820 and 1821, executors of the seller successfully sued
Grundy for the two installments with interest. On August 30, 1823, Grundy
brought suit in Tennessee to enjoin enforcement of the judgment and rescission of the contract on the grounds of fraud and misrepresentation. Among
other things, Grundy charged that 265 acres were subject to significant flood-
ing, despite the seller's assertions otherwise. The circuit court decided in Grundy's favor in 1826. The case was appealed to the U.S. Supreme Court, which
then rendered two decisions on this private matter while Grundy was a sitting
U.S. senator. In *Boyce's Executors v. Grundy,* 28 U.S. 210 (1830), the Court, in an
opinion written by Justice William Johnson, affirmed the judgment in Grun-

dy's favor and, interestingly, praised Randal McGavock as a witness. Among other things, the Court dismissed the charge that Grundy was tardy and inconsistent in raising the issue of misrepresentation. Subsequently, the Court, through Justice Joseph Story, reviewed the Circuit Court's adjudication of Grundy's recovery of damages and interest, with Francis Scott Key representing Grundy.[2]

The charge that Grundy was tardy in bringing his misrepresentation claim reflects a recurrent theme in his financial dealings, negligence or inattention to details. For whatever reason, Grundy did not keep good financial records. In the Greenville Springs project in Harrodsburg, documents were not recorded, and partners complained that the busy Grundy did not even sign basic agreements. A more serious problem emerged in his dealings with Henry Clay.

The long relationship and close collaboration in the War of 1812 between Grundy and Clay had led Clay from time to time to refer legal and collection matters in Tennessee to his former colleague. In 1813 Clay, who was the executor for the estate of his father-in-law, Thomas Hart, asked Grundy to assist in the collection of two notes totaling $4,000 to $5,000. Grundy agreed, but extraordinarily, he did not send Clay an accounting until January 13, 1827—fourteen years later—and then only after Clay's son-in-law James Erwin brought pressure. Erwin, the son of Andrew Erwin, was preparing to file suit against Grundy on Clay's behalf. According to Erwin, Grundy had offered his twelve-month note for such a balance as might be claimed. After Erwin claimed a large balance, Grundy "wonderfully" recalled that he had collected and sent to Clay the "largest part" of the amount due, even though he had no receipts or records. Erwin wrote that Grundy, without ready cash, only sought to gain time and that one should give little weight to Grundy's statements relating to his financial affairs.[3]

Grundy's own letter to Clay is a curious mixture of defensiveness and bravado. Written with the help of his son-in-law Jacob McGavock, the letter purports to explain what had happened more than a decade earlier with respect to the notes and came up with a balance due of only $174. Grundy assured Clay that the matter "has given me more uneasiness than any pecuniary matter of my whole life." Clay appears to have handled the matter with his usual grace, advising his son-in-law to let the matter rest and that he would effect a final adjustment when Grundy came to Washington in the fall of 1827. We know nothing of the settlement, except that it came just as political lines further separated the two. As Clay became even more the leader of anti-Jackson forces, the shared experiences of the past receded. Clay's references to Grundy after this period are far fewer and less friendly.[4]

Grundy continued to practice law, in which he was much more successful than in keeping financial records. Indeed, his legal career reached its peak in this period, and he reduced his courtroom commitments only when he joined the Senate in 1829. One case in Illinois in 1825 epitomized Grundy's success as a criminal advocate and led one observer, Joseph Gillespie, later a distinguished judge, to write more than fifty years later of his stirring performance.[5]

The trial of Palemon Winchester, a young lawyer, packed the courtroom in Edwardsville, a small town largely populated by newcomers from southern states. Winchester, the nephew of General James Winchester, Grundy's friend and erstwhile opponent in 1811, was accused of murdering Daniel H. "Rarefied" Smith, the recorder of Pike County and a deft caricaturist and wit. Winchester and Smith had quarreled over some of Smith's drawings, and according to two prospective witnesses, Winchester had approached Smith with a knife in his hand. Spectators in the courtroom anticipated high drama, with a talented prosecution team opposed by Grundy and Henry Starr. Grundy's fame already rested on his mastery of the spoken word—in public speeches as well as in the courtroom. The *Vandalia (IL) Intelligencer* reported that "curiosity was on tiptoe, and every ear was open to hear the big gun, . . . we all expected an intellectual feast, and we were not disappointed."[6]

An admiring observer noted that Grundy's mastery was manifest throughout the trial. In jury selection he sought and obtained a jury composed entirely of Tennesseans. His confidence was such that he accepted a juror born and raised in Tennessee who had already formed the opinion that Winchester was guilty. Grundy arranged for Winchester's wife, children, and other relatives to attend the trial and sit by the defendant. He also asked his old friend Governor Ninian Edwards to be seated at the front of the court.[7]

The trial lasted three days. The prosecutor, Benjamin Mills, pronounced the defendant's case to be so desperate that he had brought one of the most eminent lawyers in the United States all the way from Nashville. Warming to his task, Mills noted that Grundy had ridden to Edwardsville, a distance of four or five hundred miles, on horseback in mid-March, when his horse would sink to its knees in mud almost every step of the way. A man of Grundy's abilities and age would not have been willing to endure such a hardship if he was not being paid a large fee.

Grundy's defense of Winchester turned the tables on the prosecutor's claims. He said first that Mills's statement was what one might expect from "cold-blooded Yankees," who looked upon money as the motivation for human action. He had initially refused to go to Edwardsville to defend Winchester, even though his children and General Winchester's had played together and attended the same school. But his little flaxen-haired daughter Malvina had thrown her arms around his neck and said, "Pa, you must go." Judge Gillespie remembered, "As he said this, Mr. Grundy burst into tears and boo-hooed aloud, while his whole band of company and criers and weepers blubbered aloud which communicated to the jury, all of whom cried. And in truth and in fact, there was hardly a dry eye in the courtroom." Grundy then apologized for his emotional outburst and said that "from a consideration of feeling, of duty and affection, I was induced to come here to defend this case—the son of my old friend and this is why I am here now. No money could have induced me to come." Grundy later demolished the credibility of the two witnesses by showing that they had been drunk and incapable of perceiving what took place when Smith died. But his opening remarks had set the stage. The jury acquitted Winchester in less than twenty minutes.[8]

Grundy's reputation led not only to travel to distant courts but also to unusual trials. A troubling case took place in Triana, Alabama, some time in the late 1820s. A young man had left the village, gun on shoulder, to hunt partridge. He had raised his gun as a man on horseback passed by and killed the traveler. Accused of murder, the hunter claimed that he had shot at a hawk. The young man and the victim had never met, and the prosecution could not present a motive. The trial featured "wondrous powers" by Grundy and acquittal of the hunter, although many believed that a "reckless" young man had indulged in a "foolish" experiment.[9]

Grundy lost an early bulwark in 1824, when his mother died in Washington County, Kentucky, at age ninety-one. Elizabeth Burkham Grundy had signed her will by mark on March 1, 1818, and amended it by codicil on April 1, 1823; both the will and the codicil were in Felix's handwriting. The will was proved in Springfield on June 14, 1824. She bequeathed thirteen slaves to various children and grandchildren and directed that the remainder be sold at public auction, with the important proviso that only her surviving children could be purchasers.[10]

Happier events occurred, for Felix and Nancy Grundy enjoyed a new stage of life, marked by marriages and grandchildren. Their oldest daughter, Louisa, and her husband, Jacob McGavock, lived nearby on Cherry Street, now Fourth Avenue, and Jacob was well on his way to becoming one of Tennessee's wealthiest citizens. Jacob McGavock's assistance in the collection matter for Henry Clay reflected the deepening business and personal relationship Grundy enjoyed with McGavock and, later, with another son-in-law, John M. Bass. The deaths of three McGavock grandchildren did not mitigate the joy Felix and Nancy felt on the births of Anne, born April 2, 1820, Randal William, born August 10, 1826, and Edward Jacob, born December 17, 1828, as well as seven more to come. Their daughter Eliza Mayson too had several children, including Frances, born in 1821, and Felix Grundy Mayson.[11]

Moreover, even as grandchildren arrived, the Grundys still had children at home. Felicia Ann, their youngest child, born June 26, 1820, was not as old as her niece Ann McGavock. Malvina Grundy, a student at the Nashville Female Academy, in 1825, at age fifteen, welcomed General Lafayette to the academy on behalf of the hundred-plus students. More marriages also took place. Accounts of Nashville after Grundy moved there in 1808 emphasize that the Grundy house was a social center, with young merchants and students drawn to Grundy's seven attractive daughters. Four of Grundy's daughters wed in their teens, and the other three before they reached twenty-three. The third daughter to marry, Margaret, married Doctor Edward G. Rawlings on October 24, 1822. On May 12, 1825, John Rodgers Grundy, who had opened a law partnership in Nashville with James Collingsworth, married Jane Eliza Caswell in Spring Hill, Tennessee, thirty miles south of Nashville. The young couple soon presented the first grandchild to bear the Grundy name, Mary Eliza, born on September 1, 1826, in Spring Hill.[12]

Notwithstanding a busy law practice, a burgeoning family, and various investment and civic pursuits, Grundy's interest in politics never waned. In 1824 he counseled James K. Polk in his decision to run for Congress, which was justified when Polk defeated Andrew Erwin and other candidates in the Sixth Congressional District in 1825. Grundy may have been interested in running for Congress himself at the time. Sam Houston, a military leader who had been elected to Congress in 1823, expressed concern in June 1825 that the busy lawyer might run against him, but Grundy did not enter the race, and Houston won reelection handily.[13]

Grundy had been involved politically in other ways. Thomas Yeatman, a son-in-law of Andrew Erwin's, had initiated a private bank, issuing notes without a state charter. To combat that, Jackson's supporters in 1825 unsuccessfully proposed a bill to outlaw private banking, with John P. Erwin writing that Grundy had some role in the effort. Erwin also reported to Henry Clay that he had found a friendly purchaser for the Erwin newspaper, since the then owner was about to sell the paper through the machinations of Grundy and others. Grundy also increasingly accepted positions in which he worked in cooperation with Jackson. When General Lafayette visited Nashville in May 1825, as part of his countrywide tour, Jackson served as president of the welcoming committee, and Grundy was one of the four vice presidents. On July 4, 1826, after a state militia review, Grundy read the Declaration of Independence to the assembled throng and paid tribute to Nashville's founders. Following the deaths of former presidents John Adams and Thomas Jefferson on July 4, 1826, Jackson and Grundy participated on a committee to recognize their accomplishments, and Grundy gave the eulogy in their honor on August 3, 1826.[14]

Grundy decided to run for Congress in 1827 against this background of increasing public identification with Jackson. Governor William Carroll advised Henry Clay on November 25, 1825, that his old friend had decided to run for Congress and should be successful. On January 28, 1826, Grundy himself let Clay know that he intended to run. Houston worried about a Grundy candidacy, writing on May 27, 1826, apparently in response to a letter from Grundy about a congressional run:

> He is the only man in the state of Tennessee, who has talent enough to embarrass me in this way. He has great peculiarity of talents which enable him to make tools of the veriest wretches that walk the earth—They are men, as timid as hares, ferocious as wolves, and servile as spaniels. . . . They even growl at their master, when he has no whip in his hand—but when they see or feel the lash they are ready to lick the hand that has inflicted stripes. Tis thus that Grundy assails me! Tis by the use of such wretches that he seeks to accomplish his ends.

Houston's letter charges that Grundy is a "rancorous (tho secret) enemy" of John H. Eaton's. The letter is overwrought—"My destruction is only necessary to the wicked—the virtuous love me"—and was probably written under the influence of alcohol, but it illuminates the prevailing perception of Grundy's political influence.[15]

Grundy soon had his chance. Houston announced in 1826 that he would run for governor in 1827, and Grundy made known his candidacy for Houston's seat. The conditions that prompted his resignation from Congress in 1814 no longer existed. Although Nancy Grundy's health remained delicate, she had recovered from the serious illness that had afflicted her in 1813–14. Most of their children were grown. In addition, the steamboat had transformed travel to Washington. Instead of traveling by horse or stage for almost eight hundred miles, a journey that took four or five weeks, Grundy could now travel to Louisville on improved roads, board a steamboat to Pittsburgh, and then take the National Road to the District of Columbia. Even the overland route was quicker now. In 1830 Grundy wrote that he had arrived "at home in eleven days and a half from Washington traveling in the Mail Stage the whole way."[16]

Grundy's opponent for Congress, the Nashville lawyer John Bell (1796–1869), had studied under Priestley at Cumberland College and practiced law in both Franklin and Murfreesboro before moving to Davidson County in 1822. Bell, a committed Jacksonian, announced his candidacy on August 26, 1826. Grundy made clear his own identification with Jackson. In a circular in October 1826 he denounced the action of the U.S. House of Representatives in electing Adams in 1825, called for a constitutional amendment that would prevent a presidential decision in the House, trumpeted his own role in nominating Jackson for the presidency, assailed the Adams administration for excessive pomp and circumstance, and lauded Jackson for his republican principles and his frugality in governmental expenditures.[17]

Grundy ran on the slogan "Jackson and Grundy" in a spirited election. Although the Erwin faction's paper, the *National Banner and Nashville Whig*, initially praised both candidates and wrote that Grundy was "well suited, by his political experience and great ability as a public speaker, to take a leading part in the councils of the nation," it supported Bell. Jackson, however, left no doubt of his preference for Grundy. As late as July 30, 1827, Jackson wrote John Coffee that he expected Grundy to win a close election. Carroll, supporting Bell, thought otherwise, concluding in May that Bell would prevail unless Jackson's influence was greater than anticipated. Carroll also advised Clay that Calhoun, Samuel Ingham, and other supporters had written Grundy that it was important for Jackson's cause in 1828 that Grundy be elected. Carroll added that the letters had produced little effect and that "Felix finds that nothing short of a Waterloo fight will insure him victory." In the event, Carroll proved a more able prognosticator than Jackson, for Bell won in August 1827 with a margin of more than one thousand votes.[18]

Grundy, of course, continued to practice law throughout this period. His participation in two murder trials in the same week in the circuit court in Nashville in late November 1826 demonstrated his versatility. In the first, Burrell Cornwall, drunk, killed Owen Hughes with a dirk, the defense claiming verbal provocation by Hughes. In the second, George Nelson shot and killed William Brown, the defense counsel arguing that Brown, drunk, had violently thrown stones at Nelson's house and thus given Nelson the right of self-defense. Despite the similarities in these two cases, the results diverged. In the first case the defendant was found guilty of murder and hanged. In the second case, however, the jury brought in a verdict only of manslaughter. Grundy succeeded in both cases, as the prosecutor of Cornwall and as the defense counsel for Nelson. A notable aspect of the Nelson case is that the arresting officer cautioned Nelson to say nothing until he could obtain the benefits of legal counsel. This respect for the rights of the defendant anticipated the U.S. Supreme Court in *Miranda v. Arizona,* 384 U.S. 436 (1966), which upheld a defendant's right to counsel prior to police questioning.[19]

In March 1827 the week-long trial of A. F. Keeble for murder in the circuit court of Rutherford County showcased Grundy's use of character witnesses. A five-man prosecution team led by the attorney general, Samuel Laughlin, opposed six defense counsel, including Grundy and his son John Rodgers. The state brought forth nineteen witnesses, but Grundy produced thirty-two in rebuttal. He then presented fifty-five witnesses as part of the defense case, against thirteen for the prosecution. We do not know the details of the case, but the verdict was predictable: not guilty of murder but guilty of manslaughter. In a Maury County case, Grundy and James K. Polk defended Edwin Mitchell, a seventeen-year-old on trial for murder. The jury entered a finding of manslaughter but, along with the grand jury and various citizens, petitioned the governor for an executive pardon for Mitchell.[20]

Life otherwise rushed on for Grundy. He played an active role at Cumberland College, now known as the University of Nashville, and became a close adviser to its president, Phillip Lindsley. Somewhat fewer than one hundred students paid $150 each for "board, tuition, room rent, servants, wages, library and firewood" annually and benefited from instruction from President Lindsley and five professors and a library of two thousand volumes. The board of trustees, no longer the small band of Grundy and four others, was made up of twenty-three civic leaders, including Jackson, Carroll, and Houston, as well as Grundy.[21]

Upon his return from a trip in 1828, Grundy received a surprising answer when he asked a Nashvillian whether anything notable had occurred while he was gone. Not recognizing him, the man responded, "Not too much, except that Judge Grundy's daughter had run away and gotten married." As it was told some years later,

> One of the most prominent men in Nashville had a very beautiful daughter about fifteen years old. A young man from Louisiana came here . . . to go to

school, and fell very much in love with this young lady. . . . The young lady
went to the Nashville Academy and she used to meet the young man nearly
every day on her way from school. She . . . wrote a note to the young man
and told him to come to . . . [a] party prepared to run away and marry her.
. . . There were four inches of snow on the ground. . . . The young lady left the
party and met him.

They married in Winchester. There are variants of the story, but the romantic
tale is true enough. Martha Ann Grundy married Van Perkins Winder on December 7, 1828, when she was sixteen and he was nineteen and a student at the
University of Nashville. Winder, from a prominent Maryland family, became a
successful sugar planter in Louisiana.[22]

Two other children married during the same period. James Priestley, a lawyer and captain in the Nashville Guards as early as October 1827, exchanged
vows with Eliza Hogg, daughter of Major John Hogg, of Trenton, Tennessee,
on May 13, 1828. On January 7, 1829, just a month after Martha's elopement,
Malvina Grundy, aged eighteen, wed the lawyer John Meredith Bass, son of
Peter Bass and destined to be one of Nashville's outstanding leaders. Thus by
early 1829, when Felix was fifty-three and Nancy was forty-nine, the Grundys
had only two daughters at home, thirteen-year-old Maria and eight-year-old Felicia, but seven married children and numerous grandchildren.[23]

After Grundy's defeat in his run for Congress in 1827, Grundy quietly advised Jackson from time to time, participated in political events, wrote pro-
Jackson documents, and helped Jackson rebut charges in the national press.
Overton, White, Eaton, and Lewis formed the innermost circle of Jackson advisers, but Grundy, along with Sam Houston and George W. Campbell, was
considered close to the potential president. The Nashville Central Committee,
which supported Jackson's campaign as early as April 1827, included Grundy
and a large number of Middle Tennesseans.[24]

The 1828 presidential campaign proved to be one of the most bitter in American history. Martin Van Buren and John C. Calhoun joined forces to support
Jackson in the Democratic Republican Party. Jackson and his Democrats, as
we will call the Democratic Republicans, adhered to the traditional verities—
states' rights, agrarian values, minimum government, and retirement of the national debt. The National Republicans, represented by John Quincy Adams in
his reelection bid but increasingly identified with Henry Clay and his American System, supported internal improvements, tariffs, and encouragement of
commercial and manufacturing activity. When the votes were counted, Jack-

son's campaign against the corrupt bargain of 1824 gave him a decisive victory in the Electoral College, 178–83. In the popular vote, Jackson had 647,276 votes, and Adams, 508,064, the largest number voting in the presidential election to that time. The campaign, however, left a bitter residue. The vitriol hurled against Jackson and his wife, Rachel, deeply wounded him; it helped trigger her death before the inauguration and provided a poisoned and partisan backdrop for Jackson's presidency.

Following the election, Grundy wrote Jackson a prescient letter on November 20, 1828. He advised the president-elect that William H. Crawford had written that Georgia could not support either Jackson's vice-presidential candidate, John C. Calhoun, or Adams's candidate and wanted the Electoral College to consider a Georgian favorite son. Grundy intended to reply that Tennessee electors were pledged to Calhoun. More significantly, he forecast dissension among the Democrats and suggested that the only solution would be a second term for Jackson.[25]

Grundy, in Nashville, missed much of the turmoil that both preceded and followed the inauguration on March 4, 1829. He missed the furor over Jackson's first cabinet, which was generally dismissed as lacking in stature. There is no direct evidence that he was involved in the president's choice between the Tennessee senators John H. Eaton and Hugh Lawson White for the coveted post of secretary of war. The opposition press charged in 1832–33, however, that Grundy had successfully pushed Eaton for the position so that he could run for the traditionally West Tennessee Senate seat held by Eaton.

Grundy also missed the beginning of what has been called the Petticoat Affair. Official Washington divided in two camps over Margaret O'Neale Timberlake Eaton, the saucy new wife of John H. Eaton, whose alleged easy morality in the past had caused much of official Washington to snub her. On one side lined up most of formal society, including Floride, the wife of Vice President John C. Calhoun, Emily, the wife of Jackson's ward and personal secretary, Andrew Donelson, and Sarah, the wife of James K. Polk. On the other side, supporters of Peggy Eaton included Jackson, reminded of the attacks on his beloved Rachel, Postmaster General William Barry, and the widower Martin Van Buren. Congress did not return to Washington until December 1829, so much of the initial battle of the wagging heads took place among the diplomats, the cabinet, and the permanent social set of Washington. It is too easy to view this with amusement, for from this affair flowed public distress at the spectacle, personalized government, and an increasingly bitter succession struggle between Calhoun and Van Buren.

Eaton's selection as secretary of war had significant consequences in Tennessee. A new senator would have to be chosen. In addition, a gubernatorial election would occur in 1829. As a result, Jackson confronted delicate problems. William Carroll had long been at odds with the president, and Jacksonians feared the formation of an opposition party supportive of Clay and headed by Carroll. Carroll wanted to be governor again, but the incumbent, Sam Houston, wished to retain the post. Carroll needed to be satisfied, and some Jackson advisers suggested that the defeated candidate for governor should be sent to Eaton's Senate seat, which most believed Jackson wanted for Grundy. Then, to widespread shock and consternation, Houston separated from his wife, resigned as governor, and left Tennessee. With this change, Carroll successfully ran for governor in 1829.[26]

Eaton's seat open, Jackson wrote Grundy in the spring of 1829 asking him to run for the Senate. On May 22, 1829, Grundy wrote the president that he would come to the Senate if he could and believed that he had more strength than any possible opponent. Yet William E. Anderson, previously Grundy's law partner and now on the bench, "your friend and mine who is the very last man, I should have expected to oppose me—has been prevailed on to be a Candidate." Grundy surmised that Anderson, a former resident of East Tennessee, would receive nearly unanimous support in that section if Judge White supported him, and Pleasant Miller, now resident in Jackson, would do what he could for Anderson in western Tennessee. John Overton, worried about discord among Jackson partisans, thought Anderson would win, even though Grundy would have the support of Jackson, who had "made it known to Grundy long since that he wished him on the floor of Congress." Overton reported that he favored Grundy, as did the cautious Carroll.[27]

The subsequent Senate contest of 1829 has not been assessed in depth, in part because of the paucity of contemporaneous correspondence. Important questions remain unanswered, including why William L. Brown, from the small Nashville legal world, subsequently chose to enter the race against Anderson and Grundy. Yet the available evidence suggests that this election prefigured important issues of the Jackson presidency, including new alignments among Jacksonians in Tennessee, the battle against the Second Bank of the United States, and the succession struggle between Van Buren and Calhoun.

Tennessee's political alignments were shifting, particularly among nominal Jacksonians. Banking issues again played a critical role. When Tennessee banks collapsed in 1826 and 1827, after being forced to resume specie payments, Nashville businessmen launched an effort to obtain a Nashville branch of the Second Bank of the United States. With the support of Overton's newspaper, the *Nashville Republican,* and over Jackson's opposition, they persuaded the legislature to repeal the fifty-thousand-dollar tax on foreign banks imposed a decade earlier to block a similar initiative led by Grundy and Carroll. Upon petition by Carroll and others, the Second Bank did form a branch in Nashville, and John Overton became a director. The opening of the branch and the extension of credit that followed had significant repercussions. Increasingly Overton and his allies, particularly William B. Lewis, worked with the Erwin-Carroll faction, many members of which had joined Grundy and Carroll in petitioning for a branch bank in 1817.[28]

Personal ill will and jealousy exacerbated tensions among Jacksonians. The Blount-Overton group increasingly fell under the control of John Eaton and William Lewis, both of whom were close to Jackson and perceived as using their influence in the White House for personal advantage. Hugh L. White, who had been outmaneuvered by Eaton for the position of secretary of war, joined Pleasant Miller and others in opposing Jackson's cabinet appointees. White wrote Overton that other Jackson friends "feel hurt, that a limited number and those not all of the first order of men, should have his confidence exclusively." Succession issues also played a role. Lewis disliked Calhoun and supported Van Buren in various ways, a course not likely to be favored by Grundy, White, Polk, and Calhoun adherents. In addition, in the Petticoat Affair, Andrew Donelson and James K. Polk, among others, were opposed to Peggy Eaton and linked to Calhoun. These various differences ultimately led to a split among prominent Jacksonians, with Senators Grundy and White, Congressmen James K. Polk and Cave Johnson, and Jackson's secretary and nephew, Andrew Donelson, forming a new faction in opposition to Overton, Eaton, and Lewis.[29]

In the midst of these crosscurrents, Jackson wanted Grundy in the Senate to help deal with banking questions. In the spring of 1829 the president was searching for the proper approach to the Second Bank. In May he asked Grundy for his views on a new national bank, to which Grundy replied with compliments on the project and the promise of a full presentation later. Shortly thereafter, in June and July 1829, Judge John Catron, of the Tennessee Supreme Court, in a series of newspaper articles decried the ongoing credit expansion and declared that the Second Bank's charter should not be renewed. If there were to be a national bank, it should be under governmental control, with branches and directors established by state legislatures. As a result of the widespread criticism of the bank, the legislature that summer instructed its two senators to vote against rechartering the Second Bank of the United States.[30]

Jackson emphasized Grundy's potential banking role in a letter to Overton on June 8. After expressing regret that his friends Grundy and Anderson were both running for the Senate, the president gave his own assessment of Grundy: "They are both enlightened men but Grundys knowledge of men, would make him better adapted to the atmosphere of Washington than Judge Anderson for a while, and he would be better calculated to aid Judge White and myself in the change of the present incorporated Bank to that of a National Bank— This being the only way, that a re-charter to the present U.S. Bank, can be prevented." Jackson added that he intended to write Senator H. L. White about the importance of keeping Anderson on the bench. White himself later noted that Jackson had wanted to destroy private banks and then establish a U.S. bank based on government funds and that in 1829 he had wanted Grundy in the Senate so that Grundy could assist in the creation of such a bank.[31]

Jackson's opposition to banks deeply troubled or antagonized many nominal supporters, particularly merchants and businessmen in Nashville and other commercial centers. Just as anti-Jacksonians were united principally by their hostility to the president, Jackson supporters represented a wide spectrum of interests and were linked by ambition or by their personal relationships with the Hero. Jackson's election had changed the political dynamics within the state. A national administration meant less presidential involvement in Tennessee politics, jockeying for patronage plums, and negative reaction by some Tennesseans to national policies. Inevitably, too, Jackson supporters began looking beyond his presidency, and groups began to form in favor of potential successors.

Particularly evident, at least according to one politician, was the formation of a group of Van Buren supporters. In a detailed analysis of the 1829 election the Winchester lawyer James Campbell concluded that many nominal Democrats, as well as a "majority of the Williams party," had decided to support Martin Van Buren as Jackson's successor and maintained a regular correspondence with him. Some favored only a four-year term for Jackson. Even assuming some inaccuracies in Campbell's alignments, his overall thesis is suggestive. The Petticoat Affair in Washington had already exacerbated differences between Vice President Calhoun and Secretary of State Van Buren, and some key Jacksonians, such as Eaton and Lewis, appeared committed to the New Yorker. James Hamilton, Alexander's son and a close aide to Van Buren, had visited Nashville in December 1827, meeting with party leaders and numerous Nashvillians; William Carroll and Alfred Balch had identified themselves as partisans of the secretary of state. Van Buren too apparently favored more commercially supportive policies than Calhoun, and his supporters, as identified by Campbell, came from Nashville and Knoxville, not smaller towns and rural areas. When Grundy, linked with Calhoun by friendship and his wife's cousinage with the South Carolinian, urged Jackson on November 20, 1828, to consider a second term to avoid party dissension, he almost certainly had Tennessee as well as national developments in mind.[32]

Grundy thus entered the Senate contest in 1829 against a backdrop of emerging division. Critically, he enjoyed Jackson's support, but he faced a foe with strong support in East Tennessee, as well as another West Tennessee candidate, William L. Brown, who allegedly had Van Buren ties. This election, the first in which Grundy sought statewide office, required that Grundy change his electoral approach. A state contest worked to Grundy's advantage. Senators were chosen by majority vote in a joint session of the two branches of the state legislature, and Grundy had been the unquestioned master in state politics from 1819 to 1825. At the state level, politicians knew each other well, and Grundy's affability, wit, and capacity for legislative maneuvering gave him a strong following and only a few enemies. Undeniably clever and far-sighted in political thinking, he benefited from his wide range of political friends and acquaintances.

In seeking to build support, Grundy did not let electoral matters take their course. On July 28, 1829, at Carnton, Randal McGavock's home in Franklin, he wrote Tennessee's secretary of state, Daniel Graham, that for twenty years he had not enjoyed life as much as at present: "About six days hence I turned my feet out to grass literally. I have not had sock or shoe on since." Nevertheless, during this rare vacation he asked Graham to advise him in detail about successful candidates in any county. He wished to keep the matter confidential and in a revealing and almost self-evident conclusion added, "I will keep secrets well." In addition, Grundy wrote friends requesting that they inform legislators unknown to him of his qualifications, and he and his supporters tracked likely votes of legislators.[33]

White's election views could be determinative, since many East Tennesseans would follow his lead. On June 1 Overton urged White to support Grundy, emphasizing that a contest between Anderson and Grundy would distract and divide Jackson's friends and that the president "stands politically in a relation to G. that he cannot say a word against him." He further asked White to recall "when Houston was our Representative in Congress; he wanted talents; Grundy was selected to take his place, for it was found H. would not do . . . Bell beat Grundy. Since then Bell has acted well, but that but rarely happens. . . . But rest assured that he is not a man who can be relied upon, when the battle wages warm and is doubtful." Although White, upset with Jackson, held himself aloof from the contest, Grundy received votes in the east. In particular, Grundy's ties to the Cocke family benefited him. General Cocke, whose father had been defended by Grundy in the impeachment trial in 1812, persuaded at least some fellow East Tennesseans to support Grundy.[34]

The election in the legislature on October 16, 1829, resulted in Grundy's victory on the second ballot. He received 27 votes on the first ballot against 18 for Anderson and 14 for Brown. On the second ballot, Grundy received 31 votes against Anderson's 17 and Brown's 12. Grundy reported to Jackson that there was "no contest, I was the second choice of both Andersons and Browns friends, so that I could have obtained two votes to one against either." James Campbell had no doubt that the election had rested on succession issues. He concluded that the Van Buren group, including both anti- and pro-Jacksonians, had gone full tilt against Grundy. Supporting him were a large majority of the old friends of General Jackson who had no firm succession perspective and followed the president's lead. Campbell believed the legislature made the right choice: "Grundy is unquestionably the safest adviser General J could have from this state. His temperament is so different from the Genl's and his mode of attaining his objects also, he has been so long accustomed to manageing men and has so deep a knowledge of the human character that I scarcely know a man who would make a better counsellor than Grundy."[35]

In celebration of her father's election, Louisa McGavock put on a lavish party for legislators. Writing almost sixty years later, a social historian reported that the supper excelled anything she had ever seen in Nashville. A French confectioner from New Orleans prepared the meal, and the decorations included vases of beautiful artificial flowers, with a glass globe over each vase, and silver candlesticks everywhere. A large pyramid at least three feet high and made of jelly stood at the center of the long table that traversed two rooms. This reflection of the growing wealth and social maturity of Nashville provided quite a send-off for the new senator.[36]

Grundy and his supporters celebrated, but he soon turned to his new job. The future of the Second Bank of the United States loomed large. On October 22 Grundy responded to Jackson's request in May for thoughts on a new national bank. He suggested a national bank headquartered in Philadelphia with branches in each state and half of the capital to be turned over to the states for their exclusive use. Congress, not the executive, would appoint the directors of the central bank, and each state's congressional delegation would choose the directors of the state bank. This convoluted plan reflects Grundy's fear of centralized authority, in particular his fear that the executive branch might become too powerful. Grundy's proposal, presented three months after John Catron set forth his banking views, followed Catron in most respects, but instead of giving power to the state legislature, Grundy proposed relying on congressional delegations.[37]

After writing to Jackson, Grundy set out for Washington via Richmond and Norfolk. There is a suggestion, but no firm evidence, that while Grundy was in Richmond to attend the Virginia Convention in November 1829, he met with Martin Van Buren and others to discuss the Second Bank. At any rate, the future of the Second Bank would be among his concerns as he embarked on a new phase of his career.[38]

19

JACKSONIAN SENATOR

He has a mind happily tempered for political warfare.
—*The Knickerbocker*

In December 1829 Washington looked much the same as when Grundy had left it fifteen years earlier. The population of the District of Columbia had grown to eighteen thousand, but the city had the same raw, unfinished look. The White House and other buildings burned by the British had been rebuilt or largely replaced, but the Capitol's half-completed state symbolized the city. Fields and open spaces separated the scattered clusters of buildings. One visitor in 1835 wrote that to make social calls in the city, "we had to cross ditches and stiles and walk alternately on grass and pavements and strike across a field to reach a street." Most inhabitants still used horses or carriages even for short trips. Pennsylvania Avenue would be the first thoroughfare paved, in 1830, and badly at that. Visitors expressed surprise at the city's squalor, with Harriet Martineau writing that while the Capitol was splendid, the surroundings were sordid. Liquor stores abounded, as did beggars and prostitutes.[1]

The placid scene of 1812, however, had given way to an active social life. The number of permanent residents had reached a critical mass. Wives now increasingly accompanied their husbands to Washington for legislative sessions, as Nancy Grundy did for her husband's first Senate term. Shortly after they arrived in Washington, the Grundys presumably joined Jackson, Calhoun, and "about 300 gentlemen and 200 ladies" on January 8, 1830, for a ball at Carusi's Saloon, a theater purchased by a dancing master and converted to a ballroom. In the middle of cotillions and reels a small group of "chiefly foreigners" introduced the waltz, whose "motions and positions seemed rather amorous as was fully testified by the reluctance which most of the fashionables evinced in participating in it."[2]

In determining whether to accept a new dance, southerners took the lead, for Washington was a southern town. Harriet Martineau thought that the ease and frank courtesy of the southern gentry contrasted favorably with the somewhat gauche and deferential air of northern members. Jackson set the tone, and despite initial reservations, the Washington social set applauded his charm. John Tyler poked fun at Jackson's critics, writing that there was now less mock majesty at the White House, that his reception by the president had been kind and hospitable, and that "could *you old fashioned Virginians believe it,* [Jackson] . . . even went so far to *introduce his guests to each other,* a thing without precedent here *and most abominably unfashionable."* England's Martineau was taken aback, however, when she attended a White House reception at which, other than her party, all the guests were members of Congress whose last names began with the letters *J, K,* and *L.*[3]

Grundy had also changed since 1814. He was now fifty-four years old, graying, and no longer slender. He needed reading glasses. Yet even casual observers commented on his good humor and his speaking ability. A lithograph by William Brown a few years later shows a fashionably dressed and well-groomed Grundy, at ease in his position.[4]

The Knickerbocker's Washington correspondent gave a relatively complete picture: "Felix Grundy is a happy man. There is not a more jovial, benevolent face in Christendom. . . . His head is now all gray, and his step begins to falter . . . but his mind has lost nothing of its vigor, and he none of his humour. He is happy at a retort, skilful at a thrust, and good humoured even in the angriest debate. He has a mind happily tempered for political warfare." Contemporary political figures also left their impressions. A protégé and admirer of Daniel Webster's described Grundy as a persuasive speaker of imposing presence and conciliatory manner.[5]

If Grundy had changed since 1814, so had Congress. The twenty-four states furnished forty-eight senators. Political gravity now centered on the Senate, not the House, with speeches of the great orators given wide publicity. An English observer found the upper house an imposing assemblage of men exhibiting extraordinary differences. Compared with the nearly year-round legislative sessions of today, Congress did not meet often. It opened the first Monday of every December and remained in session only until March in odd-numbered years and until summer in even-numbered years. Members of both houses received eight dollars per day when in session and eight dollars for every twenty miles of travel to and from Washington. Orators debated great issues, but observers explained the long speeches by the relative lack of weighty matters. The best speakers spoke from outlines, and a member who read a prepared speech would have been hooted down. Both the galleries and the Senate itself applauded extemporaneous debate, sharpened by wit and knowledge of the subject matter.[6]

Grundy felt at home in the Senate when he arrived in 1829. His good friend Vice President John C. Calhoun presided over the upper house. Grundy could not have been closer to the two Kentucky senators, John Rowan, his former schoolmate and perhaps oldest friend, and George Bibb. Thomas Hart Benton, of Missouri, and Hugh Lawson White, the other Tennessee senator, had been colleagues in the tight world of Tennessee politics. Grundy knew both John Holmes, of Maine, and John Forsyth, of Georgia, from their days as fellow Republicans during the War of 1812, and Daniel Webster, of Massachusetts, a Federalist, had been one of Grundy's sparring partners in 1813 and 1814. Grundy, however, enjoyed something more than old friends and acquaintances, being, in the view of some in Congress, "of all the Senate, nearest the President; and the moral prestige of this relation gave a direction, a weight, a conclusion to his words, not rashly to be overlooked."[7]

Regardless of how he was perceived, Grundy never played the dominating role in the Senate that had so marked his activities in the Kentucky and Tennessee legislatures and in the House of Representatives from 1811 to 1814. Contemporary accounts give Grundy greater visibility than do modern writers, but all tend to view him, in the words of an early-twentieth-century historian, as only an "able lawyer, seasoned statesman, resourceful parliamentarian." Grundy was a significant senator, capable and respected, serving as chairman of the Post Office and Judiciary committees during his tenure. He was not, however, a determining figure. This was attributable in part to Grundy's service as a Jackson lieutenant, since all administration senators carried out the president's wishes, with varying degrees of independence; in part to the fact that the great triumvirate of Clay, Calhoun, and Webster dominated the Senate for most of Grundy's tenure, each speaking for a powerful bloc that had to be accommodated; and in part to the fact that Grundy, as a senator from Jackson's own state, had less maneuvering room and less of the independence from Jackson that would have given him more visibility and heft. There is also a sense that Grundy increasingly played a behind-the-scenes role, counting votes and helping shape legislation to facilitate its passage. Van Buren's autobiography refers to Grundy in these terms, and Grundy's letters to confidants in Tennessee suggest the same.[8]

It is perhaps equally important that Grundy and Jackson generally held similar political views. Jackson set out his principles as president in 1830: "The Federal Constitution must be obeyed, States' rights preserved, our national debt

must be paid, direct taxes and loans avoided and the Federal Union preserved."
Grundy shared these objectives and usually could be found in the forefront of
administration supporters.[9]

Jackson has long been identified with office rotation, even though recent historians suggest that his role may not have been as great as trumpeted. Grundy
consistently supported Jackson's appointive efforts, accepting that office was
not an entitlement and expressing little sympathy for those ousted from federal
jobs. In his speech on Foot's Resolution, begun on February 27 and continued
on March 1, 1830, Grundy defended the Jackson administration in a lengthy examination of presidential appointments. Grundy took a tough-minded stance,
referring to the variety of employment opportunities in the country and proclaiming a government employee who could not live without holding office
unfit. In the bitter Senate battles over Jackson's nomination of several newspaper editors to government jobs, Grundy stood in the front ranks. He fought
hard for the nomination of Isaac Hill, the editor of the *New Hampshire Patriot*
and a strong Republican during the War of 1812; he later wrote that except for
Levi Woodbury, no one had exerted himself more for Hill than he had.[10]

Grundy devoted much of his tenure as chairman of the Post Office Committee to the difficult task of justifying actions in a department that offered
opportunities for patronage and government contracts. On April 28, 1830, in a
24–21 vote, the Senate accepted a motion made by Grundy to postpone the ren-
dition of names and offices of those removed, and almost a year later, on February 28, 1831, by an identical vote, it concurred with Grundy that a select committee had no authorization to investigate Post Office removals. Grundy also
led a partially successful effort to defend Postmaster General William T. Barry
against charges with respect to corruption in his department. Barry could not
have been totally pleased, however, since Grundy concluded that Barry was an
incompetent administrator, though not personally corrupt. Anticipating the
Hatch Act, Grundy accepted that officeholders had a right to vote but argued
that they should be dismissed from public employment if they became partisans in elections.[11]

On the removal of eastern Indians across the Mississippi, we know less than
we would like. Grundy left no written record of his feelings about Indians, but
since two of his brothers died at Indian hands and the third in an Indian war,
he probably shared the hostility exhibited by early Kentucky contemporaries.
Did Grundy share Jackson's paternalistic view that removal was the only way to
protect the Indians? Did he even care? States such as Georgia insisted that their

jurisdiction extended over the Indian lands within their borders. If the federal government did not remove the Indians, it would have to protect the Indians from the states, which would be particularly difficult for states' rights–minded Jacksonians. Moreover, most southerners and westerners opposed special enclaves for Indian nations, envisioning Indian assimilation within the American culture and legal system.

The Jacksonians Hugh Lawson White in the Senate and John Bell in the House chaired the committees responsible for Jackson's Indian Removal Act. The bill did not specifically call for transfer of the Indians, but authorized the president to exchange Indian land in the East and the South for public land across the Mississippi, with no forced removals. The bill passed the Senate, 28–19, on April 26, 1830, but encountered major difficulty in the House. House legislators echoed Senate opponents in attacking the bill for its immorality and its violation of Indian rights and anticipated high costs and in attacking Jackson's unwarranted usurpation of executive power. Despite these charges and the fervor with which opponents assailed Jackson, the bill narrowly passed the House. Grundy lined up votes behind the scenes. He wrote Daniel Graham on May 22 that the final vote would be taken the following day and that the Jackson forces were "making a Murfreesboro push" to secure passage, adding that it would take him three days to tell Graham what he could not write. The revised bill was approved by the Senate, and Jackson signed it on May 28, 1830.[12]

The role of the federal government in funding internal improvements aroused intense controversy in the Jacksonian era. Grundy's moderate stance roughly mirrored Jackson's, reflecting a centrist position between southern states' righters, who generally opposed federal improvements, and the National Republicans, who supported Clay's American System. Grundy was no doctrinaire, and years earlier, in 1811, he had objected to federal funding of the Erie Canal because of its sectional favoritism, not because of constitutional scruples. In Tennessee, commercial interests throughout the state and East Tennesseans in general favored internal improvements, and Grundy supported federal aid for some initiatives, including improvements to the Cumberland River.[13]

The Maysville Road vote and veto reflected the battle lines on internal improvements. The Maysville Road was to connect Maysville and Lexington, Kentucky, as part of the great National Road, begun in 1811, and proponents sought federal funding. Apart from federal support for what some perceived as local benefits, the road was to be constructed not only in Henry Clay's state but also to his hometown. On May 15, 1830, the Senate passed the bill by a vote of

24–18. Grundy voted against the bill, as did the Kentucky senator George Bibb. John Rowan, the other Kentucky senator, cast his ballot for the bill, but only pursuant to instructions from the Kentucky legislature.[14]

Jackson vetoed the bill on May 27, 1830, notwithstanding support for the measure by important constituencies and such eminent Jacksonians as Amos Kendall. Jackson expressed concern about the bill's constitutionality, but his principal concern appears to have been that expenditures for the road would keep him from attaining his cherished goal of paying off the national debt. Van Buren, Jackson's confidant on the veto, painted a memorable picture of arriving at the White House the morning of the veto message and finding a disconsolate group made up of Grundy, Eaton, Lewis, and William T. Barry seated at a breakfast table, all fearing the effects of the veto on the Democrats in the western states. This little scene reflects Van Buren's political astuteness and may even have occurred, though it does not square with a contemporaneous account of the veto by Grundy. On May 22, 1830, Grundy wrote to Daniel Graham that the "Tug of real war" would commence the following week, when Jackson presented his veto arguments, which Grundy described as "able, sensible and convincing" and distinguishing between local and national objectives. Grundy could not resist self-praise, adding that the president's message would justify his own course, since it would sanction Grundy's favorable votes on the continuation of the Cumberland Road and the Portland and Ohio Canal, and his opposition to the Maysville Road.[15]

Grundy judged that the veto would not harm Jackson. On July 31 Grundy gave Jackson a detailed review of the regional and state effects of the Maysville veto, concluding that although "your friends may not be numerically increased their attachment is now of a stronger texture." Grundy then returned to his favorite theme, dissension within the Democratic Party, saying that Jackson's enemies were perplexed and placing their hopes on a schism among Jackson's friends.[16]

Office rotation, Indian removal, and internal improvements constituted major political issues, but Jackson's first term is identified by his veto on July 10, 1832, of the bill to recharter the Second Bank of the United States. On the other major issues of Jackson's first term Grundy generally held views similar to those of Jackson, but that is by no means clear with respect to rechartering the Second Bank. Grundy had more experience with banking legislation than most of his colleagues. He had supported a state bank in the battle over the Kentucky Insurance Company in 1805, he had been in the vanguard of those seeking a Nashville branch for the Second Bank of the United States in 1817, and he had been the recipient of Jackson's ire when he successfully pushed for a Tennessee state bank in 1820. In 1814 Grundy expressed his view that a federally established bank would be constitutional, a position affirmed by Chief Justice John Marshall in *McCulloch v. Maryland,* 17 U.S. (4 Wheaton), 316–437, but not fully accepted by Jackson. When many Jefferson Republicans opposed all banks, Grundy took a different view, accepting the importance of credit in an expanding economy but seeking a way to minimize the concentration of economic power in the hands of the few. Grundy also supported state banks, for their profit potential and especially for their local control.

Grundy presumably appreciated the benefits of the Second Bank's operations. Under Nicholas Biddle, its precociously talented but arrogant leader, the bank provided financial stability and credit. It held, without interest, all government deposits but derived its strength through its own notes and control of state bank notes accumulated in the ordinary course of business. (In 1830 the Second Bank issued almost 40 percent of all bank notes in circulation in the country.) A forerunner of the mixed private and public institution of the twentieth century, it benefited from the federal subsidy without significant governmental oversight. Private stockholders owned 80 percent of the bank and controlled the board and management. The government appointed five of the twenty-five directors, but its only real authority was its power over its deposits.[17]

When Biddle, egged on by Clay, Webster, and other bank supporters, decided to push for recharter in 1832, four years before its original charter was to expire, Grundy's position appeared ambiguous. In 1829 the Tennessee legislature had instructed the state's two senators to vote against rechartering the bank, but two years later the junior senator chose to remain silent. The *National Banner and Nashville Whig* reported on October 5, 1831, that Grundy had carefully refused to oppose recharter at a public meeting. After the congressional session opened, Biddle's agent in Washington, Thomas Cadwalader, provided an analysis of likely senatorial reaction to recharter. Relying on input from probank Treasury Secretary Louis McLane and others, he reported on December 21, 1831, that "Grundy would work for us strongly *bye* and *bye,* but now would be contra."[18]

Whether Cadwalader's report in December 1831 accurately reflected Grundy's position or not, the Tennessean had become a pronounced bank opponent by the following summer. The recharter bill passed both houses, but Grundy voted against it in a Senate vote of 28–20 in mid-June. He did not speak in the debates but became an enthusiastic supporter of Jackson's famous bank veto of July 10, 1832. What occasioned Grundy's stance?

One student of recharter believes that as many as sixteen senators who voted against rechartering the bank actually favored the bank and that they supported Jackson on party grounds, just before his reelection bid. Certainly this argument would have resonated with Grundy, a loyal Democrat. But he had other, more pressing considerations. As we shall see, from 1831 until his reelection in 1833 Grundy confronted a senatorial context in which Jackson's views could be decisive. He could join Jackson on this issue at little political cost. In addition, the pro-Jackson forces were splintering, and the Overton group not only generally supported the bank but also backed Grundy's senatorial opponent, John Eaton. By contrast, Hugh Lawson White and James K. Polk, who were strongly linked with Grundy in the other pro-Jackson faction, lined up in opposition to the Second Bank.[19]

Grundy's enthusiasm for the veto, however, went further than political realism or party factionalism. Jackson portrayed the veto—and the bank issue generally—as a struggle against the concentration of privilege and power in the aristocratic few, the heirs of the Federalists. No characterization could have more clearly reflected Grundy's core political principles. Unlike Jackson, he could support state banks in Kentucky and Tennessee because such banks did not have "aristocratic" exclusivity. Like Jackson, he would oppose artificial inequalities of wealth and power generated by privileged treatment. When Jackson led the battle against Nicholas Biddle and a national bank that had, and used, concentrated financial strength, Grundy happily joined the fray.[20]

Not only legislation required Grundy's attention in the Senate. The House had impeached the federal judge James H. Peck, of Missouri, the Senate receiving Peck's submission to trial on May 12, 1830. Grundy, whose retention of detailed notes on his Senate speech suggests the importance attached to this matter, voted with the majority for acquittal; the vote was 22–21. With Senator William Marcy, of New York, he also led the effort to establish a law library in the Library of Congress, which was effected by legislation signed by Jackson on July 14, 1832. Support for the law library afforded a welcome respite from more weighty matters, since Grundy now confronted the consequences of his seeming acceptance of the doctrine of nullification.[21]

20

NULLIFICATION

The Republican Party throughout the nation; may they be as harmonious
in action as they are united in principle.

—Felix Grundy

When Grundy entered the Senate he could have had little inkling
that the issue of nullification would loom so large, fixing the nationalistic character of the Jackson administration, heavily influencing the political
fortunes of various presidential contenders, and jeopardizing his own tenure as
a U.S. senator. Grundy's close friendship with John C. Calhoun would be part
of a difficult political equation.

As most observers noted, Grundy was a careful and cautious politician, particularly astute in judging both people and the ramifications of decisions. He
was also a good-natured man who liked most people, who separated professional from personal relationships, and who characteristically refused to let a
political issue or legal dispute cloud his relationship with another political or
legal warrior. In ordinary times Grundy's political caution and his friendly relations with adversaries went together. But with Andrew Jackson, for whom
politics was personal, there was never an ordinary time. By 1824 Grundy had
been forced to take sides between Henry Clay and Andrew Jackson, and that
bitter enmity inevitably took its toll on Grundy's previously close relationship
with the Kentuckian. Now, beginning in 1830, Grundy confronted a similar
choice between Jackson and Calhoun, with more serious political implications
for him.

John C. Calhoun largely elicited awe from his contemporaries. The Scots-
Irish South Carolinian possessed remarkable gifts of intellect, discipline, and
will that had been enhanced and polished at Yale and Tappan Reeve's law
school in Litchfield, Connecticut. He appeared to be a self-made man of iron,
and his erect, spare frame, his fierce look, and the force of his tightly presented

arguments brooked little dissent. He dominated South Carolina, and even his many opponents accorded him unwilling respect.

This talented man harbored intense ambition. He supported Jackson in 1828, and as vice president he could reasonably be viewed as Jackson's successor. Calhoun, however, had two major problems. First, the general public never warmed to him, accurately perceiving that he lacked the affability and human touch that distinguished politicians like Clay and Grundy. Second, he walked a precarious line between the northern and southern wings of the Democratic Party. States' rights, which was not an issue for most of the country in the 1820s, lurked under the surface. To appear as a more moderate nationalist in the North, Calhoun kept from the public his hardening views on the rights of states.

Political observers assumed that Grundy supported Calhoun as Jackson's successor. In 1828 Grundy had scotched Georgia's plan to substitute another vice-presidential candidate for the South Carolinian, and Grundy had long been known to be a good friend of Calhoun's. Martin Van Buren described Grundy as "quite devoted where he took a liking" and observed that Grundy and Calhoun had formed friendly relations during the War of 1812 that had never been entirely obliterated despite the enmity that arose between Jackson and Calhoun. Grundy barely knew Van Buren in 1830, and, not surprisingly, he initially favored Calhoun over Van Buren in the increasingly evident division over a successor to Jackson.[1]

The nullification controversy surfaced in 1830. Calhoun and Jackson both believed in states' rights, but Calhoun, who had certainly thought longer and harder than Jackson on legal and constitutional questions, quietly propounded nullification. Under the Constitution, a compact among preexisting independent states, the federal government had been given only specific, delegated powers. If the national government legislated in areas not delegated by the states, then the federal law had no effect and indeed was unconstitutional. But this broad generalization brought with it a raft of questions. What specifically were the powers given up by the states and the powers retained by the states? Who made such determinations? the Supreme Court? the states? If a state were to decide, how would the decision be made? by its legislature? by a convention? Most ominously, if a state purportedly concluded that a federal law was unconstitutional, what were the state's remedies? The United States, of course, ultimately answered the question of nullification in the maelstrom of civil war, but its prewar orators and political theorists recognized that the Constitution left fundamental matters unresolved. Jefferson, through his authorship of the drafts of the Kentucky Resolutions in 1798, left no doubt that he believed that a state had a right to declare a federal law null and void, and Madison, the Father of the Constitution, seems to have been of the same persuasion. The South Carolina exposition in 1828, secretly authored by Calhoun, set forth a theory of nullification in response to the tariff and other wrongs South Carolina believed it suffered.

In 1830 Calhoun's position, even if it had not been publicly announced, was reasonably clear, while Jackson's was not. Yet the issue was not on many minds. It came front and center largely as a consequence of efforts by Calhoun to counter politically Clay's American System. The system featured protective tariffs for manufacturers, a national bank for commerce, internal improvements for the West, and distribution of federal surpluses to the states. Jacksonians wanted to counter Clay, but the division between the southern and northern wings of the Democratic Party made finding a common position difficult. A particular obstacle to Democratic unity was the protective tariff; southerners, led by Calhoun, almost universally opposed a tariff that was not based on revenue objectives, while Van Buren and his New York and Pennsylvania constituencies favored it. If it was not handled carefully, the tariff could split the party.

Calhoun sought to establish an alliance between southerners and westerners that would rest on a low tariff and a land policy that encouraged emigration to the West. While southerners and westerners might differ among themselves on other matters, they could find common ground on these issues. Most importantly, Van Buren supporters would be discomfited. Calhoun, who had extensive support in both the South and the West, could rely on many of Grundy's closest associates in Kentucky and Tennessee. Apart from his respect and friendship for Calhoun, Grundy would find the strategy appealing because he opposed a protective tariff on principle and favored a graduated system of land prices in the West.

The catalyst for the launch of Calhoun's initiative proved to be a motion by the Connecticut senator Samuel Foot. Noting a report from the commissioner of the Land Office that 72 million acres of federal land already surveyed remained unsold, Foot called in December 1829 for an inquiry into the suspension of surveys, abolition of the surveyor general's office, and the closing of some regional land offices. This seemingly innocuous motion set in train a series of speeches that covered almost all the subjects that would preoccupy the Senate during Grundy's years there: land policy, debt reduction, internal improvements, and most important, the nature of the Union.

Thomas Hart Benton, a senator from Missouri and a friend of Grundy's since 1807, launched this far-reaching and principled discussion. Contemporaries gave remarkably uniform assessments of Benton, finding him vain, bombastic, and more than a little envious of those accorded more success. He had a harsh and unpleasant voice, and visitors to the Senate gallery tended to leave when he rose to speak. But Benton was also determined, hardworking, and a good writer who, notwithstanding earlier ties to Henry Clay and a feud with Jackson, now strongly supported the president. He charged that Foot's resolution reflected a tight-fisted public-lands policy that reduced emigration to the West and helped ensure a docile and impoverished workforce in the East. Coupled with a protective tariff, the policy facilitated the growth of eastern manufacturing prowess and political power. He urged the South, with its Jeffersonian traditions, to become once again the protector of the West.[2]

Benton favored a land policy with no limits on surveys and the sale of lands on exceedingly generous terms. His graduation approach, first put forward in 1824, would lower per-acre land prices annually until all land was sold. Although Grundy and many westerners shared Benton's views, others, like Governor Ninian Edwards in Illinois, believed that the lands should become the property of the states where they lay. Easterners tended to the view that land should be sold at the highest possible prices for the benefit of the U.S. Treasury, with excess proceeds distributed to the states after the public debt had been extinguished. Since the same stance could be applied to the tariff, most southerners opposed a redistribution scheme, since the South would pay more for eastern manufactured goods than they would receive back through redistribution. In his first message to Congress, Jackson, who had made elimination of the national debt a priority, favored a redistribution policy. Perhaps inevitably, since each of the three main approaches to the land policy appealed to a different section of the country, no law resulted.

Robert Hayne, of South Carolina, the senior senator from South Carolina, took up Benton's cause, arguing that the protective tariff and a revenue-producing public-lands policy could only injure the West and the South. Webster defended the East and lauded the federal government's land policy, which since the Northwest Ordinance of 1787 had contributed to the growth of a prosperous and largely non-slaveholding West. Webster's defense angered Hayne, who over two days eloquently defended the South, slavery, and his view of the states' rights. Critically, he said that if the federal government passed a law that was injurious to a state, the state, by its legislature or convention, could nullify the law unless and until the law was declared constitutional by three-fourths of the states.

Webster's reply to Hayne was a great speech and dramatic theater—delivered by "Godlike Daniel" wearing Revolutionary War colors, a blue coat and a white cravat. Webster first denied that he had attacked slavery, having referred to it only in defense of the Northwest Ordinance, and stated that he viewed slavery as part of the original bargain creating the Union. Then, in the most familiar part of this brilliant oration, Webster rejected the South Carolina doctrine and stated clearly and unequivocally that the federal government was not a product of sovereign states but, rather, "the people's government, made for the people, made by the people, and answerable to the people." No single state had the authority to nullify a federal action.[3]

Webster's speech, with stunning flights of rhetoric and exaltation of the linkage between liberty and the Union, circulated widely and had a significant long-term effect. In the short term, however, it changed little. Benton found the speech too elaborately composed. Edward Livington, the New York–born senator from Louisiana, joined Webster in rejecting nullification but attacked the federalism of New England and defended Jackson policies.[4]

In this context Grundy made his first major speech in the Senate, which began on February 27 and continued on March 1, 1830. His lengthy and wide-ranging address covered most major topics of the day—the tariff, land policy, offices—and some that were not yet on the public mind, such as slavery. Senators and observers alike awaited his speech with interest, principally because many believed that Grundy would reflect the views of the president. Jackson, committed to states' rights, believed, as did Hayne, that consolidation of the federal government posed the greatest threat to republican liberties but had not yet spoken on nullification. The fact that Grundy, a sensitive reader of political currents, did not sense that Jackson opposed nullification suggests that Jackson had not fully formed, or at least signaled, his position by the end of February.

At any rate, Grundy proceeded with what in hindsight was a political mistake. He did not equivocate. The states, sovereign instrumentalities, preexisted the federal government and through the Constitution had given up only certain delegated powers. They necessarily retained all the powers they had not yielded to the federal government. In the event of a disagreement between the federal government and a state government over the constitutionality of a congressional action, an appropriate tribunal must decide whether the action fell within the powers delegated by the states. The Supreme Court, created by the Constitution, must be considered part of the federal establishment, with the number of its judges determined by Congress. Accordingly, it would not be a disinterested party. Similarly, a state legislature, part of the state apparatus, could not judge rightly a cause in which it was interested. Under such circumstances, the only appropriate body would be a state convention chosen for the purpose.[5]

Grundy stated that his stance rested on the voice of the people. The Constitution had been ratified by conventions, and thus only the people again acting in convention could judge whether federal action conflicted with retained sovereignty. If the convention decided that there had been constitutional overreach, congressional legislation would "cease to operate in the State." The only recourse for the federal government would be an appeal to the people in the other states acting through conventions. If three-fourths of the states decided that the law was constitutional, then the complaining state would be obliged to acquiesce; if they decided otherwise, the federal government would have to accept the people's judgment.

Grundy believed that he was setting forth a position between those of Webster and Hayne, reflecting his almost instinctive desire to find a middle ground. His views on the primacy of the people followed Webster's, but in a different setting. For Webster, the people, not the states, had established the Constitution, and subsequent action by voters in individual states would have no effect. Grundy started at a different point, with the people acting only through sovereign states. Grundy accordingly differed with Hayne mainly on process. Grundy rejected the idea that a state legislature could set aside a law, but his espousal of a convention and ultimate recourse to the decision of three-fourths of the states followed approaches previously discussed in South Carolina. Grundy did not deal with the consequences of a state's failure to accept the determination of three-fourths of the states, and thus he did not directly address secession.

Grundy's speech won plaudits, at least from the predisposed. The *Nashville Republican* wrote on March 10, 1830, that for "argument and eloquence combined," Grundy's speech had never been surpassed in the Senate. Ninian Edwards, of Illinois, a Calhoun supporter, wrote approvingly, and Calhoun lauded the speech and had copies mailed to his friends. A correspondent wrote James Madison that Hayne was jubilant that Grundy and Rowan were "fully in his tether." But concerns about Grundy's position existed, even among pronounced Grundy admirers. James Campbell wrote his brother that his constituents regarded Grundy as the "greatest man this state ever sent to Congress" but said that he could not have intended the "nullifying part" and would refer the matter to him for explanation.[6]

One voice, however, would be decisive for Grundy—that of Jackson. And when the president did speak, at the Jefferson Day dinner on April 13, 1830, Grundy realized that he had misjudged his chief's thinking. John Roane, of Virginia, officiated as president at the traditional dinner, aided by six vice Presidents, including Grundy, George Bibb, and Levi Woodbury, of New Hampshire. Jackson decided to make his position clear when he concluded that the dinner would be "a nullification affair altogether." Jackson, Andrew J. Donelson, William B. Lewis, and Van Buren agreed on the toast to be given and went to the dinner at a local establishment, the Indian Queen, happily prepared for battle. Van Buren was seated at the second table, "under the care of my subsequently warm friend Grundy whose feelings were then evidently enlisted on the side of the nullifiers altho' he took great care to avoid identifying himself with their doctrines."[7]

The suspicion that the dinner was intended to advance Calhoun's cause—and nullification—appears to have been correct. Of the twenty-four regular toasts, all but six or seven spoke of Virginia and Jefferson, voicing well-known states' rights creeds. Hayne applauded Virginia's stance on the Alien and Sedition Laws and then toasted the "Union of the States, and the sovereignty of the States." After the regular toasts, Jackson volunteered his own: "Our Union: It must be preserved." Calhoun could only follow with "The Union. Next to our liberty, the most dear." Grundy's own toast appropriately reflected his desire for party harmony. "The Republican Party throughout the nation; may they be as harmonious in action as they are united in principle." The Democratic Republican Party, however, was neither harmonious nor united.[8]

The Jefferson Day toasts showed that Calhoun's hopes for the presidency were dimming. The Eaton affair continued, and in March 1830 Jackson instructed his cabinet to support Peggy Eaton. Floride Calhoun refused to accord social respect to Mrs. Eaton, and Calhoun, knowing that the affair was further eroding his influence with Jackson, felt powerless to do anything but support his wife. More significantly, fundamental issues separated Jackson and Calhoun. The president and vice president differed in important respects, on nullification and the nature of the Union, tariff policy, the national debt, and the distribution of federal surpluses. It is unlikely that Floride Calhoun's attitude toward Peggy Eaton tipped the balance, given the magnitude of the potential areas of conflict between these two immovable Scots-Irish men. Yet the Eaton affair poisoned the atmosphere.[9]

In this personalized administration, Calhoun watched helplessly while Van

Buren, the Little Magician with muffled oars plied his charm on Andrew Jackson. Van Buren, an exceptionally adroit politician and a widower, found no difficulty in supporting Peggy Eaton and quietly offered Jackson shrewd and sensitive political judgment. Amos Kendall wrote to Francis Blair that "Van Buren glides along as smoothly as oil and as silently as a cat" and has gained the "entire confidence of the President and all his personal friends."[10]

Grundy was not among Jackson's personal friends who were won over by Van Buren. Indeed, he observed with discomfort the growing estrangement between his friends Calhoun and Jackson. Grundy strongly believed in his party amidst growing partisanship. After he became a senator, he reiterated that the only response to dissension within the party was a second term for Jackson. Grundy, Hugh L. White, and other Jacksonians decided to urge the president's reelection in all private conversations. When the division between Calhoun and Van Buren increased, "it was decided in consultation, that I should make the [public] announcement in my speech on Foot's resolution," wrote Grundy.[11]

As the chosen messenger, Grundy sent a political signal, to politicians if not more broadly. In his wide-ranging speech on March 1, 1830, he described Jackson's election in 1828 as a marriage with the West. After warmly praising "good old seasoned hickory," he proclaimed, "With him the West is contented and happy; and . . . no doubt need be entertained that next November two years she will . . . again pass through the ceremony used in such cases." Grundy's message did not go unnoticed. The future president John Tyler approvingly wrote two weeks later that Grundy had announced the president's candidacy for reelection, and a correspondent informed Henry Clay as well. On May 8 Grundy, pleased with his handiwork, wrote Ninian Edwards that Jackson was running and would win reelection.[12]

Grundy early on left no doubt that he had hitched his star to Jackson. When Tennessee's influential insider Daniel Graham wrote in March 1830 that Grundy reportedly favored Calhoun, Grundy decisively rebutted the assumption. He acknowledged his close ties with Calhoun but said that he had told the South Carolinian that he supported Jackson for a second term and would make a selection at the close of such term "without any previous commitment. I have said the same at all times and places, where the subject was named."[13]

Grundy wrote Levi Woodbury that he was vexed by the lack of party unity, and he criticized Democrats who put self-interest ahead of party, probably referring to Eaton and Lewis. He and others sought to mend the fraying relationship between Calhoun and Jackson. At an unspecified date in March 1830, before Jackson's toast at the Jefferson Day dinner, Congressmen Charles Wick-liffe, of Kentucky, called a meeting of Jacksonians friendly to Calhoun in order to facilitate a greater understanding between the president and the vice president. Senators White and Grundy, of Tennessee, and Bibb, of Kentucky, as well as Congressmen James K. Polk, Cave Johnson, and Robert Desha, of Tennessee, and Wickliffe and Henry Daniel, of Kentucky, attended. The meeting, held in the room of George Bibb, had no result and only came to light in 1831, when the *Washington Globe,* a pro-Jackson Washington paper established by Francis Blair in 1831, charged that Calhoun partisans had met to seek the removal of Eaton as secretary of war. After the *Globe* article appeared, Grundy hastened to dispel any "improper impressions" held by the president. He wrote Jackson on September 30, 1831, that he had attended only two meetings limited to members. The subject of raising with Jackson the possible ouster of Major Eaton occurred only at the meeting in Senator Bibb's room, to which Grundy had been invited without knowing the object. One member raised the matter, another opposed it, and the subject was dropped after Grundy joined those in opposition.[14]

Throughout this period, Calhoun, his plans for the future going awry, tried to preserve his relationship with Jackson. He later wrote that he had consistently supported the administration, appealing to the witness of Grundy and White, "both devoted friends of General Jackson, both men of great capacity, and both having ample opportunities of forming a correct opinion of my course."[15]

Unfortunately for Calhoun, another development put a capstone on his relations with the president. As President Monroe's secretary of war, Calhoun had been a member of the cabinet in 1818, when Jackson exceeded orders, launched a campaign in Spanish Florida in pursuit of Seminole Indians, and, among other things, summarily executed two British subjects. The ensuing criticism had deeply offended the ever-touchy Jackson, who formed a mistaken belief that Calhoun had been his supporter in the cabinet, and Calhoun did not correct the impression. William H. Crawford, of Georgia, who was no friend of Calhoun's and the man Jackson blamed for the criticism in 1818, provided damning information with respect to Calhoun's role to a Van Buren ally. Through the agency of William B. Lewis, this information came to the president's attention as he was becoming convinced that Calhoun and his friends were conspiring against him. Jackson, who probably had been biding his time, confronted his vice president on May 13, 1830, with evidence of "base hypocrisy." Calhoun squirmed but ultimately had to concede that he had not supported Jackson in 1818. Gloating and expressing revenge, Jackson used this contretemps with Calhoun as a reason for severing their relationship.[16]

The Eaton affair, with its negative implications for Calhoun, continued even after Congress adjourned in 1830. Once back in Tennessee, Jackson continued to press for the acceptance of Peggy Eaton. Friends and political allies provided some support in Nashville, but their misgivings led Jackson angrily to write the city off. However, in Franklin, his hometown, Eaton found more acceptance, as Jackson enthusiastically reported. Unfortunately, what position the Grundys took, other than to assume a low profile, is not known. Socially and politically the Grundys were close to the Calhouns, the Polks, and the Donelsons, yet Grundy would soon be confronting a senatorial election, and Jackson's help would be critical. In Franklin, Randal and Sally McGavock publicly associated with the Eatons.[17]

Notwithstanding the Eaton affair and the estrangement between Jackson and Calhoun, Grundy enjoyed a happy and productive summer in 1830. Most of Grundy's surviving correspondence is political, but two letters from Grundy to Levi Woodbury, his Senate seatmate, show great warmth and regard. He wrote that upon his return to Nashville he had found his family well and his constituents in good humor and that he had never been happier. Grundy emphasized anew his desire for party harmony, regretting "the excessive feelings" still "indulged" in South Carolina. At the same time, Jackson wrote William B. Lewis that "our friend Mr. Grundy says he will abandon" Calhoun unless the South Carolinian used his influence to suppress nullification.[18]

Grundy's sanguine outlook rested in part on the "good humor" of his constituents. He had reason to feel confident. James Campbell wrote his brother, the U.S. treasurer, on May 8, 1830, asking him to tell Grundy that he continually received compliments for having voted for Grundy in the senatorial election. He reported that excepting "Old Hiccory," Grundy was the most popular man in Tennessee. He said that White was also well liked, the people speaking of him with serious and sober dignity, "but they always laugh when Grundy's name is mentioned and say he is a proper man."[19]

That summer, Grundy participated in another divisive criminal trial, which brought him full circle with the president and the family of Patton Anderson. More than nineteen years had passed since Grundy incurred Jackson's ire in defending David Magness for the killing of Patton Anderson. William Preston Anderson, Patton's brother, had prospered in Franklin County, Tennessee, while his son Rufus King Anderson, a dapper, handsome man, had developed a reputation for violence much like that of his late uncle. Rufus Anderson, an

Alabama state senator, claimed that his brother-in-law Thomas Paine Taul, an attorney in Winchester, the Franklin County seat, had abused his wife, Anderson's sister Caroline, who had just died in childbirth. Others surmised that the genesis of Anderson's anger had been Caroline's transfer of valuable Nashville property to Taul, thereby depriving Anderson and his siblings of real estate they expected to inherit. Whatever the cause, in August 1829 Rufus, incensed, had walked up to Taul at noon on court day in Winchester and, with little warning, shot him; Taul had died two days later.[20]

The killing and the related trial divided the county. Taul had many adherents, and his father, Micah, was one of Winchester's leading lawyers. Political tensions surfaced as well, since Anderson strongly supported his old friend Jackson, now in the White House, and Micah Taul aligned himself with Henry Clay. Both sides spared no expense. Micah Taul employed Samuel Laughlin as a special prosecutor to assist the state, and William P. Anderson hired several counsel, most notably Grundy. The trial lasted eighteen days in July 1830. The defense offered as many as a dozen witnesses, who principally testified that the deceased had been a dangerous man, even though Taul, with a long history of illness, had weighed less than one hundred pounds. Grundy had his usual success, obtaining an acquittal in less than an hour.[21]

Micah Taul, bitter at the loss of his last son, claimed that the Anderson family had bribed the jurors and that Grundy had tried to divert the jury's attention and demonize the deceased. The leading student of the trial, Jackson's biographer, A. S. Colyar, who had studied under Micah Taul, rejected Taul's charge and concluded that the jurors had been carried into "great error by the eloquence of the most wonderful criminal lawyer the United States ever produced." Rufus King Anderson, however, gained only four years from Grundy's eloquence: a man he had threatened and pursued shot him to death in Alabama in 1834.[22]

The summer of 1830 constituted only a brief hiatus from political worries for Grundy. When Congress resumed, he confronted the implications of the estrangement between Jackson and Calhoun. He revealed his fears in a lengthy letter to Daniel Graham in January 1831. "One thing, I fear, is certain," he wrote, "the misunderstanding between the President and Vice President cannot be healed—I have done all, I could, to bring them together and have not succeeded—I am afraid to go much further. If men want to differ, a peacemaker may make himself odious by interfering too much—I have given to each my full views on the subject and protrayed [sic] all the consequences . . . neither seemed anxious to find a remedy." Grundy reported that he had told Calhoun that in a public quarrel he would support Jackson and that publishing correspondence between the president and the vice president could only injure the party.[23]

Despite Grundy's advice, the unhappy Calhoun decided to place his case before the people. If he could not regain the president's favor, at least he could publicly justify his position and perhaps strike a public blow against Van Buren. In late January 1831 Grundy tried to soften the adverse effects of publication. He and his longtime friend and ally Senator Richard M. Johnson, of Kentucky, first called on Francis Blair, with whom they "enjoyed a cordial intimacy," and asked him to place Calhoun's publication, along with comments denying that it was an attack on Jackson, in the *Globe*. Blair refused, saying that nothing Calhoun might say could avoid a ruinous rupture with Jackson.[24]

Grundy's second initiative was, strangely enough, with John Eaton, still smarting from the continuing exclusion of his wife from polite society but viewed as a trustworthy friend of the president's. Grundy informed Eaton that Calhoun intended to publish the correspondence. He hoped, however, that the accompanying appeal could be framed in such a way that the president would not feel obligated to reply, thereby avoiding further animosity. Grundy proposed that after obtaining Calhoun's consent, he and Eaton review the draft and eliminate passages that might be offensive to Jackson. The following evening, the two Tennesseans met at Grundy's lodgings and went over the intended publication. Eaton said he thought that if all the changes were made, Jackson would not feel obligated to reply to the publication.[25]

As the meeting concluded, Grundy and Eaton agreed that Eaton would see the president and explain what had happened and that Grundy would see Calhoun and obtain his concurrence to the changes and then inform Eaton to that effect. Grundy did as agreed, and Calhoun went forward with publication on the assumption that Jackson had been advised per Grundy's agreement with Eaton. But Eaton had his revenge for the Petticoat Affair. In Eaton's own words, "I did not communicate the subject to the President, because, upon reflection, I thought it improper to do so. From Mr. Grundy I received a note the next day, stating that all was right which I understood to mean that the suggestions offered had been adopted." When Eaton subsequently received a printed copy with the request that it be submitted to Jackson, he again gave Jackson nothing. Eaton thus had two opportunities to prepare Jackson for the publication but chose not to do so, while allowing Grundy and Calhoun to believe that he had.[26]

Calhoun's correspondence appeared on February 17, 1831, in the *Washing-*

ton Telegraph, the pro-Calhoun paper edited by Duff Green. The publication took Jackson by surprise and, notwithstanding the tone, offended him. The press took over the issue, Jackson and Calhoun broke completely, and Grundy and Calhoun could only have felt blindsided and betrayed by Eaton. Two years later Grundy took great pains to present his account of what transpired, publishing his final version in the *National Banner and Nashville Whig* on June 24, 1833, during his reelection campaign. He and Eaton, who released his own statement in March 1831, differed in relatively unimportant particulars. The drafts of Grundy's account preserved among his private papers, however, set forth his assessment of mistakes made, which he did not include in the published version of what transpired. The first error was the disclosure by the *Telegraph* of Grundy and Eaton's role; the second was "Major Eaton's publishing a statement detailing private conversations and subjecting my conduct to misconstruction."[27]

Grundy's continuing efforts to prevent or at least ameliorate a break between Jackson and Calhoun deserve credit. He put himself in a dangerous position, at odds with his reputation for caution. Jackson, outraged by the whole affair, criticized Grundy and wrote that he was "thunderstruck when I saw the publication and on inquiry found out the source and those concerned." Even though Jackson's irritation appears extreme, particularly in light of Eaton's duplicity, it is clear that Grundy impaired his relationship with Jackson.[28]

Only one further point should be drawn from the publication imbroglio. Martin Van Buren, writing many years later, still smarted over Grundy's role in the affair and the publication of the Calhoun correspondence. In his view, Calhoun had intended not only to exculpate himself but also to demonstrate a Van Buren plot to destroy the vice president. Van Buren wrote that his own feelings required him to write about the roles of Johnson and Grundy. Johnson, "the friend of the human race," had been naive and not sufficiently astute to perceive the publication's injurious effect upon Van Buren. The experienced Grundy, however, had had too strong a taste for political maneuvering not to realize the full implications of the publication. Grundy had known little about Van Buren, had never been unfriendly to him, and given his general amiability would have tried to avoid the quarrel if he could have done so. Under the circumstances, however, Grundy had confined his efforts to the support of his two old friends, Calhoun and Jackson, and left Van Buren to face the potential storm. Although Van Buren wrote that he later became quite attached to Grundy and learned of the Tennessean's "fondness for the strategical branch of political warfare," his statement in his autobiography that he had "controlled" his feelings with respect to Grundy's agency does not ring true and suggests the depth of the political significance of this episode.[29]

Even though the publication of the Calhoun correspondence effectively ended Calhoun's quest for the presidency, the final steps occurred somewhat later. By 1831 the Jackson cabinet barely functioned. While Jackson had supported Peggy Eaton for more than two years, the families of various cabinet members were among her most obstinate opponents. Even worse in Jackson's view, this could only be part of a grand conspiracy headed by Vice President Calhoun and three cabinet members, John Berrien, John Branch, and Samuel Ingham, all Calhoun partisans. The ever-deft Van Buren provided Jackson a way out, proposing in April 1831 that he resign from his post as secretary of state and that the cabinet be dissolved. To the hoots of the press and the unhappiness of Peggy Eaton and the dismissed cabinet officers, Jackson acted exactly as Van Buren recommended. The president perhaps unwisely retained his postmaster general, the Kentuckian William Barry, but soon he had a new, more harmonious cabinet. The one major disappointment for Jackson occurred when Hugh Lawson White refused to resign as a senator from Tennessee to become secretary of war, thereby depriving Jackson of an opportunity to promote the dismissed Eaton to replace White as senator.

Calhoun, the clear loser in the cabinet reorganization, publicly acknowledged his support of nullification in his Fort Hill address on August 3, 1831. Unhappy and angry, he in effect gave up electoral hopes in New York, Pennsylvania, and other northern states, thereby limiting his future role to that of the leader of the southern region. In late 1832 Calhoun resigned the vice presidency and returned to the Senate, but not before he took one spiteful step. On January 26, 1832, after maneuvering that allowed him to do so, he cast the tie-breaking vote rejecting Jackson's nomination of Martin Van Buren as the U.S. minister to Great Britain. After the vote, at least according to Benton, Calhoun gloated, "It will kill him, sir, kill him dead." Grundy, more prescient, wrote on January 22 that he was saying to all Van Buren's enemies that if Van Buren was rejected for the post as minister, he ought to become vice president.[30]

For Grundy, all these changes created a series of political problems, particularly with respect to his reelection as senator. In his letter of January 24, 1831, stating that the misunderstanding between Jackson and Calhoun could not be healed, Grundy asked Daniel Graham to find out county candidates' views with respect to the upcoming Senate race. At approximately the same time, he wrote two friendly letters to Ephraim Foster, perhaps having received intimations that Foster was considering challenging Grundy for his Senate seat.[31]

If Grundy needed any reminder of political thin ice, he received it from various quarters in the spring of 1831, several months after the publication of the Calhoun correspondence in February. Samuel Gwin sent mixed messages in a letter in late May. On the one hand, he reported a long conversation with Jackson, who supported Grundy's reelection and remained "highly favorable towards you, no matter how some others may be around him. He emphatically remarked to me that he never forgot *old friends*." On the other hand, Gwin warned Grundy about Duff Green, editor of the *Telegraph,* and made clear the danger to Grundy from lingering perceptions about his relationship to Calhoun. Also in May, Grundy received a letter from Richard M. Johnson, who expressed distress at the blowup in Washington and "very great anxiety" for Grundy's political prosperity. Johnson gave Grundy pointed advice in the event that White accepted the post of secretary of war: Grundy should take a decided stance in support of Eaton for White's Senate seat, since it would strengthen his support from the old Hero and his closest friends.[32]

Grundy in fact was already strengthening his political fences. First, he sought to set the record straight with respect to his part in the publication of Calhoun's correspondence. He sent a clarifying letter to Eaton on May 12, 1831, and had asked Gwin to meet with Green to ensure that Green understood Grundy's exact role. Certainly mindful of the implications for himself, he wrote Hugh Lawson White on May 17, 1831, urging him to accept the post of secretary of war, reporting enthusiasm in Nashville for the proposed new cabinet and saying that "it affords the first clear sunshiny political weather I have seen for some time."[33]

Second, Grundy declared to all and sundry that he had maintained an independent stance with respect to the Calhoun–Van Buren split. In a generally innocuous letter to his constituents on May 9, Grundy declared that Tennessee congressmen should not take the side of any presidential aspirant, but should follow the party, and specifically that he would say nothing to the prejudice of Van Buren or Calhoun. More significantly, he asked Calhoun to verify his, Grundy's, loyalty to Jackson and to reaffirm Grundy's specific role in the publication imbroglio. Calhoun obliged, writing that soon after his arrival in Washington the previous winter Grundy had expressed his regret concerning the differences between Jackson and Calhoun but that, to ensure full understanding, Grundy had emphasized in several conversations that "however sincere your friendship to me, if we should be opposed, I must expect to find you in opposition to me, as you preferred General Jackson to all others." Grundy, for his part, made sure that this letter was made available to Jackson and other Tennessee political leaders.[34]

As part of this program, Grundy supported Van Buren for vice president in 1832 once Jackson made his position known. On February 4, 1832, upon being asked for confirmation of an earlier conversation, Grundy wrote Jackson that all of the members of his mess shared his own view that had Mr. Van Buren's nomination as minister to Great Britain been confirmed, he would have opposed Van Buren's candidacy. As a result of the Senate action, however, he and his messmates supported the New Yorker for vice president.[35]

Third, differing only in degree, not kind, from his earlier position as an administration defender, Grundy wrapped himself more closely in the Jackson mantle, taking no chances that would further challenge the president's goodwill. He acted partly by choice, since Grundy and Jackson shared Jeffersonian views and opposed Clay's American System. Grundy was a party man, and he worried that without Jackson the Democratic Party could splinter. In other respects, Grundy had little room to maneuver politically. Tennessee did not lack for talented, ambitious politicians, and Jackson's support would be critical in the upcoming senatorial election.

Finally, Grundy had to distance himself from his earlier views with respect to nullification. Adverse national developments triggered by the Tariff Bill helped him significantly. After Calhoun's break with Jackson, unhappy South Carolinians rose up against the tariff, which enshrined protectionist principles of Clay's American System. Grundy, whose constituents also opposed the tariff, maintained strong anti-tariff credentials, speaking against it on several occasions and voting against the Tariff Bill in July 1832. Unlike many southerners, Grundy saw no constitutional objection to tariffs and favored a system based solely on the need to raise revenues. He opposed protection for manufacturers on principle, which is not surprising in an egalitarian who disdained governmental support for a favored few.[36]

South Carolina responded to the Tariff Bill with the Nullification Convention of 1832, which declared the tariff laws of 1828 and 1832 null and void and directed that no duties be collected in its ports. Jackson, predictably, thundered, and in his Nullification Proclamation of December 10, 1832, he made clear to the nation, and to South Carolina in particular, that he would not tolerate nullification and would enforce the laws. His proclamation set forth a nationalistic theory, highly pleasing to Daniel Webster, that rejected the view that the Union was a compact of preexisting sovereign states. (The proclamation confused most and upset many, particularly in the South, since Jackson had appeared to propound the South's theory of preexisting sovereign states as recently as the previous week.)

No other states rallied to South Carolina's side, although historians have recently suggested that there was more sympathy for Calhoun's position than has been generally assumed. Most Tennesseans opposed South Carolina. The nullification crisis was averted by the passage of two bills, both signed by Jackson on March 2, 1833, that together constituted the Compromise of 1833. The olive branch was the Compromise Tariff, largely engineered by Clay, which provided for a gradual reduction of duties to 20 percent over nine and one-half years. The committee of seven members chosen by the Senate president pro tem, Hugh Lawson White, to negotiate a compromise included Clay as chairman, Grundy, Calhoun, Webster, John M. Clayton, William C. Rives, and George Dallas. The sword, equally important and of particular interest to Jackson, was the Revenue Collection Bill, or Force Bill, which authorized using the military to collect duties in ports of a nullifying state and to transfer to federal courts any cases that might arise from the controversy.[37]

One of five members of the Judiciary Committee, Grundy led the administration's push for the Force Bill, exercising with humor all his political skills to ensure passage of a measure that was generally detested in the South. Some of his friends of longest duration, such as Calhoun, George Bibb, and George Poindexter, opposed the bill, and others, such as Thomas Hart Benton, straddled the fence. Jackson made clear what he thought should be done: "lay *all* delicacy on this subject aside and compell every mans name to appear upon the journals that the nullifiers may *all* be distinguished from those who are in support of the laws, and the union . . . I have confidence you will push the bill, the whole bill, and nothing but the bill." Grundy and Jackson collaborated on the wording of the bill, as well as on tactics of passage. Not satisfied with the prospect of a close win for the president, Grundy asked Daniel Webster to speak for the Force Bill. Although the drama of the Webster-Calhoun speeches has been marked in history, Grundy, in fact, closed the Senate debate on behalf of the Judiciary Committee. The Force Bill passed in the Senate on February 20, 1833, by a vote of 32–1. The only southerners to vote for the bill were Rives, of Virginia, John Forsyth, of Georgia, Grundy and White, of Tennessee, and Josiah S. Johnston and George A. Waggaman, of Louisiana. Except for John Tyler, the dissenter, no other southerners voted.[38]

Grundy performed impressively on the Force Bill. All his smoothness, however, could not obscure the fact that he was shifting his position from that expressed on February 27 and March 1, 1830. Motivated by his political need to be identified with Jackson and by his distress at the no longer theoretical risk of nullification, he discarded his earlier views to the degree necessary. Grundy demonstrated his changed stance in two principal ways. First, when Calhoun presented resolutions stating that the federal union was a compact of sovereign states, limited to the powers delegated by such states, Grundy countered with his own resolutions, thereby blocking consideration of Calhoun's. Grundy continued to accept that the government was one of delegated power and adhered to the compact theory of the formation of the Union, but he now maintained that the federal government had the power to impose duties, as well as exclusive power over tariffs, and that no state could nullify the Tariff Bill. Unlike in 1830, when Grundy had seen no limit to the questions subject to state nullification, Grundy now distinguished between exclusive and non-exclusive powers.[39]

Second, Grundy's speeches in support of the Force Bill necessarily focused on the execution of federal laws and attributed to the Supreme Court an authority that he earlier had not accepted. In 1830 Grundy had ignored what would happen if the federal government did not acquiesce in a state's nullification. In 1833 he had to address a real—and not theoretical—question. He could not equivocate, and he made clear that preservation of the authority of the federal government required the Force Bill. In his closing speech he declared that South Carolina possessed no constitutional right to obstruct execution of the tariff laws and that only the federal judiciary could decide their validity. When the chips were down, Grundy cast his lot with Jackson and the Union.

Grundy's change of position did not go unnoticed and gave rise to gibes and political jeers. Most recognized, however, that Grundy's support for the administration was, in the words of Richard Ellis, "explained mainly by his pending reelection and not from any conviction that it was the right thing to do." Characteristically, Grundy responded to the criticism with humor. Van Buren reported that one of the most amusing scenes he ever witnessed in the Senate occurred when Henry Clay tried to implicate Grundy

in Mr. Calhoun's nullification scheme. The bantering vivacity and persistency of the arraignment, with the earnestness and vigor of the defense, and the invincible good nature of the parties called out frequent bursts of applause and laughter. The accused described with his finger an imaginary line between himself and Mr. Calhoun, who sat quite near him, declared in the strongest terms his warm regard for that gentleman, referred with satisfaction to the many political battles they had fought, side by side, against the federalists during the war, then, pointing to the line of nullification as he had indicated it, admitted that he had some times been found near it but affirmed with great solemnity and obvious sincerity that he had never in a single instance passed it. . . . This position he very successfully sustained to the end of the debate to the great entertainment and amusement of the Senate, not excepting Mr. Calhoun himself.

Less amusing fallout was inevitable, however. Pleasant Miller charged Grundy with self-seeking expediency, and the *Richmond Whig and Public Advertiser,* a nullification organ, castigated his apostasy, calling him a "parasite of the tyrant." John Randolph, as acerbic as ever, wrote that many who were less acquainted with Grundy would be surprised that he supported measures fraught with danger for liberty, whereas those who were aware of his "spaniel properties" would not be surprised. Davy Crockett viewed Grundy as the "general's pet."[40]

The long-term cost to Grundy of his change of position on nullification proved to be greater than the predictable comments of political foes. During his ensuing reelection campaign and after, opponents castigated him for selfishness, opportunism, and lack of principle. While the 1830s became a decade of intense vituperation, and James K. Polk and others were subjected to similar attacks, Grundy consistently received the same charge: unprincipled opportunism. Before the nullification crisis, critics pilloried him for ambition and maneuvering, the tactical logrolling accepted in politics. After the crisis, at least among his foes, his willingness to compromise and bargain was viewed in a more critical light.

Grundy's views on nullification posited in Foot's Resolution paralleled those of his mentor George Nicholas in 1798 and in his mind only expressed widely held views in Kentucky and Tennessee. When, probably to his great surprise, a crisis arose from the nullification doctrine, Grundy, confronting a real issue rather than a theoretical one, demonstrated his allegiance to the Union and to Jackson. As a leading student of this period on Tennessee history stated, "Regardless of his reasons, he handled his problem with honor and ability, while at the same time he retained the friendship of both Calhoun and Jackson. A less able man could not have done that."[41]

21

REELECTION

*A strong hold he has upon the good opinions of the great body
of the people.*

—William Carroll

*G*rundy's reelection bid for the Senate became inextricably caught up in
the continuing clash of competing factions in Tennessee. His ultimate
success in 1833 came only after a deadlocked legislature in 1832 and intensive management by Grundy and his allies. The victory would cement the leadership of the state Democratic Party by Grundy and James K. Polk until Grundy's death in 1840.

Even though political factionalism was increasing among nominal Jacksonians in Tennessee, key Jackson backers still sought electoral unity in Tennessee. Grundy's term in the Senate did not end until 1832, and some Jackson advisers hoped that he would not be challenged. John Coffee, who so vigorously
opposed Grundy for Congress in 1811, wrote Jackson in July 1831 that he was
pleased that Carroll would not oppose Grundy and create undesirable division
and thought that Grundy would continue to do well. The strife Coffee feared,
however, came to pass. Ephraim Foster (1794–1854), a wartime aide to Jackson
and son of Grundy's old friend Robert C. Foster, saw a political opportunity
and challenged Grundy. Foster, financially Nashville's most successful lawyer,
largely represented commercial interests and acted with the backing of the Erwin-Carroll faction.[1]

A lengthy article by "CJF," presumably Foster, in the *Nashville Republican
and State Gazette* on October 6, 1831, opened the campaign. Comparing Grundy's speech on the Foot Resolution with the writings of Calhoun and Hayne,
"CJF" maintained that Grundy favored nullification. A lengthy rebuttal signed
"Justice," presumably Grundy, appeared in the same paper two days later. After
expressing surprise that opinions previously applauded should now be considered dangerous, the writer asked, "Is Mr. Grundy's seat in the Senate wanted

for another?" He then claimed that all parties admitted some ill-defined right to resist the unauthorized oppression of the general government but said that Webster and Hayne offered polar solutions, one viewing the Supreme Court as the final arbiter on all questions respecting the power of the general and state governments, the other looking to the state legislatures. "Justice" aligned himself with Jackson's fear of consolidation of federal power and tried to stake out a middle position between Webster's and Hayne's, calling for a special state convention. The compromise position, which Grundy had set forth in his speech on Foot's resolution on March 1, 1830, would avoid "hastily plunging the country into civil war, with all its dire calamities." "Justice" concluded: "If his opinion be wrong, it is fortunate for him that his enemies can show only one error and that too a speculative opinion delivered in a speech in an extended and excursive debate. If he has erred, he has with Jefferson and others whose political errors have heretofore been considered as allied to public virtue."

For approximately five weeks, until Grundy left for Washington, the *Nashville Republican and State Gazette* published exchanges between "CJF" and "Justice." On October 13 "CJF" forcefully set forth his view, based on the meaning of the words used: "If Mr. Calhoun is a nullifier, you are one—if Mr. Hayne is a nullifier, you are one—if you are a nullifier, they are nullifiers—so you are all nullifiers together or you are not nullifiers." Although this author at times overplayed his position, denying, for example, that Grundy could find countenance for his doctrines in the opinions of Jefferson or Madison or in the Kentucky or the Virginia Resolution, he had the better of the argument. Under the circumstances, "CJF"'s success is not surprising and suggests that Grundy would have been better advised to offer no defense, to be above the fray.

The exchange attracted notice as well as speculation. William Donelson wrote to Grundy's ally Andrew Donelson on October 23, 1831, that the attack on Grundy had occurred just as the legislation was sitting and a short time after the return of Judge Overton. "There is some mistery in it," he said. One "mistery" was whether the Blount-Overton group would run John Eaton for the Senate, accentuating the growing divide among Jacksonians. Eaton, by now out of Jackson's cabinet, arrived in Middle Tennessee during the legislative session. Eaton's defense of his conduct had been widely publicized and, according to Governor Carroll, "produced a strong sympathy in behalf of Major Eaton. . . . Even Colonel Erwin speaks in high terms of it, and says that he would prefer Eaton for the Senate to Grundy." Foster encouraged an Eaton candidacy in order to weaken Grundy's support. Nevertheless, with Grundy's term not expiring until March 1833, Eaton not formally in the race, and a difficult choice confronting it, the legislature did not choose a senator in 1831.[2]

The campaign accelerated in 1832, with all expecting the issue to be decided in a specially called legislative session in the fall. Grundy mounted an innovative campaign, laying the groundwork for the future organization so well employed by James K. Polk. His electoral activities rested on several pillars. First and foremost, he sought press support. He had done this in Kentucky during the Kentucky Insurance fight and in his congressional campaign in 1811. Francis Blair's *Globe,* in Washington, and many Tennessee Jacksonian papers, including the *National Banner and Nashville Whig,* did back Grundy in 1832. The influential *Nashville Republican and State Gazette,* however, opposed the incumbent senator, attacking him for nullification, his ties to Calhoun, his failure to speak on behalf of Van Buren's nomination for minister to Great Britain, and his signature on a petition to cease Sunday mail delivery. Second, Grundy campaigned hard. He built support groups in various regions, traveling extensively. When opponents charged that Grundy had returned from Washington through East Tennessee for political purposes and overcharged the government for travel costs, Grundy's indignant reply only underscored that his travels had enabled him to build his political base. Grundy's legal reputation, his affability, and his legal and political travels throughout the state provided the foundation for his political effort.[3]

Third, Grundy recognized the value of political organization in the use of local committees, get-out-the-vote campaigns, and party rallies. Most importantly, he used "instructions" as a political tool. In order to ensure that existing legislators voted the right way, Grundy persuaded supporters to organize political gatherings on his behalf and to submit written resolutions asking legislators to vote for him. In Sumner County, where Grundy allegedly enjoyed more popularity than in any other county, more than one thousand people signed Grundy's instructions. Printed instructions reflected the extensive organizational effort. In the view of opponents, this transgressed public opinion, since the resolutions were obtained by solicitors sent out to scour the country. Fourth, and related to the third approach, was the use of the presidential franking privilege to deliver Grundy's speeches throughout the state, achieved with the assistance of Andrew J. Donelson and ostensibly approved by the president himself.[4]

The use of the presidential frank fit neatly into Grundy's larger plan to appear to be Jackson's candidate. Jackson did appear to favor Grundy over Foster. On June 10, 1832, Jackson stated that while he wished to avoid interference with the purity of state elections, he believed it was only just to note that he had often expressed his satisfaction with Grundy's performance as a senator. In addition, notwithstanding political tensions, personal relations between Jackson and Grundy appear to have been warm. In a letter to Grundy on August 20, 1832, Jackson expressed concern about Grundy's health and commented on other nonpolitical matters. Jackson's letters to Grundy at this time usually are signed "your friend," in contrast to earlier communications.[5]

Circumstances changed after backers put forward John Eaton's name. There is some suggestion that Foster supporters promised Eaton that they would switch to Eaton after a few ballots if Eaton entered the race. At any rate, Eaton's entry forced Jackson to express his preference. According to Jackson's confidant John C. McLemore, Grundy "is saying" that Jackson only had a personal friendship with Eaton, while politically he preferred Grundy. Jackson made clear to David Burford on September 10, 1832, that his friendly relations with Eaton, a friend of twenty years, had not changed and rejected the view that he had a previous preference for Grundy. Jackson wrote McLemore that he would be pleased to see Eaton in the Senate. In a position statement to a political committee, Jackson noted that Grundy had ably supported the administration but that the Tennessee legislature now had an opportunity to chastise administration enemies by electing Eaton. He cited the example of New Hampshire, where Democrats had put aside their favorite, Levi Woodbury, to elect Isaac Hill, the Jackson appointee rejected by the Senate. Adding salt to Foster's wound, Jackson concluded that Tennessee would be ably served by either Grundy or Eaton. Other factors may have influenced Jackson as well. There are suggestions that Jackson remained irritated at Grundy's earlier peacemaking efforts on behalf of Calhoun, while one historian wrote that Eaton would be more easily controlled. And, too, Jackson could compensate Eaton for the loss of his cabinet position and rebuke the slanderers of Mrs. Eaton.[6]

In Washington no one doubted Jackson's preference for Eaton. Duff Green, in the *Telegraph,* wrote that Jackson had traveled to Nashville to superintend Eaton's interest. Tennesseans believed that Grundy was being abandoned, and one reported that Grundy himself felt "used up."[7]

The Senate election took place on October 5 amid great anticipation. Each of the three main factions in Tennessee now had a senatorial candidate, Eaton and Grundy representing the two pro-Jackson groups and Foster enjoying the support of the Erwin-Carroll bloc. After eighteen ballots on October 5 and twelve on October 6, no candidate had a majority, and the election was postponed until 1833, after the expiration of Grundy's term and a state election of legislators. The vote showed the influence of Eaton and the factions in Tennessee: Eaton had 14 votes on the first ballot, compared with 24 for Foster and 21 for Grundy. By the final ballot, Eaton had 18; Foster, 22; and Grundy, 20. The result satisfied no one.[8]

The election of 1833 took place after the nullification crisis and the Compromise of 1833, in which Grundy played a leading part. There is some evidence that Grundy, active in Washington, did not engage significantly in the political maneuvering attendant to his reelection until he returned to Nashville in late March 1833. The Senate choice would be made in October, but by a new group of state senators and representatives, seated after elections in August. Writing to Andrew Donelson on March 31, Grundy said that he found the prospects decidedly in Foster's favor, since pro-Foster candidates had been nominated in most counties. In both Davidson and Knox counties Foster backers were unopposed. Grundy believed that he could win only by contesting the county elections, "for with the people I have the strength." Perhaps miffed by the failure of local Democrats to promote candidates who would vote for him, Grundy wrote that he would not contest county elections or encourage others to do so. He would continue as a candidate, but only as an unconcerned spectator.[9]

Grundy nevertheless decided to pursue the contest. In early May he provided Jackson an update on election prospects, viewing Foster as his opposition. Clear-eyed as always, the incumbent senator believed that despite Foster's initial advantage, the election was now equally balanced, and he continued to rely on the "people." Grundy also advised Jackson that the Armstrongs, the McLemores, and the Donelsons, close friends and relatives of Jackson's, supported Grundy candidates.[10]

Eaton, whose late candidacy had occasioned consternation in the Grundy camp in 1832, did not actively campaign in 1833. He had left Nashville, and his election as president of the board of the Ohio and Chesapeake Canal Commission in June 1833 increased the political confusion in Tennessee. Regardless of Eaton's uncertain candidacy, Grundy faced strong opposition from Foster. He responded to a variety of hostile press charges, detailing his role in the publication of Calhoun's papers in 1831, responding to factual issues raised by Colonel Robert Armstrong concerning favorable comments about John C. Calhoun made by Cave Johnson, and clarifying his resignation from Congress in 1814. Grundy also had to defend himself for suggesting in 1832 that Tennessee was ruled by a "name" (Jackson), a jocular remark treated as impudence by newspaper editors.[11]

Grundy, however, confronted time and again the unavoidable issue of nullification and his change of stance. He wrote Jackson, "I am charged with nullification and you know . . . that it is wholly untrue." To meet the issue head-on, Grundy asked Jackson to answer four questions concerning his conduct, saying that he would publish Jackson's responses or use them in some other way, at his discretion. Jackson responded on May 19 that while he did not wish to be charged with interference in the election, justice required him to say that Grundy's opposition "to the absurd and wicked doctrines of Nullification and Secession" had been "highly useful and energetic" and that no one could have manifested a "greater zeal to give effect to administration measures."[12]

Grundy tracked the state legislative contests closely. On August 6, 1833, he wrote Jackson that he had lost Davidson County and that he considered his chances very doubtful. He complimented his opponent, saying that if elected, Foster would vote well, and he emphasized that his own feelings toward Jackson and the administration had not changed. By the next day, however, Grundy's spirits had risen. He wrote Jackson that the mail had brought reports of greater electoral strength in West Tennessee than anticipated. His prospects strengthened further as East Tennessee results became known, with Grundy writing Cave Johnson that he had received ten certain and two probable votes in that region. In addition, Grundy supporters organized public meeting in counties that had Foster or Eaton candidates to force legislators to shift to Grundy, who was considered more popular with voters. James K. Polk arranged a meeting in Columbia that brought the Maury County delegation to Grundy. On September 26, 1833, Polk confidently wrote Cave Johnson that Grundy's election was reasonably secure, with twenty-seven votes likely on the first ballot.[13]

The election took place on October 8, 1833, with Eaton now in Nashville. When Grundy appeared strong, John Bell was brought in at the last minute to unite the Eaton and Foster supporters; Bell, however, could not exceed twenty-three votes. The overflowing lobby cheered when Grundy achieved victory with thirty-three votes on the fifty-fifth ballot, votes from both Eaton and Foster going to Grundy; some suggested that Foster preferred Grundy over Eaton.[14]

The most telling summary came from Governor William Carroll, an adept politician, in a letter to Martin Van Buren:

> It is but justice to him [Grundy] to say, that his success was owing to his own ability in managing such things, and to a strong hold he has upon the good opinions of the great body of the people. He is now firmly fixed in his position for six years and to say that he will not hold a commanding influence during that period in our state would be doing him great injustice. He travels much throughout the State, is mild and social in his intercourse, and makes strong

impressions wherever he goes. I mention these things because in a long conversation with Mr. Grundy just before he left home, I found that his feelings were very kind towards yourself and I know you can easily adopt such a conciliatory course toward him as will not preserve but increase those feelings.

Even the *Nashville Republican and State Gazette* responded to the election gracefully.[15]

This two-year election struggle had lasting repercussions. Ephraim Foster, previously a nominal Jacksonian but sympathetic to the Erwin-Carroll group, took umbrage at his treatment by the president. Foster soon emerged as a leader in the anti-Jackson movement in Tennessee and ultimately the Whig Party, joined by other Jacksonians opposed to Jackson's influence on Tennessee, his economic policies with respect to the U.S. Bank and internal improvements, and his choice of Van Buren as vice president in 1832.[16]

As Foster and like-minded Jacksonians moved toward the Erwin group, which had always been anti-Jackson and close to Henry Clay, the composition of the Democratic leadership in Tennessee shifted. The Blount-Overton faction collapsed. John Overton died on April 9, 1833. John Eaton, appointed governor of the Florida Territory in 1834 and then minister to Spain in 1836, lost any remaining influence. William B. Lewis became identified with the U.S. Bank. The Grundy-Polk group thus became the core of the Democratic Party in Tennessee. As groups coalesced in favor of or opposed to Van Buren, Carroll, a strong supporter of the Little Magician, became more and more identified with Grundy and Polk. For the remaining years of Grundy's life the bitter clash between Whigs and Democrats would constitute Tennessee politics.

22

LAND AND SLAVERY

Were the question submitted to me, whether slavery should be introduced,
I should, unhesitatingly, decide against it.

—Felix Grundy

*P*olitics and law still dominated Grundy's life in the 1830s, but increasingly he devoted time and energy to more personal pursuits, including large-scale land speculation. The abolition movement and the growing political focus on slavery, however, cast a lengthening shadow.

In 1830 Grundy described himself as one of a group of elderly gentlemen, even though he was not yet fifty-five. In that period early death was not unusual, and many of Grundy's grandchildren died young. Yet Grundy sustained a major shock on August 8, 1832, when his daughter Margaret Ann Camron Rawlings passed away in Mississippi at age twenty-six, the first of his adult children to die. Less than four years later, on June 6, 1836, his oldest son, John Rodgers, died at age thirty-two. John Rodgers Grundy had practiced law briefly with his father before partnering with others in Nashville and in Dresden, Tennessee. He had moved to Columbus, Mississippi, in 1836 and died unexpectedly, leaving his wife and nine-year-old daughter.[1]

When he was in late middle age, Grundy's life followed well-defined contours. On social issues, as in politics, he tended toward the middle. Compared with such contemporaries as Jackson, Clay, and John Rowan, Grundy appears to have been a model of sobriety and propriety. To a biographer's chagrin, there are no references to colorful exploits, whether horse racing, dueling, excessive drinking, or womanizing. Grundy seems always to have been in control both in his personal life and on the legislative floor. Only his wit, his humor, and his oft-noted affability kept him from the stern rectitude that marked John C. Calhoun.

Good humor and moderate habits did not soften Grundy's stance on some social issues. He opposed dueling, which he spoke against on February 20, 1833, as a practice that was "contrary to the laws of God" and abhorred by public sentiment. Grundy favored imprisonment for those convicted of dueling and enthusiastically supported a proposed law that would ban duelists from ever holding federal office. To his grandchildren's complaint, he banned card playing in his house; there is no evidence that he bet at cards or at the track, despite his knowledge of horses.[2]

Although he had a reputation for being temperate, Grundy was no teetotaler. Conviviality in early Kentucky and Tennessee invariably involved a glass of whiskey or Madeira. A traveler to those states in 1821 reported with astonishment that most little towns substituted liquor shops for churches and that the "quantity of liquor drank in the western states is immense. Morning drams almost universal." Sam Houston summarized a night of drinking on May 6, 1832, when friends dropped by to show their support in a House disciplinary proceeding (in which Grundy spoke in Houston's defense) by commenting that Speaker of the House Andrew Stevenson was sleeping on the lounge, Balie Peyton was "out of commission," and Felix Grundy had "ceased to be interesting."[3]

Yet on the issue of temperance Grundy became a crusader. Largely driven by religious zeal, the national temperance movement proved remarkably successful. The average American reduced his consumption from seven gallons of alcohol per year in 1825 to 1.8 gallons by the late 1840s. Voluntary associations such as the American Temperance Society, founded in 1826, took the lead. Grundy initially played no role. He did not, for example, help launch the Nashville Temperance Society in 1829. But on February 24, 1833, Lewis Cass, as president, and Grundy and nine other vice presidents formed the Congressional Temperance Society, of which Grundy later served as president. In the late 1830s he emerged as a national spokesman, with New England temperance programs highlighting his judgment that 80 percent of all crimes committed in the country could be traced to drink.[4]

Grundy became a national temperance leader for one major reason—family alcoholism. A statement by him published in 1839 included one comment full of pathos: "What is the most frequent and saddest grief that ever hung upon the hearts of parents? It is the dissipation and intemperance of their children." Grundy spoke from experience. James Priestley Grundy, born in 1807, showed great promise, practicing law with his father and then in a very successful partnership with Edwin H. Ewing until January 1837 and engaging in political activities. We do not know when his alcohol problems became acute, but he "killed himself by drinking," dying on May 6, 1844, at age thirty-eight.[5]

Grundy continued his keen interest in financial opportunities, particularly land investment. In the 1830s he shifted his focus from real-estate development to large-scale speculation. Arkansas first beckoned Grundy and other Nashville investors in the 1830s. Lands along the Mississippi River offered big returns from cotton, particularly after Arkansas joined the Union as a slave state in 1836. Grundy, who consistently favored the sale of public lands at reduced prices, encouraged two of his sons-in-law, Jacob McGavock and John M. Bass, to buy land in Mississippi County, Arkansas. It is unclear how much land, if any, Grundy acquired in Arkansas. On March 14, 1834, he filed a memorandum with the General Land Office listing more than twenty-five hundred acres, for which he would be issued patents, all apparently to be conveyed to other individuals. I have found no evidence of patents issued to him, although his sons-in-law, Bass and McGavock, made major investments beginning in 1833, with Bass alone acquiring approximately twenty-three hundred acres from the land offices in Little Rock and Helena. Grundy's will, however, refers to slaves and other property that he held with Bass and McGavock in Arkansas.[6]

Arkansas whetted Grundy's appetite. He soon embarked on an ambitious venture involving Tennessee land, the mayor of Washington, DC, Boston financiers, and a search for European investors. Records in the Munroe Papers at the Connecticut Historical Society provide a rare window into the scale of Grundy's ambition and vision and the details and pitfalls of nineteenth-century land speculation. The revision of the Tennessee Constitution in 1834 offered Grundy his opportunity. Tennessee previously had taxed all lands alike, without regard to their actual value. This tax system had been at the core of the self-interested Blount faction, which had been able to acquire and hold for speculation the best lands in Tennessee. The new constitution prescribed ad valorem taxation and eliminated the principal reason for not acquiring lands of lesser value.[7]

Grundy recognized the speculative opportunity arising from the constitutional change and acquired rights for the entries to eighty-five thousand acres in Franklin and Warren counties, in south-central Tennessee. The lands had not yet been surveyed, a prerequisite to the issuance of patents in Tennessee. On November 9, 1835, Grundy entered into an agreement with John Stump and Frederic H. Stump under which Grundy would own two-thirds of the patents, and the Stumps, one-third. Grundy agreed to direct the occurrence and timing of the surveys and to advance $30 for each five thousand acres. The Stumps would arrange for the surveys to be made and the patents to be issued to Grundy and the Stumps in the agreed proportion. Grundy sent $255 to his son James on December 22, 1835, and asked him to advise the Stumps to begin work.[8]

Grundy, who was authorized to sell the lands under the agreement with the Stumps, advised his friend William A. Bradley, the mayor of Washington, DC, that significant acreage could be acquired at prices ensuring large profits. He asked Bradley to recommend a financing source that would reimburse him for the cost of surveys and arrange the sale of the lands. Grundy and his partners would receive half of the profits, and the financier would receive the other half. He told Bradley that he had already secured a two-thirds interest in eighty-five thousand acres and that he probably could obtain thirty-five thousand more.

Bradley contacted Samuel Barrell, a Bostonian, who was Bradley's partner in another land venture. After agreeing on terms with Grundy, Barrell invited another New England financier, Edmund Munroe, to join the investment group. In a long letter to Munroe on February 15, 1836, Barrell detailed the operation of Tennessee law and referred to Grundy as the only individual of enterprise who had focused on the opportunities arising from the constitutional change. Barrell also wrote that Grundy had reported that whites cultivated a great proportion of the improved lands in Tennessee and that slavery was on the decline.[9]

The agreement between Barrell and Grundy provided that Grundy would transfer half of his two-thirds interest, or 28,333.5 acres of the 85,000 already secured, for payment in cash of $5,510, the total amount he had paid for his interest. Of the additional 35,000 acres, Grundy would transfer half of his interest for what he would pay, estimated to be between 5¢ and 10¢ per acre. Future lands would be split two-thirds for the investors and one-third to Grundy, with the investors reimbursing Grundy for the entire cost. All the lands would be sold by Barrell, with profits to be divided in accordance with the ownership interests. In a separate document, Mayor Bradley agreed to take one-tenth of Barrell's rights and obligations.

Barrell advised Munroe that this would be a safe but profitable investment and that he was optimistic that Grundy could obtain good title to more than 500,000 acres of land at no more than five cents per acre. He said that Grundy "is a very cautious man" but that he probably could procure 2–3 million acres in all. Despite Barrell's optimism, Munroe initially declined to invest because of the scarcity of money. Barrell, undeterred by Munroe's reluctance and convinced that money would become available because the government would distribute its surplus revenue, closed the initial transaction on April 30, 1836, giving Grundy notes maturing in six months for the whole amount due and undertaking to sell all 120,000 acres.[10]

Grundy, caught up by Barrell's enthusiasm, expanded the venture's scope. After two days of negotiation he and Stump agreed on August 15, 1836, to add 300,000 acres to the program. Grundy committed to advancing all funds and urged Stump to move quickly, since from three to four months of work would be required, and others would be taking advantage of the change in the law. Barrell, however, soon incurred problems: he could not sell the lands. Writing to Grundy on September 4, 1836, he said that the "very stiff" money market in New York and Boston cost about 2 percent a month, and he attributed the cause to the Specie Circular, under which Secretary of the Treasury Levi Woodbury required gold and silver for the purchase of public lands. Barrell wrote again on September 17, reiterating his embarrassment at his inability thus far to sell the 120,000 acres but now questioning the business deal. He thought it unfair that Grundy would receive 75,000 acres under the new arrangement, since Colonel Stump was to perform duties originally to have been undertaken by Grundy.[11]

Despite the financial malaise, Barrell found a like-minded promoter who undertook to settle New England families on up to 620,000 acres and so advised Grundy on October 7, 1836. This proposal must have erased the doubts of Edmund Munroe, who reversed his position and, as reflected in a letter of October 17, agreed to become a partner jointly with Barrell. Accordingly, Barrell, presumably encouraged by the resettlement proposal and Munroe's change of heart, authorized Grundy on October 17 to draw three thousand dollars in ninety days and to acquire up to 500,000 more acres. In early 1837 Grundy revised his agreement with Barrell to give Barrell a greater interest but also moved forward to complete the surveys and obtain clear title to the additional 500,000 acres.[12]

This arrangement represented the peak of Grundy's land speculation in south-central Tennessee. Grundy would be entitled to more than 150,000 acres under the arrangement, with all his costs to be reimbursed by Barrell and Munroe. The open question was how quickly Barrell could find buyers for 620,000 acres of Tennessee land. The next three years proved doleful for the venture. Barrell sold only small portions of the land, and the idea of relocating New Englanders to Tennessee came to naught. Barrell arranged with another financier, Joshua Dodge, to sell the lands in Europe, but the Panic of 1837 intervened. On April 29, 1837, Barrell advised Grundy that business had almost entirely ceased in Boston, that Munroe had stopped payment on obligations (though not his smaller ones to Grundy) and lands were worthless as security. Grundy, who meanwhile continued to expedite surveys and title, wrote Barrell on May 7, 1837, that Dodge would have grants for 300,000 acres available for sale but that in Nashville too money was "not to be had in any way."

Grundy confronted the promoter's nightmare—that Barrell and Munroe would not honor their notes. On June 1, 1837, he admitted his "perplexities," reported that he had already staked his private credit, and confessed that the "possibility of a paper drawn by me, being protested strikes me with horror." Three days later Grundy wrote again, saying that grants for 308,000 acres had been issued in Barrell's name and sent to him. He pointed out that Munroe's ultimate wealth would be of little use to Grundy if Munroe did not honor Grundy's drafts, and he put the matter strongly to Barrell: "I have enough of trouble, about my own business . . . you should put this matter of money to rest, by any sacrifice." Despite their own differences, Barrell and Munroe protected Grundy. First Barrell assuaged Grundy's concern and promised to cover any drafts not honored by Munroe. Second, and more fundamentally, Munroe ultimately honored Grundy's drafts. Grundy and Stump accordingly continued their Tennessee efforts, and by 1838 patents had been issued for a total of 722,664 acres.[13]

The lands continued unsold during the remainder of Grundy's life. Dodge failed to sell the lands in Germany. Other efforts to find purchasers abroad also failed, even though Barrell himself went to Europe. Barrell, frustrated, became increasingly testy when he was importuned by Grundy and Bradley, and he displayed impatience with Grundy for not promptly arranging for the correction of defective grants and certificates. Barrell's London correspondents could not help, pessimistically commenting in July 1840 that purchasers could not be found for American investments. Grundy's claims to the unsold lands would complicate the settlement of his estate.[14]

Grundy devoted a significant amount of time and energy to this major Tennessee land speculation. He originated the idea, arranged for effective Tennessee implementation, and located and persuaded Boston financiers to finance the purchase of more than seven hundred thousand acres. It appears that Grundy was reimbursed for his costs but did not profit from the venture. Although assigning responsibility cannot be carried too far, the financial crisis surrounding the depression of 1837 seems to have been the primary cause of the failure to sell the lands. Ironically, the banking policies pursued by Jackson and Van Buren faithfully championed by Grundy, contributed in no small part to that financial crisis.

* * *

During these same years, Grundy confronted, almost for the first time, the political implications of slavery. He was not a major slave owner himself, but his participation in the slave economy makes clear that he took slavery for granted, as an integral component of southern life.

Grundy grew up in a slave-owning world, but there is little evidence of his views about slavery before the 1830s. Kentucky constitutionally protected slavery, and Grundy's constituents, otherwise both egalitarian and antigovernment, looked to the state to protect slavery. By the time of the second Kentucky constitutional convention, in 1799, the twenty-four-year-old Grundy already owned seven slaves, and he voted to prohibit a future legislature from preventing the importation of slaves to Kentucky. Grundy's mentor George Nicholas encapsulated the views of many of his contemporaries when, in preparing for the convention elections, he wrote, "I never did approve of slavery, but I have thought that the removing of it in a proper manner, would be attended with great difficulties; and the doing of it in an improper manner, would produce greater evils to the country, than it would remove."[15]

Tennessee proved equally hospitable to slavery. Unlike East Tennessee, where topography encouraged the growth of small farms, West Tennessee had rolling, arable land conducive to larger-scale agriculture. As early as the first census of 1790–91 slaves represented 19 percent of the population of Davidson County. Although East Tennessee succeeded in 1812 in persuading the legislature to prohibit for five years the importation of slaves into Tennessee for sale, the legislation had little long-term effect. In 1860 slaves constituted 24.8 percent of Tennessee's population.[16]

Grundy, an urban dweller, made his living primarily from the practice of law and land investments and only indirectly from slavery. He did not operate farms for any appreciable period, in contrast to Polk, Jackson, Clay, and Calhoun, who presided over large-scale plantations with many slaves. Grundy, however, used skilled slave craftsmen in the construction of Grundy Place, in Nashville, and received at least one slave as a legal fee. He also owned house servants. The census records for Davidson County show that he owned nine slaves in 1820 and ten slaves in 1830, with the age-distribution patterns suggesting that most of the slaves, at least the males, were with the Grundys for many years.[17]

Grundy's personal relationships with blacks were paternalistic. In 1817 he and Judge James Trimble provided security for a free black, Trim Meyers, when he received a license to operate an ordinary. Grundy purportedly was devoted to Ambrose, his manservant, who traveled to and from Washington with Grundy and is buried near Grundy in the family plot. Notwithstanding Grundy's later doubts about successful integration of blacks into white society, he politically supported free blacks. In the Kentucky constitutional convention in 1799 Felix favored voting rights for Indians and free blacks. In Tennessee, where free blacks could vote in all elections from 1796 to 1835, he and other politicians assiduously courted the black electorate.[18]

Grundy did participate in the slave economy. It is ironical that the first correspondence between Felix Grundy and Andrew Jackson in the Library of Congress comprises two slave bills of sale, for a mother and daughter sold by Grundy to Jackson for six hundred dollars. Records in Middle Tennessee counties evidence an occasional purchase or sale of slaves by Grundy. Moreover, there are two revealing transactions with sons-in-law. The first reflects an effort to assist Ramsey Mayson in 1818, less than two years after Mayson married Grundy's second daughter without Grundy's consent. Grundy agreed on April 18, 1818, that on October 1 of that year he would furnish Mayson with "ten Negro Slaves, none to exceed forty years of age, four at least to be likely fellows." Mayson agreed to take the slaves to the Alabama Territory or the state of Mississippi and arrange contract labor for five years beginning January 1, 1819. Grundy and Mayson agreed to bear all costs and share all profits equally, with the slaves to be returned to Grundy when the contracts expired. Whether the agreement was ever put into effect is not known.[19]

The second transaction arose after Grundy's sons-in-law, Jacob McGavock and John M. Bass, acquired large cotton-growing tracts in Arkansas in the 1830s. Bass asked his father-in-law to acquire slaves for his Arkansas land. On December 19, 1835, Grundy wrote that he was confident that he could make purchases on good terms. Bass sent funds, and on March 31, 1836, Grundy, in Washington, purchased a family of five from a seller in Fairfax County, Virginia, for fifteen hundred dollars.[20]

Grundy's acceptance of slavery was characteristic of that very different time. At least until the 1830s all parties more or less accepted slavery as part of the constitutional bargain of 1787, even as national pressures for abolition were building. Grundy first examined slavery at length when he spoke on Foot's Resolution on February 27 and March 1, 1830. He unequivocally adopted a libertarian view, proclaiming that "were the question submitted to me, whether slavery should be introduced, I should, unhesitatingly, decide against it; for such is my devotion to liberty and the rights of man, that I would have no agency in subjecting the person or will of one man to the dominion of another."[21]

These words, however, could not mask Grundy's judgment that the problem was too deep-seated for resolution, a position much like that adopted by George Nicholas thirty-one years before and similar to the stances taken by both Jefferson and Madison. Grundy, positing a fairly standard border-state view, argued that slavery was an inherited institution. Slavery had its sanction in history, whether in classical times or in the biblical worlds of the Old and New Testament. Jesus had enjoined slaves to be obedient to their masters, making clear that it was not sinful to own slaves. Blame for slavery in the United States should not be attributed to the slaveholder but instead "to those who produced this state of things." The British merchants and the slave traders of the eastern states were culpable for bringing slaves to the South. The avarice and cupidity of some of their citizens had prevailed over justice and humanity. This was a standard argument and was not restricted to southerners. The New Yorker James Fenimore Cooper, a critic of slavery but a defender of the South, asserted in 1828 that the entire country was involved in the guilt of slavery, charging that slaveholders, as a body, "are just as innocent of the creation of slavery, as their fellow citizens of New York or Connecticut."[22]

Although Grundy insisted that he did not advocate slavery, he saw no way to end the institution; slavery was a cruel misfortune for which there was no workable solution. He feared that free blacks could not be integrated successfully into white society and believed that "these general notions about the liberation of slaves are idle and visionary, when attempts are made to reduce them to practice." He acknowledged the well-meaning efforts of philanthropists but did not believe that moving blacks to Africa or to Canada was the answer to the slavery question. In 1836 Samuel Barrell wrote that Grundy believed slavery was on the decline in Tennessee. Unfortunately, there is no other evidence to support this view, which is perhaps questionable in light of the evidence that the South was more committed to slavery in the early nineteenth century than it had been at the time of the Revolution.[23]

Like most Jacksonians, Grundy opposed the abolitionists, whose efforts could only be divisive and divert focus from other political goals. Efforts to abolish slavery had a pedigree even in the South, as reflected in the emancipation discussions in Kentucky in the 1790s. The yeoman farms and mountains of East Tennessee harbored Quakers and Presbyterians of an antislavery bent; indeed, the Upper South as a whole as late as 1827 reported four to five times the number of antislavery adherents found in the free states. Two of the earliest newspapers favoring emancipation appeared in Jonesboro and Greenville, Tennessee, in 1819 and 1822, respectively. Nevertheless, abolitionism only arose in force in the 1830s, and mainly in the North, just as the opening of cotton lands in West Tennessee, Arkansas, and Texas led to the demand for more slaves in the South. In Tennessee, the antislavery movement of the 1830s differed qualitatively from the earlier emancipation effort, being founded less on Christian principles and democratic egalitarianism and more on distrust of blacks and fears of slave uprisings.[24]

The American Anti-Slavery Society initiated a major campaign in the mid-1830s to send abolitionist tracts to southern states and the District of Columbia. The fight over what became known as the "gag rule" began in the House of Representatives, where an unattractively ambitious freshman Congressman, James Hammond, of South Carolina, sought to enhance his career by proposing that the House not consider petitions to abolish slavery in the District. John C. Calhoun, who in 1837 would pronounce slavery a positive "good," also favored rejection of the mailings. In January 1836, asserting that the petitioners were fanatics, he urged the Senate to ban all such memorials as an insult to the South. Grundy, among others, argued that citizens had an unequivocal right to petition, but he said that Congress, with no obligation to consider the submissions, could simply table them. Grundy and three other southern Democrats joined in the 36–10 rejection of Calhoun's position on March 9, 1836.[25]

Although Grundy followed his party's lead in rejecting Calhoun's position, he opposed the abolitionists. He feared that discussing the petitions could lead the free states to attempt to remove constitutionally protected property in the slaveholding states, which would lead to dissolution of the Union. Grundy also rejected any change in the District of Columbia. If slavery was abolished, the District would become a haven for runaway slaves and thus an unfit site for the nation's capital.[26]

Grundy's anger at the abolitionists never abated. Some of this was attributable to party loyalty, since the Jackson and Van Buren Democrats believed that party success depended on the continued suppression of the slavery question. Some, however, reflected the moderate Grundy's real concern that abolitionists did not understand or perhaps even care about the implications of the course they were pursuing. Grundy displayed his animosity in a lengthy political letter on January 18, 1838, sent to political correspondents throughout Tennessee. Referring to an anti-abolitionist resolution just adopted, Grundy said he hoped that it would "discourage the incendiary proceedings of these Fanatics; who show, by their reckless course that they are wholly regardless of consequences; altho' the destruction of the union should be produced." He claimed that President Van Buren would be more successful than anyone else in putting down this "dangerous and disorganizing spirit." Grundy's position reflected not only his personal view but the view of the Democrats in Tennessee, who were now in a political battle with the Whig Party.[27]

23

BATTLES WITH THE WHIGS

The most brilliant wit in the Senate.

—*Boston Post*

*G*rundy's public service from his reelection to the Senate in 1833 until his death in 1840 featured nearly continuous strife with the emerging Whig Party, particularly in Tennessee. The Panic of 1837, induced by Jacksonian banking uncertainties, exacerbated the political issues confronting Grundy and his protégé James K. Polk.

The Twenty-third Congress convened on December 2, 1833. Grundy's reelection gave him more independence, enhancing his political stature in Washington and his leadership role in Tennessee. Unlike John Bell and Ephraim Foster, however, who had also endured electoral slights from the president, Grundy continued to display his loyalty to Jackson and Democratic principles, particularly in the battles over the deposit-removal plan.[1]

During the summer recess of 1833 Jackson formulated the final details of his plan to remove government deposits from the Second Bank of the United States. Overcoming the objections of advisers who thought Congress should be involved, as well as the opposition of two successive secretaries of the treasury, Jackson in August 1833 ordered the Treasury to cease depositing government funds in the Second Bank and place them instead in state banks. The new secretary of the treasury, Roger Brooke Taney, began the implementation of Jackson's plan on September 26, 1833, within a week of his appointment. After October 1, 1833, government deposits would be made in selected state banks, and regular government expenditures would reduce and ultimately eliminate the government fund at the Second Bank. Jackson's decision produced a storm of protest. Nicholas Biddle, convinced that distress in business circles would bring about not only restoration of the deposits but also the rechartering of the Second Bank, reduced discounts, collected balances from state banks, and in general greatly restricted the credit that sustained the economy.[2]

When Congress convened in December, it appeared that anti-Jacksonians would control the Senate as it confronted the deposit-removal plan. After Clay and his National Republicans raised the cry "King Andrew," Calhoun and his forces, who had worked with Clay on the Compromise Tariff earlier that year, joined the opposition, even though many Calhounites opposed a national bank. The third anti-Jackson bloc, led by Daniel Webster, also appeared securely in the national bank camp, particularly since Webster saw no problem in accepting a retainer from the bank while pursuing the bank's legislative interest. Webster, however, saw an opportunity. The ambitious New Englander had worked closely with Grundy on the Force Bill and displayed little personal hostility to Jackson. Moreover, Jackson's nullification stance had impressed and pleased many northerners, perhaps nowhere more clearly demonstrated than in Harvard College's decision to award Jackson a honorary degree just six months earlier. Webster saw an opportunity to preserve his independence by siding with Jackson on critical issues and perhaps bid for the succession by creating a new Unionist party made up of those who disliked Van Buren and Clay.[3]

Webster suggested to Grundy that he and his supporters collaborate with the Jacksonians on committee organization, thereby giving the Democrats a potential advantage in the bank-deposit struggle. After consulting with Jackson, Grundy temporized in order to obtain input from Van Buren, proposing on December 12 that consideration of the committees be postponed until December 16. Grundy's motion passed, 28–13, thanks to the votes of Webster and nine other senators hitherto assumed to be voting with Clay and Calhoun. Consternation prevailed among the anti-administration forces, Clay urging Senator John M. Clayton to "come to us. And do not let anything keep you away."[4]

Van Buren returned to Washington on Saturday, December 14, 1833, and went to the White House the next morning, where he found the president and Grundy in deep conversation by the fireplace. Grundy presented the situation and raised the possibility of collaboration. Van Buren, instantly recognizing the political threat to his succession, opposed such a collaboration, which was reminiscent of the difficult coalitions of the 1820s. Jackson and Grundy acquiesced, thus ending the brief collaboration and the possibility of a Unionist party. Webster joined the anti-Jackson forces, and Clay, Calhoun, and Webster—the Great Triumvirate—with disparate interests and objectives, united against Jackson.[5]

The principal battle of the new session was Jackson's opposition to the Second Bank. Jackson may not have grasped the full implications of his bank-deposit plan, but Biddle made by far the greater miscalculation. When financial failures multiplied in January 1834, Biddle felt confident that his policy of "discipline" (Webster's maladroit word) for the people would be successful. But when the governor of Pennsylvania, where the Second Bank was located, denounced the bank's actions, it signaled the end of the struggle. The exercise of its power made clear even to some bank partisans that perhaps Jackson's view— that the placement of so much economic and financial power in the hands of an unelected few was incompatible with democracy—was right.[6]

Even when it was apparent that the Second Bank had overreached and that the unyielding Jackson could outlast it, Jackson's enemies in Congress continued to castigate the president, making political capital of his so-called tyrannical actions. Harkening back to the Revolution, they identified themselves as Whigs, comparing King Andrew to George III. Ultimately, Clay used his majority in the Senate to pass a resolution of censure of the president on March 28, 1834, by a vote of 26–20.

Grundy, who was not a leader in the bank-deposit plan, distinguished himself before and after the censure vote with witty and logical speeches in support of Jackson. On January 30, 1834, he gave an extended speech upholding the president's constitutional authority, pointing to precedents involving Alexander Hamilton, Albert Gallatin, and William Crawford, and rejecting the opposition argument that the secretary of the treasury had authority independent of the president. With respect to future bank deposits, Grundy suggested that the logical approach would be first to decide whether the Second Bank should be rechartered and then, only if it was decided that it should be, determine whether it should receive deposits. He emphasized that he opposed rechartering and ringingly encapsulated his stance: "The bank must go down, or we will have in our country a great moneyed power that will rule the government. . . . The true question . . . is, whether the people . . . are to be governed by the constituted authorities influenced by the public will, or by an unfeeling corporation placed entirely beyond their control." The administration press applauded the speech, with the *Boston Post* calling Grundy "one of the ablest supporters of the administration, and the most brilliant wit in the Senate" and the *Washington Globe* describing the presentation as unanswerable.[7]

Following his censure, Jackson sent a written message of protest on April 17. Senator George Poindexter, of Mississippi, objected to receiving Jackson's message. In contrast, Georgia's John Forsyth proposed that the censure resolution and Jackson's protest be submitted to state legislatures. Grundy joined Forsyth and launched an attack on the new Whigs, who had misappropriated a term that had great meaning in America. He emphasized repeatedly that the current Whigs were the Federalists of the War of 1812, who only twenty-two years earlier had been the opponents of patriots like Jackson and Grundy. Indeed, the term *Whigs* mischaracterized Jackson's opposition, which included friends of the Second Bank, nullifiers, tariff supporters, and states' righters.[8]

The struggle over rechartering the Second Bank and implementation of the deposit plan reached its climax in the House, where, unlike in the Senate, the Democrats enjoyed a fragile majority. Polk led the fight for the administration. The death knell for the bank sounded in April 1834, when the House, by a vote of 134–82, approved resolutions against rechartering.

Jackson's victory over the Second Bank and increasing national partisanship inevitably contributed to the growth of party feeling in Tennessee. Two issues in particular exacerbated differences among nominal Jacksonians in the state and sharpened the emerging clash between Whigs and Democrats: banking issues and the presidential succession.

The Whig Party in Tennessee did not spring into existence overnight. It originated in the Andrew Erwin group. Significantly, William B. Lewis and the remnant of the Overton faction, motivated by ties to the national bank, also supported the Whigs. But most important, increasing numbers of prominent Tennesseans opposed Jackson, his policies, and especially his autocratic tendencies. No greater evidence exists of Jackson's polarizing force than the fact that almost all the Whig leaders in Tennessee had left the Democratic Party at least in part because of personal hostility toward Jackson. These included Newton Cannon and the celebrated Davy Crockett, who had said that "to turn against Jackson was the unpardonable sin." John Bell and Ephraim Foster smarted from Jackson's support for Grundy in the congressional race in 1827 and the Senate contest in 1832–33, respectively. In 1833 and 1834 they remained nominal Jacksonians, but in the battles to come Bell would be the de facto leader of the Whigs, and Cannon and Foster his able lieutenants.[9]

The 1834 contest for the post of Speaker of the House provided a harbinger of the future. Based on early readings of House members by Grundy and others, Polk concluded in late autumn 1833 that with the support of Jackson and particularly Martin Van Buren, who controlled the New York delegation, he could be Speaker. One formidable adversary could be his fellow Tennessean and erstwhile Jacksonian John Bell, who might garner Whig and anti–Van Buren Democratic votes. Polk's candidacy would necessitate delicacy, since he would be required to reassure Van Buren of his loyalty at the same time that he was seeking the support of the nullifiers. Grundy provided critical help, using his ties with Calhoun and the nullifiers generally for the benefit of his protégé. When the Calhoun forces recognized that Van Buren favored Polk, however, the moment passed, and Bell won on the tenth ballot.[10]

John Bell's success over Jackson's candidate, including an open appeal for Whig votes, led Polk and Grundy and their allies into an effort in Tennessee that summer to cast Bell as a Jackson apostate. Building on Polk's personal hostility to Bell, their efforts encompassed both banking policy and the presidential succession. The Democrats painted Bell as a national-bank advocate, and Bell's supporters among the Nashville commercial elite favored such a bank. In particular, they charged that Bell was for *a* bank, if not *the* bank. When Jackson made clear at a celebratory dinner in his honor on August 13, 1834, that he opposed a national bank of any kind, Bell, Foster, and other nominal Jacksonians recognized that lines had been drawn. Foster allegedly declared, "We are broke down. Grundy and Polk are to rule this State; the Bank will have to go down."[11]

Despite differences on banking issues, the lines separating Jacksonians had not yet been fully drawn. The catalyst for the final break was Martin Van Buren. Although Grundy had endorsed Van Buren for vice president in early 1832, he had made no commitment concerning the Jacksonian succession at the time of his reelection to the Senate in 1833. Van Buren and Grundy may have had friendly relations, but as Van Buren acknowledged in his autobiography, they had barely known each other as recently as 1830. Van Buren supporters had opposed Grundy for the Senate in 1829; in addition, the remnants of the Blount-Overton group, which had just tried to terminate Grundy's Senate career, favored Van Buren. As a capstone, many Tennesseans, particularly those with links to Calhoun, distrusted Van Buren, a New Yorker with a reputation for deviousness. (As a result, there are suggestions, but little firm evidence, that after Calhoun's downfall Grundy flirted with the idea of a Unionist party and supporting other presidential candidates.)

Countering these considerations loomed Jackson's clear support of his vice president and the linkage of the Grundy/Polk group to Jackson. Grundy also recognized the desirability of retaining strong ties to the northern wing of the Democratic Party, buttressing strict constructionist, proslavery policies just as the abolition movement was beginning to be heard. At William Carroll's suggestion after Grundy's reelection victory in 1833, Grundy and Van Buren met and apparently reached an understanding, including that Polk would be the administration favorite for Speaker of the House. In August 1834 Jackson wrote Van Buren: "Grundy told me the other day he would go the whole *hog* for you, and this openly and boldly whenever it became necessary." For Grundy, however, it would become necessary only when conditions demanded a choice; until then he would preserve his options and, as always, focus on party unity.[12]

Everything came to a head when Senator Hugh Lawson White (1773–1840) decided to run for president. White was an almost cadaverous East Tennessean of serious purpose and demeanor, the son of the founder of Knoxville. He rarely spoke, partly because of a pronounced stammer, but when he did, people listened to the Cato of the Senate. He harbored ambitions to succeed Jackson and was disappointed when John Eaton became secretary of war in Jackson's first cabinet. His disappointment turned to envy when Jackson made clear that he wanted Van Buren to succeed him. An opponent of the Second Bank, a stalwart Jacksonian, and a states' rights slave owner, White dismissed two proposals from Tennesseans early in 1834 that he run for president.[13]

In December 1834 Duff Green urged Grundy and Polk to support White, but Grundy said he was not prepared to act on the subject. Then, at the invitation of the East Tennessee congressman James Standifer, probably acting at the instigation of Bell, the Tennessee congressional delegation, except for Grundy and Polk, met in Washington to consider a White candidacy for the presidency. Ultimately the entire delegation, except Grundy, Polk, and Cave Johnson, who had attended the meeting for informational purposes, asked White if he would allow his name to be considered. White consented. Jackson, whose hostility to his candidacy had angered White, soon blasted the East Tennessean. Although the White supporters opposed Van Buren, they also were responding to Jackson's Nullification Proclamation, his Force Bill, and his removal of bank deposits. As Donald Cole has pointed out, White's candidacy reflected Jackson's diminishing influence in Tennessee's politics.[14]

Grundy and Polk treaded a fine line. Both acknowledged their friendship for White, and some White supporters believed that they had committed to back him. But both Grundy and Polk reiterated that their earlier support for White had been conditional on party unity. Grundy declared publicly that he had said earlier that he would "go with the party" if a candidate other than White was favored by the majority of Democrats. At their convention in Baltimore in May 1835, the Democrats, absent Grundy, Polk, and other leading Tennessee Jacksonians, endorsed Van Buren, thereby ensuring that Tennessee Democrats, led by Grundy and Polk, would unite behind their party's candidate and against a Tennessee native son. In 1836 five candidates emerged for the presidency. The mainstream Whigs nominated William Henry Harrison, who was unenthusiastically received by Massachusetts, which decided to support Daniel Webster. South Carolina put North Carolina's Senator Willie P. Mangum in the field. The Whigs hoped that White would siphon off enough southern votes from Van Buren to throw the presidential choice into the House of Representatives. The Democrats, conversely, hoped that the four other candidates would so splinter the anti–Van Buren voters that he would be elected without undue difficulty.[15]

The first test for Tennessee Democrats would be the elections in 1835 for governor, the state legislature, and the U.S. Congress. As soon as Congress adjourned in March 1835, Grundy left Washington with the Polks and the Calhounite congressman C. C. Clay, of Alabama, traveling first by private stagecoach to Wheeling and then by steamboat via the Ohio and Cumberland rivers to Nashville. Grundy and Polk plotted their strategy. Shortly after his arrival, Grundy summarized the Tennessee political scene for Jackson, reporting that extraordinary efforts had been made for White; that Carroll, the gubernatorial candidate, had publicly declared for Van Buren and would win his election; and that he, Grundy, now supported Van Buren openly, believing that "a bold course is the prudent one." His letter reflected the new political alignments: Foster and other nominal Jacksonians vigorously supported the popular White, while Carroll joined Grundy, Polk, Cave Johnson, Andrew Donelson, and John Catron in the Democratic camp. Although Grundy continually demonstrated his loyalty to Van Buren, the support came at a cost, since he now was required constantly to affirm Van Buren's reliability with respect to southern issues.[16]

The campaign in 1835 centered on the Jacksonian succession, although state issues also played a role. Grundy took the brunt of the assaults from the White forces. The *Knoxville Register* reflected a widespread view when it wrote that "of the few prominent politicians who are opposed to Judge White, Mr. Grundy is the acknowledged leader." Taking a positive stance, Grundy attributed the attacks on him solely to his refusal to relinquish his independence with respect to the presidential succession. Demonstrating again his sensitivity to public perception, he asked Jackson to answer certain questions related to the insinuations of political enemies that Grundy had been the instrument of the breach between Jackson, on the one hand, and White and Bell, on the other. Jackson replied on June 11 that he had no recollection of ever receiving a communication from Grundy calculated to do either the slightest injury and that his opposition to them had been based on their having taken positions adverse to demo-cratic principles.[17]

Belying their fierce rhetoric, both parties drew largely from the same eco-nomic base. The Whigs tended to dominate commercial centers, particularly Nashville, and enjoyed control of the press, with the notable exception of the *Nashville Union,* formed by Grundy and Polk. Yet even in the towns, many political leaders retained their Democratic allegiance. A study of the Nash-ville area suggests that no clear socioeconomic differences existed between the prominent adherents of the two political parties; family and friends were the best indicators of party choice in the 1830s and 1840s. In the countryside, small farmers—the traditional Jeffersonian yeoman—constituted the bedrock of the Democratic Party. The county court was the fulcrum of political life, and there Grundy exercised great sway through his legal reputation and his friendships. A Polk ally later declared that "Mr. Grundy . . . knows every body" in Ruther-ford County.[18]

Extensive correspondence in the late spring and summer of 1835 among Grundy, Jackson, Polk, and Cave Johnson reflects the importance attached to the Tennessee elections. Despite hard campaigning and press support in the *Union,* the Democrats failed in the August elections. Newton Cannon handily defeated William Carroll for the governorship. More ominously, and reflective of White's popularity, the Whigs took both houses in the state legislature and all but a handful of the U.S. congressional seats.[19]

The race that most mattered, however, did not occur until more than a year later. Tempers ran high in Tennessee in the presidential contest in 1836. White was popular and respected, a native son. No one questioned his adher-ence to states' rights, republican principles, and slavery. The White forces con-tinued their attacks on Grundy, since he led the party in the state, and both Van Buren and White ran as Jacksonians. Both the press and White support-ers railed at the Democrats' efforts to paint a vote for White as a vote against Jackson. Despite brave talk and extensive campaigning by the Van Buren forces, particularly after July 1836, when Congress was out of session, Tennes-seans voted overwhelmingly for their native son in 1836. White received 58 per-cent of the statewide vote, running strongly in East and West Tennessee. Mid-dle Tennessee, in particular Polk's and Johnson's congressional districts, gave more support to Van Buren. Particularly galling to Jackson was that his home precinct, Hermitage, voted 43–18 for White. White also carried Georgia. Van Buren did reasonably well in other southern states, receiving 173 electoral votes, which was enough to take the presidency without House action and gave Jackson the satisfaction of seeing his protégé in the White House.[20]

The relationship between Grundy and White—Tennessee's two senators—became noticeably frosty. Grundy wrote his son-in-law John Bass in December 1835 that White "looks and feels lonely here, the Whigs north of the Potomac will not touch him," but the two Tennesseans necessarily had to cooperate periodically. Although Grundy and White worked together harmoniously before 1834, they now engaged in mutual recrimination. In Van Buren's view, White was the only man Grundy cordially disliked, and that was because White disliked him.[21]

Martin Van Buren assumed the presidency on March 3, 1837. His predecessor could look back on a series of accomplishments, including retirement of the national debt, destruction of the Second Bank of the United States, resolution of the nullification crisis and the related tariff controversy, and his designation of Van Buren as his successor. Van Buren, less fortunate, soon confronted a different, and difficult, legacy of the Jackson years, the Panic of 1837.

Jackson's victory over the Second Bank had left open the question whether and how to provide financial credit throughout the country. Tennessee entrepreneurs, including Polk's brothers-in-law, had partially answered that question for their state in 1832. The legislature that year chartered the Union Bank of Tennessee for thirty years with a capitalization of up to $3 million, with the state providing $500,000 in bonds and appointing five directors. The state would deposit interest-bearing funds with the bank and use bank proceeds to fund schools. The Union Bank received more than $2.2 million in subscriptions and took over the financing of the cotton crop just as the branch of the Second Bank curtailed its activities. The legislature chartered other state banks in subsequent years.[22]

There is little written evidence of Grundy's role in the initiation of these banks. He had supported state banks in both Kentucky and Tennessee, however, and his opposition to Jackson and Carroll and other advocates of hard money dovetailed exactly with the views of state-bank proponents. Moreover, the Democratic leadership of Tennessee ensured that Grundy would have a say in bank affairs even, or particularly, in a year when he was up for senate reelection. Grundy's son-in-law John Bass, Nashville's mayor in 1833, also supported the Union Bank. It thus is highly likely that Grundy played some role in the formation of the bank, even if behind the scenes.

Grundy's support for the Union Bank was more evident in later years. The Union Bank was an original federal deposit bank in 1833, and Grundy interceded with his friend Levi Woodbury, secretary of the treasury, several times on behalf of the bank. In 1836 Grundy suggested to Bass certain legislative initiatives that would forbid the establishment of branches of any bank chartered in or by another state, and later he sent Bass a copy of a directive from Secretary Woodbury affecting payments to the Union Bank.[23]

Other states authorized their own banks. Soon it became clear that the financial discipline exercised by the Second Bank of the United States had been replaced by an unfettered profusion of notes issued by proliferating state banks. In 1830, 329 banks had outstanding notes totaling $61 million; by 1837, 788 banks had issued $149 million in outstanding notes. Secretary Woodbury tried to constrain speculative excess by his Specie Circular of July 11, 1836, which required that public lands be paid for only in gold and silver, the directive that so adversely affected Grundy's large-scale Tennessee land speculation with Samuel Barrell and Edmund Munroe. In 1837 tightening credit brought about acute financial distress. In Nashville the Planters' and Union banks suspended specie payments on May 25, 1837, and the next day, the Farmers and Merchants Bank of Memphis also did so. Since the state's only private bank, Yeatman, Woods and Company, had suspended on May 16, the actions by the three state banks meant that Tennessee had no specie-paying bank.[24]

The Whigs attributed the Panic to Jackson's financial policies. Clamor mounted for a new national bank that would provide financial discipline and facilitate transfers of public money. The Democrats appeared confused and rudderless. Grundy became sufficiently concerned that he wrote Woodbury on June 1, 1837, expressing great unease at the lack of a Democrat response to the financial crisis and asking Woodbury what the administration was going to recommend.[25]

The Democratic disarray engendered by the Panic of 1837 and the political ascendancy of the Whigs in Tennessee had placed Grundy in a perilous position. Grundy's senatorial term did not expire until March 4, 1839. If, however, the Whigs took control of the legislature in 1837, they would be able to choose a successor in that year (to take the seat two years later) or issue instructions to Tennessee senators with respect to substantive votes. Instructions were not extraordinary, and Alfred Balch wrote Jackson in August 1835 that Grundy, who might resign if instructed to vote contrary to his principles, could not "be gotten to open his mouth except in a corner."[26]

In 1837 the third straight year of significant political contests in Tennessee, the Whigs highlighted Grundy's role and campaigned for the election of legislators who would vote two years early for a successor to Grundy. Grundy had suggested to Polk in April that the Democrats should immediately argue that the senatorial election should not take place in 1837 as proposed by the Whigs. The Democratic position would help in the election races, since a premature election would deprive "the people of what might suit them when the time comes, when a Senator will be needed." Candidates lined up for or against Grundy. Jackson, writing just after the election, reported that he had discovered the plot against Grundy weeks earlier: *"He is the object."*[27]

The Democrats hoped to counter the Whigs and the threat to Grundy by running strong legislative candidates and persuading White backers to return to the Democratic fold. In addition, they sought a gubernatorial nominee who could prevail against the incumbent, Newton Cannon. After abortive efforts to find other candidates, Grundy and Polk offered the candidacy to General Robert Armstrong, a former Indian fighter and postmaster in Nashville who was close to Bell, Foster, and other Whigs. Grundy and other Tennessee leaders decided on a low-key election strategy for the Armstrong-Cannon gubernatorial race. Rather than run as a party governor, Armstrong would address state issues exclusively. Grundy developed this approach, supported by other Democratic leaders, on the basis that the national Democratic Party led by Van Buren would only be a liability in 1837 and that the Whigs appeared divided. With Bell and Foster supporting Armstrong, a "family quarrel" might develop among prominent White supporters. Armstrong wrote Polk that he was being governed in all things by "Carroll, Grundy, Graham, etc." There is evidence that Polk disagreed with this approach and urged an all-out war against White supporters.[28]

Grundy participated fully in the election, partly through oversight of the *Nashville Union*. The *Union* editor, Samuel Laughlin, who was effective enough when he was sober, was usually drunk in 1837, and the paper required supervision and a constant infusion of funds from Polk, Grundy, Catron, Donelson, and others. The correspondence to and from Polk during the period 1835–37 is filled with assessments of the *Union*'s financial position. Soon the *Union*'s debts became unmanageable, and Grundy and Catron took over the newspaper's books on June 16, 1837, in order to assess its financial status. Grundy and others reorganized the paper with John O. Bradford as editor, but not until J. George Harris became editor in January 1839 was the *Union* in strong hands. In addition to organizational efforts, Grundy got involved in the nitty-gritty of publication. For five days in late June 1835 Grundy was responsible for getting the paper out, and in July 1837 he agreed to review everything that appeared in the paper.[29]

Grundy's strategy of emphasizing personality, not party, failed in 1837. Cannon defeated Armstrong by nearly twenty thousand votes, and only Polk and two other congressmen withstood the Whig onslaught; even Cave Johnson was defeated, by fewer than one hundred votes. Voter turnout was high, approximately 80 percent, compared with only 55 percent in the 1836 presidential campaign, and Cannon's margin exceeded 60 percent. Grundy's only letter was matter-of-fact: "We have been defeated in this county altogether, but not badly." He advised Polk that he was leaving for Washington shortly, by the stage to Louisville, with Mrs. Grundy, his daughter Maria, and his granddaughter Ann McGavock. Jackson fumed at the results, writing both Polk and Francis Blair that all was "as I expected from the imbecile councils of the Nashville politicians" and that Grundy, who was the Whigs' object, would find out too late that "a temporising policy will not do." The Democrats suffered a rout in Kentucky and Indiana and a weakened position nationally.[30]

The strategy of running on personality in 1837 has been attacked by historians. Charles Sellers claims that the Democrats adopted a flawed strategy because of self-interest. Grundy, Carroll, and other Nashville Democratic leaders purportedly were interested in the success of the state banks and formed an alliance with John Bell and other former White backers that was designed to encourage the White supporters to vote for Armstrong. By reducing reliance on the party vote, they could ensure the triumph of candidates who would protect the state banks. There is some plausibility to this argument, since Bell had married the widow of a founder of Yeatman, Woods and Company, the leading private bank, and Grundy supported the state banks, two of which, the Union and Planters' banks, were federal depositories.[31]

Yet reliance on this argument goes too far. The Whig Party convincingly won the governor's race in 1835, and the White forces handily defeated Van Buren in 1836. As the elections approached in 1837, the Democrats were in disarray. The Panic appeared to have demonstrated the fallacies of the Jackson–Van Buren financial policies. The Democrats offered no clear message; hard-money enthusiasts contended with a variety of plans advanced by advocates of federal or state banks. Moreover, in the view of most Tennessee politicians, the Democratic Party had numerous strong candidates who could run on local strengths. Under these circumstances, the policy decision to run on personality appears sound. If the Democrats could not win on a party basis in 1835 and 1836, then as the party blamed for the Panic, why should they be expected to win in 1837.

The election had been aimed at Grundy, and in the legislature in 1837 the Whigs, with a majority of 18–7 in the senate and 49–26 in the house, followed their announced plan to select a senator two years in advance. Polk and other leaders tried to save Grundy's seat. Polk even made a special trip to Nashville during the legislative session, bringing with him an unusual letter from Grundy that gave Polk permission to use his name in the public interest, including withdrawal of Grundy's candidacy in any future election for office. The letter testified to Grundy's confidence in his friend and former pupil, as well as Grundy's willingness to act in the party's best interest.[32]

Polk arrived too late for the senatorial contest, and too late to make use of Grundy's authorization. The Democrats did not even nominate Grundy for 1839, supporting William Carroll instead. The Whigs chose Foster, despite fierce opposition from supporters of John Bell, and Foster won by a vote of 54–33 on October 21, 1837. Democrats were scathing in their criticism of the early choice of a senator, and some of the more thoughtful Whigs joined them in expressing concern. On December 16 Andrew Jackson, ever partisan, wrote Grundy that the premature election of Foster had embarrassed the Whigs greatly, and that if it were addressed now, the election would be postponed. Grundy himself appeared philosophical about the future loss of his Senate seat, writing Jackson that "on my own account I should not regret it, but for public reasons I should dislike it."[33]

The pressing financial crisis preoccupied Van Buren's Democrats during this period. The new president proposed a radical solution in a message in September 1837. He suggested divorcing governmental fiscal operations from the banking system by holding and administering all government funds in offices of the Treasury Department. The proposal would weaken state banks, but it would ensure that government funds would be available for federal operations. It also meant that regulation of banking would be left to the states and that little centralized banking direction would be provided.[34]

Van Buren's proposal created varied political parameters. In the Senate, Calhoun and his southern allies had joined the administration forces, reasoning that slavery could be better protected within the Democratic Party. Calhoun favored keeping funds in the Treasury Department, although his insistence on the use of only gold and silver as government funds put him at odds with state-bank Democrats. Grundy kept Jackson apprised of these developments in Washington. On October 2 he reported that a majority in the Senate favored "severing the Government from the Banks, of this there is no doubt," and that Calhoun at that moment was making an "able speech in favor of the Divorce Bill, as it is here called." On January 4, 1838, he voiced his considered opinion that the Democrats would carry the divorce bill in both chambers but that there "is less certainty" in the House. Grundy's optimism proved premature. The bill did pass in the Senate, but it failed in the House despite Polk's best efforts. The administration could not reconcile those who, like Calhoun, favored only specie payments with those who saw a role for state banks.[35]

Grundy also kept Jackson up to date on political developments. He praised Van Buren, referring to his decision and perseverance and, in January, noting that "Van Buren stands up to his high duties like a man, there is no flinching in him." Significantly in light of the growing evidence of abolitionism, he pointed out that the Democrats were losing strength in the North and the West but were recruiting well in the South. Convinced that the Whigs would nominate Clay to run against Van Buren in 1840, he wrote, "You once told me, Clay would throw himself upon the non Slaveholding States, I told you, that was impossible, I would not use as strong language now."[36]

Grundy's actions in the Senate had to do with matters besides the independent-Treasury bill. In a matter "I have greatly at heart," he pushed through a steamboat-safety bill. The first steamboat in western waters, the *Washington*, made its maiden voyage in 1816, but later that same year its boiler exploded, foreshadowing a dreary repetition of deaths and injury. Van Buren suggested safety legislation for steam vessels on December 5, 1837, and the next day Grundy both proposed language for such legislation and persuaded the Senate to establish a Senate select committee, which he chaired. Grundy fast-tracked the legislation, and the bill became law. On February 12, 1838, Grundy presented the administration's bill to prevent the reissuance of notes by the Second Bank of the United States. The bank directors had authorized the reissuance of approximately $10 million in notes of that bank, even though its federal charter had expired. Grundy spoke on the bill on April 16, and the Senate passed it on April 23 by a vote of 27–13. After it was passed in the House, it was signed into law on July 7, 1838. On sales of public lands Grundy joined Senator Thomas H. Benton in a plan for graduated dispositions. Grundy proposed that public land unsold for varying periods of time, from five to eighteen years, after September 15, 1836, would be reduced in price from the original $1.25 per acre to as little as 50¢ per acre on the principle that time was the true test of land value. The Senate accepted Grundy's amendment and passed Benton's bill, but the House opposed the legislation, and no law resulted.[37]

In the midst of this senatorial activity Grundy suffered yet another indignity at the hands of the Whigs. On January 18, 1838, the Tennessee General

Assembly, aiming at Grundy, instructed its senators to vote against Van Buren's independent-Treasury proposal, the divorce bill. Anticipating the legislative action, Grundy circulated among his constituents a letter of the same date in which he set forth his political principles. He portrayed Van Buren as standing against the abolitionists and their incendiary proceedings, predicted that Clay would be the Whig candidate in 1840, and applauded the general assembly for having greatly increased Tennessee's banking capital, thereby weakening the arguments used for a national bank. Most importantly, he stressed that the people of Tennessee confronted a critical decision: whether to support a high tariff, internal improvements, and a U.S. bank, thereby reversing policies of the last nine years. If Tennessee were to cease standing in the front line of Republicanism and "wear the Livery and follow in the train and at the tail of Federalism," then Grundy would rejoice at being relieved from public service.

Grundy followed his letter of January 18 with a more far-reaching public-relations approach. On February 6, 1838, he released a lengthy letter in which he stated that he would obey the instructions in good faith and vote against the divorce bill. He deferred to the legislature as expressing the public will but emphasized that he too represented the people. Accordingly, he would submit the matter to the voters as arbiters of a matter between co-agents. Grundy ultimately affirmed that he was not hostile to state banks but categorically rejected a U.S. bank as threatening the liberties of the people. He stressed that there should be a separation between the government and all banks in order to prevent public funds from being used for banking purposes.[38]

Grundy clearly intended his letter of February 6 to have wide circulation. He wrote Jackson on February 9 that friends in Washington thought that it would have a good effect not only in Tennessee but elsewhere. Approximately three thousand copies had been sent to different parts of the state, and "I should think, upon reading it, my instructors will feel a little queer." Grundy's letter had a predictable effect, pleasing his Democratic constituency and disturbing the Whigs. The *McMinnville (TN) Gazette* praised the letter's "forcible cleariness of truth" and the "vigorous and common sense style for which that gentleman is remarkable," while a Whig organ described it as an "impudent pretension that can only be based upon utter contempt for the understanding of the people."[39]

Grundy may have avoided the perils of the assembly's instructions on the independent-Treasury proposal, but he detested the position in which he had been placed. In his letter to Jackson on February 9 Grundy reflected his discouragement. Rejecting service in the House when his Senate term expired,

Grundy planned to retire from public life and repair his fortune, which had been shattered by public service. In a rare instance of bitterness, he reflected that he had received "poor compensation from the people whose interests I have endeavored to promote." At the end of May 1838 he expressed his concerns in a confidential letter to his brother-in-law, Randal McGavock. He did not regret adhering to the instructions, since the alternative, resignation, would have necessitated his abandonment of important measures under his charge. The future, however, posed more difficulty. Grundy had not decided whether to return to the Senate, and he wished to speak to McGavock as soon as he returned home. He ruminated about the obvious question, whether to return fettered and bound to vote against his own judgment, thereby inflicting injuries upon the country, which he had endeavored to serve with fidelity.[40]

Martin Van Buren gave Grundy an answer to his dilemma: the post of attorney general of the United States.

24

ATTORNEY GENERAL

Mr. Grundy . . . has done himself great credit by the manner in which he
has discharged his official duties.

—Martin Van Buren

Felix Grundy became the fourteenth attorney general of the United
States on September 1, 1838. He served in that office for fifteen months
before reluctantly yielding to entreaties of Tennessee Governor James K. Polk
to return to the U.S. Senate.

Van Buren's choice of Grundy as attorney general followed the president's
acceptance of the resignation of Benjamin F. Butler on April 11, 1838. The capable Butler, a former law student and partner of Van Buren's, had been attorney general since 1834 and had agreed to stay on during Van Buren's presidency
largely to help deal with the Panic of 1837. Van Buren first asked Judge Richard Parker, of Richmond, Virginia, to replace Butler, but Parker declined the
appointment on May 2, 1838. Van Buren then turned to Grundy. Grundy's appointment and confirmation by the Senate were announced officially on July 6
in the *Washington Globe,* and Secretary of State John Forsyth transmitted the
commission to Grundy on July 9. Tennessee papers reacted predictably: on July
16 the *Nashville Union* applauded the appointment, while the *Nashville Whig*
expressed disapproval indirectly by printing a critical editorial from the *Cincinnati Whig.* Butler expressed the Democratic view, writing Van Buren that
Grundy's appointment "would do well with the old Democracy" and would be
a "brilliant finale" to the session.[1]

Amos Kendall attributed Grundy's appointment to the political consequences of Jackson's battle against the Second Bank of the United States. That
assessment obscures the benefits to Van Buren of an offer to Grundy. Grundy
had led the fight against the Whigs in Tennessee and was close to Jackson. A
resident of a slaveholding border state and a westerner, Grundy maintained sectional balance in a party that was always seeking to minimize tension between

its northern and southern wings. He had long-standing ties to Calhoun, whose decision to work with the Democrats significantly enhanced the political possibilities for Van Buren. Renowned as a criminal lawyer, Grundy had been the chief justice of Kentucky. Perhaps most important, he was a shrewd politician of deep experience.[2]

Grundy's tenure began on September 1, 1838, the day Butler's resignation became effective. He arrived in Washington in late August, without Nancy Grundy, whose poor health kept her in Nashville. He almost certainly lodged at Mrs. Owner's boardinghouse, on Pennsylvania Avenue, where, along with his good friend John M. Robinson, a senator from Illinois, he took quarters during the congressional sessions both preceding and following his tenure as attorney general.[3]

The post of attorney general, considered the second most demanding job in the cabinet, behind that of secretary of the treasury, involved significant responsibility but little legislative support. Unlike the secretaryships of foreign affairs, the treasury, and war, the post of attorney general was not one of the original cabinet posts but was created by the Judiciary Act of 1789. Only in 1886 did Congress establish its status as fourth in cabinet rank. In contrast to today, the attorney general in 1838 had no authority over the U.S. district attorneys, who represented the United States in the district and circuit courts. Congress was slow in providing financial support for the attorney general. When John Breckinridge served as attorney general under Jefferson, he received a salary of $3,000 but had to pay for his office space, clerks, office supplies, and other office costs out of his own pocket. By the time Grundy took office, Congress provided the attorney general an annual salary of $4,000 and authorization to hire a clerk and messenger, at salaries of $800 and $500 per year, respectively, as well as an allowance of $500 for books, $733 for furniture, and $500 for contingencies. In 1822 the attorney general received his first official quarters, a single room on the second floor of the War Department building. Grundy assumed his new responsibilities in that office, but in 1839 he moved into rooms located on the second floor of the Treasury building, taking with him his clerk and messenger, as well as his law library.[4]

From these quarters, Grundy carried out his major responsibilities of presenting the government's cases in the Supreme Court and issuing opinions to the executive branch, as well as serving as a policy adviser to the president. The new attorney general had vast courtroom experience, including arguments before the Supreme Court, but soon he was presenting cases in areas of the law with which he was not familiar. In the January term of 1839 Grundy argued at least nine cases, on issues as varied as land titles from the Kingdom of Spain, duties on silk imports, breaches of contract, and a suit to recover land in Illinois that was occupied by the military. In the military-land case, *Wilcox v. Jackson,* 38 U.S. 498 (1839), both former Attorney General Butler and Grundy appeared for the government, and Messrs. Key and Webster represented the defendant. None of the nine cases presented by Grundy had broad applicability or significant implications.

Grundy devoted more time and energy to the preparation of legal opinions for the executive branch. In his fifteen months as attorney general he wrote fifty-nine advisory opinions. While this is a significant number, it does not appear to represent greater output than for other attorneys general. Grundy's successor, Henry Gilpin, a Philadelphia lawyer, wrote seventy-nine advisory opinions in a slightly shorter period of time.[5]

Most of Grundy's opinions concerned executive actions that do not warrant much discussion. Two, however, have continuing historical interest. The first related to the bequest by James Smithson, an illegitimately born English nobleman of scientific bent. On June 26, 1829, Smithson died in Genoa, Italy, leaving the bulk of his estate to his nephew. According to his will, dated October 23, 1836, if the nephew died intestate, Smithson bequeathed "the whole of my property . . . to the United States of America, to found at Washington, under the name of the Smithsonian Institution, an Establishment for the increase and diffusion of Knowledge among men." Six years later the nephew did die intestate, and President Andrew Jackson learned that an unknown Englishman had left a fortune of $500,000 to the United States. Jackson formally notified Congress of the bequest in December 1835 and explained that the executive branch lacked the authority to deal with the matter. Congress accepted the bequest and directed the president to assert and prosecute the claim. John Quincy Adams, who was not afflicted with the states' rights mentality that led many southerners to suggest that the gift be rejected, recognized the potential of such an institution. He arranged for the appointment of Richard Rush, a former ambassador to the Court of St. James and Adams's secretary of the treasury, as agent. Rush did an admirable job, and on September 11, 1838, he advised Secretary of the Treasury Levi Woodbury that he had just deposited 105 sacks of gold sovereigns worth £104,960, or approximately $500,000, in the United States Mint.[6]

The Smithson funds arrived at the Mint at almost the same time that Grundy took over as attorney general. On October 11 the secretary of the treasury requested the attorney general's opinion on the narrow and relatively insignificant question whether the Smithsonian Fund should bear the expenses of pursuing the claim. Grundy replied on November 16, 1838, in a straightforward opinion based on section 4 of the Enabling Act of July 1, 1836. He concluded that Congress intended no diminution of the funds bequeathed for the specified purposes. Based on section 4, Grundy opined that the entire bequest, without reduction, constituted the Smithsonian Fund and that all expenses of prosecuting the claim and transporting funds to the United States, as well as additional expenses incurred in the United States, should be defrayed from the congressional appropriation.

This simple opinion appears to be the only record of Grundy's involvement with the Smithsonian, but Grundy did have continuing discussions on the subject. John Quincy Adams noted in his diary on April 8, 1839, that in conversations with Grundy and Joel Poinsett on the Smithsonian issues both had spoken "fair words." As a consequence of his involvement, Grundy escaped the censure of Adams. Adams castigated President Van Buren's indifference, "the lack of assistance" from department heads except Grundy, and the opposition of Calhoun and others to the establishment of the institution.[7]

Grundy's second historically interesting opinion provoked more controversy. The Spanish schooner *Amistad* left Havana for another Cuban port on June 27, 1839, the captain having agreed to transport Messrs. Ruiz and Montez, Spanish subjects, and approximately fifty "Negroes." Documents certified that the "Negroes" were slaves, when they had in fact been kidnapped in Africa by Spanish slave traders and brought to Cuba, where they were purchased by Ruiz and Montez. On the voyage, the Africans killed the captain and took control of the vessel. They spared the lives of Ruiz and Montez on condition that the two Spaniards navigate the ship back to Africa. Ruiz and Montez misled their captors and steered the *Amistad* to the United States, where a U.S. brig took the schooner into possession off Connecticut in late August 1839. In addition to salvage claims by various American parties, Ruiz and Montez filed claims to the Africans and asked that the slaves be delivered to them or to representatives of Spain. Ten or more of the Africans had died during the trip from Cuba, and the remaining mutineers were held in the county jail in New Haven pending resolution. The case quickly aroused the attention and sympathy of abolitionists.

Secretary of the Treasury Woodbury advised Van Buren to let the judiciary take responsibility, but the president deferred to the strong views of Secretary of State John Forsyth, who believed the matter could be promptly resolved diplomatically. Forsyth, a Princeton graduate and Georgia lawyer, had been in discussion with the Spanish minister in Washington, who on September 6 by formal note requested the return to Spanish authorities of the *Amistad* and her cargo, including all slaves. The Spanish, acting under a treaty of 1795 between Spain and the United States, took the position that the United States had no jurisdiction, since all actions had occurred on a Spanish vessel outside the limits of the United States. Forsyth consulted with Woodbury, Grundy, and Postmaster General Amos Kendall, who concurred with his view that the United States should comply with the Spanish request. Thus, on September 24 Forsyth formally asked Grundy to prepare an opinion.[8]

Commentators on the *Amistad* case invariably point out that both Forsyth and Grundy owned slaves and infer that their personal views determined the cabinet decision. This view is unfair to two professional politicians. It is reasonably certain that political, not personal, considerations influenced the cabinet judgment. Van Buren's reelection the next year would depend on southern voters, and the Democratic strategy included depiction of abolitionists as incendiaries and a danger to the Union. Van Buren could hardly be seen as giving any support to abolitionists or to an uprising by purported slaves. At the same time, he would not want northerners to think that he was giving in to southern opinion or a foreign power. The *Amistad* case thus presented a problem for Van Buren's reelection campaign, and return of the *Amistad* and its slaves represented the low-risk option.

Grundy issued his opinion in November 1839, concluding that the *Amistad* and its cargo should be returned to the Spanish minister. His opinion, which set forth the arguments used by the government in legal proceedings, had two components. First, he concluded that due faith and credit must be given to the public acts of officials of other nations under the principle of comity. This principle encompassed not only judicial decisions but also executive and legislative actions. If the United States were to disregard the *Amistad* documents submitted by Spain and explore underlying factual questions, it would be "in the embarrassing condition of judging upon the Spanish laws, their force, their effect, and their application to the case under consideration." Without such comity, international law would collapse in disharmony.[9]

Grundy also addressed the issue of piracy. If the mutineers were considered pirates, they could be tried in the United States on the basis that pirates, the common enemy of all mankind, could under American law be taken into custody. Grundy reviewed various legal definitions of the crime of piracy and concluded that pirates, freebooters, did not derive protection from any government. Since the *Amistad* was a Spanish schooner, protected by Spanish papers and flag, the mutineers by definition could not be pirates.

Grundy's opinion presupposed resolution of the *Amistad* matter diplomatically, but the judiciary decided otherwise. On September 19, 1839, the U.S. district attorney presented to the United States Circuit Court the U.S. government's position that the Spanish minister's claim to the slaves should be upheld. The circuit court denied a writ of habeas corpus on September 23 but left the case to the United States District Court. Thus, by the time Attorney General Grundy issued his opinion in November, the judiciary had taken control of the case. Since the district attorney did not report to the attorney general, Grundy communicated with District Attorney William J. Holabird (and during Holabird's illness, with Ralph Ingersoll) only as Van Buren's agent. On October 30, 1839, Grundy requested a status report on the litigation, and on November 5, presumably while preparing the final draft of this opinion, he asked whether the *Amistad* had been on the high seas when it was taken by the United States Navy. More significantly, on November 15 Grundy advised Holabird and Ingersoll that the president concurred in the attorney general's opinion and wished it to be carried out. He stated, however, that "the course of the Executive is decided on, but it is deemed expedient to make no communication of it, to anyone, until the property is freed from all judicial action, he will then act promptly, in carrying out the opinion of the Attorney General—In the meantime, I have to request regular information of the progress of the Judicial proceedings."[10]

The *Amistad* case did not turn out as Van Buren's cabinet initially expected. After a contentious and widely publicized trial, the district court determined that the mutineers should be returned to Africa. Although this outcome offered a speedy end to the matter and was thus acceptable to the administration, it was not to be. Appeals were filed by various parties, including the United States on behalf of Spain. Ultimately, on March 9, 1841, the Supreme Court, with Justice Story writing the opinion and Justice Baldwin dissenting, affirmed the decision of the district court, except that it ordered the slaves set free. The Court rested its case on the somewhat narrow grounds of treaty interpretation—that the mutineers were not merchandise under the applicable provisions—and on the broad view that on the merits of the case the Africans, seeking freedom, should not be returned to Spain. With respect to the issues addressed by Grundy, Story wrote that fraud always justified deeper examination of the facts, thereby rejecting Grundy's deference to Spanish authorities, but concurred that the mutineers were not pirates.[11]

Grundy's opinion in the *Amistad* case was not so much wrong as irrelevant. Issued after the judiciary had taken jurisdiction, and not released until sometime after November 15, 1839, the opinion had no legal effect. The district court resolved the case counter to the arguments presented by the government (and by Grundy), and the Supreme Court referred to the attorney general's opinion only in passing. Although Grundy's deference to Spanish authority reflects a principle of international legal relationships that still applies today, his opinion was too narrowly cast and outside the direction of history.

The *Amistad* case highlights the ongoing advisory role of Grundy and other cabinet members. There is only meager evidence of Grundy's role as a counselor, including resolution of an assault case involving Andrew Jackson and a labored letter for Tennessee electoral consumption attempting to cast Van Buren as a war Democrat during the War of 1812. Most of Grundy's advice was political and oral, however, and there appears to be little doubt that Van Buren appreciated Grundy's judgments, as warm words in his autobiography attest. More directly, he wrote Jackson on May 29, 1839, that Grundy would leave for Tennessee shortly in fine health and spirits and that he "has done himself great credit by the manner in which he has discharged his official duties."[12]

When Grundy returned to Tennessee in June 1839, he had one major purpose: to assist his protégé James K. Polk in his race for governor. Aside from his official position and well-known talents, Grundy possessed an established political base. John Bell reminded Henry Clay of that in an optimistic letter about Whig prospects in Tennessee in May, writing that a majority in Davidson County would be a good result and observing that Grundy's connections and influence were even greater there than those of Andrew Jackson. Grundy's protégé, however, needed little help. Polk's extraordinary efforts and persistence, his organizational initiatives, his reliance on established Democratic principles, and the returning prosperity of the state enabled Polk to defeat Newton Cannon by a vote of 54,012 to 51,396. In a rare show of real emotion Grundy wrote to Polk, "You are Governor of Ten, thank God and the people for that. Keep the ship right. No doubt you will. I rejoiced all day yesterday at the Hermitage over your victory." Although the Whigs won seven congressional seats, the Democrats gained six. Importantly for Grundy's future, the Democrats regained control of the state legislature, taking fourteen senate seats to the Whigs' eleven and forty-two house seats to the Whigs' thirty-three.[13]

The Democratic success in 1839 dramatically changed the political equation in Tennessee, almost exactly reversing the position of the Whigs in 1837. Democrats now controlled the legislature, yet the Whigs White and Foster held both U.S. Senate seats, which they would presumably yield if instructed to vote contrary to their political views. On August 12 Polk, now clearly the most powerful Democratic leader in the state, wrote Jackson that there would be one or perhaps two vacant seats in the Senate and that Grundy should be returned to the Senate. The attorney generalship could be filled by another, but only Grundy had such claims to the Senate seat that other aspirants would yield. Leading Democrats concurred in Polk's judgment, but Grundy proved reluctant to leave a cabinet post he enjoyed. Grundy instead proposed adopting the Whig playbook and selecting a successor for White immediately even though White's term would not end for two years. In that event, Foster's successor could be chosen from East Tennessee, and White's from Middle Tennessee, with Grundy continuing as attorney general for two more years.[14]

Polk, resolute, saw no alternative to Grundy's acceptance of Foster's Senate seat. Applying pressure, Polk wrote President Van Buren that Grundy's election would be extremely popular in the state and that the Democratic members of the legislature could agree only on Grundy. As loyal Democrats, Van Buren and Grundy accepted Polk's argument, and Grundy reluctantly acceded to party imperatives.[15]

Events proceeded as Polk had planned. On November 14, 1839, the legislature issued instructions to its two Whig senators to vote against rechartering a national bank, against the so-called gag bill intended to prevent federal officeholders from engaging in election activity, and against distributing sales proceeds from public lands among the states. The instructions also required the senators to vote for the independent-Treasury bill and for graduated price reductions on public lands and to support the principal measures of the president. These instructions, which were anathema to Foster and White, fit Grundy's views exactly. Foster resigned, and on November 19, 1839, the legislature elected Grundy by a vote of 56–44. The legislature determined that Grundy's Senate term would date from March 1839, when his initial term in the Senate would have expired had he not accepted the post of attorney general. Grundy submitted his resignation from the post in a gracious note on December 14, 1839, and Van Buren accepted the resignation equally graciously on December 19.[16]

One hitch developed. A friend pointed out that Grundy was a resident of Washington and therefore did not meet the requirement of being an inhabitant of Tennessee. Accordingly, Grundy concluded that he could not accept the office, and to the consternation of the Tennessee legislature, on December 14 submitted a letter declining the appointment as senator. But of course all had been prearranged. On the same day that he resigned as attorney general, Grundy wrote the Tennessee senate and house of representatives that with his resignation, he was again a Tennessean in the full sense of the term. With the technical ineligibility removed, the legislature proceeded on December 14 to elect Grundy to the Senate again. This time the Whigs presented no candidate but scattered their ballots, and Grundy received fifty-seven votes. One final act remained. As predicted by Polk and others, Hugh Lawson White did not resign upon receiving notice of the instructions. Polk forced the issue, urging Thomas Hart Benton to raise the independent-Treasury bill early in the congressional session. Benton did so, and White resigned his seat on January 13, 1840. The Tennessee legislature elected Polk's choice, General Alexander Anderson, of Knoxville, to succeed White. White died on April 10, 1840.[17]

The first session of the Twenty-sixth Congress began on December 2, 1839, when Grundy was still attorney general, and was to last until July. When Grundy returned to Washington as a senator on December 31, the committee assignments had been set, and Grundy only joined the committee dealing with the legislative power of the Union to assume state debts. Grundy brought in a report, dated January 31 and submitted on February 5, 1840, rejecting the assumption of state debts by the federal government. He believed that the Whigs planned a direct or indirect assumption of state debts and that such an assumption would necessitate new revenues and bring about a high tariff. Clay derided the report, and "the whole Whig opposition was brought out," but Calhoun applauded the conclusion, sharing Grundy's concern that assumption would facilitate distribution of surplus public revenues to the states and a high tariff.[18]

His reelection to the Senate touched Grundy deeply. In his speech on the report with respect to debt assumption, the customarily cool and collected Grundy stated that the happiest day of his life occurred when he was chosen to return to his former Senate seat.[19]

25

TWILIGHT

The Lord's will, not mine, be done.
—Felix Grundy

*I*t appears fitting that Grundy characterized his reelection to the Senate as the happiest day of his life. His political life spanned over forty years, from 1799 to 1840, and for much of that period he exuberantly engaged in political battle. Even if more renowned as a criminal lawyer, Grundy defined himself early by his political ambition, and his election to the Senate in late 1839 offset his travails in the 1830s. His last years, however, afforded more than political vindication, as the threads of his life pulled together.

Andrew Jackson had dominated Tennessee politics since 1824. When Grundy enthusiastically congratulated Governor-elect Polk on August 12, he mentioned that the Old General and he were shortly going to Tyree Springs. Visitors were drawn to the popular retreat, named for an early proprietor and located about twenty miles northeast of Nashville, because of its white sulfur mineral water and its cool air (the elevation was 1,230 feet). Jackson, Grundy, General Armstrong, and George W. Campbell gathered there with family and friends for a week in August 1839. Josephus Guild, in *Old Times in Tennessee,* described a sylvan time when an elderly gardener was hired to deliver fresh melons, fruit, and flowers daily. Under the great elms in the parklike setting, a moot court took place every day after breakfast, with Grundy as chief justice and Jackson as associate justice. Young men were indicted for every trivial offense, such as failing to bow when passing a lady. To be tried was to be fined, and Grundy decreed that anyone who objected would be fined double. In a statement that is not necessarily believable, Guild wrote that not a word of politics or public affairs was heard during the pleasant week.[1]

Grundy's relaxed retreat with Jackson that summer reflected their changed relationship. Following Grundy's reelection to the Senate in 1833 over Jackson's candidate Eaton, Grundy continued to support the measures of the Jackson administration. As Eaton and Lewis joined forces with those opposed to Jackson, the president's appreciation of Grundy became more pronounced. On June 11, 1835, in the midst of Hugh Lawson White's presidential campaign, Jackson wrote to Grundy. Referring to Grundy as the able friend of the measures that had saved the country from the national bank, Jackson concluded, "Believe me, My Dear Sir, with sentiments of the greatest respect for your uniform, and talented support of the great principles of Republicanism, and of gratitude for the manly and generous manner in which you have often vindicated my character from the aspersions of my enemies. Your friend." Other letters to Grundy from Jackson express similar appreciation. Jackson too advised Van Buren that Grundy would provide good counsel on difficult matters. Grundy's later letters often refer to evenings or days at Jackson's home, the Hermitage. After a lifetime of political struggle, these two political warriors, of dramatically different styles but similar objectives, met together with a warmth and affection that had been absent in earlier periods.[2]

Grundy continued to practice law when he was not in Washington or campaigning, but on a different level. In 1838 or 1839, "S" was being tried for murder in the Hickman Circuit Court, in Columbus, Kentucky. The defense retained only Grundy, occasioning three well-known local lawyers to volunteer to assist the prosecution, since they regarded the failure to employ a local attorney as an affront. In his presentation, one volunteer prosecutor alluded to the fact that the "accused, so desperate was his case, . . . had employed the Honorable Felix Grundy, the most renowned criminal lawyer in the south." The presiding judge, stopping the speaker, admonished him for disregarding the amenities due to a member of the bar. Grundy rose and asked the court to allow the young lawyers the fullest latitude for their arguments. This, of course, further enraged them, and they warned the jury against Grundy's skill and power.

When Grundy rose to address the jury, he did so in a respectful manner. After noting that the prosecutors had paid him compliments of a doubtful character, he said that they must have supposed that their vigorous assaults would alarm him. He, however, would not be swayed from his duty. He said that he felt very much "like a sawyer [large tree] imbedded in the. . . . Mississippi; [whose] location becomes known to all navigators as dangerous, and the proud steamers steer from . . . it, the keel and flat boats [give] it a wide berth, [and], gentlemen of the jury, there come dancing along a skiff, a canoe, and a dugout, bidding defiance to the old sawyer and running ahead on to test its resisting power. What, gentlemen, do you think will be the result between them and this deeply embedded snag? The result will be told by your verdict." After the acquittal, one of the young prosecutors, Judge W. P. Fowler, addressed the court, saying that he would like the record to show that he was the skiff that tackled the sawyer, and with grace the prosecutors congratulated Grundy.[3]

Grundy appears to have enjoyed a happy and supportive family life despite some tribulations. Maria Green Reed Grundy, his second youngest daughter, married William W. Masterson, of Nashville, on September 2, 1838. The father of the bride did not attend, having gone to Washington to assume the attorney generalship. Now only Felicia, who would marry in 1842, remained with her parents. Grandchildren arrived with regularity. On June 1, 1840, thirty-four of at least forty-one grandchildren survived. Felix Grundy Winder, born on September 22, 1839, joined his cousins Felix Grundy, Felix Grundy McGavock, and Felix Grundy Mayson as grandchildren bearing his name.

Grundy provided continuing assistance to his family. At approximately the same time that he advised his son-in-law Bass with respect to the Union Bank, Grundy interceded with President Jackson to secure the post of U.S. district attorney in Nashville for his son James P., who had served in the Seminole War as captain of the Davidson County State Guards. Grundy also helped arrange for the appointment of Ramsay Mayson, his son-in-law, as postmaster at Green Hill, Wilson County, on August 30, 1838. Grundy also put in a word on behalf of his wife's nephew John McGavock, son of Randal and Sally Rodgers McGavock and Grundy's private secretary in Washington, for a position with Polk. Polk appointed McGavock aide-de-camp, with the rank of colonel in the Tennessee Militia, on January 1, 1840.[4]

James K. Polk was much like family to Grundy, and Grundy spent much of late 1839 and early 1840 dealing with a topic dear to the future president, namely, a possible vice-presidential bid. Grundy played a pivotal role in the vice-presidential maneuverings, which involved two of his close friends, Polk and Vice President Richard M. Johnson. Johnson, homespun and popular, enjoyed nationwide fame as the alleged slayer of the Indian chief Tecumseh and for his advocacy of the separation of church and state. He was also controversial because of his attachment to Julia Chinn, a slave in his family household who died in 1833, and their two daughters. Johnson's relationships did not materially affect his political career in Kentucky, but as North-South divisions began to harden in the 1830s, southern Democrats increasingly questioned whether he should be the vice-presidential candidate in 1840. In the eyes of many, including Andrew Jackson, the Kentuckian would weaken the Democrats in the South and the Southwest. In November 1839 John Catron, in Frankfort, reported that Johnson had adopted another slave mistress and lost support as vice president. He concluded that "if a long statement and many considerations will induce Grundy to urge Blair," Johnson might be dropped from the ticket in 1840.[5]

Catron's reference was meaningful. Grundy enjoyed powerful and close relationships with decision makers, notably Van Buren, Senator Silas Wright, Van Buren's adept New York strategist, and Francis Blair, the powerful editor of the *Washington Globe*. He also was known to be a close friend of Johnson, who visited him at his residence during a visit to Nashville in 1837. Finally, and suggestively, there is at least a possibility that Grundy himself had aspirations for the vice presidency. Alfred Balch, a well-informed lawyer in Nashville, wrote Polk in September 1839 that during the previous two winters Grundy had had supporters trying to "ascertain what chance he would stand to fill old Dick's place."[6]

Polk lined up supporters in Tennessee for his vice-presidential try, notably Andrew Jackson. Critical constituencies, however, were in Washington, where Grundy, still attorney general, weighed various considerations. Johnson, the sitting vice president, retained great popularity. More significantly, a number of vice-presidential candidates had emerged, including William R. King, of Alabama, and John Forsyth, of Georgia, and the selection of one of these could alienate the others and their states. By mid-November Francis Blair, an important king-maker, believed that Johnson should not run again but avoided choosing among the aspirants. Grundy and Blair, in Washington, counseled inaction until after the Whig convention in Harrisburg, Pennsylvania, on December 4, 1839. This proved to be wise advice. Surprisingly, the Whigs chose William Henry Harrison, instead of Henry Clay, as their nominee for president in 1840. By selecting a homespun Indian fighter with a pedigree similar to Johnson's, the Whigs made retaining the Kentuckian on the Democratic ticket more attractive.[7]

The Polk forces in Tennessee concluded that holding a national convention would be desirable, on the grounds that merely calling a convention might induce the vice president to step aside or that they could force Polk's nomination. Silas Wright and other New Yorkers shared Grundy's concern about a convention, since Van Buren would be renominated, and a convention might only alienate sectional groups that had their own vice-presidential favorites. Nevertheless, by the beginning of 1840 it was generally agreed that a convention would be held in Baltimore in early May. Catron thought Polk should rely principally on Aaron V. Brown and "Grundy—who got here 31st ult. . . . full of health and life."[8]

Grundy's analysis of the likely results of the convention in Baltimore led him to conclude that Polk's best chance for the vice presidency would be election in the Electoral College. For that to occur, there must be no nomination of a vice-presidential candidate at the convention, where Polk's strength would be insufficient. Grundy's assessments in part rested on Silas Wright. Wright promised Grundy that if no nomination were made at the convention, New York would support Polk in the Electoral College, where he would have significant support. Calhoun, who had decided that Polk would best represent the interests of his faction, concurred. Grundy and all the other Democratic members of the congressional delegation but the new Senator Anderson accordingly made a joint appeal to Polk on February 3. A national convention appeared certain, but the Tennesseans anticipated little positive result. They doubted that Polk's strength in some states would translate into control of those states at the convention, but they thought that his chances in the Electoral College would be very good. Aaron Brown portrayed the collective wisdom succinctly in a separate letter to Polk: "You will be stronger without than within the convention." Polk rejected this view and again urged his friends in Washington to push for his nomination in Baltimore.[9]

Grundy, exasperated by Polk's stance, wrote on March 2, 1840, that he was mortified by some letters about the vice presidency that "imply, without saying it, that we who are here, are not acting as zealously as we should." Presenting his view forcefully, he said that "my original impression was that you could not be nominated by that Convention" and that recent circumstances had corroborated that impression. "I am in an unpleasant situation. If I act as your friends at home wish, I shall assist in defeating you. . . . I will not do a foolish thing knowingly." Grundy reiterated his view to Polk on April 15, venting his frustration with those in Tennessee who had been pushing Polk for vice president, including Jackson, Andrew Donelson (until a recent trip to Washington, where he was persuaded to the no-nomination strategy), and George Harris, editor of the *Nashville Union*. Grundy, in a letter remarkable for its expressiveness, coming as it did from a normally cautious politician, again said that "my Judgment has uniformly been against a nomination at Baltimore," adding that if it had not been urged otherwise from home, "the Convention would not have met, or no nomination of Vice-President would have been made, and you would have been Vice President beyond all doubt. . . . I have at no time in my life, seen my way so clear . . . and I have never been so thwarted and vexed by opinions of a contrary character from those who have not the means of Judging, correctly." He concluded by reporting that he had just received a letter from Jackson urging the propriety of a nomination at Baltimore. "To all I have heard upon the subject, I have one answer to make—you cannot be nominated, by that Convention. That I suppose is sufficient."[10]

Grundy's annoyance was partly triggered by concern that the vice-presidential push by Polk and Jackson would result in Johnson's being selected. The vice president's strength surged in the few weeks before the convention. New Yorkers who had agreed with the Wright-Grundy approach feared that Johnson's strength with workingmen could push even their state to vote for the Kentuckian. Worries intensified as the convention approached.

To deal with the situation, on Sunday, May 3, Grundy and Wright took a 6:00 AM train to Baltimore to meet with General John Dix, the New York floor leader. Following their discussions, New York held firm against a nomination in the convention. The convention's committee on nominations, headed by Senator Clement C. Clay, of Alabama, unanimously endorsed Van Buren for president and voted against nominating a candidate for vice president, by a vote of 133–99. When Johnson's forces asked for a ballot, Grundy quickly silenced their clamor. The party had a commander in chief, and a brave one too, and "if we could get the head along, the tail would not be far behind."[11]

The conclave, called "Mr. Grundy's convention at Baltimore" by one observer, represented a triumph for Grundy beyond the success of the Wright nonomination strategy. Grundy called the convention to order and then, after Isaac Hill, of New Hampshire, took the chair, delivered the opening, or in today's parlance, the keynote address. Grundy's highly partisan speech reiterated familiar views—Whigs' misuse of the Revolutionary War term and their failure to make their principles known and Democratic opposition to a national bank. He criticized William Henry Harrison, saying that the Whigs had picked up a harmless county clerk and promoted him as a great man capable of running a government. Harrison was "caged up" by his friends, said Grundy, and not even permitted to receive or open letters, a charge that seriously nettled the candidate. More positively, Grundy urged Democrats to tell people what "we think" and come out with a clear statement of party belief.[12]

The convention results—attributed to Grundy—pleased Polk supporters, although Polk, who was in Nashville, may not have fully appreciated his narrow escape. Aaron Brown wrote that "all persons concur in stating that Grundy did wonders." Hopkins L. Turney believed that "but for the tremendous exertions, and great tack [*sic*] and management of your devoted friend, Mr. Grundy, we would have been defeated. It is due to truth to say that on that occasion, he surpassed himself."[13]

His convention labors exhausted Grundy. The sixty-four-year-old Tennessean had engaged in intensive negotiations on the no-nomination policy, opened the convention, given the keynote address, and masterminded the actual proceedings. Grundy asked a colleague to write to Polk and tell him that "I am so nearly broke down I can't write for a day or two." Yet with the reelection campaign under way, his labors were hardly over. Polk soon resolved one important issue: After extensive press attention and speculation about his vice-presidential plans, he wrote Grundy on May 27 that his name could be promptly withdrawn if his candidacy became an obstacle to a unified Democratic Party. Polk's letter crossed one from Grundy in which Grundy gave his assessment of Polk's chances, which he described as certain if there had been no national convention, slightly in favor of Polk at the close of the convention, and now "considerably Stronger" for Johnson. Polk's letter, published in the *Globe* on June 6 and interpreted as a withdrawal, enabled Grundy to focus on Van Buren's election. Grundy started electioneering even while Congress was in session, traveling to Philadelphia on July 2 with Johnson, James Buchanan, a rising star in Pennsylvania, and other administration officials, to good effect; he spoke in Philadelphia and then in Reading on July 4.[14]

In 1840 the Democratic Party united behind Van Buren and Johnson, who ultimately was on the ticket. Notwithstanding the financial malaise, Democratic leaders put on a bold front. In July, John Rowan, Grundy's oldest friend, came from Kentucky as a commissioner to adjust claims of U.S. citizens against Mexico. He reported that his friends appeared glad to see him, "Grundy, Calhoun & Benton especially," and that Grundy, in "whose calculations I have great confidence," believed that Van Buren would be reelected. Not all shared Grundy's optimism, if, in fact, the Tennessean was revealing his true feelings. In early March 1840 Duff Green offered Grundy a pessimistic assessment. He said that the administration was unaware of the change in public sentiment produced by the dogmas of the *Globe* and "the war on the credit and business of the country." According to Green, Harrison would take every state north of the Potomac and the Ohio except New Hampshire, and he might well take Virginia. Only Grundy and Calhoun could save Van Buren. Green's proposal was financial: the infusion of government credit to railroad companies through long-term contracts for transporting mail, troops, and munitions of war. What, if anything, Grundy did with Green's proposal is unknown.[15]

Polk took the lead in organizing Tennessee for a vigorous campaign. Democratic correspondence is replete with references to speeches, barbecues, and all the socializing of nineteenth-century campaigning. It went without saying that Grundy would play a major role as stump speaker, and he agreed to return from Washington through East Tennessee. Traveling with Congressmen Harvey M. Watterson and Hopkins L. Turney, Grundy spoke to large and rapt crowds. The schedule was arduous. They were in Virginia at Wytheville on July 31 and Abingdon on August 3 and in Tennessee at Blountville on August 4, Jonesborough on August 5, Greenville on August 6, Rogersville on August 7, and Rutledge on August 8. The audiences demanded long speeches; one Democratic writer described a masterly effort by Grundy at Rogersville that lasted four hours. Watterson left his impressions: "I knew Mr. Grundy well. After the adjournment of Congress in 1840 he and I left Washington in a stagecoach and passed through Abingdon, Va. . . . to make Democratic speeches from the first county in east Tennessee down to Nashville. He called me his *exhorter*. I greatly loved him. He was one of the most eloquent speakers I ever heard. If I were called upon to specify the two most eloquent speeches I have heard in my day, I should say one was made by Felix Grundy in the Democratic Baltimore convention in 1840." The other had been a speech by Henry Clay in the Senate the same year. Democratic correspondents reported enthusiasm and riveted attention, but the Whig David Campbell, previously an admirer of Grundy's talent, reported that those attending in Abingdon had found Grundy's speech a "most miserable one."[16]

The campaign in East Tennessee produced one of the sallies for which Grundy was famous. At Greenville, Grundy sat on the podium with Thomas D. Arnold, a boisterous Whig lawyer dressed in nankeen (a brownish yellow fabric first loomed in China) with blue, white, and yellow stripes. Arnold pointed to the carefully attired Grundy and compared his own Whig simplicity with the senator's ruffled shirt, gold ring, and diamond studs. Grundy replied that if he were young and handsome like his friend, he could wear anything, even Arnold's suit, which so well suited the principles of his party. But, Grundy said, "I am old, my hair is white, my face is furrowed with wrinkles and it has lost the ruddy bloom of youth. . . . I am going to my old friends and constituents . . . as a compliment to them . . . arrayed in the best possible way, to hide, as far as possible, the hideous ravages of old age." The Democratic crowd applauded wildly.[17]

The Whigs ran a campaign based on imagery and action, with bonfire rallies, coonskins, and songs. It proved hard to match, particularly since Harrison's log-cabin image resonated with the yeoman farmers and rural folk that made up the bulk of Democratic support in Tennessee. But Grundy tried hard, despite failing health. He traveled throughout the state, over a period of four months. In Murfreesboro on August 19, 1840, he gave his famous rejoinder that defending Clay for political crimes would result in another Bennett case—the only instance in which a Grundy client was hanged. In the third week of September he spoke to a thousand people at Pattersons' Mills, and he spoke at public meetings in Hartsville and Dixon's Springs. On October 8, 1840, the Democrats hosted a free barbeque in Jackson, Tennessee, that was attended by from seven thousand to ten thousand people. After Jackson made remarks, Polk spoke for two and one-half hours, and then Grundy spoke for the same length of time, to Jackson's praise. Grundy's famous wit served him well, with one attack on the Whigs in Columbia producing "almost inextinguishable laughter among the gravest and most devoted supporters of Harrison and Tyler."[18]

In 1840 Grundy focused his time and attention largely on electoral tactics and party organization. Although he decried the partisanship of the time, he vigorously adhered to the party position of opposition to Whig initiatives. Both the Democrats and the Whigs in the South claimed that their party would best protect slavery, with Whigs charging that Van Buren, a New Yorker, could not be relied on. Grundy reiterated that next to the slavery issue, the great public questions were "chartering a National Bank, establishing a high protective Tariff, a system of Internal Improvements by the General Government, and the assumption by the General Government of the State debts." Only if these national programs were forestalled could the rights of the people and the states be preserved.[19]

These unexceptional Democratic principles proved insufficient. The economy deteriorated again in 1840, approaching the levels of 1837, and the Whigs, who were better organized and better financed, effectively blamed the Democrats for the economic difficulties. They characterized the independent-Treasury system and opposition to high tariffs as Democratic failures. Harrison received 234 electoral votes to 60 for Van Buren, although the popular vote was closer, with 53 percent of the votes for Harrison and 47 percent for Van Buren. In Tennessee, the Whig candidate received sixty thousand votes, and Van Buren, forty-eight thousand. The South now had two parties.[20]

The campaign took its toll on Grundy. The lengthy speeches, from two to four hours long, would have exhausted a younger and healthier man, and by summer Grundy was seriously ill. In August, at McMinnville, he made one of his "happiest" efforts even though he was suffering from an "inveterate derangement of the bowels." Samuel Laughlin wrote that Grundy neglected the constantly disordered state of his stomach, endured much, and became emaciated and enfeebled.[21]

Although Justice Catron reported that Grundy was in good health and full of life at the beginning of 1840, it is likely that he was already fatally ill. Intensive campaigning in the summer and fall of 1840 may have sapped his strength but did not cause his death. The paucity of medical information makes a definitive diagnosis impossible, but it appears that Grundy suffered from colon cancer or possibly another abdominal or pelvic malignancy.[22]

Grundy's condition deteriorated in the late fall of 1840, with newspapers reporting after his death that he had been in extreme or excruciating pain during the last weeks of his life. He began putting his affairs in order. On November 11, 1840, he sold to John M. Bass for three thousand dollars a portion of his residence block, on which Bass subsequently built an imposing home. More significantly, he amended his will, originally signed on August 16, 1838, with a codicil executed on December 11, 1840. The codicil principally revoked the estate in fee given to his son James P. Grundy and provided that his son's share would be divided among James's present or future children when they reached the age of twenty-one. The codicil also established trusts, rather than outright bequests, for his daughters, Maria and Felicia. Jacob McGavock and John M. Bass were named executors.

Grundy's physicians, Samuel Hogg and Felix Robertson, two of his oldest and best friends, could do little except try to make the patient comfortable. By early December they despaired of his life. James K. Polk, who traveled from Columbia for a day's visit on December 9 or 10, learned on December 11 that John Bass judged the case hopeless. On Sunday, December 13, Daniel Graham wrote Polk that he had just left Grundy's home and that Jacob McGavock considered the situation desperate. On Monday the fourteenth Andrew Jackson came in from the Hermitage, prompting Grundy to show more animation and strength, to turn himself in his bed, and to speak more cheerfully than he had since Polk's visit. On Thursday, December 17, the *Union* reported that Grundy's continuing decline caused the most painful fears. And on December 19 Jackson wrote Polk that he feared that their friend was "gone."[23]

The end came on Saturday, December 19, 1840, with Grundy in perfect mind and surrounded by his wife and family. One of his tearful physicians in a choked voice told Grundy that it was his duty to tell him that he could not live much longer. Grundy returned the pressure of the hand and said, in close to his final words, "The Lord's will, not mine, be done."[24]

EPILOGUE

*G*rundy's funeral took place on Sunday, December 20, 1840, in the afternoon. It was followed by a series of memorial services in Nashville and Washington. His body initially was interred at the City Cemetery, in Nashville, but in 1890 was moved, along with the remains of Ann Phillips Rodgers Grundy and Grundy's friend and servant Ambrose, to Mt. Olivet Cemetery in Nashville.

Grundy's death occasioned numerous tributes and memorials. Andrew Jackson wrote Amos Kendall on January 2 that "our friend Grundy is no more, his death . . . is a serious loss to his country and family." John Rowan mourned his old friend in a long letter to his daughter, writing, "I am more affected at the death of my old schoolmate Mr. Grundy, than at any event of the kind." Sam Houston, soon to return to power as president of Texas, wrote General William Giles Harding that "the U.S. sustained in the death of Judge Grundy a serious loss. He was a great man. . . . His cast of genius was peculiar, but it was peculiarly Grand."[1]

Ann Rodgers Grundy outlived her husband by more than six years, dying in Nashville on January 27, 1847. Her obituary stated that she was the widow of Felix Grundy and that she was universally respected and beloved but did not mention her leadership in the formation of Nashville's first welfare organization and various other benevolent organizations in Nashville. Some measure of her character and strength is provided by the tribute on her tomb, now located at Mt. Olivet Cemetery: "Our mother, who Taught us How to Live, and How to Die."[2]

After Nancy Grundy's death, her executors sold Grundy Place to President and Mrs. James K. Polk for $6,770.17. In October 1847 lightning hit a powder magazine west of Capitol Hill in Nashville, and the resulting explosion rocked the area, badly damaging the walls on the north and west sides of the house. Partly for that reason, the Polks extensively remodeled the house, altering the exterior; only the east wall of Grundy Place remained. Sarah Childress Polk, who would outlive her husband by forty-two years, reigned in the house, now called Polk Place, until her death on August 14, 1891. During the Civil War, federal authorities ordered that Mrs. Polk and her home not be disturbed, and Polk Place became a refuge for various Confederate friends. After the State of Tennessee refused to pay the twenty-two thousand dollars asked by the Polk heirs, the property was sold, and the house demolished, in 1901. A hotel and other buildings now occupy the site.[3]

James K. Polk did not live long enough to enjoy the delights of Polk Place. Elected president in 1844, he led the country during the Mexican War and oversaw the addition of Texas, Oregon, California, and New Mexico to the United States. Grundy's protégé is regarded today as a highly successful president, ranking higher than Jackson in the most recent assessment of presidents in a poll conducted periodically among professional historians. Unusual among politicians, he adhered to his pledge to serve only one term as president. Polk died of cholera in Nashville on June 15, 1849, less than four months after relinquishing the presidency.

Death soon took its toll among Grundy's colleagues. Andrew Jackson died at the Hermitage on June 8, 1845. Jacob McGavock, Grundy's son-in-law, served as one of thirteen pallbearers. Henry Clay, vital to the end, died on June 29, 1852, after yet again trying to hold together his beloved Union. John C. Calhoun, the ironlike founder of the intellectual basis of the Confederacy, died on March 31, 1850. Cave Johnson, so close to his colleagues that in 1844 he named one son Polk Grundy Johnson, continued his distinguished career, serving again in the House of Representatives from 1839 to 1845, as Polk's postmaster general from 1845 to 1849, and as president of the Bank of Tennessee from 1854 to 1860. The postage stamp was introduced during his tenure as postmaster general. Johnson opposed secession in 1861 but reluctantly supported the Confederacy; he died in 1866. William Carroll did not run for public office again after his defeat in the gubernatorial election of 1835, but he was honored, probably at the suggestion of Grundy, with the chairmanship of the Baltimore convention in 1840. He died in 1844.

Grundy's closest friends from his early days in Kentucky ended their careers in varied ways. John Rowan, who served in the Senate from 1825 to 1831, became president of the Kentucky Historical Society in 1838 and held that position until his death on July 13, 1843. His elegant home, Federal Hill, in Bard-stown, Kentucky, is a major tourist attraction. George M. Bibb and Grundy occasionally opposed each other politically during Bibb's Senate term, from 1829 to 1835, but continued their warm friendship. After his Senate term ended, Bibb served as a judge on the Louisville Chancery Court until 1844, when he was appointed secretary of the treasury by Whig president John Tyler, serving until 1845. He then practiced law in Washington until his death on April 14, 1859. Richard M. Johnson, who served as a Kentucky senator from 1819 to 1837, and vice president during Van Buren's administration, was elected to the Kentucky legislature intermittently thereafter. A committed Baptist, Johnson established and ran an Indian boys' school, the Choctaw Academy, on his farm. He died on November 19, 1850.[4]

Exactly twenty years elapsed between Grundy's funeral on December 20, 1840, and the adoption by South Carolina of its Ordinance of Secession on December 20, 1860. Although historians apportion primary responsibility for the Civil War to political failures after 1840, earlier leaders do not escape unscathed. Grundy and similarly inclined moderate southerners accepted slavery as part of the constitutional bargain of 1787 and never were publicly forced to confront, in a serious way, the moral and political issues attendant on slavery. Grundy's statement in 1830 that he would oppose slavery *de novo* gave lip service to his egalitarian views, but he provided little leadership in dealing with what today is viewed as the principal issue of the nineteenth century.

Yet it appears unfair to judge Grundy for his failure to grapple meaningfully with slavery. Only at the tail end of his forty-year political career did slavery register on the political scale, and then largely in the context of abolitionism. Other issues loomed larger, and Grundy's significance rests in the context of the political questions that he confronted, not those that we now pose through a different prism. What, then, was his role in a larger context, and why should we study this political leader and lawyer who, though once important, is now largely forgotten? Four answers emerge.

First, Grundy's life affords a window into the questing, mobile society of early-nineteenth-century America. Successful in two states, Grundy engaged in a wider range of activities than almost all of his contemporaries, serving in the judiciary, as chief justice of Kentucky; in the executive branch, as a member of Van Buren's cabinet; and in the legislative branch, in both the House and the Senate in Washington and in two state legislatures. An entrepreneur, he was involved not only in farming, law, and periodic financial investments but also in a variety of real-estate transactions, including the Greenville Springs resort, the first residential subdivisions in Gallatin and Franklin, city lots in Nashville and elsewhere, and a large-scale venture in south-central Tennessee. His legal practice necessitated a peripatetic lifestyle but also showcased the innovations he brought to criminal trials and illustrates why he was so widely regarded as the outstanding criminal defense lawyer in the Old Southwest.

Second, Grundy lived as the United States was undergoing a transformation from a collection of thirteen states united by a document into something quite different—a nation shaped by conflicting aspirations and visions, political accommodation, and a driving entrepreneurial capitalism. Grundy's national roles in the War of 1812 and the Jacksonian period of the 1830s are well known, but he may have had greater effect in helping build the working democracies in Kentucky and Tennessee, two of the first new states to join the Union. Local and state governments, not the federal government, touched the lives of ordinary citizens, and it was at the state level that Grundy's activism was most important. In Kentucky, "indefatigable Felix" battled for judicial reform, land rights, and equal access to banking capital, while in Tennessee the "Saddle-Bags Bank" and the boundary settlement with Kentucky constituted his principal legacies. Grundy did not restrict his institutional interests to government. Active in civic life in both Kentucky and Tennessee, Grundy unceasingly supported education, particularly Cumberland College; the bargain he struck in the Tennessee legislature in 1822 gave financial footing to the University of North Carolina and colleges that would become the University of Tennessee and Vanderbilt University. Not surprisingly, his relationships with principal political figures—his warm ties with James K. Polk, his sensitive linkages with Henry Clay and John C. Calhoun, and his complicated and evolving relationship with Andrew Jackson—add illumination to the period.

Third, Grundy, a westerner of frontier stock, personified the new type of political leader produced in the post-Revolutionary period. Henceforth the United States would be led not only by aristocratic elites but also by talented men, often lawyers, who rose by merit in the rough-and-tumble democracies of the new states. Opposed to privileges for the favored few, Grundy never ceased to impugn the "aristocrats" and "federalists" who threatened egalitarian principles. Grundy's Jeffersonian political standards—minimal government, states' rights, legislative supremacy—were not unique. What was unusual was the consistency with which he adhered to these agrarian values over his forty years in politics. Not an abstract political thinker, Grundy did not challenge these beliefs but instead tried to put them into place as a practical politician, with compromise and legislative skill.

Finally, Grundy's life encourages us to recognize and think more deeply about how institutions develop in democratic societies. Economic and political theorists increasingly acknowledge that the rule of law, a system for resolving conflicting interests that is perceived as more or less fair by most citizens, is essential for democratic progress. Such a system in post-Revolutionary America was not imposed from on high; it was worked out over time in local government and state legislatures. Federal actions rarely impinged on the daily lives of settlers in Kentucky or Tennessee. They worried instead about rival land claimants or economic ruin brought about by banks over which they had no control. Grundy was their leader in dealing with formative questions. Supremely confident, imaginative, and having a brilliant wit, Grundy brought his skills as an advocate to the legislature, ensuring that the privileged few would not dominate the affairs of the new states. Ultimately, Grundy should be recognized as he viewed himself: a believer in and representative of the voice of the people.

NOTES

INTRODUCTION

1. Crabb, *Nashville*, 175; Guild, *Old Times in Tennessee*, 83–84; Judge Joseph Gillespie, quoted by John F. Darby in *St. Louis Republican*, 26 Feb. 1876, quoted in Guild, *Old Times in Tennessee*, 295–98.

2. Guild, *Old Times in Tennessee*, 84–85.

3. Quincy, *Life of Josiah Quincy*, 303; Van Buren, *Autobiography*, 382–83.

4. Wood, *Radicalism of the American Revolution*, 8; Wood, *Revolutionary Characters*; Appleby, *Inheriting the Revolution*.

5. Kirk, *John Randolph of Roanoke*, 46; *Annals of Congress*, 13th Cong., 1st sess., 252–54.

1. THE GREAT ROAD

1. Roger Burkham was transported to Virginia on unknown terms by Henry Smith, who received 1,000 acres in Accomac County, on Virginia's Eastern Shore, for transporting twenty persons, including Roger. Nell Marion Nugent, *Cavaliers and Pioneers: Abstracts of Virginia Land Patents and Grants*, 7 vols. (Richmond: Dietz, 1934–49), 2:1666–95. In 1687 Roger purchased the 200-acre farm Green's Recantation, on Quantico Creek, on the eastern side of the Nanticoke River in Somerset County, and on 7 October 1695, he purchased 30 acres of adjoining land called Friend's Discovery. Somerset County Deed Books, Salisbury, MD, MA-06, 922; SH-017, 336. Roger Berkham (listed as Berkum) married Lucia (or Anna) Jones on 20 December 1681 and had at least one son, John, born on 4 January 1682. Clayton Torrence, *Old Somerset on the Eastern Shore of Maryland* (Richmond, VA: Whitted & Shepperson, 1935), 396; Robert W. Barnes, *Maryland Marriage Evidences, 1634–1718* (Baltimore: Genealogical Publishing, 2005), 27.

John Burkham married Elizabeth West. By 1 September 1705 he had sold to his father-in-law, James West, 100 acres of his father's land, and three years later he deeded the remaining 100 acres as a gift to "my well-beloved son, Roger Burkum." Somerset County Deed Books, IK-014, 210, and SH-017, 336; and J. Elliott Russo, *Tax Lists of Somerset Co., 1736–1740* (Westminster, MD: Family Line, 1992).

2. Robert Mitchell, "Over the Hills and Far Away: George Washington and the Virginia Backcountry," in *George Washington and the Virginia Backcountry*, ed. Warren R. Hofstra (Madison,

WI: Madison House, 1998), 77; Frederick County Order Book 1, 1743–1745, 25, Winchester, VA. A deed recorded in Berkeley County, Virginia, refers to a property boundary opposite "Roger Burkum's house," near Warm Springs (now Berkeley Springs, West Virginia). Deed of Thomas Bryan Martin, Northern Neck Grants, Book Q, 1775–1778, 218–19, Land Office Records, Virginia State Library and Archives, Richmond.

3. "Virginia Troops in French and Indian Wars," *Virginia Magazine of History* 1 (1894): 378. Lloyd Dewitt Bockstruck, *Virginia's Colonial Soldiers* (Baltimore: Genealogical Publishing, 1988), 122. Frederick County Order Books 1, 1743–1745, 114; 4, 1751–1753, 168, 174, 178, 243, 493; 5, 1753–1754, 51, 66, 109, 221; 6, 1754–1755, 115, 331.

4. Frederick County Order Book 1, 1743–1745, 29; Guy Broadwater, Field Notes, 1749–1751, Survey 25, entry 120, Land Office Records, Virginia State Library and Archives. Land and other records in both Virginia and Kentucky suggest a close tie between Elizabeth Burkham and her sister, on the one hand, and Roger and his sons, Charles and Solomon, on the other. Importantly, however, Frederick County records contain several references to Joseph Burkham; in 1743, for example, Joseph was appointed overseer of a certain portion of road. Supporting the possibility that Joseph was Elizabeth Burkham Grundy's father are the names of Elizabeth Burkham Grundy's nine sons. At a time when Scots and northern English followed distinct naming patterns (the oldest son named for his paternal grandfather, the second son for his maternal grandfather), none of Elizabeth's sons was named Roger, and the second or third son was Joseph. In addition, Roger Burkham apparently had one daughter, Liddy, an abbreviation of Elizabeth, and it would be more likely that cousins, rather than sisters, would bear the same name. Elizabeth's will, written in 1818, states she was then eighty-five years old. Assuming that she was a niece of Roger Burkham's, she had three first cousins, children of Roger's: Charles, Solomon, and Liddy. Charles's son and Felix Grundy's cousin, Stephen Burkham (1762–1850), was a well-known Indian fighter. Liddy married Bartlett White.

5. "Political Portraits," 162; Leonard Wilson, "Study of the Grundy Family," London, 6 Mar. 1939, Felix Grundy Papers, 1820–1840, TSLA. Felix Grundy's father, George, is sometimes confused with another George Grundy. This other George Grundy was born before 5 January 1728 in Bolton Parish, Lancashire, England, and married Elizabeth Byron in Bolton on 3 October 1749. He moved to Baltimore, Maryland, before the Revolution and lived at Bolton Abbey, a splendid estate outside Baltimore. He had a number of descendants, several of whom corresponded in the period before the two world wars with descendants of Felix Grundy. Felix Grundy Papers, 1820–1840, TSLA.

6. Fischer, *Albion's Seed,* 608–15; James G. Leyburn, *The Scotch-Irish* (Chapel Hill: University of North Carolina Press, 1962), 180; James Webb, *Born Fighting* (New York: Broadway Books, 2004), 139.

7. Bedford County Deed Book 1, Bedford, VA, 134; George Grundy to Adam Beard, 26 June 1764, Bedford County Deed Book 2, Bedford, VA, 409; Charles McLoughlin to George Grundy, 26 June 1764, ibid., 405; John Mounts to George Grundy, 8 Jan. 1772, Bedford County Deed Book 4, Bedford, VA, 231. Bedford County licensed George Grundy to build and operate a grinding mill on the Little Otter River on 25 June 1771. Bedford County Order Book 3, Bedford, VA, 741. See also Peter Viemeister, *The Peaks of Otter* (Bedford, VA: Hamilton, 1992); and Lula Jeter Parker, *The History of Bedford County, Virginia* (Bedford, VA: Bedford Democrat, 1954).

8. Bedford County Deed Book 4, 231; Bedford County Order Book 3, 114; Bedford County Order Book 5A, Bedford, VA, 741; Bedford County Order Book 3, 262, 274. The claim of "George

Grundy and Company" was brought on 12 October 1771, in Botetourt County, formed in 1769, and was one of a number of proceedings brought by George Grundy from 1770 to 1779. Botetourt County Order Book 1, Fincastle, VA, 474; Fincastle County Order Book 1, Christiansburg, VA, 323, 343, 357, 381, 400; Fincastle County Order Book 2, Christiansburg, VA, 408, 440.

9. The dates of birth of these sons can only be estimated from available information, since no birth records or the like exist. The best evidence comes from George Grundy's will and from the tax lists in Kentucky, which only listed tithables of twenty-one years or older. John's, George Jr.'s, and Robert's names appear on the first tax lists, in 1785, and Samuel and Guardum Grundy are first listed in 1789.

The most unusual document George Grundy filed with the Bedford County Court is a power of attorney executed on 27 March 1769. Grundy appointed his "well-beloved wife Elizabeth Grundy" as his true and lawful attorney, giving her the power, in strikingly modern terms, to recover debts, take legal recourse, and act as fully as if he were present. This unusual document suggests an extraordinary if now unknown journey. It reveals a willingness by Grundy to rely on the acumen and sense of his wife and forecasts the independence and resilience that "Betty" Grundy would exhibit in Kentucky. Bedford County Deed Book 3, Bedford, VA, 255.

10. John Brown Sr. to William Preston, 5 May 1775, Lyman Copeland Draper Manuscripts, 4 QQ 15; John Breckinridge to James Breckinridge, 29 Jan. 1786, James Breckinridge Papers, Breckinridge Family Papers, 1740–1902, University of Virginia; Charles W. Bryan Jr., "Richard Callaway, Kentucky Pioneer," *Filson Club History Quarterly* 9 (Jan. 1935): 35; idem, "Addenda to Biography of Richard Callaway," ibid. 9 (Oct. 1935): 243; R. Alexander Bate, "Colonel Richard Callaway, 1722–1780," ibid. 29 (Jan. 1955): 3–20.

11. Lord Fairfax to Elizabeth Grundy and Catherine McKenny, 20 Nov. 1772, Northern Neck Grants, Book P, 1771–1775, 167, Land Office Records, Virginia State Library and Archives. Three years later, by an unrecorded deed dated 9 August 1775, the four hundred acres on the north fork of Sleepy Creek were conveyed to George Grundy for one hundred pounds by Elizabeth Grundy and "her sister," Catherine Allen. Witnesses included William Grundy and John Grundy. Berkeley County Unrecorded Deed Book No. 1, Martinsburg, WV, 58; J. E. Norris, *History of the Lower Shenandoah Valley* (Chicago: A. Warner, 1890), 234–35, 292. After the Grundys moved to northern Virginia, George Grundy placed in the 17 May 1776 *Virginia Gazette* a large and prominent notice offering a reward of six pounds for three racehorses. The three had strayed or been stolen from Grundy near Warm Springs, in Berkeley, in May 1775, after the horses had been transported from Bedford.

12. The Louisa Grundy McGavock family Bible, now in the possession of descendants in Nashville, reveals handwritten records of the births and deaths of the Felix Grundy family, including a clear birth date of 1775 for Felix. The tax lists in Kentucky, which show tithables aged twenty-one or older, first list Felix Grundy in 1795. Grundy's friendships with John Rowan and various other schoolmates make more sense if he was born in 1775 rather than 1777, since Archibald Cameron, John Rowan, John Pope, and most other fellow students were born between 1770 and 1773. Grundy's speech in 1830, referring to his earliest memory of the death of his oldest brother at Indian hands, becomes real, and not exaggerated hyperbole, if he was almost three years old at the time of his brother's death instead of nine months. In addition, "Leonidas" wrote in June 1811 that Grundy was thirty-five years old, consistent with a birth date of September 1775. *Democratic Clarion and Tennessee Gazette,* 23 July 1811.

13. Vernon F. Alex, *A Full and Complete History of Martinsburg and Berkeley County, West Vir-*

ginia, Past and Present (Hagerstown, MD: Mail Publishing, 1888), 123; James McDowell to James K. Polk, 21 Mar. 1846, James K. Polk Papers, 1795–1849.

14. George Washington, 13 Mar. 1748, in *The Diaries of George Washington,* ed. Donald Jackson and Dorothy Twohig, 6 vols. (Charlottesville: University Press of Virginia, 1976–79), 1:7, 12, 15, 18, 19; George Washington to Richard, 1749 or 1750, in *The Papers of George Washington, Colonial Series,* ed. W. W. Abbott et al., 10 vols. (Charlottesville: University Press of Virginia, 1983–95), 1:43–44; Warren R. Hofstra, "A Parcel of Barbarian's and an Uncooth Set of People: Settlers and Settlements of the Shenandoah Valley," in Hofstra, *George Washington and the Virginia Backcountry,* 87–114. Many in colonial America shared Washington's perspective. See Aron, *How the West Was Lost,* 13–15 and nn.

2. THE DARK AND BLOODY GROUND

1. Earl L. Core, *The Monongalia Story: A Bicentennial History,* 5 vols. (Parsons, WV: McClain, 1974–84), 1:179. The Grundys settled close to Fort Powers, occasionally called Simpson's Creek Fort, built in 1771, one mile north of present-day Bridgeport, West Virginia. Ibid., 346. There is some evidence that the Grundys, or at least one or more sons, intended to make their permanent residence in this part of Virginia. Melba Pender Zinn, comp., *Monongalia County (West) Virginia: Records of the District, Superior and County Courts,* 11 vols. to date (Bowie, MD: Heritage Books, 1990–), vol. 2, *1800–1808,* 234–35; Alexander Withers, *Chronicles of Border Warfare* (Clarksburg, VA: Joseph Israel, 1831), 181; Willis DeHaas, *History of the Early Settlement and Indian Wars of Western Virginia* (Wheeling, WV: H. Hoblitzell, 1851), 243.

2. Berkeley County Deed Book 5, Martinsburg, WV, 529; Gertrude Gray, *Virginia Northern Neck Land Grants,* vol. 3, *1775–1880* (Baltimore: Genealogical Publishing, 1993), 62.

3. Levi Todd, "General Levi Todd's Narrative," in *Tales of the Dark and Bloody Ground,* ed. Willard Rouse Jillson (Louisville, KY: Dearing, 1930), 3; Chinn, *Kentucky, Settlement, and Statehood,* 209–11; Hening, *Statutes at Large,* 10:35–41.

4. There is an extensive and expanding literature on Indian and European interaction in the Great Lakes region and areas further south. Seminal was White, *Middle Ground.* For recent views, see Daniel P. Barr, ed., *The Boundaries between Us: Natives and Newcomers along the Frontiers of the Old Northwest Territory, 1750–1850* (Kent, OH: Kent State University Press, 2006); and, as always concerning early Kentucky, Aron, *How the West Was Lost.*

5. Barnhart, *Valley of Democracy,* 20–33; Watlington, *Partisan Spirit,* 8–11; Robert L. Kincaid, *The Wilderness Road* (Indianapolis: Bobbs-Merrill, 1947). One traveler in 1776 said of the trip: "It is too tedious to name everything that transpired in our disagreeable journey; we had to travel a small and miserable track, over mud and logs and high waters." Hickman Autobiography, Reuben T. Durrett Collection, Codex 94.

6. "John D. Shane's Interview with Benjamin Allen," ed. Lucien Beckner, *Filson Club History Quarterly* 5 (Apr. 1931): 65; Cotterill, *History of Pioneer Kentucky,* 160; Collins and Lewis, *History of Kentucky,* 1:20.

7. Meyer, *Life and Times of Colonel Richard M. Johnson,* 18; Hammon, "Early Louisville and the Beargrass Stations," 156; Chinn, *Kentucky, Settlement, and Statehood,* 211–18.

8. Jillson, *Tales of the Dark and Bloody Ground,* 91–95. For a relatively full account of the trip on the Ohio to Limestone in 1788, see Drake, *Pioneer Life in Kentucky,* 7–16.

9. John Floyd to Thomas Jefferson, 15 Jan. 1781, in Jefferson, *Papers,* 4:364–65; Nancy O'Malley,

"Frontier Defenses and Pioneer Strategies in the Historic Settlement Era," in Friend, *Buzzel about Kentuck*, 68.

10. Hickman Autobiography, Reuben T. Durrett Collection, Codex 94 (quotation); Chinn, *Kentucky, Settlement, and Statehood*, 221; Drake, *Pioneer Life in Kentucky*, 14–16.

11. Floyd to Jefferson, 16 Apr. 1781, in Jefferson, *Papers*, 5:465–68; Patrick Griffin, *American Leviathan* (New York: Hill & Wang, 2007), 183–239; Lyman Copeland Draper Manuscripts, 17 CC 24; Hammon, "Early Louisville and the Beargrass Stations," 159.

12. Petition to Congress, 15 May 1780, Papers of the Continental Congress, Series 48, 237, National Archives; Petition to Congress, 1780, ibid., 245; Barnhart, *Valley of Democracy*, 54–57, 68; Watlington, *Partisan Spirit*, 31; Chinn, *Kentucky, Settlement, and Statehood*, 222–24; Bodley and Wilson, *History of Kentucky*, 1:279. See also Watlington, "Discontent in Frontier Kentucky."

13. Report of George Rogers Clark to Governor Thomas Jefferson, 22 Aug. 1780, published in *Virginia Gazette*, 4 Oct. 1780. During the fight, "Joseph Grundy, the brother of the Honorable Felix Grundy, fell by his side." Charles Kennedy, application for pension, no. S. 13617, cert. no. 4696, 27 Aug. 1832, Trigg County, KY, in National Archives.

14. Jefferson County Bond, Apr. 1781, Reuben T. Durrett Collection; Jefferson County Order Book, Louisville, KY, 7 Aug. 1781; Chinn, *Kentucky, Settlement, and Statehood*, 239; Robert E. McDowell, "Bullitt's Lick: The Related Saltworks and Settlements," *Filson Club History Quarterly* 30 (1956): 240–69.

15. Will of Hezekiah Moss, 11 May 1782, as proved 2 July 1782, Jefferson County Courthouse, Louisville, KY; *Andrew McCall v. John and Elizabeth Grundy*, Sept. 1786, Jefferson County Minute Book A, Louisville, KY, 11–12; deposition by John Grundy, in *Wickliffe v. Nathaniel Cotton & James McKee*, Supreme Court, Bardstown District (July 1790). John filed entries between 12 December 1782 and 12 March 1784 for almost 3,000 acres, and at least 1,502 acres were surveyed for him. George filed for four separate 150-acre tracts on 12, 28, and 30 December 1782 and 2 March 1784. Two of George Grundy's tracts were withdrawn, and one is listed as located on "John Grundy's" watercourse, probably Cartwright Creek. It appears that George Grundy acquired 300 acres in his own name through the Virginia treasury warrant procedure. Jillson, *Old Kentucky Entries and Deeds*, 213. George Grundy also bought land near Bardstown. A suit in chancery in Bardstown refers to the purchase of a 400- and a 500-acre parcel by Grundy from William Bard, resolved by an agreement in 1803 recognizing the entitlement of the Grundy estate to a 400-acre tract west of Bardstown. Nelson County Deed Book 6, Bardstown, KY, 228. Jillson lists John Grundy as receiving Virginia land grants *(a)* in Jefferson County on 24 December 1782 for 825 acres on Licking Creek, on 21 April 1783 for 670 acres on Beech Fork, and on 28 July 1784 for 377 acres on Cartwright Creek and *(b)* in Nelson County on 10 October 1787 for 400 acres on Cartwright Creek and on 21 February 1787 for 50 acres on Severns Run. John Grundy also received a Kentucky land grant on 17 March 1798 for 416 acres on Caney Creek in Washington County. Jillson, *Kentucky Land Grants*, 56, 182.

16. Since the will was proved in Lincoln County on 6 March 1784 and in Jefferson County on 6 April 1784, George Grundy probably died in mid- or late February 1784. All of George Grundy's property was left to "his beloved wife Elizabeth Grundy," provided that she paid "to each of my following children upon their coming of age, one horse creature and one cow and calf, to wit, to Robert Grundy, Guardum Grundy, Samuel Grundy, Charles Grundy, Felix Grundy and Polly Grundy." Only upon Elizabeth's death or marriage would George's property be divided among his children. If Elizabeth were to remarry, she would have a child's part; she would "have the privi-

lege to live on any land I may die possessed of and make what use she may think proper of the farm so long as she may continue a widow and no longer." Jefferson County Will Book 1, Louisville, KY, 1. The will in Jefferson County was proved on the oaths of William Owens and William Allen. Other witnesses were Richard Lee, Charles Kinnet, Andrew Scott, Catherine Allen, and Elizabeth Owens. The bond for the executors Elizabeth Grundy and John Grundy was established at one thousand pounds. Jefferson County Order Book, 6 Apr. 1784. Catherine Allen was probably Elizabeth Burkham Grundy's sister, and William Allen her brother-in-law.

17. John Filson, *The Discovery, Settlement, and Present State of Kentucke* (Wilmington, DE: James Adams, 1784), 28.

18. Washington County, KY, *Bicentennial History, 1792–1992* (Paducah, KY: Turner, 1991), 11.

19. Diary of Joel Watkins, 1789, Reuben T. Durrett Collection, Codex 198; Virginia Smith Herold et al., "Joel Watkins Diary of 1789," *Register, Kentucky State Historical Society* 34 (July 1936): 233–34; "Journal of Needham Parry," ibid. 34 (Oct. 1936): 384; William A. Owens, *A Fair and Happy Land* (New York: Charles Scribner's Sons, 1975), 122; G. Glenn Clift, *The Cornstalk Militia of Kentucky, 1792–1811* (Frankfort: Kentucky Historical Society, 1957), 175; Drake, *Pioneer Life in Kentucky*, 43–70. See also Samuel Haycraft, *A History of Elizabethtown, Kentucky and its Surroundings* (1869; Elizabethtown: Hardin County Historical Society, 1975), 15.

20. Taul, "Memoirs of Micah Taul," 359–63, quotations on 363 and 359; Griffin, *American Leviathan*, 186–90.

21. Asbury, *Journals and Letters*, 2:704; John R. Finger, "Witness to Expansion: Bishop Francis Asbury on the Trans-Appalachian Frontier," *Register, Kentucky State Historical Society* 82 (Autumn 1984): 334–57. At the time of the Revolution the yearly consumption of alcohol was an estimated 3.5 gallons of pure two-hundred-proof alcohol. Rorabaugh, *Alcoholic Republic*, 8; Marshall, *History of Kentucky*, 1:244.

22. Washington County Tax Lists, Springfield, KY, 1792. The advertisement, dated 6 Mar. 1793, read: "The famous horse Belmount will spend this season half his time at the Widow Grundy's the other half at Robert Grundy's on the Rolling Fork. The terms are one bushel of grain to be delivered when the mare is brought and twenty shillings to be paid in the following articles, viz wheels, rye, corn, whiskey, oats, sugar, hemp and flax at the 'market Price.'" George Grundy Estate Papers, Washington County Courthouse, Springfield, KY.

23. George Grundy Estate Papers, Washington County Courthouse. George Grundy's executors were diligent in pursuing claims as creditor. In Kentucky, for example, the court of appeals on 2 June 1802 upheld actions of John Grundy in *Wm. Bard v. George Grundy's Devisees*, and claims were pursued outside the state. Harvey Myers, ed., *Decisions of the Court of Appeals of the State of Kentucky*, 2nd ed. (Cincinnati: Robert Clarke, 1869), 168.

24. John Grundy was a trustee of the town of Bardstown in 1785. He provided the bond when his mother acquired her first ordinary license, as well as the bond for his brother Robert when Robert was ordered on 8 March 1791 by the Nelson County court to provide support for an illegitimate child. Fees Elizabeth Grundy received until May 1786 for housing and boarding prisoners also probably were due to John's service as deputy sheriff of Jefferson and then Nelson County. Minutes of Board of Trustees, Bardstown, KY, Courthouse.

25. Matthew Walton (1759–1819) was a cousin of George Walton, a signer of the Declaration of Independence from Georgia, and attended the College of William and Mary. In part using warrants issued for his service in the Revolution at Kings Mountain and at Yorktown, he had amassed nearly two hundred thousand acres in Kentucky by 1800. Washington County, KY, *Bicentennial History*, 9–10; U.S. Congress, *Biographical Directory of the United States Congress, 1774–2005*, H.

Doc. 108-222 (Washington, DC: Government Printing Office, 2005). Walton represented Nelson County in the Virginia convention of 1788, when Virginia ratified the U.S. Constitution by a vote of 89–79. J. N. Brenaman, *A History of Virginia Conventions* (Richmond: J. L. Hill, 1902), 40. Most delegates from what became Kentucky opposed ratification. Charles Gano Talbert, "Kentuckians in the Virginia Convention of 1788," *Register, Kentucky State Historical Society* 58 (1960): 187–93.

26. *Register of Debates*, 21st Cong., 1st sess., 1 Mar. 1830, 218.

27. Arkansas Daughters of the American Revolution, Arkansas DAR GRC Report 48 (1966–67), 65–69; Mrs. Arthur A. Thompson, "The Family of Samuel Seay," *Virginia Genealogist* 27, no. 3 (1963): 129.

3. EDUCATION ON THE FRONTIER

1. Receipt from John Moore, George Grundy Estate Papers, Washington County Courthouse, Springfield, KY. In an advertisement in the *Kentucky Gazette* on 18 October 1788 a schoolteacher portrayed himself as "well-recommended" to teach "Reading, Writing and Bookkeeping; also Geometry Trigonometry and Algebra."

2. John D. Wright Jr., *Transylvania: Tutor to the West* (Lexington, KY: Transylvania University, 1975), 16–24; Records of the Board of Trustees of Transylvania Seminary, 1783–89, Reuben T. Durrett Collection, Codex 188. An invoice dated 1790 to Elizabeth Grundy from Isaac Wilson, of the "Transylvania primary," requests payment of 7 pounds, 50 shillings, for tuition for "your son 7 months." Although it is conceivable that the student was Charles, then aged seventeen or eighteen, it was almost certainly Felix, then fourteen. The widow Grundy was apparently very careful about money. She objected to this bill, and the treasurer, John Fowler, reported to her that "if any mistake should appear, it may be in raising the tuition last October." On 6 June 1791 Mrs. Grundy paid the outstanding balance. George Grundy Estate Papers, Washington County; Walter Wilson Jennings, *Transylvania: Pioneer University of the West* (New York: Pageant, 1955), 12–16.

3. "Journal of William Brown while traveling from Virginia to Kentucky 1782 and 1790," Reuben T. Durrett Collection, Codex 29; Virginia Smith Herold et al., "Joel Watkins Diary of 1789," *Register, Kentucky State Historical Society* 34 (July 1936): 234 ("we came to Beards Town—which has a very Beautiful Situation but not well improv'd the Building cheap Built"); Washington County, KY, *Bicentennial History, 1792–1992* (Paducah, KY: Turner, c. 1991), 13; Sarah B. Smith, *Historic Nelson County: Its Towns and Peoples* (Bardstown, KY: GBA/Delmar, 1983), 75.

4. Two monographs have been written on Priestley: Alfred L. Crabb, "James Priestley: Pioneer Schoolmaster," *Tennessee Historical Quarterly* 12 (Mar. 1953): 129–34; and John H. Thweatt, "James Priestley: Classical Scholar of the Old South," ibid. 39 (Winter 1980): 423–39. After Salem Academy, Priestley conducted a "celebrated" academy in Baltimore, but he was teaching again in Kentucky, at Danville, from 1807 to 1809. He was then recruited as president of Cumberland College, in Nashville, where he served from 1809 to 1814 and again from 1816 to 1821. He died in Nashville on 6 February 1821. See Birney, *James G. Birney and His Times*, 12–14, for a detailed description of the curriculum offered by Priestley at Danville.

5. The George Grundy Estate Papers, Washington County, show that Elizabeth Grundy paid nine pounds, ten shillings, to Thomas on 18 May 1793 "for the boarding of Felix Grundy for the term of nine months and a half." There is no indication where Thomas lived. Census records show an Edwin Thomas in Bardstown and one in Lexington, so Grundy spent 1792–93 either at Salem Academy with an instructor other than Priestley or, more likely, in Lexington, in the first year of his legal apprenticeship with George Nicholas. Herring and Longacre, "Felix Grundy," 363; Capps,

Rowan Story, 4; William Littell, in *Kentucky Gazette,* 23 Jan. 1806; Livingston, "Biographical Letter from John Catron," 73. William Allen, an early historian of Kentucky, wrote that he had been a student of Priestley's at Cumberland College along with two sons of John Rowan "and a son of Felix Grundy." Allen, *History of Kentucky,* 350.

6. *Dictionary of American Biography,* s.v. "Rowan, John"; Capps, *Rowan Story.* See also Stephen Fackler, "John Rowan and the Demise of Jeffersonian Republicanism in Kentucky, 1819–1831," *Register, Kentucky State Historical Society* 78 (Winter 1980): 1–26.

7. Pope to Grundy, 30 Mar. 1837, McGavock Family Papers, 1797–1897. Among other Grundy friends from Salem Academy were John Allen and John Simpson. John Allen (1771–1813) was a prominent young lawyer and politician until he was killed at the Battle of River Raisin while serving as colonel of the First Rifle Regiment of the Kentucky militia. John Simpson, who served in the Kentucky House and was speaker in 1810 and 1811, was also killed at River Raisin.

8. *U.S. Magazine and Democratic Review,* Oct. 1838, 163.

9. William Pollard to Charles Biddle, 30 Jan. 1797, Nicholas Biddle Papers, 1681–1933, as quoted in Eslinger, *Citizens of Zion,* 65. The travails of early settlers due to the land laws in Kentucky are well described in Watlington, *Partisan Spirit,* 11–23; Eslinger, *Citizens of Zion,* 63–67; and Aron, *How the West Was Lost,* 70–89.

10. John Breckinridge to Col. Joseph Cabell, 10 May 1793, *Register, Kentucky State Historical Society* 3 (Sept. 1905): 20.

11. Francis B. Heitman, *Historical Register of Officers of the Continental Army* (Baltimore: Genealogical Publishing, 1967), 413; Dupre, "Political Ideas of George Nicholas"; Hugh Blair Grigsby, *History of the Virginia Federal Convention of 1788,* 2 vols. (Richmond: Virginia Historical Society, 1891), 2:284–95. Nicholas's father, a noted lawyer and colony treasurer, was president of Virginia's Revolutionary convention in 1775, and George studied law under George Wythe at William and Mary. Nicholas married Mary Smith, of a well-known family of Scots-Irish descent; her brother Robert served as secretary of state under Jefferson from 1809 to 1811, and her brother Samuel was a general in the Maryland militia and a U.S. congressman or senator for forty years, from 1793 to 1833. As attorney general, Grundy attended Samuel Smith's funeral in Baltimore on 25 April 1839.

12. Coward, *Kentucky in the New Republic,* 13; Harrison, *Kentucky's Road to Statehood,* 74–75; Allen, *History of Kentucky,* 240–41.

13. McAfee, "Life and Times of Robert B. McAfee," 217–23. The leading scholar Richard Ellis notes that Nicholas, Breckinridge, and James Brown "established a debating society and held moot courts in which young lawyers discussed the intricacies of the law and received instruction in Coke and Blackstone." Ellis, *Jeffersonian Crisis,* 141.

14. Allen, *History of Kentucky,* 251–53; Thomas Humphrey, *History of Daviess County* (Utica, KY: McDowell, 1980), 122.

15. Lewis Condict, "Journal of a Trip to Kentucky in 1795," *Proceedings, New Jersey Historical Society,* n.s., 4 (1919): 120; Staples, *History of Pioneer Lexington,* 104; Herndon J. Evans, *The Newspaper Press in Kentucky* (Lexington: University Press of Kentucky, 1976), 2. Samuel R. Brown contrasted Lexington at the time of his visit in 1817 with the town as it had been twenty years earlier: in 1797 Lexington "contained about fifty houses, partly frame and hewn logs, with the chimneys outside; a village lot could have been purchased for $30, and a good farm in its vicinity for $5 an acre. The best farmers lived in log cabins, and wore hunting shirts and leggings." *Sketch for Western Gazeteer,* quoted in Kerr et al., *History of Kentucky,* 1:525. See also Friend, *Along the Maysville Road.*

16. "Journal of Needham Parry," *Register, Kentucky State Historical Society* 34 (Oct. 1936): 383; Staples, *History of Pioneer Lexington*, 108.

17. McAfee, "Life and Times of Robert B. McAfee," 219.

18. Aron, *How the West Was Lost*, 124–29; Eslinger, *Citizens of Zion*, 80.

19. Barnhart, *Valley of Democracy*, 80–90; Ellis, *Jeffersonian Crisis*, 121–27; Harry Innes to Jefferson, 27 Aug. 1791, in Jefferson, *Papers*, 22:86–87.

20. Barnhart, *Valley of Democracy*, 90–105.

21. According to Humphrey Marshall, "to establish upon a candidate that he was a *Federalist* was the equivalent of his exclusion from office." Marshall, *History of Kentucky*, 2:333.

22. George Nicholas, *A Letter From George Nicholas of Kentucky to his Friend in Virginia* (1798; Louisville, KY: John P. Morton, 1926); George Washington to Bushrod Washington, 8 Mar. 1798, in *The Writings of George Washington, 1745–1799*, ed, John C. Fitzpatrick, George Washington Bicentennial Edition, 39 vols. (Washington, DC: Government Printing Office, 1941–44), 36:185.

23. *U.S. Magazine and Democratic Review*, Oct. 1838, 163; Allen, *History of Kentucky*, 241.

4. FELIX GRUNDY, ESQUIRE

1. Washington County, KY, *Bicentennial History, 1792–1992* (Paducah, KY: Turner, c. 1991), 8–13; Washington County Order Book, Springfield, KY, 4 June 1795. Elizabeth Grundy's former home was identified later in 1795 in county records as "Widow Grundy's old place." Washington County Order Book, 5 Nov. 1795; Eslinger, *Citizens of Zion*, 103.

2. In the 1799 tax lists for Washington County John Grundy is shown as owning 5,516 acres (including 625 acres in Nelson County) and 18 slaves. In addition to numerous transactions in Washington and Nelson counties, John Grundy acquired land in other counties, including Green and Hardin. John had first married Elizabeth McIntyre, apparently in Virginia. After her death, he married Jenny Briggs, daughter of William Briggs, pursuant to a marriage bond issued on 3 May 1785. Jenny Grundy died on 26 February 1794, and John then married Jean Speaks, daughter of John and Rebecca Speaks, on 25 August 1794.

3. The 1799 tax lists for Washington County show George Grundy owning 350 acres and 2 slaves and Robert Grundy owning 350 acres and 6 slaves, both on Rolling Creek. Guardum Grundy owned an unspecified number of acres and 2 slaves, and Samuel Grundy owned 660 acres on Cartwright Creek and 16 slaves.

4. Hubbard Taylor to James Madison, 23 May 1793, in "The Letters of Hubbard Taylor to President James Madison," *Register, Kentucky State Historical Society* 36 (1938): 113–14.

5. Ibid.; Butler, *History of the Commonwealth of Kentucky*, 455–56; George Houston, *Memories of Eighty Years* (Morganfield, KY: Sun Point, 1904), 6, 19; François A. Michaux, *Travels to the West of the Alleghany Mountains, in the States of Ohio, Kentucky and Tennessee and Back to Charleston, by the Upper Carolinas . . . Undertaken in the Year 1802*, in *Early Western Travels, 1748–1846*, ed. Reuben Gold Thwaites, 32 vols. (Cleveland, OH: Arthur H. Clark, 1904–7), 3:247, 248; Taul, "Memoirs of Micah Taul," 359. Taul wrote that "the people indulged in almost all sorts of amusements, playing cards, fives or ball, throwing long bullets." Years later, Grundy purportedly said of Andrew Jackson, "The general is a sportsman and must always have a cock in the pit." Quoted by John Clayton, 5 Sept. 1844, in *Niles Weekly Register*, 14 Sept. 1844, and reported in Peterson, *Olive Branch and Sword*, 91.

6. Michael Cook and Bette Anne Cook, *Pioneer History of Washington County, Kentucky* (Ow-

ensboro, KY: Cook & McDowell, 1980), 226, 229, 231; Washington County Deed Book A, Springfield, KY, 345; Washington County Order Book, 5 Nov. 1795, 7 Apr. 1796.

7. Washington County Order Book, 7 July 1796, 2 Dec. 1796, 4 Apr. 1797, 3 Apr. 1798, 3 Apr. 1799.

8. Ireland, *County Courts in Antebellum Kentucky,* 79; Rohrbough, *Trans-Appalachian Frontier,* 49–53.

9. See, e.g., the deposition by Grundy in *Pottinger v. Beall,* Nelson Circuit Court, Bardstown, KY, 1806, with respect to land in Green County.

10. Levin, *Lawyers and Lawmakers of Kentucky,* 400–401; Aron, *How the West Was Lost,* 85–86.

11. The description of this lawsuit is derived from records in *Walton v. Henry Banks, Gilbert Imlay and Henry Lee,* Bardstown, Kentucky District Court, 1797, Henry Banks Papers, 1781–1817. General Henry Lee (1757–1845) was the son of Stephen Lee, an early settler of Kentucky who died in Mason County in 1791. General Henry Lee served in the Revolution, represented Kentucky in the Virginia legislature, and was an active land speculator. Lucy Lee, "General Henry Lee," *Register, Kentucky State Historical Society* 1 (Sept. 1903): 82–88; Eslinger, *Citizens of Zion,* 58–59; Lyndall Gordon, *Vindication: A Life of Mary Wollstonecraft* (New York: HarperCollins, 2005).

12. Samuel Haycraft, *A History of Elizabethtown, Kentucky and its Surroundings* (1869; Elizabethtown: Hardin County Historical Society, 1975), 203; J. Stoddard Johnston, "The Duel between John Rowan and Dr. James Chambers," *Register, Kentucky State Historical Society* 10 (Sept. 1912): 27–28; Parks, *Felix Grundy,* 6; Levin, *Lawyers and Lawmakers of Kentucky,* 169.

13. *Kentucky Gazette,* 7 June 1788; Calvin Morgan Fackler, *Early Days in Danville* (Louisville, KY: Standard Printing, 1941), 113.

14. The Cub Creek influence extended beyond Nancy Grundy's relatives. David Rice, the father of Presbyterianism in Kentucky, and Caleb Wallace, a leading member of the Bluegrass establishment, were pastors at Cub Creek while the Rodgers family lived there. David Rice, who led the unsuccessful antislavery movement at the constitutional convention in 1792, had been supply minister at Cub Creek from 1767 to 1771. Caleb Wallace, born at the Caldwell Settlement in 1742, went to Princeton at the age of twenty-five, graduating in 1771 and becoming "an intimate" of James Madison. Considered a theological pupil of John Witherspoon, he was licensed to preach in May 1772 and was the pastor of Cub Creek from 1773 to 1779. He then emigrated to Kentucky, where he became an influential leader.

15. Margaret was the granddaughter of Thomas Dougherty, another Scots-Irish immigrant who came to America as part of John Caldwell's group in 1727. "The Doughertys of Kentucky," *Register, Kentucky State Historical Society* 54 (Oct. 1956): 348–67. The account of Margaret Dougherty Rodgers's captivity appears in several sources. See Florence Amelia Houston, *Maxwell History and Genealogy* (Indianapolis: C. E. Pauley, 1916), 224–26; and unpublished manuscript cited in Bucy, "Quiet Revolutionaries," 51n2.

5. POLITICAL BEGINNINGS

1. Coward, *Kentucky in the New Republic,* 63. In addition to specific citations, this outstanding study provided the framework for discussion of Grundy's role at the convention.

2. Ibid., 48.

3. Marshall, *History of Kentucky,* 2:251; *Frankfort Palladium,* 20 Nov. 1798; Chinn, *Kentucky, Settlement, and Statehood,* 553–66.

4. Dupre, "Political Ideas of George Nicholas," 201–3; George Nicholas to John Breckinridge, 17 June 1798, Breckinridge Family Papers, 1752–1904, Library of Congress; Coward, *Kentucky in the New Republic,* 116–23. Hubbard Taylor, a large Fayette County landholder and a militia and state official, wrote to his kinsman James Madison on 3 January 1799 that "abolition of slavery and the Senate, the Representation by Counties, and I fear the destruction of the Compact with Virginia will be attempted with great violence, and it is intended also by that party to Gag the Judges so that they shall not have it in their power to declare a Law unconstitutional." Hubbard Taylor, "Letters of Hubbard Taylor to President James Madison," ed. James A. Padgett, *Register, Kentucky State Historical Society* 36 (July 1938): 217.

5. Joseph A. Borome, "Henry Clay and James G. Birney: An Exchange of Views," *Filson Club History Quarterly* 35 (1961): 123; Coward, *Kentucky in the New Republic,* 123; Asa E. Martin, *The Anti-Slavery Movement in Kentucky prior to 1850* (Louisville, KY: Standard Printing, 1918), 27–32.

6. *Kentucky Gazette,* 30 May 1799.

7. *Journal of the Convention, Begun and Held at the Capitol in the town of Frankfort on Monday, the twenty-second day of July in the year of our Lord one thousand, seven hundred and ninety-nine* (Frankfort, 1799), Filson Club Historical Society, Louisville, KY; Ellen Eslinger, ed., *Running Mad for Kentucky: Frontier Travel Accounts* (Lexington: University Press of Kentucky, 2004), 180 (quotation); Nettie Henry Glenn, *Early Frankfort in Kentucky, 1786–1986* (Frankfort: privately printed, 1986).

8. Parks, *Felix Grundy,* 6; Herring and Longacre, "Felix Grundy," 364 (quotation).

9. Coward, *Kentucky in the New Republic,* 125–29.

10. Notes on constitutional convention, 29 July 1799, John Breckinridge Papers, 1760–1806.

11. Ibid., 27 July–7 Aug. 1799.

12. Ibid.; *Journal of the Convention,* 17; Coward, *Kentucky in the New Republic,* 153–55; Ellis, *Jeffersonian Crisis,* 147–48.

13. *Journal of the Convention,* 17.

14. Notes on constitutional convention, 29 July 1799.

15. *Journal of the Convention,* 36, 39, 40, 42, 43.

16. Ibid., 47; Purviance, *Biography of David Purviance,* 40; Coward, *Kentucky in the New Republic,* 137–40.

17. Martin J. Spalding, *Sketches of the Early Catholic Missions in Kentucky, 1787–1827* (Bardstown, KY, 1844), 26; Benedict J. Webb, *The Centenary of Catholicity in Kentucky* (Utica, KY: McDowell, 1884), 104. According to Webb, "Intellectually considered, Felix Grundy was one of the foremost men of his day in the whole country. He had the reputation, too, of being at all times an honest and fearless advocate of the right" (104).

18. In the twenty-six roll-call votes, Grundy voted with Breckinridge on only nine occasions. Of these nine votes, two dealt with lawyer opportunities, and the remainder were largely insignificant. John Rowan and William Logan each voted with Breckinridge thirteen times; among the young lawyers, only William Bledsoe, with eight shared votes, voted with Breckinridge fewer times than Grundy. Interestingly, Samuel Taylor and John Bailey, customarily viewed as the most implacable of Breckinridge's opponents, voted with Breckinridge on seven and eight occasions, respectively. Grundy's allies on at least the recorded votes were much as one might expect. Closest to him in voting was Robert Abell, his fellow delegate from Washington County, with whom he voted 92 percent of the time. Grundy, John Rowan, and William Logan voted together on 84 percent of the votes, while Grundy and William Bledsoe voted together on 81 percent of the votes. See *Journal of the Convention;* and Coward, *Kentucky in the New Republic,* 134–35.

6. CIRCUIT COURT REFORM

1. Samuel McDowell to John Breckinridge, 24 Dec. 1801, John Breckinridge Papers, 1760–1806; William Bradford to Breckinridge, 26 Dec. 1801, ibid.

2. Louis-Phillipe, *Diary of My Travels in America*, 115–17.

3. Breckinridge to Samuel Meredith, 7 Aug. 1797, John Breckinridge Papers, 1760–1806.

4. Harrison, "John Breckinridge and the Kentucky Constitution of 1799," 228; Allen, *History of Kentucky*, 338ff.; Ramage, "Green River Pioneers," 181–83; Coward, *Kentucky in the New Republic*, 50–54; George Houston, *Memories of Eighty Years* (Morganfield, KY: Sun Point, 1904), 6; Eslinger, *Citizens of Zion*, 74; Aron, *How the West Was Lost*, 150–54.

The phrase *Green River* is used in inconsistent and confusing ways by Kentucky historians and writers. The Green River congressional district was made up of Green and certain other counties and should not be confused with the lands south of the Green River that were originally part of the Green River military district. Similarly, the "Green River Band" included not only representatives south of the Green River but also legislators from other counties who were interested in the indebtedness due the state from sale of Green River lands.

5. *Journal of the House of Representatives for the Commonwealth of Kentucky, 1800* (Frankfort: Kentucky Historical Society, 1969); Ramage, "Green River Pioneers," 183–84; Aron, *How the West Was Lost*, 157–58; Purviance, *Biography of David Purviance*, 32. Purviance described the contest between Breckinridge and Grundy as occurring over too great a period. Both Breckinridge and Grundy served in the constitutional convention of 1799, but they were together in the legislature only in 1800.

6. *Journal of the House of Representatives for the Commonwealth of Kentucky, 1801* (Frankfort: Kentucky Historical Society, 1801), 4; Purviance, *Biography of David Purviance*, 34–38.

7. Kerr et al., *History of Kentucky*, 1:481; William Russell to Breckinridge, 5 Nov. 1802, John Breckinridge Papers, 1760–1806.

8. Tachau, *Federal Courts in the Early Republic*, 31–53. Others practitioners were James Blair, James Brown, J. Hughes, Henry Clay, John Allen, Isham Talbot, Humphrey Marshall, and John Rowan. Petition of district court councillors to Senator John Breckinridge, 1 Dec. 1802, John Breckinridge Papers, 1760–1806.

9. Kirwan, *John J. Crittenden*, 15; *Dictionary of American Biography*, s.v. "Edwards, Ninian."

10. *Journal of the House of Representatives for the Commonwealth of Kentucky, 1800*, 31 Dec. 1800; Ellis, *Jeffersonian Crisis*, 150; Clay to Breckinridge, 18 Dec. 1800, John Breckinridge Papers, 1760–1806.

11. *Journal of the House of Representatives for the Commonwealth of Kentucky, 1800*, 20 Nov. 1800; Harrison, *John Breckinridge: Jeffersonian Republican*, 109.

12. Thomas Todd to Breckinridge, 9 Nov. 1801, John Breckinridge Papers, 1760–1806; Nathaniel Hart to Breckinridge, 14, 19 Nov. 1801, ibid.; Parks, *Felix Grundy*, 14, 17; Ellis, *Jeffersonian Crisis*, 153.

13. Samuel Hopkins to Breckinridge, 21 Nov. 1801, Benjamin Howard to Breckinridge, 15 Dec. 1801, and Samuel McDowell to Breckinridge, 8 Jan. 1801, John Breckinridge Papers, 1760–1806.

14. Samuel Hopkins to Breckinridge, 21 Nov. 1801, ibid.; Robert McAfee to Breckinridge, 24 Nov. 1802, ibid.

15. Robert Breckinridge to John Breckinridge, 2 Dec. 1802, and T. L. Turner to John Breckinridge, 8 Dec. 1802, ibid.

16. Christopher Greenup to Breckinridge, 27 Dec. 1802, and Matthew Walton to Breckinridge, 16 [Jan.?] 1803, ibid. An itinerant Methodist minister described meeting in Springfield about this time the "far-famed Felix Grundy," "then a distinguished man at the bar, and afterward, a distinguished politician and . . one of the steadfast friends of General Jackson." He reported that the "Hon. Robert Wickliffe was the antagonist of Grundy," as manifest first in a paper war, then at the bar, and finally on opposite sides in politics. Rev. Jacob Young, *Autobiography of a Pioneer; or, The Nativity, Experience, Travels, and Ministerial Labors of Rev. Jacob Young, with Incidents, Observations and Reflections* (Cincinnati: Swormstedt & Poe for the Methodist Episcopal Church, 1857), 70–71. Wickliffe, born in Pennsylvania in 1775, studied under Nicholas, practiced in Lexington, and served as a U.S. attorney from 1808 until 1819. Tachau, *Federal Courts in the Early Republic*, 75–76.

17. Thomas Todd to Breckinridge, 22 Dec. 1802, John Breckinridge Papers, 1760–1806. Todd, who referred to "much warmth, party spirit and discontent among the members of the delegation," blamed the "friends of the district system refusing to extend the Courts." Todd to Breckinridge, 30 Dec. 1802, ibid.

18. Innes to Breckinridge, 23 Dec. 1802, James Blair to Breckinridge, 14 Dec. 1802, James Brown to Breckinridge, 13 Jan. 1803, Samuel Hopkins to Breckinridge, 26 Jan. 1803, and Achilles Sneed to Breckinridge, 30 Dec. 1802, ibid. Micah Taul, writing of this time, reported that "Mr. Brown was probably 35 to 40 years of age, a gentlemen of high literary and legal attainment, a good speaker but not eloquent . . . a man of towering and majestic person, very proud, austere and haughty in fact repulsive in his manner and exceedingly unpopular. . . . Mr. Clay, Mr. Bibb and Mr. Bledsoe had come to the bar a short time before; they were all three great favorites with the people, and considered very promising." Taul, "Memoirs of Micah Taul," 343. Hopkins also noted that Matthew Lyon and John Caldwell were supporters of the circuit court legislation.

19. Hopkins commented, "Edwards is coined into a Circuit Judge which I suppose will satisfy him." Hopkins to Breckinridge, 26 Jan. 1803, John Breckinridge Papers, 1760–1806.

20. Innes to Breckinridge, 19 June 1803, and Breckinridge to Innes, 22 June 1803, ibid. Breckinridge had given Daveiss the letter because he did not think the observations on circuit court change were private or personal. "Of one fact I am positive which is that no man living with my permission except Mr. Daveiss can have the contents of your letters." Breckinridge to Innes, 22 June 1803.

21. Framers of the Ohio Constitution in 1802 gave the common-pleas judiciary a "hybrid composition . . . adopting a similar feature of Pennsylvania's judicial system. Each of the county common pleas courts consisted of a presiding judge and two or three associates, understanding that the presiding judge would be a lawyer, and the associates lay people." Donald F. Melhorn Jr., *Lest We Be Marshall'd: Judicial Power and Politics in Ohio, 1806–1812* (Akron, OH: University of Akron Press, 2003), 24.

7. GRUNDY AND CLAY

1. Louis-Philippe, *Diary of My Travels in America*, 118; Grundy to Harry Innes, 8 Feb. 1803, Harry Innes Papers, 1752–1816. Grundy asked for delay in making payment to "Fairfax's Executors," noting that he had not removed all of his papers from Springfield and that he had "no more money at this time, my removing to this place has drained me of cash." Nelson County Deed Book 6, Bardstown, KY, 192, 232.

2. The Bardstown Pleiades, purportedly initiated by James Priestley, met periodically; its meet-

ing place also served as a center for the study of classical languages. Members over the years included John Rowan; William Pope Duval, the future first territorial governor of Florida; Charles A. Wickliffe, a future Kentucky governor from Grundy's base in Washington County; Ninian Edwards; Ben Hardin; and John Pope.

3. On 13 October 1804 Grundy was accorded the allowance for the previous year. Nelson County Record Book B, Bardstown, KY, 148. Hardin grew up three miles east of Springfield. Grundy, who had long known young Hardin, found him one day in 1798 or 1799 lounging in a billiard parlor. Billiards was then a very popular recreation—"a game pursued with fanatical devotion in the early days of Nashville." Parton, *Life of Andrew Jackson,* 1:390. Grundy soon persuaded Hardin to study for a year under an accomplished teacher rather than waste his gifts. The event was sufficiently important to Hardin that his biographer included it in his biography. Little, *Ben Hardin,* 15, 27; Levin, *Lawyers and Lawmakers of Kentucky,* 196.

4. McAfee, "Life and Times of Robert B. McAfee," 222.

5. Grundy was listed as one of eighteen apprentices in Lexington Lodge No. 1 in 1802; Henry Clay was a junior Warden. J. Winston Coleman Jr., *Masonry in the Bluegrass* (Lexington, KY: Transylvania, 1933), 52. The election of Felix Grundy, General William Henry, and Thomas Wallace to the Transylvania board of trustees was announced in the *Kentucky Gazette* on 12 October 1802, but minutes of the board meeting on 2 April 1804 indicate that on 2 April 1803 Colonel James Morrison was elected a trustee in "the room of Felix Grundy." John Bradford, *The Voice of the Frontier: John Bradford's Notes on Kentucky,* ed. Thomas D. Clark (Lexington: University Press of Kentucky, 1993), 239; Benjamin Howard to Breckinridge, 22 Dec. 1803, John Breckinridge Papers, 1760–1806.

6. In 1786, and until the early nineteenth century, a British pound was equivalent to $3.33 in Virginia currency. Hugh Blair Grigsby, *The History of the Virginia Federal Convention of 1788,* 2 vols. (Richmond: Virginia Historical Society, 1891), 2:177. In early Kentucky, tobacco was an important currency, with county officer fees so determined. In 1792 one pound of tobacco was valued at "one penny current money." Edmund L. Starling, *History of Henderson County, Kentucky* (Henderson: privately printed, 1887), 111.

7. Hammond, *Banks and Politics in America,* 169–70; Aron, *How the West Was Lost,* 158–62.

8. Felix Grundy was one of those "said to have been youthful protégés of this benevolent gentlemen, who seems to have been a sort of impresario for budding politicians." George Rawlings Poage, *Henry Clay and the Whig Party* (Chapel Hill: University of North Carolina Press, 1936), 3.

9. William T. Barry to Doctor John Barry, 2 Aug. 1803, William Taylor Barry Papers, 1785–1835; Mayo, *Henry Clay,* 150–52.

10. A description of Clay's background is presented in Remini, *Henry Clay,* 2–14. Only two of Clay's brothers survived to maturity.

11. *Nashville Union,* 1 Feb. 1841.

12. *Kentucky Gazette,* 23 Jan. 1806.

13. Meyer, *Life and Times of Colonel Richard M. Johnson,* 50–55; Robert Grayson to Breckinridge, 18 Nov. 1804, John Breckinridge Papers, 1760–1806; Joseph H. Daveiss to Thomas Jefferson, 28 Mar. 1806, Thomas Jefferson Papers, 1606–1902.

14. The first vote taken for U.S. senator on 15 November showed 40 votes for John Adair, 24 for Thruston, and 21 for John Brown. In the Kentucky house, there were 30 votes for Adair, 18 for Thruston, and 14 for Brown. The votes were not entirely sectional: 22 of the votes from south of the Kentucky River went to Adair, compared with 14 for the Bluegrass candidates. Conversely, Adair

received only 8 votes from north of the river, while Thruston and Brown together received 18. It was reasonably clear that Bluegrass votes would be sufficient to defeat Adair if the Bluegrass bloc could be maintained. After six votes in the house that day, Clay, recognizing the inevitable, skillfully persuaded the Brown voters to support Thruston; only Joel Watkins, of Grundy's base in Washington County, switched his vote from Brown to Adair. The house was deadlocked at 30 votes each, and Thruston's strength in the Senate was sufficient to give him the majority vote required, 44–43. Jack Jouett to Breckinridge, 24 Dec. 1804, John Breckinridge Papers, 1760–1806. Clay's management was praised as "artful," an amusing counterpoint to the description of Grundy's efforts as "intriguing" and "conniving." T. L. Turner to Breckinridge, 2 Dec. 1804, and Robert Grayson to Breckinridge, 18 Nov. 1804, ibid.

15. Remini, *Henry Clay*, 35–37; Innes to Breckinridge, 20 Dec. 1804, John Breckinridge Papers, 1760–1806.

16. William Russell to Breckinridge, 1 Mar. 1806, John Breckinridge Papers, 1760–1806. Russell (1758–1825) was a wealthy planter and respected veteran of Kings Mountain and Guilford Court House, who would subsequently command a regiment of regulars at Tippecanoe. His father had been a distinguished frontier leader and Revolutionary War general and an early backer of Daniel Boone. Faragher, *Daniel Boone*, 89–90; Anna Russell des Cognets, *William Russell and His Descendants*, 2nd ed. (Princeton, NJ: privately printed, 1960), 43–55. W. L. Stevenson, an opponent of all banks, wrote John Breckinridge in 1806 that "sufficient to say you are blamed for General Russell's vote" and "what your sentiments . . . on the subject may be I know not . . . Parker roundly reported that you were hostile to the bank." Stevenson to Breckinridge, 5 Jan. 1806, John Breckinridge Papers, 1760–1806.

17. "A Poor Farmer," *Kentucky Gazette*, 29 Jan. 1805; Mayo, *Henry Clay*, 160; Hammond, *Banks and Politics in America*, 169.

18. *Kentucky Gazette*, 23 Jan. 1806; George Bibb to Grundy, 5 Feb. 1827, Felix Grundy Papers, 1807–1899, SHC.

19. Felix Grundy, "Address to the People of Kentucky," *Bardstown Western American*, as reprinted in *Kentucky Gazette*, 16 Apr. 1805; Aron, *How the West Was Lost*, 158–61.

20. *Kentucky Gazette*, 29 Jan., 30 Apr. 1805; Aron, *How the West Was Lost*, 158–59.

21. Aron, *How the West Was Lost*, 159; Royalty, "Banking, Politics and the Commonwealth of Kentucky," 12–20. According to Royalty, "Grundy's amendment would possibly have been successful if the question had been simply the elimination of the bank or its continuation under the existing charter, but the possibility of regulation as an alternative divided the anti-bank party enough to defeat repeal." Ibid., 17–18.

22. Clay to Breckinridge, 22 Dec. 1804, in Clay, *Papers*, 1:166–67; Brown to Clay, 12 Mar. 1805, in Clay, *Papers*, 1:179; Aron, *How the West Was Lost*, 158–59; Remini, *Henry Clay*, 35–37.

23. "A Poor Farmer," *Kentucky Gazette*, 29 Jan. 1805; Grundy to the people of Kentucky, reprinted from *Bardstown Western American* in *Kentucky Gazette*, 16 Apr. 1805.

24. Grundy to Clay, 4 Feb. 1805, in Clay, *Papers*, 1:171. Grundy said that he and Clay had their differences in opinion on the bank but "that difference ought not to induce either of us, however, to wish, or even permit a false statement to be made to the prejudice of either." Grundy stated that an unknown person had charged Grundy with saying that the bank "had actually issued paper to three times the amount of the money in their Coffers." Grundy said that he had not made such a statement; on the contrary, he had spoken respectfully of bank management. He had said, however, that the bank had the power to issue notes to any amount and that given the great profits arising to

stockholders, some portion of the profits must have derived from issuance of paper above the sums actually deposited.

25. The congressional recommendation, signed in Washington by John Boyle, Matthew Walton, John Fowler, Thomas Landford, and M. Lyon, states that Grundy "is of fine character and unimpeachable integrity. He was bred to the law and in the course of seven or eight years practice in his profession has distinguished himself both as an advocate and a Lawyer, he is active industrious and persevering in all his pursuits and we have no hesitation to say that if the trust should be reposed in him he will execute it with talents and fidelity." Letter to Jefferson, 28 Feb. 1805, Thomas Jefferson Papers, 1606–1902; Walton to Jefferson, 19 Apr. 1805, received 21 May 1805, ibid.; Breckinridge to Albert Gallatin, 25 Apr. 1805, and Gallatin to Breckinridge, 11 July 1805, John Breckinridge Papers, 1760–1806; Parks, *Felix Grundy,* 25; Royalty, "Banking, Politics and the Commonwealth of Kentucky," 25. Breckinridge's letter, dated 24 April 1805, is not at the Library of Congress and is unknown to the editors of *The Papers of Thomas Jefferson,* at Princeton. Gallatin's letter to Breckinridge on 11 July enclosed a commission for Grundy as land agent in Louisiana. He also set forth a procedure for issuance of a commission to another person in the event that Grundy refused the commission offered him.

26. William Morton to Thomas and John Clifford, 31 Aug. 1805, Clifford Family Papers, 1727–1832, as quoted in Mayo, *Henry Clay,* 171; Royalty, "Banking, Politics and the Commonwealth of Kentucky," 25–26.

27. William Stevenson to Breckinridge, Jan. 1806, John Breckinridge Papers, 1760–1806; Aron, *How the West Was Lost,* 159–60; Remini, *Henry Clay,* 37–40. For the actual breakdown of votes in this period, see Royalty, "Banking, Politics and the Commonwealth of Kentucky."

28. Innes to Breckinridge, 24. Dec. 1805, John Breckinridge Papers, 1760–1806.

29. Ibid.; Aron, *How the West Was Lost,* 160–61.

30. F. L. Turner to Breckinridge, 20 Dec. 1805, John Breckinridge Papers, 1760–1806.

31. For a good account of this maneuvering, see Royalty, "Banking, Politics and the Commonwealth of Kentucky," 28–36. Littell amusingly summarized these events in the *Kentucky Gazette,* 30 Jan. 1806.

32. The two from south of the Green River were Robert Ewing, for Logan and Christian counties, and Jesse Richardson, for Pulaski, Wayne, and Cumberland. The other three were Bennett Pemberton, of Franklin County, James Thompson, of Garrard and Jessamine counties, and Philemon Waters, of Washington County. Barton, "Politics and Banking in Republican Kentucky," 95–96; *Kentucky Gazette,* 30 Jan. 1806.

33. *Randolph (TN) Recorder,* 28 June 1834, cited in Parks, *Felix Grundy,* 29–30.

34. William Littell, ed., *The Statute Laws of Kentucky,* 5 vols. (Frankfort: William Hunter, 1809–19), 3:390–401; Royalty, "Banking, Politics and the Commonwealth of Kentucky," 37; Barton, "Politics and Banking in Republican Kentucky," 94–100; Aron, *How the West Was Lost,* 160–61.

35. Mayo, *Henry Clay,* 177; Russell to Breckinridge, 1 Mar. 1806, John Breckinridge Papers, 1760–1806. Russell was so impressed by Grundy that in 1809 he named his fourth son Felix Grundy Russell. Des Cognets, *William Russell and His Descendants,* 53.

8. CHIEF JUSTICE

1. *Journal of the House of Representatives for the Commonwealth of Kentucky, 1806* (Frankfort: Kentucky Historical Society, 1806), 60ff. The nominees of the Kentucky House of Representatives

for the U.S. Senate seat were Grundy, Pope, Adair, Samuel Hopkins, and Fortunatus Cosby. Clay, *Papers,* 1:254.

2. All analyses of cases and caseload are derived from reported opinions of the Kentucky Court of Appeals for 1805–8. Those opinions are in three Kentucky reports, known as the Hardin Reports, prepared by Martin Hardin in 1810. For fuller exposition, see Martin Hardin, *Report of Cases Argued and Adjudged in the Court of Appeals of Kentucky, 1805–1808* (Frankfort: Johnston & Pleasants for Hardin, 1810).

3. Innes to John Breckinridge, 27 Dec. 1801, John Breckinridge Papers, 1760–1806; Kerr et al., *History of Kentucky,* 1:482–83. The legislature did not generously compensate itself; in 1796 legislators received $1.50 for each day of service. Ibid., 312.

4. John C. Doolan, "The Court of Appeals of Kentucky," *Green Bag* 12 (Aug. 1900): 346.

5. There is no evidence that Grundy ever bought a house in Frankfort or nearby, but he must have been in attendance at court for much of the time from February to June (opinions in the spring term were issued from 18 April to 5 June) and in the fall. The view that Grundy's decision to leave for Tennessee was partially due to dissatisfaction with service on the court is buttressed by the experience of his colleagues. Ninian Edwards, appointed to the court on 13 December 1806, succeeded Grundy as chief justice but resigned in May 1809 to become the first governor of the Illinois Territory. William Logan followed Edwards as the fourth judge on 11 January 1808 but resigned 19 days later. Finally, George Bibb, commissioned a judge on 31 January 1808, became chief justice on 30 May 1809 but resigned in March 1810.

6. The biographer of Ben Hardin gave a somewhat different background for Grundy's move: "The son of a prominent citizen and an old personal friend was arrested, at Nashville, on a criminal charge. Judge Grundy was engaged to defend the youth, which he did successfully. His talent made a most favorable impression on the Tennesseans and, in turn, he was so won by their kindness and attention, and the prospect of professional advantages" that he moved to Nashville. Little, *Ben Hardin,* 172–73. Daveiss advised Andrew Jackson in September 1808 that he intended to practice law in Nashville, but in fact he remained in Kentucky. Daveiss to Jackson, 28 Sept. 1808, in Jackson, *Papers,* 2:553; Daveiss to John Overton, date unknown, John Overton Papers, 1797–1833, TSLA. Daveiss also noted that his residence in Kentucky was about as close to Nashville (150 miles) as to Frankfort. Harry Innes assessed the legal establishment in Tennessee in December 1804 as follows: "In Tennessee there is a want of abilities. Mr. G. W. Campbell of the House of Representatives is considered one of the first—yet I think there is one superior, Mr. Jenkin Whiteside, still he lacks dignity or respectability for a judge." Innes to Breckinridge, 20 Dec. 1804, John Breckinridge Papers, 1760–1806.

7. Grundy to Samuel Williams, 12 Aug. 1809, Washington County Deed Book C, Springfield, KY, 437; Grundy to William Logan, 13 Sept. 1808, Felix Grundy Papers, Kentucky Historical Society. Ben Hardin's daughter Lucinda, later the wife of Kentucky governor John L. Helm, recalled seeing Felix Grundy on one of his visits to Kentucky when she was a schoolgirl. "It was at Dr. Ben Harrison's residence, in Bardstown. When I first saw him I took him for a red-faced Irishman . . . when he saw me, and was told I was Ben Hardin's daughter, he ran and caught and kissed me." Little, *Ben Hardin,* 177.

9. GREENVILLE SPRINGS

1. *Beck v. Grundy,* 19 Jan. 1799, and *Grundy v. Beck,* Oct. 1799, Washington County Circuit Court; Nelson County Deed Book 16, Bardstown, KY, 343; Jillson, *Kentucky Land Grants,* 182.

The purchase of 1,480 acres was registered on 6 November 1800 in Nelson County Deed Book 7, Bardstown, KY, 628. The acquisitions on Buffalo Creek included 200 acres bought by Grundy in 1800 from the executors of his father's estate, 100 acres bought from a Henry Floyd, and 240 3/4 acres between Witherroe's Run and Buffalo Creek acquired from his brother John on 28 January 1805 for 577 pounds. Nelson County Deed Book 12, Bardstown, KY, 117; Nelson County Deed Book 8, Bardstown, KY, 111; Oakes, *Ruling Race*, 61.

2. Fortescue Cuming, *Sketches of a Tour to the Western Country* (Philadelphia, 1810), 211–12; J. Winston Coleman Jr., *The Springs of Kentucky* (Lexington: Winburn, 1955), 13–19. All information on the development of the Harrodsburg resort is from Mercer County Circuit Court records, Harrodsburg, KY, package G10; and Van Arsdall, "Springs at Harrodsburg." Grundy's role as the initial developer of Greenville Springs is not described in the histories of the springs of Kentucky, such as that by Coleman.

3. Head married Jane Ramsey, of Bedford County, Pennsylvania, and died in Harrodsburg, Kentucky, in March 1842. Biography of Jesse Head, Reuben T. Durrett Collection. Head received a lot and certain rights for introducing Grundy to the opportunity on the Van Arsdal farm.

4. The purchase agreement is not well drafted. The last paragraph, written in a different style and as if almost an afterthought, appears to require Grundy to pay an additional five hundred dollars to Van Arsdal "so soon as a bond given by William Duval to Grundy becomes due which is sometime in the next year."

5. Mercer County Circuit Court records, Harrodsburg, KY, package G10.

6. Greenville Springs subsequently was used as a residence—U.S. Supreme Court Justice John Harlan lived there as a boy, from 1834 to 1841—and was the locale for various girls' schools and colleges. The core of the property today is the site of the Beaumont Inn and remains a lovely place.

10. TENNESSEE AND CONGRESS

1. François A. Michaux, *Travels to the West of the Allegheny Mountains, in the States of Ohio, Kentucky and Tennessee and Back to Charleston, by the Upper Carolinas . . . Undertaken in the Year 1802*, in *Early Western Travels, 1748–1846*, ed. Reuben Gold Thwaites, 32 vols. (Cleveland, OH: Arthur H. Clark, 1904–7), 3:250–53; John M. Bass, "Half An Hour With Some Early Visitors to Tennessee," *American Historical Magazine* 5 (Apr. 1900): 99–114; George M. Martin, "Recollections of 1799," in *The First Presbyterian Church of Nashville: A Documentary History*, ed. Wilbur F. Creighton Jr. and Leland R. Johnson (Nashville: Williams Printing, 1986), 6–9.

2. Randal McGavock to James McGavock, 10 May 1805, McGavock Papers, 1760–1888.

3. Asbury, *Journals and Letters*, 3:251–52; Clayton, *History of Davidson County, Tennessee*, 201; *Democratic Clarion and Tennessee Gazette*, 27 Sept. 1808. The property was offered for sale by W. Sneed. Grundy purchased a 100-acre tract in Davidson County on 26 December 1809 for $15 per acre and sold the land on 4 September 1812 for the same price. Davidson County Deed Books, Nashville, G, 573, and K, 285; Williamson County Deed Book 13, Franklin, TN, 618, 620 (3 Feb. 1810). He paid $640 for 640 acres on the western side of the South Harpeth and $360 for 80 acres on the eastern side. Ibid. The Williamson County Tax Book, 1800–1813, Franklin, TN, 273–74, shows Grundy as owning 1,120 acres on the South Harpeth River in 1810 and 640 acres in 1811. See also Wills, *History of Belle Meade*, 21, 23; *Democratic Clarion and Tennessee Gazette*, 9 Apr. 1811.

4. Crabb, *Nashville*, 21. Shrewd and determined, James McGavock emigrated from Glenarm, Northern Ireland, about 1754, served as a captain in the Virginia militia in the French and Indian

War, signed the Fincastle Resolutions, and was a leading revolutionary on the southwestern frontier of Virginia. Rev. Robert Gray, *The McGavock Family* (Richmond, VA: William Ellis Jones, 1903), 1–3; Emory G. Evans, "Trouble in the Backcountry," in *An Uncivil War: The Southern Backcountry during the American Revolution,* ed. Ronald Hoffman, Thad W. Tate, and Peter J. Albert (Charlottesville: University Press of Virginia for Capital Hill Historical Society, 1985).

5. *Nashville Union,* 11 Jan. 1841.

6. David McGavock to James McGavock, 20 Aug. 1805, McGavock Papers, 1760–1888; Caldwell, *Sketches of the Bench and Bar,* 52–60.

7. Jackson, *Papers,* 2:172–74; Grundy to Daniel Graham, 22 May 1828, Felix Grundy Papers, 1807–1899, SHC.

8. *Democratic Clarion and Tennessee Gazette,* 2 Nov. 1810. The best account of the Magness case is found in Gary Alan Webb, "The Magness Trials," *Williamson County Historical Society Publication* 15 (1984): 21–33. See also Benton, *Thirty Years' View,* 1:736.

9. Parton, *Life of Andrew Jackson,* 1:344; Jackson, *Papers,* 2:255; James A. Crutchfield and Robert Holladay, *Franklin, Tennessee's Handsomest Town: A Bicentennial History, 1799–1999* (Franklin: Hillsboro, 1999), 66–67.

10. William Preston Anderson to Jackson, 17 Nov. 1810, in Jackson, *Papers,* 2:255–56; Parton, *Life of Andrew Jackson,* 1:344.

11. Buell, *History of Andrew Jackson,* 1:235–36. Magness's two brothers, one of whom was only fourteen at the time of the shooting, were also tried in Franklin, in 1811 and 1812, and acquitted.

12. Carlton C. Simms, ed., *A History of Rutherford County* (Murfreesboro, TN: privately printed, 1947), 26; Fanny Noailles Dickinson Murfree, *Hardy Murfree, 1752–1809* (Murfreesboro, TN: privately printed, nd); *Democratic Clarion and Tennessee Gazette,* 21 July, 24 Jan., 19 May 1809.

13. Thomas Hart Benton to Henry Clay, 18 Sept. 1810, in Clay, *Papers,* 1:490–91. Benton was a first cousin, once removed, of Clay's wife, Lucretia. Benton years later benefited politically from his relation to Clay. A former Kentucky congressman wrote of Benton's election to the Senate from Missouri: "Col. Benton was *not popular* but was considered a man of talents and being allied to Mr. Clay by marriage (he was a cousin of Mrs. Clay) received then, with the aid of a few men, myself among the rest, the vote of Kentuckians who were members." Taul, "Memoirs of Micah Taul," 502; *Democratic Clarion and Tennessee Gazette,* 9 July 1811.

14. Sellers, *Market Revolution,* 170. The role of land speculation in Tennessee development and politics has been studied in various works, including Abernethy, *From Frontier to Plantation,* and most recently Ray, *Middle Tennessee,* 1–17, 43–56. See also Masterson, *William Blount;* Driver, *John Sevier;* and Buckner F. Melton Jr., *The First Impeachment: The Constitution's Framers and the Case of Senator William Blount* (Macon, GA: Mercer University Press, 1998).

15. George W. Campbell to Jenkin Whiteside, 7 Feb. 1811, Brown-Ewell Family Papers, 1781–1984; *Democratic Clarion and Tennessee Gazette,* 25 Jan. 1811; "Leonidas," ibid., 23 July 1811. Tennessee was thoroughly Republican, and every candidate a Jeffersonian. As "A Citizen" wrote in 1808, "It is true that of all objects, that of ascertaining that your candidate is immovably attached to Democratic Republic Principles, is the most important." *Carthage Gazette,* 19 Sept. 1808, quoted in Kristofer Ray, "Land Speculation, Popular Democracy and Political Transformation on the Tennessee Frontier, 1780–1800," *Tennessee Historical Quarterly* 61 (Fall 2002): 173; *Democratic Clarion and Tennessee Gazette,* 25 June 1811; Ray, *Middle Tennessee,* 95–112.

16. *Democratic Clarion and Tennessee Gazette,* 2 July 1811, August 1811.

17. *Democratic Clarion and Tennessee Gazette,* 9, 23 July 1811. Martin's letter sets forth the following: "The charges which he has brought against us (reduced to some sort of order) are these. First, that we are a gang of Yazooites: and therefore we hate Mr. G who is all of a sudden the great antagonist of Yazooism. Second, that we are an excommunicated tribe of Federalists; and therefore we hate Mr. G who is the very pink of republicanism. Third, we are a set of litigious dogs, who Mr. G as a lawyer has had occasion to thrash and therefore we hate Mr. G who is no doubt a most correct and unimpeachable attorney. Fourthly, lastly and generally, that we are a pack of fellows without honor, without principle, without love for our country; and therefore we hate Mr. G who is full of honor, full of principles and loves his dear country (just at this moment) beyond all the things of this world—fees not excepted." Durham, *James Winchester,* 99–100.

18. William P. Anderson to John Coffee, 30 July 1811, John Doak to Coffee, 2 Aug. 1811, and John Drake to Coffee, 1 Aug. 1811, John Coffee Papers, 1770–1917.

19. *Democratic Clarion and Tennessee Gazette,* 2 July, 11 Aug. 1811. In Rutherford County Winchester had 698 votes to Grundy's 296, and in Maury County Roberts had 532 votes to 467 for Grundy.

11. WAR HAWK

1. Watts, *Republic Reborn,* 240ff. The *Democratic Clarion and Tennessee Gazette,* in endorsing Grundy in January 1811, reported two important local objectives: trade down to Mobile and removal of the Indians scattered throughout Tennessee. George W. Campbell, a Tennessee congressman from 1803 to 1809 and a War Hawk senator in 1811, wrote Jenkin Whiteside that taking possession of West Florida was "perilously interesting to the Western country." Campbell to Whiteside, 7 Feb. 1811, Brown-Ewell Family Papers, 1781–1984. See also Weymouth T. Jordan, "The Public Career of George Washington Campbell," *East Tennessee Historical Society Publications* 10 (1938): 3–18; and Jordan, *George Washington Campbell of Tennessee.*

2. *Democratic Clarion and Tennessee Gazette,* 24 Jan., 19 May 1809; Grundy to Isaac Shelby, 25 Mar. [1807?], Isaac P. Shelby Papers, 1792–1893.

3. *Democratic Clarion and Tennessee Gazette,* 19 Nov. 1811; Grundy to Jackson, 24 Dec. 1811, in Jackson, *Papers,* 2:274–76. In a letter of 18 November to Tennessee's Governor Blount, Grundy wrote that "something must be done, or we shall loose [*sic*] our respectability abroad and even cease to respect ourselves." *Knoxville Gazette,* 18 Dec. 1811.

4. McCaughey, *Josiah Quincy,* 45.

5. Perry M. Goldman and James S. Young, *The United States Congressional Directories, 1789–1840* (New York: Columbia University Press, 1973), 50–51; "Journal of Governor John Sevier," ed. John H. Dewitt, *Tennessee Historical Magazine* 6 (Apr. 1920): 41–43. Tom Kanon first pointed out that Grundy was not part of the War Mess. Kanon, "James Madison, Felix Grundy, and the Devil," 449.

6. Clay's persuasive charm and talent are described in Remini, *Henry Clay,* 75–85.

7. *Annals of Congress,* 12th Cong., 1st sess., 403–14, 558; Pratt, *Expansionists of 1812,* 134–38. Grundy also wrote Andrew Jackson on 12 February 1812 that he opposed an appropriation for the New York "Mammoth Canal," for "which no other purpose could be answered, except to increase the power of the northern Section of the Union." Jackson, *Papers,* 2:283. The Tennessee legislature had asked its congressional delegation to support the measure. Grundy said that they were "no doubt mistaken" and that he would act on his own responsibility in opposing the Erie Canal.

8. Congressman Samuel Taggart described four parties with overlapping membership in Congress: a war party, "who sincerely aim at war as the result of the present measures"' an antiwar group, who "not only oppose war but all preparations for it"; "the scarecrow" or "Presidential party," who vote for war measures without any sincere intention to go to war but in hopes that Great Britain "may be intimidated by the din of our preparations to relax her system"; and finally the antiadministration parties, which contain parts of the first two parties. He further surmised that if those whose object was war could not obtain it, they "will be nearly all anti-administration men." Taggart to John Jackson, 20 Jan. 1812, in Taggart, "Letters of Samuel Taggart," 376–79. On war groupings, see Wilentz, *Rise of American Democracy*, 153–59; and Hickey, *War of 1812*. For a listing of articles on the War Hawks, see Latimer, *1812: War with America*, 426n102. Augustus Foster, the British minister in Washington in 1811, saw the War Hawks as the raucous manifestation of an inspired national pride and believed that war was "as necessary to America as a duel is to a young [naval] officer to prevent his being bullied and elbowed in society." Quoted in Rutland, *Presidency of James Madison*, 95–96.

9. Parks, *Felix Grundy*, 60–61; Taggart to Jackson, 30 Dec. 1811, in Taggart, "Letters of Samuel Taggart," 375–76; Randolph to Frances Scott Key, 12 Sept. 1813, in Garland, *Life of John Randolph*, 2:20 ("great allowance is to be made for men under the *regime* of Clay, Grundy and Co.; and besides a few individuals only are answerable for the consequences of this tortuous policy"); *Annals of Congress*, 13th Cong., 1st sess., 253; Marshall Smelser, *The Democratic Republic, 1801–1815* (New York: Harper & Row, 1968), 208–9, 221; Brant, *James Madison: The President, 1809–1812*, 391; "Letters of Edward Coles," *William and Mary Quarterly*, 2nd ser., 7 (1927), 162–63; Kanon, "James Madison, Felix Grundy, and the Devil," 435.

10. Quincy, *Life of Josiah Quincy*, 303.

11. James A. Green, *William Henry Harrison: His Life and Times* (Richmond, VA: Garrett & Massie, 1941), 128–31; Stagg, *Mr. Madison's War*, 177–87; Wilentz, *Rise of American Democracy*, 148–53.

12. Jordan, *George Washington Campbell of Tennessee*, 93–100; Stagg, *Mr. Madison's War*, 84; Grundy to Jackson, 28 Nov. 1811, in Jackson, *Papers*, 2:271; Anthony Butler to Jackson, 12 Oct. 1811, ibid., 267.

13. *Annals of Congress*, 12th Cong., 1st sess., 376ff.

14. The much-quoted sentence reads, "We are about to ascertain by actual experiment how far our republican institutions are calculated to stand the shock of war and whether, after foreign danger has disappeared, we can regain our peaceful attitude without endangering the liberties of the people." Ibid., 423. See also Henry Adams, *History of the United States During the First Administration of James Madison*, 2:137; and Watts, *Republic Reborn*, 244–46.

15. *Annals of Congress*, 12th Cong., 1st sess., 422ff.

16. Andrew Jackson, offering assistance to William Henry Harrison on 28 November 1811, stated that "this hostile band which must be excited to war, by the secret agents of Great Britain must be destroyed." Andrew Jackson Papers, 1775–1860. A British traveler in 1817 commented on how terrible the Indian threat appeared to Lexingtonians, even though most had experienced the threat secondhand, through the stories of their elders. John Palmer, *Journal of Travel in the United States of North America, and in Lower Canada, Performed in the year 1817* (London: Sherwood, Neely, & Jones, 1818). Grundy stated "Yes, Mr. Speaker, in one individual has fallen, the honest man, the orator and the soldier . . . I mean the late commander of the cavalry; you, sir, who have often measured your strength with his on forensic debate can attest that he in a good degree was the

pride of the Western Country, and Kentucky claimed him as a favorite son . . . and sir, war once declared, I pledge myself for my people—they will avenge the death of their brethren." *Annals of Congress,* 12th Cong., 1st sess., 425.

17. See Pratt, *Expansionists of 1812,* 138–52; and Latimer, *1812: War with America,* 31. Latimer's study is the first British assessment of the War of 1812 since 1968. Both Pratt and Latimer attribute the war largely to the drive to acquire Canada.

18. *Annals of Congress,* 12th Cong., 1st sess., 449.

19. Mayo, *Henry Clay,* 473; Kirk, *John Randolph of Roanoke,* 46.

20. Ravenel, *Life and Times of William Lowndes,* 119.

21. *Annals of Congress,* 12th Cong., 1st sess., 611–13.

22. Ibid., 730ff., 787, 794; Saul Cornell, *A Well-Regulated Militia* (New York: Oxford University Press, 2006).

23. *Annals of Congress,* 12th Cong., 1st sess., 999; Rutland, *Presidency of James Madison,* 89; Mayo, *Henry Clay,* 445; Ketcham, *James Madison,* 515. Samuel Taggart described the opposition of the "wise western warriors" to the navy bill as a matter of calculation. "The more distressing the war on the coast the more probable would it tend to enrich and populate the western states." Taggart to Jackson, 6 Feb. 1812, in Taggart, "Letters of Samuel Taggart," 381.

24. Grundy to Jackson, 12 Feb. 1812, in Jackson, *Papers,* 2:283; *Annals of Congress,* 12th Cong., 1st sess., 1136–46; Grundy to Joseph Phillips, 22 Feb. 1812, published in the *Nashville Banner,* 14 Nov. 1896. Grundy's efforts with respect to avoidance of a high tax on stills won him high praise from the *Democratic Clarion and Tennessee Gazette,* which noted on 6 May 1812 that the "faithful representative had saved them [his Tennessee constituents] from an unjust tax."

25. Brant, *James Madison: The President 1809–1812,* 391–92; Ravenel, *Life and Times of William Lowndes,* 90 ("Mr. Monroe has given the strongest assurances that the President will cooperate zealously with Congress in declaring war if our complaints are not met by May next"); Grundy to Jackson, 24 Dec. 1811, in Jackson, *Papers,* 2:274; Taggart to Jackson, 30 Dec. 1811, in Taggart, "Letters of Samuel Taggart," 375–76. Taggart also said of Grundy that "he is a man of whom you must form a very erroneous idea if you compare him to a northern Democrat," and "there is no doubt but so far as respects the state of Tennessee he can effect it, for he manages that state at pleasure" (375, 376).

26. Grundy to Jackson, 12 Feb. 1812, in Jackson, *Papers,* 2:283. Senator George Bibb wrote John Crittenden on 16 April 1812, "The Kentuckians are impatient, Congress firm . . . with a proper minister of war we might now have been prepared for war." Coleman, *Life of John J. Crittenden,* 1:15–16. Taggart to Jackson, 28 Jan. 1812, in Taggart, "Letters of Samuel Taggart," 379–81. Madison wrote Jefferson on 7 February 1812, "With a view to enable the Executive to step at once into Canada, they have provided after two months delay, for a regular force requiring 12 to raise it, and after 3 months for a volunteer force, on terms not likely to raise it at all for that object." *The Writings of James Madison,* ed. Gaillard Hunt, 9 vols. (New York: G. P. Putnam's Sons, 1900–1910), 8:175–77.

27. Grundy to Joseph Phillips, 22 Feb. 1812, published in the *Nashville Banner,* 14 Nov. 1896.

28. Grundy to Jackson, 12 Feb. 1812, in Jackson, *Papers,* 2:283.

29. Taggart to Jackson, 21 Mar. 1812, in Taggart, "Letters of Samuel Taggart," 390–91. Taggart believed that a junto of five to ten from both houses "manage the affairs of the nation at pleasure," with this "violent party" having a "complete ascendancy over" Madison, who was preoccupied by his election. Taggart to Jackson, 26 Apr. 1812, ibid., 394. See also Gaillard Hunt, "Joseph Gales on the War Manifesto of 1812," *American Historical Review* 13 (Jan. 1908): 303–10; Albert Carr, *Com-*

ing of War, 325–26; *Annals of Congress,* 13th Cong., 1st sess., 254; and Remini, *Henry Clay,* 91–92. Sean Wilentz concludes that Madison, no pacifist, had decided for war at least by April 1812. Wilentz, *Rise of American Democracy,* 153–56.

30. *Annals of Congress,* 12th Cong., 1st sess., 1587–98, 1407–14; Buel, *America on the Brink,* 151–53.

31. *Annals of Congress,* 12th Cong., 1st sess., 1546–64; Hunt, "Joseph Gales on the War Manifesto of 1812"; Charles M. Wiltse, "The Authorship of the War Report of 1812," *American Historical Review* 49 (Jan. 1944): 253–59; Watts, *Republic Reborn,* 265–74; Calhoun, *Papers,* 1:109–24; manuscript of the War Manifesto, 12-A-C5, RG 233, Records of the House of Representatives, National Archives.

32. Remarks, 17 July 1841, in Calhoun, *Papers,* 15:623–28; *Congressional Globe,* 27th Cong., 1st sess., 1841, 10, no. 14:215 (17 July 1841). When the House vote occurred, it was something of a non-event. John Sevier's diary notation for Thursday, 4 June 1812, reads, "Pleasant day wt to the House passed the declaration of war against G. Britain etc." Dewitt, "Journal of Governor John Sevier," 47. Grundy to Jackson, 5 June 1812, Andrew Jackson Papers, 1775–1860.

33. Grundy to Jackson, 5 June 1812, Andrew Jackson Papers, 1775–1860; William Lowndes's commonplace (historical) notebook, 11–12, William Lowndes Papers, 1787–1842, cited in Mayo, *Henry Clay,* 522–23.

12. CONGRESS AT WAR

1. Jackson to the Second Division, 7 Mar. 1812, in Jackson, *Papers,* 2:290–91. In May 1812 Grundy stated in the House that after a declaration of war, the country's inquiry would be whether one was "for your country, or against it." *Annals of Congress,* 12th Cong., 1st sess., 1410.

2. Jefferson to Madison, 19 Feb. 1812, in *The Republic of Letters: The Correspondence between Thomas Jefferson and James Madison, 1776–1826,* ed. James Morton Smith, 3 vols. (New York: Norton, 1995), 3:1688. Grundy's lack of involvement in military matters was manifest with respect to the dismissal of Tennessee soldiers in 1813. In March 1813, after the secretary of war, with no notice, had ordered Jackson's volunteers disbanded, Jackson wrote Grundy from the field that his soldiers, who had been "solicited, entreated and urged by your eloquence," were being infamously treated and would ask why of Grundy, "of the President, and the incumbent who must have been drunk when he wrote." Jackson to Grundy, 15 Mar. 1813, in Jackson, *Papers,* 2:385. Grundy, who had learned of the dismissal before Jackson, had written a letter on 15 February 1813, published in the Nashville press, saying that he could not "account for the proceeding. I know of no cause," but he had been unable to reverse the decision.

3. *Annals of Congress,* 12th Cong., 2nd sess., 355–62; Ravenel, *Life and Times of William Lowndes,* 121–24.

4. Quincy's remarks do not appear in the printed report of his speech but are referred to by Grundy and others. *Annals of Congress,* 12th Cong., 2nd sess., 600; McCaughey, *Josiah Quincy,* 54; *Daily National Intelligencer,* 30 Jan. 1813. Grundy claimed in 1814 that 6,257 Americans had been impressed by the British. ibid., 9 Mar. 1814. This was the same number included in a report by President Madison in January 1812. Madison's report is characterized as shoddy in Latimer, *1812: War with America,* 14–19, 31–32.

5. *Annals of Congress,* 12th Cong., 2nd sess., 960–67, 1048–55; Calhoun, *Papers,* 1:148–49; *Daily National Intelligencer,* 30 Jan., 10 Feb. 1813. Grundy's letter on Federalist discomfort with the

bill included thanks for "a very acceptable present." Grundy to unidentified recipient, 13 Feb. 1813, Special Collections, University of Tennessee, Knoxville. See also *Annals of Congress,* 12th Cong., 2nd sess., 1055, 1339–42.

6. Josiah Quincy to his wife, 16 Feb. 1813, in Quincy, *Life of Josiah Quincy,* 303.

7. *Nashville Whig,* 3 Mar. 1813. Sevier, a fellow congressman, wrote Robertson in February 1813 that he was "much pleased with your friend Grundy, ... a very useful and active member ... you will not be better represented should you change him for another." Sevier went further and said that it would be gratifying to him personally if Robertson would attend the polls at the time of election, as "I am informed he will meet a strong opposition." Sevier to Robertson, 25 Feb. 1813, *American Historical Magazine* 5 (July 1900): 278–79; Robertson to Capt. John Davis, 9 Mar. 1813, in Putnam, *History of Middle Tennessee,* 602. Putnam in 1859 referred to Grundy as "a man of quick discernment, acute discrimination, firm decision, learned, ingenious, eloquent." Ibid. The results were as follows: in Davidson County, 929–42; in Williamson, Cannon's home county, 892–200; in Rutherford, 454–54; in Lincoln, 446–21; and in Bedford, 556–440. *Nashville Whig,* 7 Apr. 1813.

8. *Nashville Whig,* 16 Sept., 14 Oct. 1812; Quincy, *Life of Josiah Quincy,* 332; Daniel Webster to Isaac P. Davis, 6 Jan. 1814, in Webster, *Papers,* 1:159–60.

9. Grundy to his daughters, 27 June 1813, and Grundy to Louise Grundy, 19 Dec. 1812, Felix Grundy Papers, 1807–1899, SHC.

10. *Annals of Congress,* 13th Cong., 1st sess., 26, 219–29; Remini, *Daniel Webster,* 108–10; Buel, *America on the Brink,* 178–81.

11. *Annals of Congress,* 13th Cong., 1st sess., 225–26; Buel, *America on the Brink,* 180–81.

12. *Annals of Congress,* 13th Cong., 1st sess., 234–36, 251–65; Calhoun, *Papers,* 1:177.

13. Discussing a bill encouraging enlistments, Grundy said on 6 January 1814: "I now repeat, that those who systematically oppose the filling of the loans and the enlistment of soldiers, are in my opinion guilty of moral treason. By this I by no means intend to censure those who, in the exercise of a constitutional right, expose their opinions freely against the expediency of having declared the war, or those who from choice withhold their own money from the public service; but those are intended who, after the respective laws were passed, exerted their influence to prevent others carrying them into effect." *Annals of Congress,* 13th Cong., 2nd sess., 993; *Daily National Intelligencer,* 27 Jan. 1814; *Annals of Congress,* 13th Cong., 2nd sess., 1534. Years later, Grundy noted that the doctrine had become "canonical," stating that "although, like other truths, it was disputed and questioned when first advanced, now none seem to controvert it." *Register of Debates,* 21st Cong., 1st sess., 1 Mar. 1830, 218.

14. Grundy to Jackson, 26 July 1813, in Andrew Jackson Papers, 1775–1860; *Annals of Congress,* 13th Cong., 2nd sess., 500–504; Brant, *James Madison: Commander in Chief, 1812–1836,* 197.

15. *Nashville Whig,* 4 Jan. 1814. The vote was 85–57 in the House and 20–14 in the Senate. *Annals of Congress,* 13th Cong., 2nd sess., 549–62.

16. *Annals of Congress,* 13th Cong., 2nd sess., 1057; *Daily National Intelligencer,* 20 Jan. 1814, 2; Francis Scott Key to John Randolph, 20 Jan. 1814, in Garland, *Life of John Randolph,* 2:30; *Daily National Intelligencer,* 1 Feb. 1814; Brant, *James Madison: Commander in Chief, 1812–1836,* 241; Stagg, *Mr. Madison's War,* 429.

17. *Annals of Congress,* 13th Cong., 2nd sess., 1532–42.

18. Grundy to John Overton, 6 Mar. 1814, John Overton Papers, SHC; "Mercator," in *Boston Gazette,* 14 Apr. 1814.

19. *Annals of Congress,* 13th Cong., 2nd sess., 1942–56, 2002; Watts, *Republic Reborn,* 277–79; Catterall, *Second Bank of the United States,* 8–9.

20. *Clarion and Tennessee State Gazette,* 19 July 1814; *Nashville Whig,* 19 July 1814; Grundy to unidentified recipient, 8 Sept. 1829, published in *National Banner and Nashville Daily Advertiser,* 21 June 1833; Grundy to Robert Wood, 21 Nov. 1826, Special Collections, Filson Club Historical Society, Louisville, KY; Grundy to Messrs. McEwen, 20 Sept. 1826, in the possession of Lillian Stewart, Franklin, TN.

13. RETURN TO NASHVILLE

1. *Nashville Whig,* 24 May 1815; Parton, *Life of Andrew Jackson,* 2:329. Grundy had previously delivered the oration at the Nashville courthouse welcoming Jackson and Tennessee soldiers back from the Creek War. *Nashville Whig,* 16 May 1814; Colyar, *Life and Times of Andrew Jackson,* 1:192.

2. Jacob McGavock to Joseph McGavock, 7 Jan. 1816, in McGavock, *Pen and Sword,* 24; Gen. Calvin Jones to unidentified recipient, 21 May 1818, in Calvin Jones Papers, 1783–1929. Jones reported that the tavern where he stayed was run by a Frenchman and was "a very large establishment but as dirty as you can imagine or a scotchman could claim." He also reported on financial conditions. A former student now practicing medicine at Carthage was making $3,000 per year. "Living" was cheap. At Sparta he was charged for board 67.5¢ cents per day.

3. Byrd Douglas, *Steamboatin' on the Cumberland* (Nashville: Tennessee Book Company, 1961), 3–11; *Nashville Whig and Tennessee Advertiser,* 13 Mar. 1819; William E. Beard, *Red Letter Days in Nashville* ([Nashville], c. 1925), 107; Howe, *What Hath God Wrought.*

4. *Nashville Whig,* 19 July 1814; Marcus B. Winchester to Gen. James Winchester, 12 June 1816, James Winchester Papers, 1787–1853.

5. Grundy acquired 100 acres in Sumner County, Tennessee, on 25 December 1815 but sold 550 acres in Nelson County, Kentucky, to William P. Duval, a fellow member of the Bardstown Pleiades and later the territorial governor of Florida. Certificate 751, in *First Land Grants of Sumner Co., Tenn., 1786–1833,* ed. Helen C. Marsh and Timothy R. Marsh (Greenville, SC: Southern Historical Press, 2003), 155. In 1816 Grundy, in Greenville Springs, asked his friend George Bibb to maintain tax payments on the 550 acres in Nelson County and 1,400 acres in Green County but then to transfer the 550 acres to Duval. Grundy to George Bibb, 16 July 1816, Felix Grundy Papers, Kentucky Historical Society. In the fall of 1814 Grundy purchased a certificate issued in 1787 for 1,000 acres that could not be identified and gave notice that he intended to apply to the Commission of West Tennessee for a new certificate. *Nashville Whig,* 25 Oct. 1814; John Stokes to Grundy and Ewing, 3 Mar. 1815, Davidson County Deed Book K, Nashville, TN, 561; Grundy to George Poindexter, 30 Jan. 1825, Felix Grundy Papers, 1807–1899, SHC.

6. Data on the lots were obtained from Davidson County Deed Books; the purchase of lot 40 from John Overton is recorded in Davidson County Deed Book M, Nashville, 513, and the sale to Washington Hannum is recorded in Davidson County Deed Book O, Nashville, 211. Goodstein, *Nashville,* 25.

7. Sumner County Deed Book 7, Gallatin, TN, 40; Sumner County Deed Book 9, Gallatin, TN, 135; *Nashville Whig,* 3 Apr. 1819; Durham, *Old Sumner,* 131–32.

8. *Nashville Whig and Tennessee Advertiser,* 30 Jan. 1819; James A. Crutchfield and Robert Hol-

laday, *Franklin Tennessee's Handsomest Town: A Bicentennial History, 1799–1999* (Franklin: Hillsboro, 1999), 83; *Franklin (TN) Review Appeal*, 24 July 1969; indenture between Grundy and McGavock, 13 Nov. 1824, in the author's possession.

9. Goodstein, *Nashville*, 44–70; Charles Albert Snodgrass, *The History of Freemasonry in Tennessee, 1789–1943* (Nashville: Ambrose, 1944), 38, 67–68, 425; Guy Miles, "The Tennessee Antiquarian Society of the West," *East Tennessee Historical Society, Publications* 18 (1946): 87–106. Twenty-two members attended meetings, including William Carroll, Grundy, Ralph Earl, John Overton, Patrick Darby, Alfred Balch, Thomas Washington, Oliver Hayes, Francis B. Fogg, Sam Houston, Judge Haywood, and William L. Brown. Ibid., 96–97. See also Caldwell, *Sketches of the Bench and Bar*, 20.

10. Noah M. Ludlow, *Dramatic Life As I Found It* (1880; Bronx, NY: B. Blom, [1966]), 112–13, 118–22, 166–70, 387–89. Converting a salthouse into a theater, Ludlow offered the "finest ladies" five-act comedies or tragedies on backless benches less than ten inches wide. The ladies, according to Ludlow, "had not been corrupted with fast times, sensational dramas, and easy, cushioned chairs." See also Sarah Sprott Morrow, "A Brief History of Theater in Nashville, 1807–1970," *Tennessee Historical Quarterly* 30 (Summer 1971): 178–89.

11. Clayton, *History of Davidson County, Tennessee*, 266–69; Sarah Foster Kelley, *Children of Nashville* (Nashville: Blue & Gray, 1973), 76; *Nashville Whig*, 21 July 1817, 3. For a history of the Nashville Female Academy, see Crew, *History of Nashville, Tennessee*, 399–405.

12. Grundy to Robert Wood, 21 Nov. 1826, Special Collections, Filson Club Historical Society, Louisville, KY. *The Nashville Whig* published the constitution of the Female Bible and Charitable Society of Nashville on 5 May 1817. The other teachers were Mrs. Mittie Moore, Nathan Ewing, and Samuel Ament. McGavock, *Pen and Sword*, 27; biography of Samuel Ament (1801–91), in *Biographical Cyclopedia of the Commonwealth of Kentucky* (Chicago: John M. Grisham, 1896); Goodstein, *Nashville*, 59; Bucy, "Quiet Revolutionaries," 42–43.

13. Clayton, *History of Davidson County, Tennessee*, 199–202. Before completing the house, Grundy appears to have occupied a plantation six miles north of Nashville on Mill Creek. *Clarion and Tennessee State Gazette*, 25 May 1819. He advertised the sale of his farm in the *Nashville Whig* on 2 January 1822, noting that it had "a good orchard, several excellent springs, and a distillery." Macdonald-Millar, "Grundy-Polk Houses, Nashville," 281. In 1835 a young Kentuckian wrote: "On one of the hills overlooking a greater part of the city is a dark clump of cedars, in the midst of which is a neat family mansion. It looks very pretty and graces the city with its green and rural freshness." Henry Weller, *Narrative of a Journey through Kentucky and Tennessee in 1835* (Louisville, KY: Contre Coup, 1997), 33.

14. Mary Sue Smith, *Davidson County, Tennessee, Deed Book H, 1809–1821* (Bowie, MD: Heritage Books, 2000), 120. For a useful discussion of African-American labor in Nashville, see Anita S. Goodstein, "Black History on the Nashville Frontier, 1780–1810," *Tennessee Historical Quarterly* 38 (Winter 1979): 401–20.

15. John Grundy's will, dated 3 March 1814, was proved in Washington County, Kentucky, on 9 May 1814. George Grundy's will, signed 1 September 1811, was proved in Washington County on 13 February 1815.

16. Calhoun to Grundy, 12 Dec. 1816, Felix Grundy Papers, 1807–1899, SHC.

17. On 10 November 1812 Jacob McGavock wrote his father, Hugh McGavock, in Max Meadows, Virginia, that he had spent the weeks traveling in Kentucky, his business taking him principally "to Bairdstown and Springfield with Miss Rogers, sister to Aunt Sally, and a daughter of Mr.

Grundys, who were on a visit to some of their relations." Quoted in McGavock, *Pen and Sword*, 21. The wedding was performed by the Reverend Gideon Blackburn on a Tuesday evening. *Clarion and Tennessee State Gazette,* 18 May 1819.

18. *Nashville Whig,* 14 July 1823. Information about Grundy's joining the church was revealed by a land speculator, Patrick Darby, as part of a continuing "paper war" between Darby and Grundy. Among other things, Darby believed that Grundy was behind a movement to oust him from the Presbyterian church in Nashville, which the pastor, Reverend Allan Campbell, denied. On one occasion, Governor William Carroll asked Grundy how he had stood a sermon of three and a half hours by Gideon Blackburn, founder of the First Presbyterian Church in Nashville, titled "What Shall It Profit a Man." Grundy paid Blackburn real or facetious tribute by saying, "I could have stood it until twelve that night if he had continued." *The First Presbyterian Church* (Nashville: Foster & Parkes, 1915), 51. H. M. Queener, "Gideon Blackburn," *East Tennessee Historical Society, Publications* 6 (1934): 23; *Christian Herald,* 1 June, 28 Dec. 1816. The sole purpose of the North American Bible Society was to encourage circulation of the Bible without note or comment. *American Quarterly Register* (Boston), Aug. 1831, 4; James H. Atherton to Mary Anne Atherton, 24 Nov. 1831, Tennessee Historical Society Collection, TSLA; Rev. V. F. O'Daniel, *The Father of the Church in Tennessee, or the Life Times and Character of the Right Reverend Richard P. Miles, O. P., The First Bishop of Nashville* (Washington, DC: Dominicana, The Press of St. Mary's Industrial School, 1926), 301; Ben J. Webb, *The Centenary of Catholicity in Kentucky* (Utica, KY: McDowell, 1884), 240.

14. CRIMINAL LAWYER

1. Lyman Copeland Draper Manuscripts, 26 CC 41; Caldwell, *Sketches of the Bench and Bar,* 57, 60. Watterson said of stump orators, "He who could not relate and impersonate an anecdote to illustrate and clinch his argument, nor 'make the welkin ring' with the clarion tones of his voice, was politically good for nothing." Henry Watterson, *"Marse Henry": An Autobiography,* 2 vols. (New York: Doran, 1912), 1:8.

2. Guild, *Old Times in Tennessee,* 83–84.

3. *Nashville Whig and Tennessee Advertiser,* 10 Nov. 1817.

4. Jefferson to Edmund Pendleton, 26 Aug. 1776, in Jefferson, *Papers,* 1:505; Michael Jonathan Millender, "The Transformation of the American Criminal Trial 1790–1875" (PhD diss., Princeton University, 1996), 155–59; Kerr et al., *History of Kentucky,* 1:312.

5. White, *Messages of the Governors of Tennessee,* 2:15–19; *Journal of the Tennessee Senate, General Assembly, 1st Sess.* (Nashville: G. Wilson, 1821), 86–99.

6. *National Banner and Nashville Whig,* 9 Dec. 1826; Millender, "Transformation of the American Criminal Trial," 159. This attitude was reflected in civil cases. See, e.g., *Owen's Administrator v. Grundy and Rucks,* 16 Tenn. 436 (1835) at 438–39.

7. *Clarion and Tennessee State Gazette,* 19 Oct. 1819; *Nashville Whig,* 3 Nov. 1819. The indictment stated that Charles L. Bennett had struck William T. Hay on the right ear with an axe and then, using a bandana, choked and strangled him to death. Tennessee Supreme Court Clerk Records, 1810–1955, Record Group 191, Ser. V, Vol. 1 (1817–1920), 903. On southern attitudes affecting criminal justice, see Dickson D. Bruce Jr., *Violence and Culture;* Wyatt-Brown, *Southern Honor;* and Ayers, *Vengeance and Justice.* One other defendant named Bennett was hanged in Tennessee during Grundy's lifetime. See *James R. Bennett v. State,* 8 Tenn. 134 (1827). It appears unlikely that

Grundy was involved in this case, but the absence of counsel names renders uncertain any final conclusion.

8. Anderson to Jackson, 17 Nov. 1810, in Jackson, *Papers,* 2:255–56.

9. Taul, "Memoirs of Micah Taul," 617.

10. Caldwell, *Sketches of the Bench and Bar,* 57–60; Phelan, *History of Tennessee,* 362; Judge Joseph Gillespie, quoted by John F. Darby in *St. Louis Republican,* 26 Feb. 1876, quoted in Guild, *Old Times in Tennessee,* 295–98; Joseph Etter, *Sketches of U.S. Senators* (Washington, DC, 1839), 30; Laughlin, "Sketches of Notable Men," 73–75; John C. Spence, *The Annals of Rutherford County,* vol. 1 (1799–1828; Murfreesboro: Rutherford County Historical Society, 1991), 172. Samuel H. Laughlin (1796–1850) first met Grundy in 1815 and appears to have regarded him as a mentor. Laughlin practiced law, served as editor of the *Nashville Union* when Grundy was a U.S. senator, and played an active role in Democratic politics. His success would have been greater had he been more temperate. His life is presented in Frank B. Williams Jr., "Samuel Hervey Laughlin, Polk's Political Handyman," *Tennessee Historical Quarterly* 24 (Winter 1965): 356–92.

11. Seigenthaler, *James K. Polk,* 23; Arnow, *Flowering of the Cumberland,* 125; Sadakat Kadri, *The Trial: A History from Socrates to O. J. Simpson* (New York: Random House, 2005), 286.

12. Foote, *Bench and Bar,* 155–57; "Old Virginia," 20 Feb. 1832, in *Nashville Republican and State Gazette,* 10 Mar. 1832, concluded: "His manner is that of a plain western farmer; and when he rises, you never think of restraint ... for his whole manner is so simple, and republican, that you are entirely at ease in an instant. His eloquence seems to me, better fitted for our institutions than any speaker I ever heard—because he divests every subject his mind touches, of every thing like mystery and brings his conclusion home to the comprehension, the business and the bosom of all men. When he speaks all understand all he says. ... In the plainness and perspicuity of his style and the ease and simplicity of his manner, he has no superior in either House of Congress."

13. Laughlin, "Sketches of Notable Men," 75; Calhoun to Grundy, 12 Dec. 1816, Felix Grundy Papers, 1807–1899, SHC. Guild, *Old Times in Tennessee,* also emphasized his "vein of strong common sense" (293).

14. Laughlin wrote that "his knowledge of the affairs of the world and of the human heart was such as has seldom been surpassed." Laughlin, "Sketches of Notable Men," 74. See also Levin, *Lawyers and Lawmakers of Kentucky,* 67–68; and John Haywood, *Civil and Political History of the State of Tennessee, with Biographical Sketch of Judge John Haywood,* ed. Col. A. S. Colyar (reprint, Knoxville, TN: Tenase, 1969), 12–13.

15. Phelan, *History of Tennessee,* 362; Caldwell, *Sketches of the Bench and Bar,* 58; Guild, *Old Times in Tennessee,* 293, 294.

16. Laughlin, "Sketches of Notable Men," 74.

17. Livingston, "Biographical Letter from John Catron," 79.

18. Saunders, *Early Settlers of Alabama,* 199.

19. *Nashville Gazette,* 25 Nov. 1820, 16 June 1821.

20. Grundy to Jackson, 27 June 1822, in Jackson, *Correspondence,* 3:163; Grundy to Ninian Edwards, 20 Feb. 1825, Ninian Edwards Papers, 1798–1833; Clark, "A. O. Nicholson of Tennessee," 9; Nancy Grundy to Mrs. Margaret M. Reed, 11 Mar. 1826, Francis McGavock Papers, 1784–1854. Nancy Grundy's sister wrote her daughter that "a cheerful countenance is one of a woman or man's greatest accomplishments—but for your Aunt Grundy's constant cheerfulness what would your uncle with all his great talents have been?" Margaret M. Reed to Isabella E. J. Clay, 23 Jan. 1828, Sidney P. Clay Collection, 1783–1846.

21. Parks, *Felix Grundy,* 100; Caldwell, *Sketches of the Bench and Bar,* 74. Elihu Washburne, who heard Grundy argue before the Supreme Court in March 1840, described him as a "great lawyer and a distinguished statesman. No man of his time had so great a reputation as a criminal lawyer in the West and Southwest." Edwards, *Papers,* 235n.

22. Receipt from Felix Grundy, 9 Apr. 1808, in the estate of Elizabeth Macon, in the author's possession; "Memoirs of James Norman Smith (1789–1875)," bk. 2, 159–62, Wallace Alexander Jones Genealogical Collection; Grundy to Levi Woodbury, 7 July 1830, Levi Woodbury Family Papers, 1638–1914; Guild, *Old Times in Tennessee,* 72. 77.

23. Caldwell, *Sketches of the Bench and Bar,* 82; *Nashville Whig,* 12 June 1822, 15 Nov. 1824, 8 Apr. 1826. Guild remembered that "the great firm of Rucks, Anderson & Grundy of Nashville existed for years, doing a sweeping and profitable practice." Guild, *Old Times in Tennessee,* 451. See also *National Banner and Nashville Whig,* 3 May 1828; and *Nashville Republican and State Gazette,* 2 Dec. 1830.

24. Arnow, *Flowering of the Cumberland,* 314; Durham, *Old Sumner,* 11; Russell Fowler, "Milton Brown, 1804–1883: West Tennessee's Man for All Seasons," *West Tennessee Historical Society Papers* 50 (1996): 7–26; John Bruce to Polk, 23 Mar. 1846, James K. Polk Papers, 1795–1849; Jenkins, *Life of James Knox Polk,* 45–46; Sellers, *James K. Polk,* 59.

25. Jenkins, *Life of James Knox Polk,* 45–46.

15. THE PANIC OF 1819

1. Abernethy, "Early Development of Commerce and Banking," 312–13; Ray, *Middle Tennessee,* 78–83. Directors of the Nashville Bank included John H. Eaton, William B. Lewis, and Ephraim H. Foster. Sellers, "Banking and Politics in Jackson's Tennessee," 65.

2. Sellers, "Banking and Politics in Jackson's Tennessee," 64–67; Hugh Lawson White, *Memoir,* 19–23.

3. Sellers, "Banking and Politics in Jackson's Tennessee," 66. Jackson later wrote that this effort to obtain a branch was due to the "arristocratic [*sic*] few in Nashville." Jackson to Thomas H. Benton, June 1832, in Jackson, *Correspondence,* 4:445–46.

4. *Nashville Whig and Tennessee Advertiser,* 7 Feb. 1818. Grundy wrote in his letter to Jones that "any number from seven to thirteen, might be selected from the following, and the choice could not be a bad one. Jenkin Whiteside, *Andrew Hayes,* Randal McGavock, *John P. Erwin, Thomas H. Fletcher, James Stewart,* Felix Robertson, Robert Weakly, Elihu S. Hall, Alfred Balch, *William Carroll, Thomas Hill,* George W. Gibbs, Robert C. Foster, *Samuel Zelford.* Those printed in italics are merchants; the others, substantial freeholders, and men of intelligence." Hugh Lawson White, *Memoir,* 21–22.

5. Rothbard, *Panic of 1819,* 3–15.

6. Ibid.; Sellers, *Market Revolution,* 136.

7. *Nashville Gazette,* 26 June 1819; Sellers, *James K. Polk,* 66–67; Parks, "Felix Grundy and the Depression of 1819," 20–22; Ray, *Middle Tennessee,* 124–28.

8. *Nashville Whig and Tennessee Advertiser,* 10 Apr. 1819. The *Clarion and Tennessee Gazette* reported on 6 April 1819 that Grundy had announced his candidacy on Saturday, 3 April. Sellers, "Banking and Politics in Jackson's Tennessee," 67; Parks, *Felix Grundy,* 106; Saunders, *Early Settlers of Alabama,* 94.

9. White, *Messages of the Governors of Tennessee,* 2:22. Grundy received 991 votes, compared

with 1,163 votes for William Williams and 928 for Col. Thomas Williamson. *Nashville Whig and Tennessee Advertiser,* 7 Aug. 1819. See also *Nashville Whig,* 28 Nov. 1825.

10. The resolutions introduced on 25 September 1819 included (1) that a joint committee be formed to investigate the condition of banks; (2) that banks extend discounts; (3) that banks be prohibited from levying on notes not acquired in the ordinary course of business; (4) that creditors generally be prohibited from enforcing debts in gold and silver; and (5) that a law be passed abolishing imprisonment for debt under certain circumstances. *National Register,* 30 Oct. 1819; Sellers, "Banking and Politics in Jackson's Tennessee," 67; Parks, "Felix Grundy and the Depression of 1819," 22–23.

11. Pleasant M. Miller (1773–1849) was born in Lynchburg, Virginia, studied law under Archibald Stewart, in Staunton, Virginia, and moved to Tennessee in 1796. Miller later relocated to western Tennessee and opposed both Jackson and Grundy. Russell Fowler, "Pleasant M. Miller, 1773–1849: The Last of the Titans of Tennessee's Founding Age," *West Tennessee Historical Society Papers* 49 (1995): 23–45; Emma Inman Williams, *Historic Madison* (Jackson, TN: Madison County Historical Society, 1946), 65; Howell, "Felix Grundy."

12. *Acts of a Public or General Nature Passed at the Full Session of the Thirteenth General Assembly of the State of Tennessee* (Nashville: Sublett, 1819), 44; Parks, "Felix Grundy and the Depression of 1819," 22; Rothbard, *Panic of 1819,* 68–70; Sellers, "Banking and Politics in Jackson's Tennessee."

13. Parks, *Felix Grundy,* 114; *Nashville Whig,* 24 Nov. 1819; Samuel Cole Williams, *Beginnings of West Tennessee,* 98–104. As a U.S. congressman Grundy had pushed for legislative action to establish claims by North Carolinians under the agreement of cession of Tennessee. *Annals of Congress,* 12th Cong., 2nd sess., 1159–60.

14. Sellers, *James K. Polk,* 70; Parks, *Felix Grundy,* 117; Guild, *Old Times in Tennessee,* 460–61; Abernethy, *From Frontier to Plantation,* 266; *Nashville Whig,* 11, 16, 23 June 1823.

15. Guild, *Old Times in Tennessee,* 460–61.

16. *Niles Register,* 20 Oct. 1821; Sydnor, *Development of Southern Sectionalism,* 101; *Nashville Whig,* 4 Sept. 1822.

17. William Robertson Garrett, *History of the South Carolina Cession and the Northern Boundary of Tennessee* (Nashville: Southern Methodist Publishing House, 1884), 19ff.; Bayless E. Hardin, "The Kentucky Boundary," *Register, Kentucky State Historical Society* 44 (Jan. 1946): 1–32. A more recent history of the boundary dispute is found in C. Edward Skeen, *1816: America Rising* (Lexington: University Press of Kentucky, 2003), 163–65.

18. Kerr et al., *History of Kentucky,* 1:518. On 9 November 1804 a bill with respect to the boundary between Kentucky and Tennessee was presented in the Kentucky House of Representatives and referred to a select committee of Grundy and seven others. *Journal of the House of Representatives for the Commonwealth of Kentucky, 1804* (Frankfort: Kentucky Historical Society, 1804).

19. Gov. Joseph McMinn to Daniel Graham, 12 Jan. 1819, in "Correspondence of Gov. Jos. McMinn," *American Historical Magazine* 4 (Oct. 1899): 319, 331.

20. Samuel Cole Williams, *Beginning of West Tennessee,* 105–7.

21. McMinn to Graham, 26 Dec. 1819, in "Letters and Papers of Gov. Jos. McMinn," *American Historical Magazine* 5 (Jan. 1900): 48, 56; Kerr et al., *History of Kentucky,* 1:520.

22. John J. Crittenden to Richard M. Johnson, 5 Jan. 1820, Special Collections, Filson Club Historical Society, Louisville, KY. Grundy and Brown were influenced by their conclusion that Alexander and Munsell had done a first-rate job and by the facts that they had heard no major ob-

jections to the Alexander and Munsell line, that the Walker line was miles north of 36°30' N, and that, not surprisingly, no one in Tennessee was arguing that the Walker line was too far north. "Report of Grundy and Brown to the Governor of Tennessee," 17 Apr. 1820, in *Nashville Whig*, 31 May 1820.

23. Coleman, *Life of John J. Crittenden*, 1:39–40. For Crittenden's report to the Kentucky legislature, see ibid., 48–56.

24. *Clarksville Gazette*, date unknown, quoted in the *Nashville Whig*, 1 Mar. 1820; *Clarion and Tennessee Gazette*, 15 Feb. 1820; Graham to McMinn, 16 Feb. 1820, quoted in Parks, *Felix Grundy*, 133.

25. John H. Eaton to John Overton, 3 Apr. 1820, John Overton Papers, 1797–1833, TSLA.

26. *Nashville Whig*, 10 May 1820.

16. LEGISLATIVE LEADERSHIP

1. Sellers, *Market Revolution*, 138; Abernethy, "Andrew Jackson and the Rise of Southwestern Democracy," 67; Goodstein, *Nashville*, 38–39. When Jenkin Whiteside died in 1822, his heirs noted that "very much of his property" was encumbered by mortgages and that they hoped to satisfy debts "in property, at fair value," since "payment in money is known to be impracticable." *Nashville Whig*, 8 Jan. 1823, 3, and 10 May 1820; *Murfreesboro Courier*, date unknown, quoted in *Nashville Whig*, 24 May 1820. The *Clarion and Tennessee Gazette*, on 20 June 1820 reported "the pain of witnessing a number of execution sales by the sheriff. We saw property which 18 months ago cost $1800 sold for $265, property which then was worth $7000 sold for $1000; property which was then worth $500 sold for $60."

2. *Clarion and Tennessee Gazette*, 23 May, 20 June 1820; Rothbard, *Panic of 1819*, 70 ff.; Sellers, "Banking and Politics in Jackson's Tennessee," 68; *Clarion and Tennessee Gazette*, 18, 20 June 1820; *Knoxville Register*, 20 June 1820; *Clarion and Tennessee Gazette*, 17 June 1820.

3. *Acts Passed at the Session of the General Assembly of the State of Tennessee* (Knoxville, 1820), 9; Parks, "Felix Grundy and the Depression of 1819," 19–43; Rothbard, *Panic of 1819*, 73–74. A minimum-appraisal law, also recommended by Governor McMinn, was not included in the bill sent to the legislature.

4. *Daily National Journal*, 21 Apr. 1830; *Journal of the Tennessee Senate, General Assembly, 2d Sess.* (Murfreesboro: Sublett, 1820), 87–89; William B. Lewis to Jackson, 15 July 1820, in Jackson, *Papers*, 4:376–78.

5. John Bowen to Calhoun, 13 Jan. 1821, in Calhoun, *Papers*, 5:552; *Knoxville Register*, 18 July 1820.

6. *Clarion and Tennessee Gazette*, 8 Aug. 1820; Sellers, "James K. Polk's Political Apprenticeship," 38. The original named directors were John McNairy, George Gibbs, David McGavock, John Catron, Nathan Ewing, R. C. Foster, James Stewart, Jesse Wharton, Andrew Hynes, Thomas Washington, and Joseph T. Elliston. In addition to three named directors' declining election, McNairy declined the presidency. Beard, "Joseph McMinn," 164.

7. Ray, *Middle Tennessee*, 124–32; Miller to John Gray Blount, 2 Jan. 1821, in Blount, *Papers*, 4:319; Sellers, "Banking and Politics in Jackson's Tennessee," 71; *Nashville Whig*, 4 Sept. 1822.

8. *Townsend v. Townsend*, May term 1821, in Jacob Peck, ed., *Tennessee Reports*, 1:1–21; Parks, "Felix Grundy and the Depression of 1819," 41–42; *Knoxville Register*, 5 June 1821, 6 Aug., 13 Oct., 14 Nov. 1823.

9. *Journal of the Tennessee House of Representatives, General Assembly, 1st Sess.* (Nashville: G. Wilson, 1821), 6–27, 49–53; White, *Messages of the Governors of Tennessee,* 1:642–58. See also Beard, "Joseph McMinn."

10. White, *Messages of the Governors of Tennessee,* 2:15; Sellers, *James K. Polk,* 71; Sellers, "Banking and Politics in Jackson's Tennessee," 71–74. Carroll deserves fuller treatment than he has hitherto been accorded by historians. His years as governor are reviewed in Gabriel Hawkins Golden, "William Carroll and His Administration," *Tennessee Historical Magazine* 9 (Apr. 1925): 9–30, and in Harriet Stern, "William Carroll," in *Governors of Tennessee,* vol. 1, *1790–1835,* ed. Charles Crawford (Memphis: Memphis State University Press, 1979), 119–47.

11. Abernethy, *From Frontier to Plantation,* 238; Bergeron, *Antebellum Politics in Tennessee,* 2–3; Parks, "Felix Grundy and the Depression of 1819," 37–43.

12. Sellers, "James K. Polk's Political Apprenticeship," 40–43; Parks, "Felix Grundy and the Depression of 1819," 38–41.

13. Herring and Longacre, "Felix Grundy," 369; Ray, *Middle Tennessee,* 128–39.

14. Parks, *Felix Grundy,* 164–65; Sellers, *James K. Polk,* 58; Sellers, *Market Revolution,* 165–66.

15. James Campbell to Col. David Campbell, 23 Oct. 1821, Campbell Family Papers, 1731–1969.

16. Rothbard, *Panic of 1819,* 242–45. For a summary of the Kentucky experience, see Wilentz, *Rise of American Democracy,* 288–90.

17. Parks, *Felix Grundy,* 106; Sellers, "Banking and Politics in Jackson's Tennessee," 67–69; *Nashville Whig,* 7 June 1820; *Clarion and Tennessee Gazette,* 18 July 1820.

18. *Nashville Whig,* 28 Feb. 1821. The trustees were Priestley, Grundy, Robert C. Foster, James Roane, and Alfred Balch. *Clarion and Tennessee Gazette,* 21 Nov. 1820. East Tennessee College, founded in 1807, had reopened in 1820 after being closed since 1809.

19. Memorial of the Trustees of the University of North Carolina, in White, *Messages of the Governors of Tennessee,* 2:32–36; *Nashville Whig,* 31 July 1822.

20. Daniel Graham to William Polk, 25 Nov. 1821, Polk Family Papers, 1767–1859.

21. Murphey was not enthusiastic: "This is a dreadful trip to me; but I see clearly, all will be lost there if I do not go." Murphey to Thomas Ruffin, 18 May 1822, in Murphey, *Papers,* 1:239.

22. Marvin Downing, "John Christmas McLemore: 19th Century Tennessee Land Speculator," *Tennessee Historical Quarterly* 42 (Fall 1983): 254, 261; Murphey to Ruffin, 30 June 1822, in Murphey, *Papers,* 1:242.

23. "Old Tennessee is inferior, very inferior to North Carolina for Farming. I am, upon the whole, very much pleased with the People; they are shrewd, active, intelligent, united in favour of all their Men of talents, so that every thing Valuable is made the most of.... There is an able Bar at this place.... There are 26 lawyers here, and Courts sit nine months in the Year." Murphey noted that he could make twenty-five thousand dollars if he stayed until Christmas, when the "Harvest will be over.... It is rich now and not more than twenty Men have their sickles in it." Murphey to Ruffin, 21 July 1822, in Murphey, *Papers,* 1:245, 248.

24. Murphey to Ruffin, 1 Aug. 1822, ibid., 251; Ruffin to John Haywood, 18 Aug. 1822, ibid., 254.

25. Murphey to Ruffin, 18 Aug. 1822, ibid., 253 (quotation); Murphey to Haywood, 18 Aug. 1822, ibid., 253–58. The bill conferred almost absolute power on the commissioners. The two commissioners signed the agreement with the North Carolina representative on 26 August 1822, only three

days after the legislature adjourned. White, *Messages of the Governors of Tennessee,* 2:37; Hamer, *Tennessee,* 1:364–67; Murphey to Haywood, 18 Aug. 1822, in Murphey, *Papers,* 1:259, 254.

26. Paul K. Conkin, *Peabody College* (Nashville: Vanderbilt University Press, 2002), 21–22. The trustees—John McNairy, William Hume, Felix Grundy, John Bell, William L. Brown, Francis B. Fogg, and Henry Crabb—also set forth an ambitious plan for Cumberland, including completion of the central building and purchase of more equipment and books. *Nashville Whig,* 14 June 1824.

27. Murphey to Haywood, 18 Aug. 1822, in Murphey, *Papers,* 1:258–59.

17. ANDREW JACKSON FOR PRESIDENT

1. Carroll to Clay, 1 Feb. 1823, in Clay, *Papers,* 3:360.

2. Eaton to Grundy, 2 Apr. 1826, Felix Grundy Papers, 1807–1899, SHC. On 16 February 1818 Clay purportedly urged Grundy to return to Washington, writing, "Have you not got tired of making money? And disposed to come back here? I should be very glad to see you. . . . I declined accepting the appointment of director of the Bank of the United States, because, there being some subjects likely to come on before Congress relating to the institution." The letter, not found, is quoted in an undated newspaper clipping (in the author's possession) describing letters in a scrapbook owned by Jacob McGavock Dickinson.

On 7 July 1822 Clay wrote to Grundy asking him to serve as one of two Kentucky commissioners charged with settling issues between Kentucky and Virginia that had been outstanding since Kentucky's separation from Virginia in the eighteenth century. Clay to Grundy, 7 July 1822, in Clay, *Papers,* 3:249. Grundy's response, not found, presumably was negative, since Hugh Lawson White ultimately was chosen to represent Kentucky.

3. Parks, *Felix Grundy,* 166.

4. Grundy to Jackson, 13, 16 June 1810, 19 Mar. 1811, Andrew Jackson Papers, 1775–1860; Parks, *Felix Grundy,* 166. Jackson may have met Grundy when *Grundy's Executors v. Harmon* was decided in 1799 by Jackson as a justice of the Washington District Superior Court. (The case, dealing with the estate of George Grundy, involved the application of conflict of laws.) Jackson, *Legal Papers,* 169; Abernethy, *From Frontier to Plantation,* 293.

5. Grundy to Jackson, 24 Dec. 1811, in Jackson, *Papers,* 2:274.

6. Grundy to Jackson, 2 Jan. 1819, in Jackson, *Correspondence,* 6:469. For other evidence of strain, see Grundy to Jackson, 26 July 1813, Andrew Jackson Papers, 1775–1860; Jackson to Grundy, 15 July 1813, in Jackson, *Papers,* 2:410. See also memorandum, ibid., 2:409.

7. *Democratic Clarion and Tennessee Gazette,* 21 Oct. 1812.

8. Nathaniel McNairy, who suggested in 1814 that Grundy defend Jacob Thompson in Mississippi, had fought a duel with John Coffee as an outgrowth of Jackson's fatal duel with Charles Dickinson. He was the brother of John McNairy, who had brought Jackson to Tennessee in the 1780s but was now antagonistic. The McNairys, enemies of Jackson at least since the Dickinson duel, were good friends and associates of Grundy's. David McGavock, whose quarrel with Jackson warranted mention in the first great biography of Jackson (Parton, *Life of Andrew Jackson,* 1:266), was the brother of Randal McGavock, a close friend of Grundy's and since 1811 his brother-in-law, as well as uncle to Jacob McGavock, Grundy's son-in-law. Finally, Grundy worked closely with William Carroll and other members of the Andrew Erwin faction.

Boyd and Nathaniel McNairy remained bitter enemies of Jackson's and according to Jackson used Thomas Hart Benson as a foil against him. Jackson, *Papers,* 2:413n2. Boyd McNairy, whose enmity apparently began when he traveled with Jackson from North Carolina, studied medicine in Lexington, where he first met Grundy and Henry Clay. W. H. Sparks, *The Memories of Fifty Years* (Philadelphia: Claxton, Remsen & Heffelfinger, 1870), 147.

9. It is difficult to assess Jackson's actions without constant reference to his personality and temperament. See Burstein, *Passions of Andrew Jackson.*

10. Jackson's nephew and ward, Andrew Jackson Donelson, had resigned from the military, and Jackson advised him to study law at Transylvania, in Lexington, Kentucky, apparently over Donelson's objections. Jackson told his nephew that there was no one in Nashville with whom he could be placed: "I could see no beneficial prospect for your study of the law here or at Nashville—in short there was no legal character of sufficient standing in morality and law knowledge, who was in the habit of taking in legal students, under whom I could have placed you, to have received those benefits I wish—I hate a quack of any kind." Jackson to Donelson, 26 Apr. 1822, in Jackson, *Papers,* 5:176. In a separate letter to Donelson, Jackson set forth his view of lawyers: "But as lawyers, unconnected with politics, they (Thomas Barry and Jessie Bledsoe) are both men of great talents—It is their Legal knowledge, abstracted from politicks, that I wish you to learn—not the absurd doctrine that the Legislature is the people." Jackson to Donelson, 11 Oct. 1822, ibid., 220.

11. Sellers, "Jackson Men with Feet of Clay," 540–46; Sellers, *Market Revolution,* 172–74. Sellers's position has been accepted by most Jackson historians. See, for example, Remini, *Andrew Jackson and the Course of American Freedom,* 48–52.

12. Miller to John Overton, 27 Jan. 1822, John Overton Papers, 1797–1833, TSLA; Sellers, "Jackson Men with Feet of Clay," 541.

13. John Overton to Samuel Overton, 23 Feb. 1824, and Miller to John Overton, 27 Jan. 1822, John Overton Papers, 1797–1833, TSLA. For a discussion of Lewis's role, see Louis R. Harlan, "Public Career of William Berkeley Lewis," *Tennessee Historical Quarterly* 7 (Mar. 1948): 12–21.

14. Sellers, "Jackson Men with Feet of Clay," 542; Grundy to Jackson, 27 June 1822, in Jackson, *Correspondence,* 3:163.

15. Benton to Clay, 12 July 1822, in Clay, *Papers,* supplement, 115. Benton also said that Grundy's "deportment seems to be suspicious, for he has abstained from making any declarations to me, although I have given him many opportunities. He is in fact vehemently suspected by all our friends here, notwithstanding the voluntary pledges which they know that he has made." This certainly suggests that Clay's principal supporters in Tennessee wanted Grundy's aid and may previously have received some indications that it would be forthcoming.

16. Clay to Return J. Meigs, 21 Aug. 1822, in Clay, *Papers,* supplement, 117; Sellers, *Market Revolution,* 172–75.

17. Benton to Clay, 23 July 1823, in Clay, *Papers,* 3:460; Carroll to Clay, 1 Feb. 1823, ibid., 360.

18. *Nashville Whig,* 14 July 1823; *Constitutional Advocate,* 3, 10 Sept. 1822.

19. Abernethy, *From Frontier to Plantation,* 262–69; Guild, *Old Times in Tennessee,* 461.

20. Jackson to Coffee, 15 Apr. 1823, in Jackson, *Papers,* 5:270. Thomas Perkins Abernethy wrote that "it was under these circumstances that the General turned against his old friend and against the majority of the leading men of Tennessee to ally himself with a notorious shyster and support the principle that absentee claimants had the right to evict occupants of long standing." Abernethy, *From Frontier to Plantation,* 267. See also *Nashville Whig,* 14 July 1823. Darby clearly refrained from going further and did not suggest that Grundy's objective was to slander Jackson as well as Darby.

21. Jackson, *Papers,* 5:277–78; Jackson to Coffee, 24 May 1823; *Nashville Whig,* 11 Aug. 1823.

For other instances of potential corruption with respect to use of depreciated bank notes, see Remini, *Andrew Jackson and the Course of American Freedom,* 12–38.

22. Sellers, "Jackson Men with Feet of Clay," 548–50. Since Virginia, the most populous state, was likely to support William Crawford, of Georgia, for president in 1824, the caucus was viewed as unfavorable to Jackson. William Brady and Thomas Williamson to Jackson, 20 Sept. 1823, in Jackson, *Papers,* 5:296; Jackson to Brady and Williamson, 27 Sept. 1823, ibid., 299; Leota Driver Maiden, "Colonel John Williams," *East Tennessee Historical Society, Publications* 30 (1958): 7–46. The caucus resolution is set forth in White, *Messages of the Governors of Tennessee,* 2:62–65.

23. Darby to James G. Dana, 26 Dec. 1827, in *Trenton (NJ) True American,* 19 Jan. 1828, as quoted in Jackson, *Papers,* 5:307.

24. *Journal of the Tennessee House of Representatives, General Assembly, 1st Session* (Murfreesboro, TN: Norvell & Sublett, 1823), 76–77; *Nashville Whig,* 6 Oct. 1823. Davy Crockett, as a member of the Tennessee House, voted for Williams and described the election in his autobiography. Crockett, *Life of Colonel David Crockett,* 138. See also Wilentz, *Rise of American Democracy,* 244–45.

18. ELECTION TO THE SENATE

1. Grundy sold 200 acres in Green County, Kentucky, on 28 June 1819 to John Hall, of Sumner County, Tennessee, for $864, and 425 acres in the same county on 19 March 1821 to Alfred Lomax, of Nashville, for $2,550. Green County Deed Books, Greensburg, KY, 9, 318, and 10, 172. Similarly, on 11 May 1822 he transferred 320 acres on Spring and Hurricane creeks, in Wilson County, Tennessee, although the 1828–29 lists in Wilson County show that he still owned 285 acres. Wilson County Deed Book K, Lebanon, TN, 441. In 1823 he subdivided land in Washington County, Kentucky, in order to obtain clear title to 311 acres, although there is no evidence of any subsequent sale. Washington County Deed Book H, Springfield, KY, 172.

Felix and Nancy Grundy had various land dealings with family members and others in Green County, presumably through inheritance or because her family lived there. Green County Deed Books, Greensburg, KY, 8, 273, and 9, 382. John Rodgers Jr. mortgaged various tracts of land in 1819 and 1821 and apparently lost this property in 1823. Green County Deed Books, 9, 126 and 136, and 10, 50. Rodgers died of tuberculosis in August 1823. Margaret Rodgers Reed to John Rodgers, 6 Sept. 1823, in the author's possession.

2. Grundy to Poindexter, 30 Jan. 1825, Felix Grundy Papers, 1807–1899, SHC. Justice Johnson stated: "Indeed, if we are to believe the testimony of Randal McGarvick [*sic*], and its clearness, fullness and fairness speaks its own eulogism; a case of more general or more vital misrepresentation, can seldom occur, or a case of more absolute devotion to misplaced confidence." *Boyce's Executors v. Grundy,* 28 U.S. 221; *National Banner and Nashville Whig,* 24 Feb. 1827. For other Grundy financial issues, generally resolved in his favor, see *Nashville Bank v. Grundy and Hays,* 19 Tennessee 256 (1838); *Nashville Republican and State Gazette,* 4 July 1832; *Nashville Bank v. Hays and Grundy,* in *Nashville Republican and State Gazette,* 6 July 1832.

3. Clay to Grundy, 7 Apr. 1813, in Clay, *Papers,* 1:781; James Erwin to Clay, 15 Jan. 1827, ibid., 6:69.

4. Grundy to Clay, 13 Jan. 1827, ibid., 6:60; Clay to James Erwin, 1 Feb. 1827, ibid., 155.

5. Judge Joseph Gillespie, quoted by John F. Darby in *St. Louis Republican,* 26 Feb. 1876, quoted in Guild, *Old Times in Tennessee,* 295–98.

6. *Vandalia (IL) Intelligencer,* date unknown, as reported in *Nashville Whig,* 16 Apr. 1825. The best account of the trial is Guild, *Old Times in Tennessee,* 295–98.

7. Grundy to Ninian Edwards, 20 Feb. 1825, Ninian Edwards Papers, 1798–1833.

8. Judge Joseph Gillespie, quoted by John F. Darby in *St. Louis Republican,* 26 Feb. 1876, quoted in Guild, *Old Times in Tennessee,* 295–98.

9. Foote, *Bench and Bar,* 154–55.

10. The will of Elizabeth Grundy is in Washington County Will Book D, Springfield, KY, 21–23.

11. Nancy Grundy's sister Margaret wrote Jacob McGavock's brother Randal, in Virginia, on 20 November 1834 that "Mr. Grundy and my sister love your brother Jacob as well as their own son." Carnton Plantation Archives, Franklin, TN. Louisa and Jacob's house, constructed in the 1820s, was a two-story red brick house, built on the street. Jacob McGavock bought the house lot from Grundy on 14 December 1822 for $3,600, Grundy having purchased it in 1815 for $1,500. *Nashville Tennessean Magazine,* 3 Oct. 1971.

12. *Nashville Whig,* 24 Jan. 1825.

13. Sellers, *James K. Polk,* 95–98; Houston, *Autobiography,* 32, 35; Sam Houston to John H. Houston, 30 June 1825, in Houston, *Writings,* 5:3.

14. John P. Erwin to Henry Clay, 12 Dec. 1825, in Clay, *Papers,* 4:900–901. Grundy was the chairman of a thirteen-person committee for the gala reception held for Jackson on 16 April 1825, upon Jackson's return from Washington following Adams's election. *Nashville Whig,* 9 Apr. 1825. After Jackson was elected to the Cumberland College board of trustees on 27 March 1825 and professorships were created in honor of Jackson and Lafayette, Jackson worked with Grundy and ultimately sought Grundy's advice on a letter soliciting funds from the "citizens of New Orleans to endow the professorships." Jackson to Grundy, 30 May 1826, in Jackson, *Papers,* 6:174. See also *A Selection of Eulogies, Pronounced in the Several States, in Honor of Those Illustrious Patriots and Statesmen, John Adams and Thomas Jefferson* (Hartford, CT: D. F. Robinson and Norton & Russell, 1826). The *Nashville Republican* reported on 5 August 1826 that a very large audience had attended the oration, even though the "weather was inclement and bad" and necessitated postponement from 11:00 AM until 2:00 PM. *Nashville Republican,* 8 July 1826; Burstein, *America's Jubilee,* 247.

15. Carroll to Clay, 25 Nov. 1825, in Clay, *Papers,* 4:847; Grundy to Clay, 28 Jan. 1826, ibid., 5:64; Sam Houston, "Concerning Expected Trouble with Felix Grundy," 27 May 1826, in Houston, *Writings,* 1:63–64. On 5 February 1827 George Bibb wrote to Grundy from Frankfort, Kentucky, and congratulated the people of Tennessee "that you have again taken the political theater, I congratulate them, because I have known you long as a firm undeviating Republican, willing to aid the Federal government in the exercise of the just and necessary powers conceded and granted by the states to the Federal government, but unwilling to divert the states of their rights and sovereignty by construing away those powers which they have never granted nor intended to grant." Felix Grundy Papers, 1807–1899, SHC.

16. Grundy to Levi Woodbury, 7 July 1830, Levi Woodbury Family Papers, 1638–1914.

17. Parks, *John Bell of Tennessee;* circular to the voters of Rutherford, Williamson, and Davidson counties, in the author's possession; Grundy to Messrs. McEwen, 20 Sept. 1826, in the possession of Lillian Stewart, Franklin, TN.

18. James R. White to James Polk, in Polk, *Correspondence,* 1:72; Jackson to Coffee, 30 July 1827, in Jackson, *Papers,* 6:372–73; Carroll to Clay, 3 May 1827, in Clay, *Papers,* 6:515; John P. Erwin to Clay, 12 Aug. 1827, ibid., 892.

19. *National Banner and Nashville Whig*, 9 Dec. 1826. The Supreme Court of Tennessee affirmed Cornwall's conviction, emphatically rejecting that drunkenness could so impair a defendant's mental state as to provide a defense. *Burrell Cornwall v. The State of Tennessee*, 8 Tennessee 147 (1827).

20. *National Banner and Nashville Whig*, 24 Mar. 1827, 11 July 1829, 9 June 1822. See also the acquittal of Nathaniel Rodgers, ibid., 16 Jan. 1829.

21. Ibid., 5 Jan., 6 Apr. 1828.

22. Thomas, *Old Days in Nashville*, 50.

23. *National Banner and Nashville Whig*, 27 Oct. 1827.

24. Grundy was the president at a "sumptuous dinner" held in honor of Alexander Hamilton's son at the Nashville Inn in December 1827. Ibid., 5 Jan. 1828; Remini, *Andrew Jackson and the Course of American Freedom*, 108–9, 409n30. Members of the Nashville Central Committee included Overton, Lewis, Campbell, Alfred Balch, Tom Claiborne, John Catron, Robert Whyte, John McNairy, William L. Brown, Robert C. Foster, Joseph Phillips, Daniel Graham, Jesse Wharton, Edward Ward, Felix Robertson, John Shelby, Josiah Nichol, and William White. At about this time, John Overton, unquestionably Jackson's closest friend and adviser, said that there were only three men in which Jackson had thorough confidence: John H. Eaton, Judge White, and Overton. Overton to White, 1 June 1829, John Overton Papers, 1797–1833, TSLA. Overton, however, was in part trying to assuage the hurt feelings of White, who felt that Eaton and William B. Lewis had far too much influence over Jackson.

Grundy engaged in a letter exchange rebutting alleged discussions between Jackson and Stephen Decatur. The correspondence originator wrote, "I wrote to Grundy in preference to my other friends in Nashville because I knew he had more *tact* and judgment about such matters than any of them and I knew he would attend promptly to my letter. If I had written to Claiborne or Sam Houston there would have been some flourish about the matter that would have spoil'd the whole affair." John Campbell to James Campbell, 13 Dec. 1827, Campbell Family Papers, 1731–1969. See also James Campbell to Col. David Campbell, 21 Oct. 1827, ibid., with respect to Grundy's authorship of "inflammatory" resolutions in the Tennessee General Assembly concerning the presidential race.

25. Grundy to Jackson, 20 Nov. 1828, in Jackson, *Papers*, 6:534; Mooney, *William H. Crawford*, 314.

26. John C. McLemore to Donelson, 5 Apr. 1829, Andrew Jackson Donelson Papers, 1779–1943; Moore, "Political Background of the Revolt against Jackson," 47–50; Hamer, *Tennessee*, 1:278.

27. Grundy to Jackson, 22 May 1829, in Jackson, *Papers*, 7:236–37; Overton to White, 30 May 1829, John Overton Papers, 1797–1833, TSLA. See also Carroll to Jackson, 25 May 1829, in Jackson, *Papers*, 7:239–41.

28. Bergeron, *Antebellum Politics in Tennessee*, 4; Moore, "Political Background of the Revolt against Jackson," 54; James Edward Murphy, "Jackson and the Tennessee Opposition," *Tennessee Historical Quarterly* 30 (Spring 1971): 50–69; McCormick, *Second American Party System*, 226; Sellers, *James K. Polk*, 197–99. Alexis de Sarcy (an assumed name) assessed the anti-Jackson Tennesseans as follows: "Col. Williams and General Cocke are firm . . . Carrol I think has sent in his adhesion, but Jackson and he hate each other so cordially . . . but little will be necessary to produce discord again—you must set some agent of competent powers at that work, some of the Erwin's perhaps, as they are all of them intimate and confidential with Carrol." Alexis de Sarcy to Clay, 11 Feb. 1830, in Clay, *Papers*, 8:176–77; Coffee to Jackson, 9 July 1831, in Heiskell, *Andrew Jackson and*

Early Tennessee History, 3:520; James Campbell to John Campbell, 18 Oct. 1829, Campbell Family Papers, 1731–1969.

29. Van Buren, *Autobiography,* 341; White to Overton, 28 June 1829, John Overton Papers, 1797–1833, TSLA. Pleasant Miller broke with Jackson principally over cabinet appointments. Russell Fowler, "Pleasant M. Miller, 1773–1849: The Last of the Titans of Tennessee's Founding Age," *West Tennessee Historical Society Papers* 49 (1995): 40–41; Ellis, *Union at Risk,* 59, 68–69; Cole, *Presidency of Andrew Jackson,* 48. The role of William B. Lewis is critically assessed in Louis R. Harlan, "Public Career of William Berkeley Lewis," *Tennessee Historical Quarterly* 7 (Mar. 1948): 3–37, 118–51.

30. Grundy to Jackson, 22 May 1829, in Jackson, *Papers,* 7:236; *Nashville Republican,* 12, 26, 30 June, 3, 7 July 1829; Sellers, *James K. Polk,* 173–75.

31. Jackson to Overton, 8 June 1829, in Jackson, *Papers,* 7:270–72. Jackson believed that Anderson should stay on the bench, both because any replacement would lack Anderson's talent and because Anderson, a poor man, would spend one-third of his Senate salary on expenses and have only $800 to $1,000 to support himself and his family in Tennessee. Hugh Lawson White, *Memoir,* 311.

32. Those identified included Carroll, Fletcher, Bell, William C. Brown, William E. Anderson, and "I believe H. L. White, Cave Johnson, Pryor Lee, Standifer, Huntsman, the Bradford connexion and the Tipton connexion." James Campbell to John Campbell, 18 Oct. 1829, Campbell Family Papers, 1731–1969.

33. Grundy to Daniel Graham, 28 July 1829, Felix Grundy Papers, 1807–1899, SHC; Grundy to Col. Kincannon, 6 Sept. 1829, Felix Grundy Papers, 1820–1840, TSLA; Archibald Yell to James K. Polk, 9 Sept. 1829, in Polk, *Correspondence,* 1:274.

34. Overton to White, 1 June 1829, John Overton Papers, 1797–1833, TSLA; Thomas, *Old Days in Nashville,* 56.

35. W. M. Berryhill to Donelson, 16 Oct. 1829, Felix Grundy Papers, 1807–1899, SHC; Grundy to Jackson, 22 Oct. 1829, in Jackson, *Papers,* 7:505–6; James Campbell to John Campbell, 18 Oct. 1829, Campbell Family Papers, 1731–1969. Campbell provided a breakdown of how all legislators voted.

36. Thomas, *Old Days in Nashville,* 57.

37. Grundy to Jackson, 22 Oct. 1829, in Jackson, *Papers,* 7:505–6.

38. Ibid.; Henry Clay to Nicholas Biddle, 14 June 1830, in Clay, *Papers,* 8:223–24; Hammond, *Banks and Politics in America,* 355, 370–71; Journal of Hugh Blair Grigsby, 1806–1881, 22 Nov. 1829, Virginia Historical Society, Richmond.

19. JACKSONIAN SENATOR

1. Martineau, *Retrospect of Western Travel,* 1:143–44; Thomas Clark, *Footloose in Jacksonian America: Robert W. Scott and His Agrarian World* (Frankfort: Kentucky Historical Society, 1989), 87. Clark found Washington remarkable for dogs and grog shops. Clark also noted that given the strangers in the city and the number of men at a distance from their families and wives, "the sexes are not scrupulous about illicit intercourse." Ibid.

2. Clark, *Footloose in Jacksonian America,* 68–69.

3. John Tyler to John Rutherfoord, 14 Mar. 1830, in Tyler, *Letters and Times of the Tylers,* 3:63; Martineau, *Retrospect of Western Travel,* 1:152–57. "One fancies one can tell a New England member in the open air by his deprecatory walk." Ibid., 145.

4. Diary of Reverend Patrick Sparrow, 18 Apr. 1836, W. Keats Sparrow Papers; *Workingman's Advocate,* 17 Dec. 1831, 3–18, American Periodical Series Online, 1740–1900, http://proquest.umi. com. The correspondent for the *Workingman's Advocate* described Grundy on 5 Dec. 1831: "I perceive the celebrated Felix Grundy of Tennessee. His profile is not strongly marked, and you would not imagine, from his personal appearance, that he was very intellectual. He has the appearance of a good jolly farmer" (4).

5. "A Peep At Washington," *The Knickerbocker,* 14 June 1834, 439, http://proquest.umi.com; March, *Reminiscences of Congress,* 198.

6. Martineau, *Retrospect of Western Travel,* 1:178–79; Nathan Sargent, *Public Men and Events in the United States: From the Commencement of Mr. Monroe's administration, in 1817, to the close of Mr. Fillmore's administration, in 1853,* 2 vols. (1875; New York: Da Capo, 1970), 1:46; Edward S. Abdy, *Journal of a Tour of the United States,* 3 vols. (London, 1835), 2:3: "The Federal government has comparatively little to do; and oratory finds a double stimulus in the form of fame and dollars. No wonder, therefore that three days are sometimes allotted to one speech, and three months to one subject." Grundy and other senators also had the support of a clerical force. H. C. Williams "acted as sort of an amateur private secretary" to Grundy and referred to a colleague, George Matthews Head, a son of Grundy's old friend Rev. Jesse Head, as part of the group. Williams to Col. S. M. Sterling, 26 Dec. 1875, Felix Grundy Papers, 1820–1840, TSLA. In addition, John McGavock, a son of Randal and Sally Rodgers McGavock, served as private secretary to his uncle. William S. Speer, ed., *Sketches of Prominent Tennesseans* (Nashville: Albert B. Tavel, 1888), 4.

7. March, *Reminiscences of Congress,* 95.

8. Bowers, *Party Battles of the Jackson Period,* 271.

9. Jackson to Van Buren, 15 May 1830, in Van Buren, *Autobiography,* 322.

10. *Register of Debates,* 21st Cong., 1st sess., 1 Mar. 1830, 216–18. Grundy took the same view five years later, stating that he saw no impropriety in replacing men who had held office for a time with men who were equally well qualified. Ibid., 23rd Cong., 1st sess., 18 Feb. 1835, 531; Leonard D. White, *Jacksonians,* 319–20; Grundy to unidentified recipient, 18 May 1830, Levi Woodbury Family Papers, 1638–1914.

11. Parks, *Felix Grundy,* 243; *Philadelphia Aurora,* 11 Oct. 1834; *Register of Debates,* 23rd Cong., 1st sess., 30 Jan. 1834, 433; Leonard D. White, *Jacksonians,* 337.

12. Remini, *Andrew Jackson and His Indian Wars,* 226–38; Grundy to unidentified recipient, 17 Apr. 1830, in the possession of Mrs. Edward McGavock, Nashville; Grundy to Daniel Graham, 5 Apr., 22 May 1830, Felix Grundy Papers, 1820–1840, TSLA.

13. *Register of Debates,* 22nd Cong., 1st sess., 22 June 1832, 1121; Grundy to Graham, 5 Apr. 1830, Felix Grundy Papers, 1820–1840, TSLA.

14. Howe, *What Hath God Wrought,* 357–59. See also Friend, *Along the Maysville Road.*

15. Van Buren, *Autobiography,* 325–26; Carlton Jackson, "The Internal Improvement Vetoes of Andrew Jackson," *Tennessee Historical Quarterly* 25 (Fall 1966): 261–79; Grundy to Graham, 22 May 1830, Felix Grundy Papers, 1820–1840, TSLA; *Register of Debates,* 21st Cong., 1st sess., 22 May 1830, 453–55.

16. Grundy to Jackson, 31 July 1830, Andrew Jackson Papers, 1775–1860; Cole, *Presidency of Andrew Jackson,* 66.

17. Wilentz, *Rise of American Democracy,* 364–67. There are numerous useful accounts of the Second Bank of the United States and the "Bank War" between Jackson and Biddle. See esp. Schlesinger, *Age of Jackson;* Hammond, *Banks and Politics in America;* Catterall, *Second Bank of the United States;* and Remini, *Andrew Jackson and the Bank War.*

18. Cadwalader to Biddle, 21, 25 Dec. 1831, in Biddle, *Correspondence,* 147–50, 155–57. Louis McLane believed that a number of men friendly to the Second Bank—John Forsyth, Willie Mangum, and Felix Grundy—would support the government at this time. Munroe, *Louis McLane,* 319.

19. Wilburn, *Biddle's Bank,* 11–16.

20. Wilentz, *Rise of American Democracy,* 370. Throughout the 1830s the Tennessee Whig press generally recognized that Grundy accepted the constitutionality of a national bank and charged his opposition to the Second Bank to expediency. See *Knoxville Register,* date unknown, as quoted in *Nashville Republican,* 16 July 1835; see also *Nashville Whig,* 27 Apr. 1838.

21. Felix Grundy's opinion, 31 Jan. 1831, Felix Grundy Papers, 1807–1899, SHC; John Quincy Adams, *Memoirs,* 31 Jan. 1831, 8:306.

20. NULLIFICATION

1. Van Buren, *Autobiography,* 382. Although Calhoun and Nancy Rodgers were second cousins, they had not yet met in 1829. Calhoun to John Rodgers, 28 Mar. 1825, in Calhoun, *Papers,* 10:14.

2. *Register of Debates,* 21st Cong., 1st sess., 18 Jan. 1830, 25–27. One observer wrote that "Benton's egotism was so vast, so towering, so part and parcel of the man, that it was not at all offensive, and never excited disgust." Oliver Dyer, *Great Senators of the United States Forty Years Ago (1848 and 1849)* (1889, Freeport, NY: Book for Libraries, 1972), 207. Harriet Martineau, however, did not like Benton "by instinct nor analysis." Martineau, *Retrospect of Western Travel,* 1:179.

3. *Register of Debates,* 21st Cong., 1st sess., 8 Dec. 1829, 74; Howe, *What Hath God Wrought,* 370–72.

4. Peterson, *Great Triumvirate,* 179–80; Benton, *Thirty Years' View,* 1:142.

5. *Register of Debates,* 21st Cong., 1st sess., 1 Mar. 1830, 210–14.

6. Parks, *Felix Grundy,* 186; Grundy to Edwards, 18 May 1830, Ninian Edwards Papers, 1798–1833; Calhoun to Christopher Van Deventer, 20 Mar. 1830, in Calhoun, *Papers,* 11:140; Brant, *James Madison: Commander in Chief, 1812–1836,* 481; James Campbell to his brother, 8 May 1830, Campbell Family Papers, 1731–1969.

7. Parton, *Life of Andrew Jackson,* 3:284; Remini, *Andrew Jackson and the Course of American Freedom,* 233–36; Van Buren, *Autobiography,* 414–15.

8. Van Buren, *Autobiography,* 414–15; *National Intelligencer,* 19 Apr. 1830; Parks, *Felix Grundy,* 176.

9. See Marszalek, *The Petticoat Affair.*

10. Amos Kendall to Francis Blair, 25 Apr. 1830, Blair and Lee Papers, 1764–1946.

11. Grundy to Daniel Graham, 5 Apr. 1830, Felix Grundy Papers, 1820–1840, TSLA.

12. *Register of Debates,* 21st Cong., 1st sess., 1 Mar. 1830, 219; Tyler to John Rutherford, 14 Mar. 1830, in Tyler, *Letters and Times of the Tylers,* 3:62; Josiah Johnston to Clay, 14 Mar. 1830, in Clay, *Papers,* 8:181–83. In a letter of 8 May 1830 to Ninian Edwards, Grundy stated four "certainties" about Jackson: (1) he would run again; (2) his popularity was increasing; (3) his reelection was "as certain as his life, and he is in excellent health"; and (4) "his standing is of a peculiar character, his ministers and his Congress may all become unpopular, and still his hold on the affections of the people not be weakened." Ninian Edwards Papers, 1798–1833. See also Grundy to unidentified recipient, 17 Apr. 1830, in the possession of Mrs. Edward McGavock, Nashville.

13. Grundy to Graham, 5 Apr. 1830, Felix Grundy Papers, 1820–1840, TSLA.

14. Grundy to Levi Woodbury, 7 July 1830, Levi Woodbury Family Papers, 1638–1914; Charles Wickliffe to Hugh L. White, Felix Grundy, et al., 24 Dec. 1831, Blair and Lee Papers, 1764–1946; John Quincy Adams, *Memoirs,* 20 Feb. 1832, 8:477; White, Grundy, et al., response to Wickliffe, Blair and Lee Papers, 1764–1946; *Niles Register,* 25 Feb. 1832; Grundy to Jackson, 30 Sept. 1831, Andrew Jackson Papers, 1775–1860.

15. Calhoun, *Papers,* 11:479, 481.

16. Just three days before the Jefferson Day dinner, on April 10, 1830, with all documentation in hand, Jackson wrote his old friend John Coffee of evidence of the "base hypocracy of the great secret agent . . . under the most positive assurance of his friendship." Jackson to Coffee, 10 Apr. 1830, in Jackson, *Correspondence,* 4:134; Cole, *Presidency of Andrew Jackson,* 81; Marszalek, *Petticoat Affair,* 127.

17. Marszalek, *Petticoat Affair,* 131–35; Burke, *Emily Donelson of Tennessee,* 1:231–97. On 24 October 1830 Jackson wrote Mary Eastin, a niece of Rachel Jackson's, "One word more, has judge Overton, Randal McGavock, Samuel Donelson, General Coffee and thousand more injured their standing and character by associating with Major Eaton and his family. I think not." Jackson, *Correspondence,* 4:186. Shortly before her death on 8 November 1879, Peggy Eaton told a newspaper reporter that in 1829 "I went out to Randal McGavock's very often. He was a great friend of my husband and of General Jackson. Mrs. McGavock was a noble woman and treated me, very kindly. I remember one of her sons very well, John McGavock, for he was a great favorite with General Jackson." Mrs. J. T. Wallace, "A Bit of Franklin's Early History," *Franklin (TN) Review Appeal,* date unknown, Carnton Plantation Archives, Franklin, TN.

18. Grundy to Woodbury, 24 Aug. 1830, Levi Woodbury Family Papers, 1638–1914; Bowers, *Party Battles of the Jackson Period,* 129; Grundy to Jackson, 1 Sept. 1830, Andrew Jackson Papers, 1775–1860; Jackson to William B. Lewis, 25 Aug. 1830, in Jackson, *Correspondence,* 4:177.

19. Grundy to Woodbury, 7 July, 24 Aug. 1830, Levi Woodbury Family Papers, 1638–1914; Solomon Clark to Woodbury, 10 July 1830, ibid.; James Campbell to his brother, 8 May 1830, Campbell Family Papers, 1731–1969.

20. Saunders, *Early Settlers of Alabama,* 94; Timothy R. Brock, "The Killing of Thomas P. Taul," *Franklin County Historical Review* 15, no. 1 (1984): 3–16.

21. Thomas Taul to Henry Clay, 18 Jan. 1827, in Clay, *Papers,* 6:31–33; Taul, "Memoirs of Micah Taul," 601–27.

22. Taul, "Memoirs of Micah Taul," 601–27; A. S. Colyar, "Winchester: The Present and the Past in an Old Tennessee Town," *Franklin County News,* 3 Oct. 1884, quoted in Brock, "Killing of Thomas P. Taul," 14; Saunders, *Early Settlers of Alabama,* 95.

23. Grundy to Graham, 24 Jan. 1831, Felix Grundy Papers, 1807–1899, SHC.

24. Cole, *Presidency of Andrew Jackson,* 81–82; Van Buren, *Autobiography,* 377.

25. Eaton statement, *Washington Globe,* 26 Mar. 1831; Van Buren, *Autobiography,* 378.

26. Eaton statement, *Washington Globe,* 26 Mar. 1831.

27. Grundy, notes on Eaton and *Globe* publication, Felix Grundy Papers, 1807–1899, SHC. John Quincy Adams noted that Eaton's letter confirmed Grundy's account and added, "It seems probable that this letter of Eaton's is published to pacify Jackson's irritation upon seeing a statement that Calhoun's pamphlet had been exhibited previous to its publication to his bosom friends without meeting any objection from them." John Quincy Adams, *Memoirs,* 28 Mar. 1831, 8:350.

28. Jackson to Andrew Donelson, 24 Mar. 1831, in Jackson, *Correspondence,* 4:251–54. Jackson also wrote, "In the meantime you can ask judge Grundy where he was, when by his invitation Eaton

called at his lodgings, and who was in consultation with him at mr. Inghams, and from whom he got the manuscript he read to major Eaton that evening, and why it was that I was not made acquainted with the intended publication of Calhouns Book." Ibid. See also Moore, "Political Background of the Revolt against Jackson," 52. According to Moore, "It also appears that Eaton used the situation to advance his own position at Grundy's expense. Had Jackson become completely alienated from Grundy, because of the Seminole affair, it is entirely possible that the latter would have followed Calhoun's example in becoming an ally of the Whig party, if not a permanent member" (52–53).

29. Van Buren, *Autobiography,* 377–83. Van Buren also gave an account of his personal relationship with Calhoun at this time. Calhoun had arrived somewhat unexpectedly at a dinner for thirty given by Van Buren in February 1831. Van Buren surmised that Grundy had exacted a controlling influence "over Calhoun's attendance at the dinner which was not only numerous and brilliant, but, with the exception of Mr. Calhoun, lively and jocular." Calhoun, at Van Buren's request, "took Mrs. Grundy in to dinner and placed her between him and myself." Calhoun had remained constrained, and Van Buren had interpreted Calhoun's demeanor as suggesting that their future relationship would depend on what happened with respect to publication of Calhoun's correspondence. Ibid., 750.

30. Benton, *Thirty Years' View,* 1:219; Remini, *Henry Clay,* 383–85; Grundy to John Overton, 22 Jan. 1832, John Overton Papers, 1797–1833, TSLA. Grundy also reported to Overton that Calhoun "declares, he will not be a candidate for President or Vice President."

31. Grundy to Graham, 24 Jan. 1831, Felix Grundy Papers, 1807–1899, SHC. The letters to Foster have not been found, but Foster's friendly response suggests that they were about the relationship between Jackson and Calhoun. Foster to Grundy, 25 Jan. 1831, ibid.

32. Samuel Gwin to Grundy, 25 May 1831, ibid.; Richard M. Johnson to Grundy, 12 May 1831, *American Historical Magazine* 5 (Apr. 1900): 132. Johnson also said that "if Judge White refuses the office, I want you to be taken into the Cabinet. Without flattery, I think you better qualified than most men to manage a department."

33. Grundy to John Eaton, 12 May 1831, Felix Grundy Papers, 1807–1899, SHC; Samuel Gwin to Grundy, 25 May 1831, ibid.; Hugh Lawson White, *Memoir,* 248.

34. Grundy to Solomon Clark, 9 May 1831, Felix Grundy Papers, 1820–1840, TSLA. Calhoun further stated: "I, at all times regarded you as the decided friend of General Jackson in preference to myself or any other individual but, at the same time, as being of friendly feeling towards myself personally." Calhoun to Grundy, 8 June 1831, Felix Grundy Papers, 1807–1899, SHC.

35. Grundy to Jackson, 4 Feb. 1832, Andrew Jackson Papers, 1775–1860. Grundy's messmates included Messrs. Buckner, Hall, Isaacs, Blair, Standifer, Johnston, Lyon, Boon, Carr, McCarty, and Thompson.

36. Bergeron, "Tennessee's Response to the Nullification Crisis," 35–37, 44. Bergeron concluded that the statement in Freehling's *Prelude to Civil War* that Tennessee was "mildly anti-tariff . . . and passionately pro-Jackson" (239) was at best a gross oversimplification. *Register of Debates,* 22nd Cong., 1st sess., 15 Feb. 1832, 393ff., and 13 July 1832, 1293; Parks, *Felix Grundy,* 188–91; Howe, *What Hath God Wrought,* 400–401.

37. Wilentz, *Rise of American Democracy,* 379–89; Ellis, *Union at Risk,* 158–82; Bergeron, "Tennessee's Response to the Nullification Crisis," 44; Comegys, *Memoir of John M. Clayton,* 76–83; Peterson, *Olive Branch and Sword,* 70–82. See also Daniel Webster to Nathan Appleton, 17 Feb. 1833, in Webster, *Papers,* 3:216–17, for Grundy's support of Clay's tariff compromise.

38. Jackson to Grundy, 13 Feb. 1833, *American Historical Magazine* 5 (Apr. 1900): 137; Jackson to Grundy, 7 Feb. 1833, Andrew Jackson Papers, 1775–1860; Ellis, *Union at Risk,* 160–77; Cole, *Presidency of Andrew Jackson,* 167–72.

39. *Register of Debates,* 22nd Cong., 2nd sess., 20 Feb. 1833, 192–93. Grundy made no judgment concerning whether a state could nullify a non-exclusive power.

40. Ellis, *Union at Risk,* 172–73; Van Buren, *Autobiography,* 382; Pleasant Miller to Calhoun, Nov. 1832, in Calhoun, *Papers,* 11:683–84; *Richmond Whig and Public Advertiser,* 8 Mar. 1833; John Randolph to Samuel P. Carson, 21 [June?] 1833, John Randolph of Roanoke Papers, 1781–1860; Crockett, *Life of Colonel David Crockett,* 248.

41. Moore, "Political Background of the Revolt against Jackson," 54.

21. REELECTION

1. Coffee to Jackson, 9 July 1831, in Heiskell, *Andrew Jackson and Early Tennessee History,* 3:520; Atkins, *Parties, Politics, and the Sectional Conflict,* 29.

2. William Donelson to Andrew J. Donelson, 23 Oct. 1831, John Coffee Papers, 1770–1917; Atkins, *Parties, Politics, and the Sectional Conflict,* 30. On 6 December 1831 Jackson wrote Martin Van Buren that Eaton would be "elected Senator next year if he will accept." Jackson, *Correspondence,* 4:379–80.

3. Grundy to Sam Turney, *Nashville National Banner,* 29 Sept. 1833. The canvassing for votes and development of party organization in the South are described in Cooper, *South and the Politics of Slavery,* 23–42.

4. *Nashville Republican and State Gazette,* 28 Sept., 1 Oct. 1832; Parks, *Felix Grundy,* 206–7; John McLemore to Jackson, 25 Sept. 1832, in Jackson, *Correspondence,* 4:476; Cheatham, *Old Hickory's Nephew,* 105.

5. Atkins, *Parties, Politics, and the Sectional Conflict,* 29–30; Jackson to Ephraim H. Foster, 22 June 1832, in Jackson, *Correspondence,* 4:451–52; Jackson to Grundy, 20 Aug. 1832, Andrew Jackson Papers, 1775–1860.

6. *Nashville Republican and State Gazette,* 1 Oct. 1832; Carroll to Jackson, 3 Dec. 1833, in Heiskell, *Andrew Jackson and Early Tennessee History,* 3:528; Jackson to David Burford, 10 Sept. 1832, in Jackson, *Correspondence,* 4:473–74; McLemore to Jackson, 25 Sept. 1832, ibid., 476–77; Jackson to McLemore, 29 Sept. 1832, ibid., 477; Jackson "To A Committee," Sept. 1832, ibid., 478–79; Moore, "Political Background of the Revolt against Jackson," 54.

7. *United States Telegraph,* 15 Sept. 1832; Duff Green to Calhoun, 4 Oct. 1832, in Calhoun, *Papers,* 11:664; Pleasant Miller to Calhoun, Nov. 1832, ibid., 683–84. Another observer wrote that Jackson had attended the legislature in Nashville on 19 September 1832. "The legislature seems to hold out . . . the screws will be applied . . . Grundy feels that. . . . he is 'used up.' It is sacrificing one devoted partisan for one more devious . . . will be some mouthings, but General Jackson's popularity can stand anything." Lunsford Yandell to Susan Yandell, 19 Sept. 1832, Yandell Family Papers, 1823–1877. See also John Quincy Adams, *Memoirs,* 26 Dec. 1833, 9:60.

8. W. A. Wade wrote that despite the shifting of votes, the strength of candidates was Grundy, 23; Foster, 20; and Eaton, 17. Wade to Maj. William Campbell, 2 Oct. [1832], Campbell Family Papers, 1731–1969; *National Banner,* 6, 8 Oct. 1832; Balie Peyton to McLemore, 5 Oct. 1832, John Overton Papers, 1797–1833, TSLA. See also Durham, *Balie Peyton of Tennessee,* 14–15. The future Virginia governor David Campbell expressed disappointment that the legislature would "put out

a man of decided talent and send a cipher"; he thought that if Jackson approved of the opposition to Grundy, he was lacking in judgment. David Campbell to Maj. William Campbell, 20 Oct. 1832, Campbell Family Papers, 1731–1969.

9. Grundy to Andrew Donelson, 31 Mar. 1833, Travellers Rest Archives, Nashville.

10. Grundy to Jackson, 6 May 1833, in Heiskell, *Andrew Jackson and Early Tennessee History,* 3:527.

11. Grundy to William Barry and Francis Blair, 21 June 1833, Blair and Lee Papers, 1764–1946; Marszalek, *Petticoat Affair,* 208; Grundy to Burford, 15 June 1833, Special Collections, University of Tennessee, Knoxville; *Nashville National Banner,* 28 June 1833; *To the public; A publication of Col. Robert Armstrong . . . to . . . Felix Grundy,* printed broadside, 24 July 1833, Library of Congress, American Memory, http://memory.loc.gov/ammem/index.html, portfolio 174, folder 32. Grundy did not directly refute the allegation but suggested such a comment had been made in jest. Grundy's jocularity regularly got him in trouble, as in a dispute with Charles Biddle over an alleged slighting remark. Parks, *Felix Grundy,* 212–13.

12. Grundy to Jackson, 6 May 1833, Andrew Jackson Papers, 1775–1860; Jackson to Grundy, 19 May 1833, Felix Grundy Papers, 1807–1899, SHC.

13. Grundy to Jackson, 6 Aug. 1833, Blair and Lee Papers, 1764–1946; Grundy to Jackson, 7 Aug. 1833, in Heiskell, *Andrew Jackson and Early Tennessee History,* 3:527; Grundy to Cave Johnson, 29 Aug. 1833, Cave Johnson Papers, 1833–1948; Sellers, *James K. Polk,* 205–6; Polk to Johnson, 26 Sept. 1833, in Polk, *Correspondence,* 2:110.

14. Sellers, *James K. Polk,* 206; Terry Cahal to Polk, 8 Oct. 1833, in Polk, *Correspondence,* 2:113; W. A. Wade to Maj. William Campbell, 10 Oct. 1833, Campbell Family Papers, 1731–1969; McKellar, *Tennessee Senators,* 201; Carroll to Jackson, 9 Aug. 1833, in Heiskell, *Andrew Jackson and Early Tennessee History,* 3:517. For a different assessment of Jackson's preference, see Arda S. Walker, "John Henry Eaton, Apostate," *East Tennessee Historical Society Publications* 24 (1952): 26–43, suggesting, mistakenly in my view, that Jackson favored Grundy.

15. Carroll to Van Buren, 11 Nov. 1833, Martin Van Buren Papers, 1787–1910; *Nashville Republican and State Gazette,* 10 Oct. 1833.

16. Foster to David Hubbard, 7 June [1833?], David Hubbard Papers, 1807–1871. William Carroll wrote Jackson that Judge Anderson, Grundy's former law partner, had been a leader in trying to induce Eaton to enter the contest in 1833 but that Anderson had said that in a race between Grundy and Eaton he would support Grundy. In an unusually hostile tone, Carroll wrote, "I know of no one in the stability of whose political friendship or sound principles on public measures I have less confidence than in Judge A. He is activated by a restless ambition, is subject to the control of weak men, and . . . is wholly deficient in moral *stamina.*" Carroll to Jackson, 3 Dec. 1833, in Heiskell, *Andrew Jackson and Early Tennessee History,* 3:528. Polk's brother-in-law wrote in October 1833 that when he was in Nashville he had had evidence of a "perfect understanding between Bell, Eaton, Armstrong and Foster." James Walker to Polk, 20 Oct. 1833, in Polk, *Correspondence,* 2:117.

22. LAND AND SLAVERY

1. Grundy to Levi Woodbury, 7 July 1830, Levi Woodbury Family Papers, 1638–1914; Margaret Rodgers Reed to Isabella Reed Clay, 23 Jan. 1828, Sidney P. Clay Collection, 1783–1846.

2. McKellar, *Tennessee Senators,* 197. According to Grundy, "Those who fought duels were generally the young and high-spirited, whose sole ambition was to get into power and place; and when

they found themselves forever excluded by the passage of such a law, they would be cautious how they infringed its penalties." *Register of Debates,* 22nd Cong., 2nd sess., 20 Feb. 1833, 662. See also *Congressional Globe,* 25th Cong., 2nd sess., 1838, 6, no. 19:293 (9 Apr. 1838), where Grundy voted to prohibit giving or accepting a challenge for a duel in the District of Columbia. Grundy did have a racehorse named for him: on 1 August 1833 the *American Turf Register* referred to a race in Nashville on 7 May in which W. B. Gower's chestnut colt Felix Grundy had won his first heat (one mile) but failed in the third day's concluding race.

3. Robert V. Remini, ed., "A New York 'Yankee' in Tennessee, 1821," *Tennessee Historical Quarterly* 37 (Fall 1978): 282; Houston, *Autobiography,* 68.

4. Howe, *What Hath God Wrought,* 166–68; "Agreement February 14, 1833, of Congressmen Desiring to Form a Congressional Temperance Society, 22nd Congress, 2nd Session," Felix Grundy Papers, Virginia Historical Society; "Temperance Meeting at the Odeon, September 22, 1839," circular, Brown University, Providence, RI.

5. "Temperance Meeting at the Odeon, September 22, 1839"; Clayton, *History of Davidson County, Tennessee,* 121; Memoirs of William Calhoun Love, transcribed by Donald E. Collins, TSLA. Married to the daughter of John Hogg, of Trenton, in Gibson County, Tennessee, James Priestley Grundy moved to Trenton in the 1840s, perhaps living on the two hundred acres given to him by his father in 1829 as an expression of the "natural love and affection he bore his son." Jonathan K. Smith, *Genealogical Abstracts from Early Land, Chancery and Other Records of Gibson County, Tennessee* (Np: Smith, c. 1998), 12.

6. Wills, *History of Belle Meade,* 37; General Land Office, Department of the Interior, to B. B. Eskridge, Pecan Point, AR, 25 May 1881, in the author's possession; Arkansas Land Records, RG 49, Records of the Bureau of Land Management, National Archives.

7. Samuel B. Barrell to Edmond Munroe, 15 Feb. 1836, Henry Smith Munroe Papers, 1804–1934. The Munroe Papers are the source of much of the narrative in this chapter with respect to Grundy's land speculation activities in south-central Tennessee.

8. The terms of the original agreement between Grundy and the Stumps are described in the Henry Smith Munroe Papers, 1804–1934. An agreement between Grundy and John Stump dated 18 July 1837 is filed in Loose Papers, 1830–052, Franklin County Archives, Winchester, TN.

9. Samuel Barrell reported that no individual could "enter, *in his own name,* more than five thousand acres of the public lands" but that the "universal practice which is now sanctioned by law" for an individual to obtain any acreage desired is to procure entries in various names and then have the entries assigned to himself. Barrell to Munroe, 15 Feb. 1836, Henry Smith Munroe Papers, 1804–1934.

10. Barrell to Munroe, 30 Apr. 1836, ibid.

11. Grundy to Barrell, 15 Aug. 1836, and Barrell to Grundy, 4 Sept. 1836, 17 Sept. 1836, ibid.

12. Grundy advised Barrell in February 1837 that the survey of 100,000 acres had been completed and that Colonel Stump thought that the survey of the whole 500,000 acres would be completed in four months. Barrell to Munroe, 24 Feb. 1837, ibid.

13. Munroe wrote Barrell on 17 May, "I shall not condescend to hold further communication with you on the subject of your drafts on me." Ibid. Grundy to S. L. Barrell and Edmund Munroe, 1 June 1837, Grundy to Barrell, 4 June 1837, Barrell to Grundy, 1 July 1837, Grundy to Barrell, 14 July 1837, and Schedule of Tennessee Lands, 1838, ibid.

14. Barrell to Grundy, 16 Jan. 1839, ibid.; A Mr. Maxcy was authorized to sell lands at not less than 50¢ per acre for a commission of 10 percent. Barrell to Grundy, 30 Apr., 25 July 1839, and Bar-

rell to Munroe, 30 Jan. 1840, ibid. In a letter dated 12 April 1840, for example, Barrell wrote to Grundy, "You will excuse me for entertaining the opinion that, under the circumstances, Mr. Munroe and myself are more competent to judge of the expediency of procrastinating the negotiation with my London correspondent to the period I have designated than either yourself or Mr. Bradley." He noted that he had invested "upwards of 12 1/2 cents per acre" for his proportion of the lands. Ibid. See also Barrell to Grundy, 18 Aug. 1840, and unnamed London correspondent to Barrell, 20 July 1840, ibid.

A controversy arose between Grundy's heirs and Frederick Stump as to how much of the amounts due Grundy had paid Stump upon the purchase by Barrell and Munroe. John M. Bass proposed a division of all lands among the parties, but apparently no agreement was reached. Some lands were apparently sold in 1846. Dr. A. Anderson to Barrell, 25 Nov. 1846; Bradley to Barrell, 19 Dec. 1846, ibid. Franklin County records reflect various efforts to resolve the legal tangle created by the land venture. Loose Papers, 1860-025, Franklin County Archives. On 6 February 1882 Felix's grandson James P. Grundy, a resident of Hamilton County, Texas, sold his residual interests in the coal properties for one hundred dollars. Franklin County Deed Book 9, Winchester, TN, 310.

15. *Kentucky Gazette,* 30 Mar. 1799; Dupre, "Political Ideas of George Nicholas," 210–11; J. W. Coleman Jr., *Slavery Times in Kentucky* (Chapel Hill: University of North Carolina Press, 1940).

16. Edward Michael McCormack, *Slavery on the Tennessee Frontier* (Nashville: Tennessee American Revolution Bicentennial Commission, 1977), 17; Anita S. Goodstein, "Black History on the Nashville Frontier, 1780–1810," *Tennessee Historical Quarterly* 38 (Winter 1979): 401–20; Fitz, "Tennessee Antislavery Movement."

17. Dusinberre, *Slavemaster President,* 2003. In the 1820 census there were two male slaves in the age group 26–45, one in the age group 14–26, and two under 14, as well as two female slaves in the age group 14–26 and two under 14. In 1830 there were three male slaves in the age group 24–55, one in the age group 24–36, two in the age group 10–24, and one under 10, as well as two females slaves in the age group 10–24 and two under 10.

18. Davidson County Minute Book, 1817, 120, as quoted in Goodstein, *Nashville,* 91; Bobby L. Lovett, *The African American History of Nashville, Tennessee, 1780–1830* (Fayetteville: University of Arkansas Press, 1999), 68.

19. Bills of sale from Grundy to Jackson, 13, 16 June 1810, in Jackson, *Papers,* 2:559–60; agreement between Grundy and Ramsey Mayson, 18 Apr. 1818, Carnton Plantation Archives, Franklin, TN.

20. Grundy to Nancy Grundy and John Bass, 20 Feb. 1836, Whiteford R. Cole Papers, 1818–1951, in which Grundy reported that he had visited a slave agent named Skinner, in Baltimore, but did not plan to use Skinner's services; sales contract between Grundy and Thomas Jones, of Fairfax County, 31 Mar. 1836, in the possession of Margaret Lindsley Warden, Nashville.

21. *Register of Debates,* 21st Cong., 1st sess., 1 Mar. 1830, 215.

22. Ibid., 215–16; Howard R. Floan, *The South in Northern Eyes, 1836–1861* (Austin: University of Texas Press, 1958), 116–18; James Fenimore Cooper, *Notions of the Americans: Picked up by a Traveling Bachelor,* new ed., 2 vols. (Philadelphia: Carey, Lea & Blanchard, 1836), 2:257–76. Jefferson's views, perhaps encapsulated in his remark that he would go to great lengths to end slavery "in any practicable way," are summarized in Wilentz, *Rise of American Democracy,* 136–37. See also Freehling, *Road to Disunion,* 121–31.

23. *Register of Debates,* 21st Cong., 1st sess., 1 Mar. 1830, 215–16; Barrell to Munroe, 15 Feb. 1836, Henry Smith Munroe Papers, 1804–1934; Howe, *What Hath God Wrought,* 147–60.

24. Lester C. Lamon, *Blacks in Tennessee, 1791–1970* (Knoxville: University of Tennessee Press, 1981), 8; McCormack, *Slavery on the Tennessee Frontier;* Sellers, *Market Revolution,* 127; Cooper, *South and the Politics of Slavery,* 58. An excellent recent study on the antislavery movement in Tennessee emphasizes that the explosion of antislavery voices in the years 1833–35 showed little concern for blacks. Founded on political and economic fears of non-slaveholding whites, the antislavery petitions favored the colonization and expulsion of freed blacks and were pessimistic about the coexistence of blacks and whites. Fitz, "Tennessee Antislavery Movement," 18–19.

25. *Register of Debates,* 24th Cong., 1st sess., 9 Mar. 1836, 779; Miller, *Arguing about Slavery,* 117; Earle, *Jacksonian Antislavery,* 42–48; Freehling, *Road to Disunion,* 322–27.

26. Nathan Sargent, *Public Men and Events in the United States: From the Commencement of Mr. Monroe's Administration, in 1817, to the Close of Mr. Fillmore's Administration, in 1853,* 2 vols. (1875; New York: Da Capo, 1970), 1:306–7; Earle, *Jacksonian Antislavery,* 42–48; *Register of Debates,* 24th Cong., 1st sess., 8 Mar. 1836, 751ff.

27. Grundy to D. R. Gooch, 18 Jan. 1838, Felix Grundy Papers, 1820–1840, TSLA. Grundy's anger did not prevent him from even-handed appraisal of such adversaries of the South as John Quincy Adams. James Freeman Clarke, *Anti-Slavery Days* (New York: J. W. Lovell, 1883), 153–54.

23. BATTLES WITH THE WHIGS

1. John Quincy Adams recounts meeting Grundy in the Senate chamber on 26 December 1833 after listening to Clay object to the deposit-removal plan. When Adams mentioned that he had expected to hear from Grundy, the Tennessean replied, "No, not upon this subject." Adams remarked that "perhaps it was not quite so important that he should give proof of zealous patriotism now as it was last winter," in response to which Grundy "laughed, and said, no; it was of no consequence at all." Adams continued, "He knew my allusion was to his re-election . . .—which he succeeded in effecting in spite of Jackson's interference to supplant him by John H. Eaton." John Quincy Adams, *Memoirs,* 9:60.

2. Wilentz, *Rise of American Democracy,* 392–96. See also Kendall, *Autobiography,* 391.

3. Van Buren, *Autobiography,* 673–75; Norman D. Brown, *Daniel Webster,* 56–58; Niven, *Martin Van Buren,* 356.

4. Van Buren, *Autobiography,* 675–77; Niven, *Martin Van Buren,* 356–58; Norman D. Brown, *Daniel Webster,* 56–58; Clay to James Brown, 14 Dec. 1833, in Clay, *Papers,* 8:675; Clay to John Clayton, 12 Dec. 1833, ibid., 674.

5. Van Buren, *Autobiography,* 677–79; Niven, *Martin Van Buren,* 356–58; Cole, *Presidency of Andrew Jackson,* 184–203. Cole suggests that Louis McLane, Lewis Cass, Edward Livingston, and Grundy were sympathetic to a new unionist party.

6. Biddle, *Correspondence,* 219; Bowers, *Party Battles of the Jackson Period,* 303–19. Bowers described the situation succinctly: "The feeling was germinating that Jackson was not far wrong in the conclusion that a moneyed institution possessing the power to precipitate panics to influence governmental action, was dangerous to the peace, prosperity, and liberty of the people" (318–19).

7. *Congressional Debates,* 23rd Cong., 1st sess., 1834, 416ff.; *Boston Post,* date unknown, quoted in *Nashville National Banner,* 22 Feb. 1834; *Washington Globe,* 12 Feb. 1834, quoted in Parks, *Felix Grundy,* 227–28.

8. *Congressional Debates,* 23rd Cong., 1st sess., 1834, 1557–58.

9. Phelan, *History of Tennessee,* 357–59; John E. Harkins, "Newton Cannon, Jackson Neme-

sis," *Tennessee Historical Quarterly* 43 (Winter 1984): 357; Abernethy, "Origin of the Whig Party in Tennessee," 508.

10. Sellers, *James K. Polk,* 237–41; Willie Mangum to John Bell, 15 June 1835, in Mangum, *Papers,* 2:349–50.

11. R. M. Burton to Polk, 27 Aug. 1834, in Polk, *Correspondence,* 2:461. Burton also told Polk that "Mr. Grundy was at Murfreesboro last week and corpsed the Bank, had the funeral dirge of *A Bank* sung and left the place." Atkins, *Parties, Politics, and the Sectional Conflict,* 35; Jackson to Van Buren, 16 Aug. 1834, in Jackson, *Correspondence,* 5:282–83.

12. Sellers, *James K. Polk,* 250–53; Jackson to Van Buren, 16 Aug. 1834, in Jackson, *Correspondence,* 5:282–83; Cooper, *South and the Politics of Slavery,* 142–45. According to William Freehling, in *The Road to Disunion,* "Poor Van Buren already in enough southern trouble because Jackson was such a bear to follow, faced charges that he was disloyal to slavery from every Southern direction" (297).

13. Hugh Lawson White, *Memoir,* 245–51; Cole, *Presidency of Andrew Jackson,* 255.

14. McCormac, *James K. Polk,* 75; Stephen D. Byas, "James Standifer, Sequatchie Valley Congressman," *Tennessee Historical Quarterly* 50 (Summer 1991): 90–97; Hugh Lawson White, *Memoir,* 253–64; Sellers, *James K. Polk,* 259–62; Cole, *Presidency of Andrew Jackson,* 255.

15. Grundy, statement dated 5 June 1835, *Nashville Union,* 8 July 1839.

16. Sellers, *James K. Polk,* 269; Grundy to Jackson, 28 Mar. 1835, Andrew Jackson Papers, 1775–1860. Polk ran unopposed in 1835 and 1837. His efforts on behalf of the party are summarized in Joseph M. Pukl Jr., "James K. Polk's Congressional Campaigns of 1835 and 1837," *Tennessee Historical Quarterly* 41 (Summer 1982): 105–23.

17. *Knoxville Register,* date unknown, as quoted in *Nashville Republican,* 16 July 1835; Grundy to Jackson, 30 May, 6 June 1835, Andrew Jackson Papers, 1775–1860; Francis Blair to Grundy, 10 June 1835, ibid.; Jackson to Grundy, 11 June 1835, in Jackson, *Correspondence,* 5:353–54. Davy Crockett described Jackson's animosity and the nature of campaigning in 1835 in his *Life of Colonel David Crockett,* 246–50. See also Robert Cassell, "Newton Cannon and State Politics, 1835–1839," *Tennessee Historical Quarterly* 15 (Dec. 1956): 30.

18. John W. Childress to Polk, 20 Dec. 1837, in Polk, *Correspondence,* 4:299–300; Folsom, "Politics of Elites," 376; Carroll Van West, "The Democratic and Whig Political Activists of Middle Tennessee," *Tennessee Historical Quarterly* 42 (Spring 1983): 3–17.

19. Paul H. Bergeron, "James K. Polk and the Jacksonian Press in Tennessee," *Tennessee Historical Quarterly* 41 (Fall 1982): 257–77; Jackson to Grundy, 5 Oct. 1835, Felix Grundy Papers, 1807–1899, SHC; Grundy to Jackson, 30 May 1835, ibid.; Samuel H. Laughlin to Polk, 21 Oct. 1835, in Polk, *Correspondence,* 3:344–45; Atkins, *Parties, Politics, and the Sectional Conflict,* 48–49.

20. Only 55 percent of eligible voters went to the polls, a lower turnout than in future contests between Whigs and Democrats but higher than the Tennessee turnouts of 40 percent in 1828 and 28 percent in 1832. See Bergeron, *Antebellum Politics in Tennessee,* 56–63; and Atkins, *Parties, Politics, and the Sectional Conflict,* 52–54. One student observed that the voters in Tennessee in 1836 were "Pro-White," not necessarily "anti-Van Buren." James Edward Murphy, "Jackson and the Tennessee Opposition," *Tennessee Historical Quarterly* 30 (Spring 1971): 67.

21. Grundy to John M. Bass, 19 Dec. 1835, Whitefoord R. Cole Papers, 1818–1951; Hugh Lawson White, *Memoir,* 253; Van Buren, *Autobiography,* 382. In 1839 an observer of the Senate contrasted the two Tennessee senators, concluding, "A few short sessions ago, how trustingly they confided in each other! now they engage in mutual recrimination." Joseph Etter, *Sketches of U.S. Senators*

(Washington, DC, 1839), 39. Of Grundy, Etter wrote: "Mr. Grundy is a graceful speaker, voluble and ever ready; prone to utter, or to hear, things that are pleasant. He is experienced, and by reason thereof, cautious; and aiming generally to assume the position best calculated for his powers—that of defence. A certain natural bluntness and candor, however, belong to his character which will sometimes break out in spite of studied restraint. His manner is warm and effective. . . . As regards their temperment, from experience and from physiognomy, I should say, that to Mr. GRUNDY belong fire, animation and impetus, on every occasion" (37–38).

22. Larry Schweikart, "Tennessee Banks in the Antebellum Period, Part I," *Tennessee Historical Quarterly* 45 (Summer 1986): 121–22; Sellers, *James K. Polk,* 206–9.

23. Sellers, *James K. Polk,* 207–9; Grundy to Bass, 9, 16 Feb. 1836, Whitefoord R. Cole Papers, 1818–1951. See also Grundy to Woodbury, 16 May 1837, Levi Woodbury Family Papers, 1638–1914; John Pope to Grundy, 30 Mar. 1837, McGavock Family Papers, 1797–1897.

24. Sharp, *Jacksonians versus the Banks,* 27; Atkins, *Parties, Politics, and the Sectional Conflict,* 57.

25. Grundy presented his own views on the crisis in his letter to Woodbury. He pointed out that a major problem was the government's inability to meet demands because its money was tied up in Secretary Taney's depository banks. Accordingly, Grundy offered his own "unmatured opinion": that Congress should direct the issuance of treasury bills, with or without interest, payable in short periods of up to three years, in sufficient number to meet the needs of the Treasury. Grundy to Woodbury, 1 June 1837, Levi Woodbury Family Papers, 1638–1914. In October Grundy predicted to Jackson that a bill to issue treasury notes would pass. Grundy to Jackson, 2 Oct. 1837, Andrew Jackson Papers, 1775–1860.

26. Balch to Jackson, 26 Aug. 1835, Andrew Jackson Papers, 1775–1860; Grundy to Jackson, 5 Nov. 1835, Blair and Lee Papers, 1764–1946.

27. Grundy to Polk, 25 Apr. 1837, in Polk, *Correspondence,* 4:101; John F. Gillespy to Polk, 7 July 1837, ibid., 170; Alfred Flournoy to Polk, 15 July 1837, ibid., 179; Aaron V. Brown to Polk, 18 July 1837, ibid., 182; Jackson to Polk, 6 Aug. 1837, ibid., 199.

28. Grundy to Polk, 25 Apr. 1837, ibid., 101; *Nashville Union,* 11 July 1837; Gillespy to Polk, 5 May 1837, in Polk, *Correspondence,* 4:112; Grundy to William Trousdale, 14 Apr. 1837, William Trousdale Papers, 1790–1872; Catron to Polk, 7 July 1837, in Polk, *Correspondence,* 4:168: "Our affairs here stand curiously. The policy ardently sought to be observed by the candidates for the Legislature and for Gov on our side is of the neutral character—no excitement, or contestation that will cement the neutral White men to their old associates. . . . I have great faith in Grundy's Judgment of results and he is in an attitude to have his full attention bestowed on the subject. He avers, if the whole ticket is carried in Davidson and the Gov's election carried, that the Legislature and the State will naturally return to their old friends"; Atkins, *Parties, Politics, and the Sectional Conflict,* 62–65; Daniel Graham to Polk, 19 July 1837, in Polk, *Correspondence,* 4:186; Polk to Andrew Donelson, 12 July 1837, ibid., 175; John W. Childress to Polk, 11 July 1837, ibid., 173; Robert Armstrong to Polk, 16 July 1837, ibid., 182; Powell Moore, "James K. Polk: Tennessee Politician," *Journal of Southern History* 17 (Nov. 1951): 497–98; McCormac, *James K. Polk,* 114.

29. Catron to Polk, 7 July 1837, in Polk, *Correspondence,* 4:168–70; Bergeron, "James K. Polk and the Jacksonian Press in Tennessee"; Robert Beeler Satterfield, "The Uncertain Trumpet of the Tennessee Jacksonians," *Tennessee Historical Quarterly* 26 (Spring–Winter 1967): 83–89.

30. Sellers, *James K. Polk,* 325; Grundy to Polk, 4 Aug. 1837, in Polk, *Correspondence,* 4:196; Jackson to Polk, 6 Aug. 1837, ibid., 199; Jackson to Blair, 16 Aug. 1837, Andrew Jackson Papers,

1775–1860; Polk to Blair, 16 Aug. 1837, in Polk, *Correspondence,* 4:210; Bergeron, *Antebellum Politics in Tennessee,* 49.

31. Sellers, *James K. Polk,* 324–26. Polk received a letter from the Democratic stalwart Josephus C. Guild, who informed the Speaker "as a matter of some astonishment . . . that a very great portion or majority of Smith [County] seems to be in favor" of establishing a U.S. Bank. Guild to Polk, 11 July 1837, in Polk, *Correspondence,* 4:174.

32. Parks, *Felix Grundy,* 310; Grundy to Polk, 17 Oct. 1837, in Polk, *Correspondence,* 4:260.

33. Parks, *Felix Grundy,* 310–13; *Nashville Union,* 31 Oct., 14 Nov. 1837; Jackson to Grundy, 16 Dec. 1837, *American Historical Magazine* 5 (Apr. 1900): 138; Grundy to Jackson, 2 Oct. 1837, Andrew Jackson Papers, 1775–1860.

34. Grundy to Woodbury, 1 June 1837, Levi Woodbury Family Papers, 1638–1914; Sharp, *Jacksonians versus the Banks,* 10–19.

35. Grundy to Jackson, 2 Oct. 1837, 4 Jan. 1838, Andrew Jackson Papers, 1775–1860.

36. Ibid. Grundy's January letter is dated 1837, but from the context and specific references it is clear that Grundy wrote the letter in 1838.

37. Grundy to Jackson, 4 Jan. 1838, Andrew Jackson Papers, 1775–1860; *Congressional Globe,* 25th Cong., 2nd sess., 1838, 6, no. 19, appendix, 299–304 (11 Apr. 1838); ibid., nos. 20–21:319–24 (20–23 Apr.); ibid., no. 19:292–93 (9 Apr. 1838); Parks, *Felix Grundy,* 288–91; *Nashville Union,* 8 Mar. 1838. On 27 April 1838 the *Nashville Whig* reported that Hugh Lawson White had exacted modest revenge on Grundy. White had made the closing speech in opposition to Grundy's bill on the Second Bank's notes, in which he included Grundy's 1814 report affirming the constitutionality of a U.S. bank and the memorial requesting a branch in Nashville. Grundy, according to the *Whig,* "was mortified and colored up" and forced to concede that he believed in the constitutionality of a U.S. bank.

38. *Niles National Register,* 10 Mar. 1838; A. V. Brown to Grundy, 8 Feb. 1838, Felix Grundy Papers, 1807–1899, SHC. See also *Nashville Whig,* 14 Feb. 1838.

39. Grundy to Jackson, 9 Feb. 1838, Andrew Jackson Papers, 1775–1860; *McMinnville (TN) Gazette,* date unknown, as quoted in *Nashville Union,* 22 Mar. 1838; *Nashville Whig,* 7 Feb., 2 Mar. 1838; *Nashville Union,* 20 Feb. 1838 (quoting Grundy's letter in its entirety); *Franklin (TN) Review,* date unknown, as quoted in *Nashville Whig,* 12 Mar. 1838.

40. Grundy to Jackson, 9 Feb. 1838, Andrew Jackson Papers, 1775–1860; Grundy to Randal McGavock, 29 May 1838, Felix Grundy Papers, 1807–1899, SHC.

24. ATTORNEY GENERAL

1. Niven, *Martin Van Buren,* 433–35; Van Buren to Benjamin F. Butler, 11 Apr. 1838, Martin Van Buren Papers, 1787–1910; Richard E. Parker to Van Buren, 2 May 1838, ibid.; *Nashville Union,* 16 July 1838; *Nashville Whig,* 16 July 1838; Butler to Van Buren, 9 July 1838, Martin Van Buren Papers, 1787–1910.

2. Kendall, *Autobiography,* 422; Niven, *Martin Van Buren,* 434–36. Niven concluded that Grundy brought real strength to the administration.

3. Grundy to Butler, 26 July 1838, quoted in William Allen Butler, *A Retrospect of Forty Years, 1825–1865* (New York: Charles Scribner's Sons, 1911), 90–91; Perry M. Goldman and James S. Young, *The United States Congressional Directories, 1789–1840* (New York: Columbia University Press, 1973), 217ff.

4. Niven, *Martin Van Buren,* 434; Homer Cummings and Carl McFarland, *Federal Justice: Chapters in the History of Justice and the Federal Executive* (New York: Macmillan, 1937), 10; Albert Langeluttig, *The Department of Justice of the United States* (Baltimore: Johns Hopkins Press, 1929), 4ff.; Daniel J. Meador, "The President, the Attorney General, and the Department of Justice" (paper presented at the Miller Center of Public Affairs, University of Virginia, 4–5 Jan. 1980), 4–7; Harrison, *John Breckinridge: Jeffersonian Republican,* 189; Homer Cummings, *Selected Papers of Homer Cummings,* ed. Carl B. Swisher (New York: Charles Scribner's Sons, 1939), 4–5.

5. The opinions of the attorney general were first printed and transmitted to the House of Representatives on 3 March 1841. Langeluttig, *Department of Justice,* 4. My analysis is derived from Benjamin F. Hall, comp., *Official Opinions of the Attorneys General of the United States,* 12 vols. (Washington, DC: Robert Farnham, 1852–70).

6. All factual information is derived from the opinion of the attorney general dated 16 Nov. 1838, in Hall, *Official Opinions of the Attorneys General,* 3:383–85; Nina Burleigh, *The Stranger and the Statesman* (New York: HarperCollins, 2003); and Ewing, *Lost World of James Smithson.*

7. John Quincy Adams, *Memoirs,* 8 Apr. 1839, 10:112–13, and 26 Oct. 1839, 10:138–39.

8. Jones, *Mutiny on the Amistad,* 55–60; Duckett, *John Forsyth,* 184–87; Niven, *Martin Van Buren,* 466–68; Forsyth to Van Buren, 18, 23 Sept. 1839, Martin Van Buren Papers, 1787–1910; Woodbury to Van Buren, 22 Sept. 1839, ibid.

9. Grundy's opinion, dated only "November, 1839," is found in Hall, *Official Opinions of the Attorneys General,* 3:484–92.

10. Grundy to William J. Holabird, 30 Oct. 1939, Grundy to Ralph Ingersoll, 5 Nov. 1839, and Grundy to Holabird and Ingersoll, 15 Nov. 1839, in Office of the Attorney General, letter book, B.1, RG 60, National Archives; Jones, *Mutiny on the Amistad,* 57–60; Fehrenbacher, *Slaveholding Republic,* 193–95.

11. *United States v. Amistad,* 40 U.S. 518 (1841).

12. Grundy to Andrew Donelson, 15 Nov. 1838, Andrew Jackson Donelson Papers, 1779–1943; Jackson to Van Buren, 4 Dec. 1838, Martin Van Buren Papers, 1787–1910; L. A. Gobright, *Recollection of Men and Things at Washington During the Third of a Century* (Philadelphia: Claxton, Remsen & Heffelfinger, 1869), 21–23; A. O. P. Nicholas to Grundy, 11 May 1839, *Letters Received by the Attorney General,* 60-230-1-33-2, RG 60, National Archives; *Alexandria (VA) Gazette,* date unknown, as quoted in the *Nashville Whig,* 12 June 1839; Parks, *Felix Grundy,* 324–26; Van Buren to Jackson, 29 May 1839, Martin Van Buren Papers, 1787–1910.

13. Bell to Clay, 21 May 1839, in Clay, *Papers,* 9:316–17; Grundy to Polk, 12 Aug. 1839, in Polk, *Correspondence,* 5:184; Clay, *Papers,* 9:317.

14. Polk to Jackson, 12 Aug. 1839, in Polk, *Correspondence,* 5:185–86; Samuel H. Laughlin to Polk, 20 Aug. 1839, ibid., 195–96; Grundy to Polk, 17 Oct. 1839, ibid., 264–65.

15. Polk to Van Buren, 11 Nov. 1839, ibid., 295–97.

16. White, *Messages of the Governors of Tennessee,* 3:357–61, 365–81; *Nashville Republican Banner,* 20 Nov. 1839; *Nashville Union,* 20 Nov. 1839; *Journal of the Tennessee House of Representatives, General Assembly, 1st Sess.* (Knoxville: Gifford & Eastman, 1839), 176–208; Parks, *Felix Grundy,* 326–29; Grundy to Van Buren, 14 Dec. 1839, Martin Van Buren Papers, 1787–1910; Van Buren to Grundy, 19 Dec. 1839, Felix Grundy Papers, 1807–1899, SHC.

17. White, *Messages of the Governors of Tennessee,* 3:382–89; *Nashville Union,* 16 Dec. 1839; Grundy to Polk, 1 Dec. 1839, in Polk, *Correspondence,* 5:321–22; Cave Johnson to Polk, 1 Dec. 1839, ibid., 322–23; Harvey Watterson to Polk, 1 Dec. 1839, ibid., 323–24; Thomas Hart Benton to Polk,

5 Dec. 1839, ibid., 329; Cave Johnson to Polk, 8 Dec. 1839, ibid., 333–35; Sellers, *James K. Polk,* 384; McCormac, *James K. Polk,* 168–69; White, *Messages of the Governors of Tennessee,* 3:388–401; Grundy to Polk, 13 Jan. 1840, in Polk, *Correspondence,* 5:371. Van Buren's autobiography recounts a conversation with Grundy, that "facetious and worthy man": "You ask me how he [Judge White] spends his time! I will tell you:—he sits all the day long in the chimney corner, spitting tobacco juice by the gallon, cursing everything and everybody, except his Creator—but thinking devilish hard of him!" Van Buren, *Autobiography,* 226.

18. *Congressional Globe,* 26th Cong., 1st sess., 1840, 8, no. 11:164 (5 Feb. 1840); *The Diary of Philip Hone, 1828–1851,* ed. Allan Nevins (New York: Dodd, Mead, 1927), 458.

19. *Washington National Intelligencer,* 8 Feb. 1840; Grundy to Polk, 9 Feb. 1840, in Polk, *Correspondence,* 5:389–90.

25. TWILIGHT

1. Guild, *Old Times in Tennessee,* 157–58; Grundy to Polk, 12 Aug. 1839, in Polk, *Correspondence,* 5:184; Jackson to Polk, 13 Aug. 1839, ibid., 186; Anne T. Durham, "Tyree Springs," *Tennessee Historical Quarterly* 28 (Summer 1969): 156–65.

2. Jackson to Grundy, 11 June 1835, Felix Grundy Papers, 1807–1899, SHC; Jackson to Van Buren, 4 Dec. 1838, Martin Van Buren Papers, 1787–1910.

3. Levin, *Lawyers and Lawmakers of Kentucky,* 402–4.

4. *Nashville National Banner,* 7 June 1836; Grundy to Jackson, 8 Feb. 1836, Jackson to Grundy, 17 Feb. 1836, and Grundy to John M. Bass, 18 Feb. 1836, Whitefoord R. Cole Papers, 1818–1951; *Nashville Whig,* 12 Apr. 1841; *Nashville Union,* 19 Apr. 1841; Grundy to Polk, 12 Aug. 1839, in Polk, *Correspondence,* 5:184.

5. Robert Bolt, "Vice President Richard M. Johnson of Kentucky: Hero of the Thames—or the Great Amalgamator," *Register, Kentucky State Historical Society* 75 (July 1977): 191–204; Sellers, *James K. Polk,* 399–418; Meyer, *Life and Times of Colonel Richard M. Johnson,* 317–22; Cooper, *South and the Politics of Slavery,* 130–31; Catron to Polk, 5 Nov. 1839, in Polk, *Correspondence,* 5:286.

6. *Nashville Union,* 6 May 1837; Alfred Balch to Polk, 3 Sept. 1839, in Polk, *Correspondence,* 5:223–26.

7. Cave Johnson to Polk, 1, 28 Nov. 1839, in Polk, *Correspondence,* 5:304–6, 316–17.

8. Sellers, *James K. Polk,* 406–8; Catron to Polk, 3 Jan. 1840, in Polk, *Correspondence,* 5:366–68.

9. Bolt, "Vice President Richard M. Johnson of Kentucky," 192; *Register of Debates,* 24th Cong., 2nd sess., 8 Feb. 1837, 738–39; Jackson to Van Buren, 17 Feb., 3 Apr. 1840, Martin Van Buren Papers, 1787–1910. Samuel Laughlin left his account of Polk's efforts to obtain the vice presidency in diary entries from 13 April to 4 May 1840, when he served as a delegate to the convention. Laughlin, "Diaries"; Sellers, *James K. Polk,* 406–8; Grundy et al. to Polk, 3 Feb. 1840, in Polk, *Correspondence,* 5:377; Aaron V. Brown to Polk, 4 Feb. 1840, ibid., 380–81.

10. Grundy to Polk, 2 Mar., 15, 23 Apr. 1840, in Polk, *Correspondence,* 5:399–400, 427–28, 428–29.

11. Laughlin to Polk, 2 May 1840, ibid., 433–35; Brown to Polk, 3 May 1840, ibid., 436; Laughlin to Polk, 3 May 1840, ibid., 437–38; Laughlin to Polk, 6 May 1840, ibid., 440; Sellers, *James K. Polk,* 409–14; *Niles National Register,* 9 May 1840, as reported in Sellers, *James K. Polk,* 414.

12. Humphrey Marshall Jr. to Joel R. Poinsett, 24 July 1840, in *Calendar of Joel R. Poinsett Papers in the Henry D. Gilpin Collection*, ed. Grace E. Heilman and Bernard S. Levin (Philadelphia: Gilpin Library of the Historical Society of Pennsylvania, 1941), 343, 114–15; Parks, *Felix Grundy*, 334–37; *Niles National Register*, 9 May 1840, 147–48; James A. Green, *William Henry Harrison: His Life and Times* (Richmond, VA: Garrett & Massie, 1941), 368–69; Gunderson, *Log Cabin Campaign*, 238.

13. Brown to Polk, 8 May 1840, in Polk, *Correspondence*, 5:443; Hopkins L. Turney to Polk, 7 May 1840, ibid., 442; Laughlin to Polk, 6 May 1840, ibid., 440; Garraty, *Silas Wright*, 184–85.

14. Grundy to Polk, 1 June 1840, in Polk, *Correspondence*, 5:476–77; Polk to Grundy, 27 May 1840, ibid., 470–72; Meyer, *Life and Times of Colonel Richard M. Johnson*, 445–46; Henry Horn to Grundy, 7 July 1840, Felix Grundy Papers, 1807–1899, SHC; Gunderson, *Log Cabin Campaign*, 242–43.

15. John Rowan to John Rowan Jr., 16 July 1840, in Capps, *Rowan Story*, 44–45; Duff Green to Grundy, 2 Mar. 1840, Duff Green Papers, SHC.

16. Sellers, *James K. Polk*, 423–26; J. G. M. Ramsey to Polk, 10 June 1840, in Polk, *Correspondence*, 5:484–86; Grundy to Polk, 23 Apr. 1840, ibid., 428–29; Watterson to Polk, 14 Aug. 1840, ibid., 538–39; Polk to Laughlin, 15 Aug. 1840, ibid., 539–41; Watterson, as quoted in Little, *Ben Hardin*, 175; Polk to Laughlin, 17 Aug. 1840, in Polk, *Correspondence*, 5:513–19; *Knoxville Vedette*, 15 Aug. 1840; David Campbell to his nephew, 3 Aug. 1840, Campbell Family Papers, 1731–1969.

17. Oliver P. Temple, *Notable Men of Tennessee from 1833 to 1875: Their Times and Their Contemporaries* (New York: Cosmopolitan, 1912), 58–60; Parks, *Felix Grundy*, 337–39; Arnold also had an amusing rejoinder when Grundy was speaking at Rogersville. Grundy was "very eloquent as well as pathetic and began to shed tears quite freely." After several minutes, Arnold interrupted him, saying, "Never mind, Felix Grundy, it will be my time to cry directly." John T. Mather in *Nashville American*, 27 Dec. 1899. For a variant of the "ruffled shirt" story, see Gunderson, *Log Cabin Campaign*, 238.

18. *Nashville Union*, 21, 24 Aug. 1840; *Knoxville Vedette*, 26 Sept. 1840; *Nashville Union*, 21 Sept., 20 Oct. 1840; Emma Inman Williams, *Historic Madison* (Jackson, TN: Madison County Historical Society, 1946), 8–9; Jackson to Blair, 26 Sept. 1840, in Jackson, *Correspondence*, 6:77–78; Foote, *Bench and Bar*, 158. See also Durham, *Balie Peyton of Tennessee*, 79–83.

19. Grundy to Committee of the Democratic Republican Citizens of Williamson County, 25 Aug. 1840, Lawrence O. Branch Papers, University of Virginia, Charlottesville; Cooper, *South and the Politics of Slavery*, 138–48.

20. Niven, *Martin Van Buren*, 468–72; Holt, *Rise and Fall of the American Whig Party*, 111–21; Sellers, *James K. Polk*, 424–26; Cooper, *South and the Politics of Slavery*, 147–48.

21. Samuel Laughlin wrote that Grundy's exertions in 1840, "his traveling to distant places, over-fatiguing himself—and neglecting the constant disordered state of his stomach and bowels—caused the disease to become so permanently seated, that he was compelled at length to retire to his house and shortly to be confined to his own room. He was still cheerful, apprehending no immediate danger, although he suffered much, and had become considerably emaciated and enfeebled." Laughlin, "Sketches of Notable Men," 75.

22. I am indebted to Doctor Thomas Inglesby, of Baltimore, Maryland, for his conclusion concerning the most likely cause of Grundy's death. Inglesby analyzed and weighed all the known factors about Grundy's physical condition. In particular, he noted Grundy's age at death, the absence of any recorded major illnesses, his symptoms (fatigue, increasing weakness, the constant disor-

dered state of stomach, and "inveterate derangement of the bowels"), and the course and duration of his final illness. He also took into account his clear state of mind until death, the absence of jaundice, and his temperate use of alcohol.

23. Laughlin, "Sketches of Notable Men," 75; John I. Young to Polk, 11 Dec. 1840, James K. Polk Papers, 1795–1849; Daniel Graham to Polk, 13, 14 Dec. 1840, ibid.; *Nashville Union*, 17 Dec. 1840; Jackson to Polk, 19 Dec. 1840, James K. Polk Papers, 1795–1849.

24. Laughlin, "Sketches of Notable Men," 75–76.

EPILOGUE

1. Jackson to Kendall, 2 Jan. 1841, in Jackson, *Correspondence*, 6:88–89; Rowan to Mrs. Alice Shaw, 2 Jan. 1841, in Capps, *Rowan Story*, 22–23; Houston to Harding, 17 July 1841, Harding-Jackson Papers, 1819–1911, also cited in Houston, *Writings*, 3:10–11. William Giles Harding had married Elizabeth McGavock, a daughter of Randal and Sally Rodgers McGavock, in 1840.

2. *Nashville Republican Banner*, 29 Jan. 1847; Bucy, "Quiet Revolutionaries," 42–43, 52n.

3. Bumgarner, *Sarah Childress Polk*, 92; Reports of Bass and McGavock, executors of Felix Grundy estate, Whitefoord R. Cole Papers, 1818–1951; Macdonald-Millar, "Grundy-Polk Houses, Nashville."

4. Stephen Fackler, "John Rowan and the Demise of Jeffersonian Republicanism in Kentucky, 1819–1831," *Register, Kentucky State Historical Society* 78 (Winter 1980): 1–26; John S. Goff, "The Last Leaf: George Mortimer Bibb," *Register, Kentucky State Historical Society* 59 (Oct. 1961): 331–42. See also Meyer, *Life and Times of Colonel Richard M. Johnson*.

SELECTED BIBLIOGRAPHY

Felix Grundy's life spanned sixty-five formative years of American history and included more than forty years' involvement in political and entrepreneurial activities. His service encompassed the legislative, executive, and judicial branches of government, as well as civic causes and criminal defense advocacy. There is thus no dearth of general source material for a study of Grundy and no lack of data for such peers as John C. Calhoun, Henry Clay, Andrew Jackson, and James K. Polk. Grundy himself, a cautious man, confided less to writing than many of his contemporaries and left few records of a personal or philosophical nature. John B. Hayes wrote Polk in 1839, "I hope that you are as great a man as G [Grundy] in not leaving anything, in confidence, in writing to appear in judgement against you." Hayes to Polk, 9 Jan. 1839, in Polk, *Correspondence*, 5:13.

Despite Grundy's caution, I have been able to locate and compile a larger amount of his correspondence than initially expected. Most collections yielded only one or perhaps two Grundy letters, but I was able to find several significant sources not previously examined. Other Kentucky and Tennessee contemporaries of Grundy's, including such important figures as William Carroll, left comparatively little correspondence; what exists is widely scattered.

In general, I include here only those sources that are cited twice or more in the notes or that I found particularly useful for background study. References cited infrequently (typically once) are included only in the notes.

Manuscripts

There are two primary locations for original Grundy correspondence and other papers: the Southern Historical Collection, at the University of North Carolina, Chapel Hill (SHC), and the Tennessee State Library and Archives, in Nashville (TSLA). The Felix Grundy Papers at the Southern Historical Collection include correspondence and other records kept by Grundy that were inherited by members of the Dickinson family. Grundy materials at the SHC also can be found in the McGavock Family Papers. The Tennessee State Library and Archives includes Grundy materials in the Felix Grundy Papers, the Lindsley Family Papers, the Francis McGavock Papers, the Jacob McGavock Dickinson Papers, and the Whitefoord R. Cole Papers, as well as in the Dyas Collection of the John Coffee Papers, the John Overton Papers, the David Hubbard Papers, the William Trousdale Papers, and other collections.

Two other institutions have significant Grundy holdings. The Henry Smith Munroe Papers, at the Connecticut Historical Society, in Hartford, contain correspondence relating to Grundy's large-scale land speculation in south-central Tennessee from 1835 until his death. The Library of Congress has many collections containing one or two Grundy letters, although the Felix Grundy Papers there contain fewer than ten items.

Fortunately for anyone studying Grundy, he was closely associated with most of the major political figures of the first half of the nineteenth century. Accordingly, some of his correspondence can be found in compilations of letters and other papers of such political leaders.

Few of the deed, will, order, or minute books mentioned in the text have inclusive dates. Most have never been published and can be seen only by visiting the county courthouses at the locations given in the notes.

Banks, Henry, Papers, 1781–1817. Virginia Historical Society, Richmond.

Barry, William Taylor, Papers, 1785–1835. Filson Club Historical Society, Louisville, KY.

Biddle, Nicholas, Papers, 1681–1933. Library of Congress, Washington, DC.

Blair and Lee Papers, 1764–1946. Rare Books and Special Collections, Princeton University Library.

Breckinridge Family Papers, 1752–1904. Library of Congress, Washington, DC.

Breckinridge Family Papers, 1740–1902. Alderman Library, University of Virginia, Charlottesville.

Breckinridge, John, Papers, 1760–1806. Library of Congress, Washington, DC.

Brown-Ewell Family Papers, 1781–1984. Filson Club Historical Society, Louisville, KY.

Campbell Family Papers, 1731–1969. Rare Book, Manuscripts, and Special Collections Library, Duke University, Durham, NC.

Clay, Sidney P., Collection, 1783–1846. Rare Books and Special Collections, Princeton University Library.

Clay and Overton Papers, 1747–1894. Claybrooke Collection. Tennessee State Library and Archives.

Clifford Family Papers, 1727–1832. Historical Society of Pennsylvania, Philadelphia.

Coffee, John, Papers, 1770–1917. Dyas Collection. Tennessee State Library and Archives, Nashville.

Cole, Whitefoord R., Papers, 1818–1951. Tennessee State Library and Archives, Nashville.

Dickinson, Jacob McGavock, Papers, 1851–1928. Tennessee State Library and Archives, Nashville.

Donelson, Andrew Jackson, Papers, 1779–1943. Library of Congress, Washington, DC.

Draper, Lyman Copeland, Manuscripts. Wisconsin State Historical Society, Madison.

Durrett, Reuben T., Collection. University of Chicago Library.

Edwards, Ninian, Papers, 1798–1833. Chicago Historical Society.

Grundy, Felix, Papers. Kentucky Historical Society, Frankfort.

Grundy, Felix, Papers. Virginia Historical Society, Richmond.

Grundy, Felix, Papers, 1807–1899. Southern Historical Collection. Wilson Library, University of North Carolina–Chapel Hill.

Grundy, Felix, Papers, 1820–1840. Tennessee State Library and Archives, Nashville.

Grundy, Felix, Papers, 1822–c. 1840. Library of Congress, Washington, DC.

Harding-Jackson Papers, 1819–1911. Tennessee State Library and Archives, Nashville.

Hubbard, David, Papers, 1807–1871. Tennessee State Library and Archives, Nashville.

Innes, Harry Papers, 1752–1816. Library of Congress, Washington, DC.

Jackson, Andrew, Papers, 1775–1860. Library of Congress, Washington, DC.

Jefferson, Thomas, Papers, 1606–1902. Library of Congress, Washington, DC.

Johnson, Cave, Papers, 1833–1948. Library of Congress, Washington, DC.

Jones, Calvin, Papers, 1783–1929. Southern Historical Collection. Wilson Library, University of North Carolina–Chapel Hill.

Jones, Wallace Alexander, Genealogical Collection. Tennessee State Library and Archives, Nashville.

Lindsley Family Papers, ca. 1600–1940. Tennessee State Library and Archives, Nashville.

Lowndes, William, Papers, 1787–1842. Library of Congress, Washington, DC.

McGavock, Francis, Papers, 1784–1854. Tennessee State Library and Archives, Nashville.

McGavock Family Papers, 1797–1897. Southern Historical Collection. Wilson Library, University of North Carolina–Chapel Hill.

McGavock Papers, 1760–1888. Swem Library, College of William and Mary, Williamsburg, VA.

Munroe, Henry Smith, Papers, 1804–1934. Connecticut Historical Society, Hartford.

Overton, John, Papers. Southern Historical Collection. Wilson Library, University of North Carolina–Chapel Hill.

Overton, John, Papers, 1797–1833. Tennessee State Library and Archives, Nashville.

Polk, James K., Papers, 1795–1849. Library of Congress, Washington, DC.

Polk Family Papers, 1767–1859. Library of Congress, Washington, DC.

Randolph, John, of Roanoke, Papers, 1781–1860. Small Library, University of Virginia, Charlottesville.

Robinson, John, Papers (THS). Tennessee State Library and Archives, Nashville.

Shelby, Isaac P., Papers, 1792–1893. Filson Club Historical Society, Louisville, KY.

Sparrow, W. Keats, Papers. Joyner Library, East Carolina University, Greenville, NC.

Trousdale, William, Papers, 1790–1872. Tennessee State Library and Archives, Nashville.

Trousdale, William, Papers (THS), 1828–1940. Tennessee State Library and Archives, Nashville.

Van Buren, Martin, Papers, 1787–1910. Library of Congress, Washington, DC.

Winchester, James, Papers, 1787–1853. Tennessee State Library and Archives, Nashville.

Woodbury, Levi, Family Papers, 1638–1914. Library of Congress, Washington, DC.

Yandell Family Papers, 1823–1877. Filson Club Historical Society, Louisville, KY.

Published Works, Dissertations, and Theses

Abernethy, Thomas Perkins. "Andrew Jackson and the Rise of Southwestern Democracy." *American Historical Review* 33 (Oct. 1927): 64–77.

———. "The Early Development of Commerce and Banking in Tennessee." *Mississippi Valley Historical Review* 14 (Sept. 1927): 311–25.

———. *From Frontier to Plantation in Tennessee: A Study in Frontier Democracy.* Chapel Hill: University of North Carolina Press, 1932.

———.. "The Origin of the Whig Party in Tennessee." *Mississippi Valley Historical Review* 12 (Mar. 1926): 504–22.

———. *The South in the New Nation, 1789–1819.* Baton Rouge: Louisiana State University Press, 1961.

———. *Three Virginia Frontiers.* Baton Rouge: Louisiana State University Press, 1940.

———. *Western Lands and the American Revolution.* New York: D. Appleton-Century, 1937.

Adams, Henry. *History of the United States During the First Administration of James Madison.* 2 vols. New York: Charles Scribner's Sons.

Adams, John Quincy. *Memoirs of John Quincy Adams Comprising Portions of His Diary from 1795 to 1848.* Edited by Charles Frances Adams. 12 vols. Philadelphia: J. B. Lippincott, 1874–77.

Alexander, Thomas B. "The Presidential Campaign of 1840 in Tennessee." *Tennessee Historical Quarterly* 1 (Mar. 1942): 21–43.

Allen, William B. *A History of Kentucky.* Louisville, KY: Bradley & Gilbert, 1872.

Ammon, Harry. *James Monroe: The Quest for National Identity.* New York: McGraw-Hill, 1971.

Appleby, Joyce. *Inheriting the Revolution: The First Generation of Americans.* Cambridge, MA: Harvard University Press, Belknap, 2000.

Arnow, Harriette Simpson. *Flowering of the Cumberland.* New York: Macmillan, 1963.

———. *Seedtime on the Cumberland.* New York: Macmillan, 1960.

Aron, Stephen. *How the West Was Lost: The Transformation of Kentucky from Daniel Boone to Henry Clay.* Baltimore: Johns Hopkins University Press, 1996.

Asbury, Frances. *The Journals and Letters of Frances Asbury.* Edited by Elmer T. Clark, J. Manning Potts, and Jacob S. Payton. 3 vols. Nashville: Abingdon, 1958.

Atkins, Jonathan. *Parties, Politics, and the Sectional Conflict in Tennessee, 1832–1861.* Knoxville: University of Tennessee Press, 1997.

Ayers, Edward. *Vengeance and Justice: Crime and Punishment in the Nineteenth Century American South.* New York: Oxford University Press, 1984.

Barnhart, John D. *Valley of Democracy: The Frontier versus the Plantation in the Ohio Valley, 1775–1818.* Bloomington: Indiana University Press, 1953.

Barton, Tom K. "Politics and Banking in Republican Kentucky, 1805–1824." PhD diss., University of Wisconsin, 1968.

Baylor, Orval W. "The Career of Felix Grundy, 1777–1840." *Filson Club History Quarterly* 16 (Apr. 1942): 88–110.

———. *John Pope, Kentuckian: His Life and Times, 1770–1845.* Cynthiana, KY: Hobson, 1943.

Beard, William E. "Joseph McMinn, Tennessee's Fourth Governor." *Tennessee Historical Quarterly* 4 (June 1945): 154–66.

Bemis, Samuel Flagg. *John Quincy Adams and the Union.* New York: Knopf, 1956.

Benton, Thomas Hart. *Thirty Years' View.* 2 vols. New York: D. Appleton, 1854–56.

Bergeron, Paul H. *Antebellum Politics in Tennessee.* Lexington: University Press of Kentucky, 1982.

———. "Tennessee's Response to the Nullification Crisis." *Journal of Southern History* 39 (Feb. 1973): 23–44.

Biddle, Nicholas. *The Correspondence of Nicholas Biddle Dealing with National Affairs, 1807–1844.* Edited by Reginald C. McGrane. Boston: Houghton & Mifflin, 1919.

Birney, William. *James G. Birney and His Times.* New York: Appleton, 1890.

Blount, John Gray. *John Gray Blount Papers.* Edited by David T. Morgan. 4 vols. Raleigh: North Carolina Department of Cultural Resources, 1952–82.

Bodley, Temple, and Samuel Wilson. *A History of Kentucky.* 3 vols. Chicago: S. J. Clarke, 1928.

Bowers, Claude G. *The Party Battles of the Jackson Period.* Cambridge, MA: Riverside, 1923.

Brands, H. W. *Andrew Jackson: His Life and Times.* New York: Doubleday, 2005.

Brant, Irving. *James Madison: The President, 1809–1812.* Indianapolis: Bobbs-Merrill, 1956.

———. *James Madison: Commander in Chief, 1812–1836.* Indianapolis: Bobbs-Merrill, 1961.

Brown, Norman D. *Daniel Webster and the Politics of Availability.* Athens: University of Georgia Press, 1969.

Brown, Roger. *The Republic in Peril: 1812.* New York: Columbia University Press, 1964.

Brown, William H. "Felix Grundy." In *Portrait Gallery of Distinguished Citizens, with biographical sketches, and facsimiles of original letters,* 97. Hartford, CT: E. B. & E. C. Kellogg, 1845.

Bruce, Dickson D., Jr. *Violence and Culture in the Antebellum South.* Austin: University of Texas Press, 1979.

Bruce, William Cabell. *John Randolph of Roanoke, 1773–1833.* 2 vols. New York: G. P. Putnam's & Sons, 1922.

Bucy, Carole Stanford. "Quiet Revolutionaries: The Grundy Women and the Beginnings of Women's Voluntary Associations in Tennessee." *Tennessee Historical Quarterly* 54 (Spring 1995): 40–53.

Buel, Richard, Jr. *America on the Brink: How the Political Struggle over the War of 1812 Almost Destroyed the Young Republic.* New York: Palgrave Macmillan, 2005.

Buell, Augustus. *History of Andrew Jackson.* 2 vols. New York: C. Scribner's Sons, 1904.

Bumgarner, John Reed. *Sarah Childress Polk: A Biography of the Remarkable First Lady.* Jefferson, NC: McFarland, 1997.

Burke, Pauline Wilcox. *Emily Donelson of Tennessee.* 2 vols. Richmond, VA: Garrett & Massie, 1941.

Burstein, Andrew. *America's Jubilee.* New York: Knopf, 2001.

———. *The Passions of Andrew Jackson.* New York: Knopf, 2003.

Butler, Mann. *A History of the Commonwealth of Kentucky.* Louisville, KY: Wilcox, Dickerman, 1834.

Caldwell, Joshua W. *Sketches of the Bench and Bar of Tennessee.* Knoxville: Odgen Brothers, 1898.

Calhoun, John C. *The Papers of John C. Calhoun.* Edited by W. Edwin Hemphill and Clyde N. Wilson. 28 vols. Columbia: University of South Carolina Press, 1959–2003.

Capps, Randall. *The Rowan Story: From Federal Hill to My Old Kentucky Home.* Bowling Green, KY: Homestead, 1976.

Carr, Albert. *The Coming of War: An Account of the Remarkable Events Leading to the War of 1812*. Garden City, NY: Doubleday, 1960.

Carr, John. *Early Times in Middle Tennessee*. Nashville: Stevenson & Owen, 1857.

Catterall, Ralph. *The Second Bank of the United States*. Chicago: University of Chicago Press, 1903.

Chambers, William Nisbet. *Old Bullion Benton, Senator from the New West: Thomas Hart Benton, 1782–1858*. Boston: Little, Brown, 1956.

Cheatham, Mark R. *Old Hickory's Nephew: The Political and Private Struggles of Andrew Jackson Donelson*. Baton Rouge: Louisiana State University Press, 2007.

Chinn, George Morgan. *Kentucky, Settlement, and Statehood, 1750–1800*. Frankfort: Kentucky Historical Society, 1975.

Clark, Patricia. "A. O. Nicholson of Tennessee: Editor, Statesman and Jurist." MA thesis, University of Tennessee, 1965.

Clay, Henry. *The Papers of Henry Clay*. Edited by James F. Hopkins et al. 10 vols. and supplement. Lexington: University of Kentucky Press, 1959–72.

Clayton, W. W. *History of Davidson County, Tennessee*. Philadelphia: Lewis, 1880.

Cole, Donald B. *Martin Van Buren and the American Political System*. Princeton, NJ: Princeton University Press, 1984.

———. *The Presidency of Andrew Jackson*. Lawrence: University Press of Kansas, 1993.

Coleman, Mrs. Chapman, ed. *The Life of John J. Crittenden, with Selections from His Correspondence and Speeches*. Philadelphia: J. B. Lippincott, 1873.

Coles, Harry. *The War of 1812*. Chicago: University of Chicago Press, 1965.

Collins, Lewis, and Richard H. Collins. *History of Kentucky*. 2 vols. Covington, KY: Collins, 1882.

Colyar, A. S. *Life and Times of Andrew Jackson*. 2 vols. Nashville: Marshall & Bruce, 1904.

Comegys, Joseph P. *Memoir of John M. Clayton*. Wilmington: Historical Society of Delaware, 1882.

Cooper, William J. *The South and the Politics of Slavery, 1828–1856*. Baton Rouge: Louisiana State University Press, 1978.

Cotterill, R. S. *History of Pioneer Kentucky*. Cincinnati: Johnson & Hardin, 1917.

Coward, Joan Wells. *Kentucky in the New Republic: The Process of Constitution Making*. Lexington: University Press of Kentucky, 1979.

Crabb, Alfred Leland. *Nashville: Personality of a City*. Indianapolis: Bobbs-Merrill, 1960.

Crew, H. W. *History of Nashville, Tennessee*. Nashville: Methodist Episcopal Church, South, 1890.

Crockett, David. *Life of Colonel David Crockett*. Philadelphia: W. E. Evans, 1859.

Dangerfield, George. *The Awakening of American Nationalism, 1815–1828*. New York: HarperCollins, 1965.

———. *The Era of Good Feelings*. New York: Harcourt, Brace, 1952.

Drake, Daniel. *Pioneer Life in Kentucky: 1785–1800*. New York: Henry Schuman, 1948.

Driver, Carl S. *John Sevier: Pioneer of the Old Southwest*. Chapel Hill: University of North Carolina Press, 1932.

Duckett, Alvin. *John Forsyth: Political Tactician*. Athens: University of Georgia Press, 1962.

Dupre, Huntley. "The Political Ideas of George Nicholas." *Kentucky State Historical Society Register* 39 (July 1941): 201–23.

Durham, Walter T. *Balie Peyton of Tennessee*. Franklin, TN: Hillsboro, 2004.

———. *James Winchester, Tennessee Pioneer*. Gallatin, TN: Sumner County Library Board, 1979.

———. *Josephus Conn Guild and Rose Mont*. Franklin, TN: Hillsboro, 2002.

———. *Old Sumner: A History of Sumner County, Tennessee from 1805 to 1861*. Gallatin, TN: Sumner County Library Board, 1972.

Dusinberre, William. *Slavemaster President: The Double Career of James Polk*. New York: Oxford University Press, 2003.

Earle, Jonathan H. *Jacksonian Antislavery and the Politics of Free Soil, 1824–1851*. Chapel Hill: University of North Carolina Press, 2004.

Eaton, John Henry. *The Life of Andrew Jackson*. Philadelphia: Jesper Harding, 1824.

Edwards, Ninian. *The Edwards Papers; Being a Portion of the Collection of the Letters, Papers, and Manuscripts of Ninian Edwards, Chief Justice of the Court of Appeals of Kentucky; First and Only Governor of Illinois Territory; One of the First Two United States Senators*. Edited by E. B. Washburne. Chicago: Fergus, 1884.

Ellis, Richard E. *The Jeffersonian Crisis: Courts and Politics in the Young Republic*. New York: Oxford University Press, 1971.

———. *The Union at Risk: Jacksonian Democracy, States' Rights, and the Nullification Crisis*. New York: Oxford University Press, 1987.

Eslinger, Ellen. *Citizens of Zion: The Social Origins of Camp Meeting Revivalism*. Knoxville: University of Tennessee Press, 1999.

Ewing, Heather. *The Lost World of James Smithson: Science, Revolution, and the Birth of the Smithsonian*. New York: Bloomsbury, 2007.

Faragher, John Mack. *Daniel Boone: The Life and Legend of an American Pioneer*. New York: Holt, 1992.

Fehrenbacher, Don E. *The Slaveholding Republic*. New York: Oxford University Press, 2001.

Feller, Daniel. *The Public Lands in Jacksonian Politics*. Madison: University of Wisconsin Press, 1984.

Finger, John R. *Tennessee Frontiers: Three Regions in Transition*. Bloomington: Indiana University Press, 2001.

Fischer, David Hackett. *Albion's Seed: Four British Folkways in America*. New York: Oxford University Press, 1989.

Fischer, David Hackett, and James C. Kelly. *Bound Away: Virginia and the Westward Movement*. Charlottesville: University of Virginia Press, 2000.

Fitz, Caitlin A. "The Tennessee Antislavery Movement and the Market Revolution, 1815–1835." *Civil War History* 42 (2006): 5–40.

Fladeland, Betty. *James Gillespie Birney: Slaveholder to Abolitionist*. Ithaca, NY: Cornell University Press, 1955.

Folmsbee, Stanley John. *Sectionalism and Internal Improvements in Tennessee, 1796–1845*. Knoxville, TN: East Tennessee Historical Society, 1939.

Folsom, Burton W., II. "The Politics of Elites: Prominence and Party in Davidson County, Tennessee, 1835–1861." *Journal of Southern History* 39 (Aug. 1973): 359–78.

Foote, Henry S. *The Bench and Bar of the South and Southwest*. St. Louis: Soule, Thomas & Wentworth, 1876.

———. *Casket of Reminiscences*. Washington, DC: Chronicle, 1874.

Freehling, William W. *Prelude to Civil War: The Nullification Movement in South Carolina, 1816–1836*. New York: Harper and Row, 1966.

———. *The Road to Disunion: Secessionists at Bay, 1776–1854*. New York: Oxford University Press, 1990.

French, Benjamin Brown. *Witness to the Young Republic: A Yankee's Journal, 1828–1870*. Edited by Donald B. Cole and John J. McDonough. Hanover, NH: University Press of New England, 1989.

Friend, Craig T. *Along the Maysville Road: The Early American Republic in the Trans-Appalachian West*. Knoxville: University of Tennessee Press, 2005.

———, ed. *The Buzzel about Kentuck: Settling the Promised Land*. Lexington: University Press of Kentucky, 1999.

Garland, Hugh. *The Life of John Randolph of Roanoke*. 2 vols. New York: Appleton, 1856.

Garraty, John Arthur. *Silas Wright*. New York: Columbia University Press, 1949.

Goodstein, Anita Shafer. *Nashville, 1780–1860: From Frontier to City*. Gainesville: University Press of Florida, 1989.

Guild, Josephus Conn. *Old Times in Tennessee*. Nashville: Tavel, Eastman & Howell, 1878.

Gunderson, Robert Gray. *The Log-Cabin Campaign*. Lexington: University of Kentucky Press, 1957.

Hamer, Phillip M. *Tennessee: A History, 1673–1932*. 4 vols. New York: American Historical Society, 1933.

Hammon, Neal O. "Early Louisville and the Beargrass Stations." *Filson Club History Quarterly* 52 (Apr. 1978): 147–65.

———. "Kentucky Pioneer Forts and Stations." *Filson History Quarterly* 76 (Fall 2002): 523–86.

Hammond, Bray. *Banks and Politics in America: From the Revolution to the Civil War*. Princeton, NJ: Princeton University Press, 1957.

Harrison, Lowell H. *John Breckinridge: Jeffersonian Republican.* Louisville, KY: Filson Club, 1969.

———. "John Breckinridge and the Kentucky Constitution of 1799." *Kentucky State Historical Society Register* 57 (July 1959): 209–33.

———. *Kentucky's Road to Statehood.* Lexington: University Press of Kentucky, 1992.

Hatcher, William B. *Edward Livingston, Jeffersonian Republican and Jacksonian Democrat.* Baton Rouge: Louisiana State University Press, 1940.

Heiskell, Samuel G. *Andrew Jackson and Early Tennessee History.* 3 vols. Nashville: Ambrose, 1920–21.

Hening, William W., comp. *Statutes at Large: Being a Collection of all the Laws of Virginia, 1619–1792.* 13 vols. Richmond, VA, 1809–23.

Herring, James, and James B. Longacre. "Felix Grundy." In *The National Portrait Gallery of Distinguished Americans,* 3: 361–70. New York: Hermon Bancroft, 1836.

Hickey, Donald. *The War of 1812: A Forgotten Conflict.* Urbana: University of Illinois Press, 1989.

Holt, Michael F. *The Rise and Fall of the American Whig Party: Jacksonian Politics and the Onset of the Civil War.* New York: Oxford University Press, 1999.

Horsman, Reginald. *The Causes of the War of 1812.* Philadelphia: University of Pennsylvania Press, 1962.

Houston, Sam. *Autobiography of Sam Houston.* Edited by Donald Day and Harry Herbert Ullom. Norman: University of Oklahoma Press, 1954.

———. *The Writings of Sam Houston, 1813–1863.* Edited by Amelia W. Williams and Eugene C. Barber. 8 vols. Austin: University of Texas Press, 1938–43.

Howe, Daniel Walker. *What Hath God Wrought: The Transformation of America, 1815–1848.* New York: Oxford University Press, 2007.

Howell, R. B. C. "Felix Grundy." *Tennessee Law Review* 16 (Apr. 1941): 828–42.

Ireland, Robert M. *The County Courts in Antebellum Kentucky.* Lexington: University Press of Kentucky, 1972.

Jackson, Andrew. *Correspondence of Andrew Jackson.* Edited by John Spencer Bassett. 7 vols. Washington, DC: Carnegie Institute of Washington, 1926–35.

———. *The Legal Papers of Andrew Jackson.* Edited by James W. Ely Jr. and Theodore Brown Jr. Knoxville: University of Tennessee Press, 1987.

———. *The Papers of Andrew Jackson.* Edited by Harold D. Moser et al. 7 vols. to date. Knoxville: University of Tennessee Press, 1980–.

James, Marquis. *Andrew Jackson.* 2 vols. Indianapolis: Bobbs-Merrill, 1933–37.

———. *The Raven: The Life Story of Sam Houston.* Indianapolis: Bobbs-Merrill, 1929.

Jefferson, Thomas. *The Papers of Thomas Jefferson.* Edited by Julian P. Boyd et al. 36 vols. to date. Princeton, NJ: Princeton University Press, 1950–.

Jenkins, John S. *The Life of James Knox Polk, Late President of the United States.* Auburn, NY: Alden, 1850.

Jillson, Willard Rouse. *The Kentucky Land Grants*. Louisville, KY: Standard Printing, 1925.

———. *Old Kentucky Entries and Deeds*. Louisville, KY: Standard Printing, 1926.

Jones, Howard. *Mutiny on the Amistad*. New York: Oxford University Press, 1987.

Jordan, Weymouth T. *George Washington Campbell of Tennessee: Western Statesman*. Tallahassee: Florida State University Press, 1955.

Kanon, Tom. "James Madison, Felix Grundy, and the Devil: A Western War Hawk in Congress." *Filson History Quarterly* 75 (Fall 2001): 433–68.

———. "The Kidnapping of Martha Crawley and Settler-Indian Relations prior to the War of 1812." *Tennessee Historical Quarterly* 64 (Spring 2005): 2–23.

Kendall, Amos. *The Autobiography of Amos Kendall*. Edited by William Stickney. Boston: Lee & Shepard, 1872.

Kerr, Charles, et al., eds. *History of Kentucky*. 5 vols. New York: American Historical Society, 1922.

Ketcham, Ralph. *James Madison: A Biography*. New York: Macmillan, 1971.

Kirk, Russell. *John Randolph of Roanoke: A Study in American Thought*. Chicago: University of Chicago Press, 1951.

Kirwan, Albert. *John J. Crittenden: The Struggle for the Union*. Lexington: University Press of Kentucky, 1962.

Latimer, Jon. *1812: War with America*. Cambridge, MA: Harvard University Press, Belknap Press, 2007.

Laughlin, Samuel H. "Diaries of S. H. Laughlin of Tennessee, 1840, 1843." Edited by St. George L. Sioussat. *Tennessee Historical Magazine* 2 (Mar. 1916): 43–85.

———. "Sketches of Notable Men." *Tennessee Historical Magazine* 4 (Mar. 1918): 73–78.

Levin, H., ed. *The Lawyers and Lawmakers of Kentucky*. 1897. Reprint, Easley, SC: Southern Historical Press, 1982.

Little, Lucius. *Ben Hardin*. Louisville, KY: Courier-Journal Job Printing, 1887.

Livingston, John. "Biographical Letter from John Catron." In *Portraits of Eminent Americans Now Living*, 73–80. New York: R. Craighead, 1854.

Louis-Philippe. *Diary of My Travels in America*. New York: Delacorte, 1977.

Macdonald-Millar, Donald. "The Grundy-Polk Houses, Nashville." *Tennessee Historical Quarterly* 25 (Fall 1966): 281–86.

Mahon, John K. *The War of 1812*. Gainesville: University Press of Florida, 1972.

Mangum, Willie Persons. *The Papers of Willie Persons Mangum*. Edited by Henry Thomas Shanks. 5 vols. Raleigh, NC: State Department of Archives and History, 1950–56.

March, Charles W. *Reminiscences of Congress*. New York: Baker & Scribner, 1850.

Marshall, Humphrey. *The History of Kentucky: Exhibiting an Account of the Modern Discovery, Settlement, Progressive Improvement, Civil and Military Transactions, and the Present State of the Country*. 2 vols. Frankfort, KY: George S. Robinson, 1824.

Marszalek, John F. *The Petticoat Affair.* New York: Free Press, 1997.

Martineau, Harriet. *Retrospect of Western Travel.* 2 vols. London: Saunders & Otley, 1838.

Mason, Matthew. *Slavery and Politics in the Early American Republic.* Chapel Hill: University of North Carolina Press, 2006.

Masterson, William. *William Blount.* Baton Rouge: Louisiana State University Press, 1954.

Mayer, Henry. *All on Fire: William Lloyd Garrison and the Abolition of Slavery.* New York: St. Martin's, 1998.

Mayo, Bernard. *Henry Clay.* Boston: Houghton Mifflin, 1937.

McAfee, Robert B. "The Life and Times of Robert B. McAfee and His Family and Connections." *Kentucky State Historical Society Register* 25 (1927): 5–37, 111–43, 215–37.

McCaughey, Robert A. *Josiah Quincy, 1772–1864: The Last Federalist.* Cambridge, MA: Harvard University Press, 1974.

McCormac, Eugene Irving. *James K. Polk: A Political Biography.* Berkeley: University of California Press, 1922.

McCormick, Richard P. *The Second American Party System: Party Formation in the Jacksonian Era.* Chapel Hill: University of North Carolina Press, 1966.

McDougall, Walter A. *Throes of Democracy: The American Civil War Era, 1829–1877.* New York: HarperCollins, 2008.

McFerrin, John B. *History of Methodism in Tennessee.* Nashville: Methodist Episcopal Church, South, 1886.

McGavock, Randal W. *Pen and Sword: The Life and Journals of Randal W. McGavock.* Edited by Herschel Gower and Jack Allen. Nashville: Tennessee Historical Commission, 1959.

McKellar, Kenneth. *Tennessee Senators as Seen by One of their Successors.* Kingport, TN: Southern Publishers, 1942.

McMinn, Joseph. "Letters and Papers of Governor Jos. McMinn." *American Historical Magazine* 5 (Jan. 1900): 48–66.

Meacham, Jon. *American Lion: Andrew Jackson in the White House.* New York: Random House, 2008.

Meyer, Leland W. *The Life and Times of Colonel Richard M. Johnson of Kentucky.* New York: Columbia University Press, 1932.

Miller, William Lee. *Arguing about Slavery: The Great Battle in the United States Congress.* New York: Knopf, 1996.

Mooney, Chase C. *William H. Crawford, 1772–1834.* Lexington: University Press of Kentucky, 1974.

Moore, Powell. "James K. Polk and Tennessee Politics, 1839–1841." *East Tennessee Historical Society, Publications* 9 (1937): 31–52.

———. "The Political Background of the Revolt against Jackson in Tennessee." *East Tennessee Historical Society, Publications* 4 (1932): 45–66.

———. "The Revolt against Jackson in Tennessee." *Journal of Southern History* 2 (Aug. 1936): 335–59.

Munroe, John A. *Louis McLane: Federalist and Jacksonian.* New Brunswick, NJ: Rutgers University Press, 1973.

Murphey, Archibald D. *Papers of Archibald D. Murphey.* Edited by William Henry Hoyt. 2 vols. Raleigh: North Carolina Historical Commission, 1914.

Nelson, Anson, and Fanny Nelson. *Memorials of Sarah Childress Polk: Wife of the Eleventh President of the United States.* New York: Anson D. Randolph, 1892.

Nicholson, James C. *Grundy County.* Memphis: Memphis State University Press, 1982.

Niven, John. *John C. Calhoun and the Price of Union: A Biography.* Baton Rouge: Louisiana State University Press, 1988.

———. *Martin Van Buren: The Romantic Age of American Politics.* New York: Oxford University Press, 1983.

Oakes, James. *The Ruling Race: A History of American Slaveholders.* New York: Knopf, 1982.

Parks, Joseph Howard. *Felix Grundy, Champion of Democracy.* Baton Rouge: Louisiana State University Press, 1940.

———. "Felix Grundy and the Depression of 1819 in Tennessee." *East Tennessee Historical Society Publications* 10 (1938): 19–43.

———. *John Bell of Tennessee.* Baton Rouge: Louisiana State University Press, 1950.

Parton, James. *Life of Andrew Jackson.* 3 vols. New York: Mason Brothers, 1859–60.

Peterson, Merrill D. *The Great Triumvirate: Webster, Clay, and Calhoun.* New York: Oxford University Press, 1987.

———. *Olive Branch and Sword: The Compromise of 1833.* Baton Rouge: Louisiana State University Press, 1982.

Phelan, James. *History of Tennessee.* Boston: Houghton Mifflin, 1888.

"Political Portraits with Pen and Pencil, Felix Grundy." *U.S. Magazine and Democratic Review* 3 (Oct. 1838): 161–70.

Polk, James K. *Correspondence of James K. Polk.* Edited by Herbert Weaver, Paul Bergeron, and Wayne Cutler. 10 vols. to date. Nashville: Vanderbilt University Press; Knoxville: University of Tennessee Press, 1969–.

Pratt, Julius. *Expansionists of 1812.* New York: Macmillan, 1925.

Purviance, Levi. *The Biography of Elder David Purviance, with His Memoirs: Containing His Views on Baptism, the Divinity of Christ, and the Atonement Written by Himself.* Dayton, OH: Published for the author by B. F. and G. W. Ellis, 1848.

Putnam, A. W. *History of Middle Tennessee; or, Life and Times of General James Robertson.* Nashville: Southern Methodist Publishing House, 1859.

Quincy, Edmund. *Life of Josiah Quincy of Massachusetts.* Boston: Ticknor & Fields, 1867.

Ramage, James A. "The Green River Pioneers: Squatters, Soldiers and Speculators." *Kentucky State Historical Society Register* 75 (July 1977): 171–90.

Ratner, Lorman A. *Andrew Jackson and His Tennessee Lieutenants.* Westport, CT: Greenwood, 1997.

Ravenel, Mrs. St. Julien. *Life and Times of William Lowndes of South Carolina, 1782–1822.* Boston: Houghton Mifflin, 1901.

Ray, Kristofer. *Middle Tennessee, 1775–1825: Progress and Popular Democracy on the Southwestern Frontier.* Knoxville: University of Tennessee Press, 2007.

Remini, Robert V. *Andrew Jackson and His Indian Wars.* New York: Viking, 2001.

———. *Andrew Jackson and the Bank War.* New York: Norton, 1967.

———. *Andrew Jackson and the Course of American Democracy, 1833–1845.* New York: Harper & Row, 1984.

———. *Andrew Jackson and the Course of American Empire, 1767–1821.* New York: Harper & Row, 1977.

———. *Andrew Jackson and the Course of American Freedom, 1822–1832.* New York: Harper & Row, 1981.

———. *Daniel Webster: The Man and His Time.* New York: Norton, 1997.

———. *Henry Clay: Statesman for the Union.* New York: Norton, 1991.

———. *Martin Van Buren and the Making of the Democratic Party.* New York: Columbia University Press, 1959.

Rippy, J. Fred. *Joel R. Poinsett, Versatile American.* Durham, NC: Duke University Press, 1935.

Risjord, Norman K. *The Old Republicans: Southern Conservatism in the Age of Jefferson.* New York: Columbia University Press, 1965.

Rohrbough, Malcolm J. *The Trans-Appalachian Frontier: People, Societies, and Institutions, 1775–1850.* New York: Oxford University Press, 1978.

Rorabaugh, W. J. *The Alcoholic Republic: An American Tradition.* New York: Oxford University Press, 1979.

Rothbard, Murray. *The Panic of 1819: Reactions and Policies.* New York: Columbia University Press, 1962.

Royalty, Dale Maurice. "Banking, Politics and the Commonwealth of Kentucky, 1800–1825." PhD diss., University of Kentucky, 1971.

Rutland, Robert Allen. *The Presidency of James Madison.* Lawrence: University Press of Kansas, 1990.

Satterfield, Robert Beeler. *Andrew Jackson Donelson: Jackson's Confidant and Political Heir.* Bowling Green, KY: Hickory Tales, 2000.

Saunders, Col. James Edmonds. *Early Settlers of Alabama.* New Orleans: L. Graham & Son, 1899.

Schlesinger, Arthur M., Jr. *The Age of Jackson.* Boston: Little, Brown, 1945.

Schweikart, Larry. *Banking in the American South from the Age of Jackson to Recon-struction*. Baton Rouge: Louisiana State University Press, 1987.

Seigenthaler, John. *James K. Polk*. New York: Times Books, 2004.

Sellers, Charles G., Jr. "Banking and Politics in Jackson's Tennessee, 1817–1827." *Mississippi Valley Historical Review* 41 (June 1954): 61–84.

———. "Jackson Men with Feet of Clay." *American Historical Review* 62 (Apr. 1957): 537–51.

———. *James K. Polk: Jacksonian, 1795–1843*. Princeton, NJ: Princeton University Press, 1957.

———. "James K. Polk's Political Apprenticeship." *East Tennessee Historical Society, Publications* 25 (1953): 37–53.

———. *The Market Revolution: Jacksonian America, 1815–1846*. New York: Oxford University Press, 1991.

Shackford, James Atkins. *David Crockett: The Man and The Legend*. Chapel Hill: University of North Carolina Press, 1956.

Sharp, James Roger. *The Jacksonians versus the Banks*. New York: Columbia University Press, 1970.

Sioussat, St. George L. "Some Phases of Tennessee Politics in the Jackson Period." *American Historical Review* 14 (Oct. 1908): 51–69.

Spencer, Ivor Debenham. *The Victor and the Spoils: A Life of William L. Marcy*. Providence, RI: Brown University Press, 1959.

Stagg, J. C. A. *Mr. Madison's War: Politics, Diplomacy, and Warfare in the Early American Republic, 1783–1830*. Princeton, NJ: Princeton University Press, 1983.

Staples, Charles R. *The History of Pioneer Lexington (Kentucky), 1779–1806*. Lexington: Transylvania, 1939.

Sydnor, Charles S. *The Development of Southern Sectionalism, 1819–1848*. Baton Rouge: Louisiana State University Press, 1948.

Tachau, Mary K. Bonsteel. *Federal Courts in the Early Republic: Kentucky, 1789–1816*. Princeton, NJ: Princeton University Press, 1978.

Taggart, Samuel. "Letters of Samuel Taggart: Representative in Congress, 1803–1814." Edited by George H. Haynes. *Proceedings of the American Antiquarian Society*, n.s., 33 (1923): 113–226, 297–438.

Taul, Micah. "Memoirs of Micah Taul." *Kentucky State Historical Society Register* 27 (Jan., May, Sept. 1929): 343–80, 494–517, 601–27.

Temin, Peter. *The Jacksonian Economy*. New York: Norton, 1969.

Thomas, Miss Jane. *Old Days in Nashville*. Nashville: Methodist Episcopal Church, South, 1897.

Tocqueville, Alexis de. *Democracy in America*. Edited by Phillips Bradley. 2 vols. New York: Knopf, 1945.

Tyler, Lyon G., ed. *The Letters and Times of the Tylers*. 3 vols. Richmond, VA: Whittet & Shepperson, 1884.

U.S. Congress. *Annals of the Congress of the United States, 1789–1824*. 42 vols. Washington, DC, 1834–56.

———. *Congressional Globe, Containing the Debates and Proceedings, 1833–1873*. 109 vols. Washington, DC, 1834–73.

———. *Register of Debates in Congress*. 29 vols. Washington, DC, 1825–37.

Van Arsdall, Mai Flournoy van Deren. "The Springs at Harrodsburg." *Kentucky State Historical Society Register* 61 (1963): 300–328.

Van Buren, Martin. *The Autobiography of Martin Van Buren*. Vol. 2 of *Annual Report of the American Historical Association for the Year 1918*. Edited by John C. Fitzpatrick. Washington, DC: Government Printing Office, 1920.

Van Deusen, Glyndon G. *The Life of Henry Clay*. Boston: Little, Brown, 1937.

Watlington, Patricia. "Discontent in Frontier Kentucky." *Kentucky State Historical Society Register* 65 (Apr. 1967): 77–93.

———. *The Partisan Spirit: Kentucky Politics, 1779–1792*. Chapel Hill: University of North Carolina Press, 1972.

Watts, Steven. *The Republic Reborn: War and the Making of Liberal America, 1790–1820*. Baltimore: Johns Hopkins University Press, 1987.

Webster, Daniel. *The Papers of Daniel Webster; Correspondence*. Edited by Charles M. Wiltse and Harold Moser. 8 vols. Hanover, NH: University Press of New England, 1974.

White, Hugh Lawson. *A Memoir of Hugh Lawson White, with Selections from His Speeches and Correspondence*. Edited by Nancy N. Scott. Philadelphia: J. B. Lippincott, 1856.

White, Leonard D. *The Jacksonians: A Study in Administrative History, 1829–1861*. New York: Macmillan, 1954.

White, Richard. *The Middle Ground: Indians, Empires, and Republics in the Great Lakes Region, 1650–1815*. New York: Cambridge University Press, 1991.

White, Robert H., ed. *Messages of the Governors of Tennessee*. 8 vols. Nashville: Tennessee Historical Commission, 1952–72.

Wilburn, Jean Alexander. *Biddle's Bank: The Crucial Years*. New York: Columbia University Press, 1967.

Wilentz, Sean. *Andrew Jackson*. New York: Times Books, 2005.

———. *The Rise of American Democracy: Jefferson to Lincoln*. New York: Norton, 2005.

Williams, John Hoyt. *Sam Houston*. New York: Simon & Schuster, 1993.

Williams, Samuel Cole. *Beginnings of West Tennessee*. Johnson City, TN: Watauga, 1930.

Wills, Ridley, II. *The History of Belle Meade: Mansion, Plantation, and Stud*. Nashville: Vanderbilt University Press, 1991.

Wilson, Major L. *The Presidency of Martin Van Buren*. Lawrence: University Press of Kansas, 1984.

Wiltse, Charles M. *John C. Calhoun.* 3 vols. Indianapolis: Bobbs Merrill, 1944–51.

Windrow, John Edwin. *John Berrien Lindsley.* Chapel Hill: University of North Carolina Press, 1938.

Wisehart, M. K. *Sam Houston, American Giant.* New York: Van Rees, 1962.

Wood, Gordon S. *Creation of the American Republic, 1776–1787.* Chapel Hill: University of North Carolina Press, 1969.

———. *The Purpose of the Past.* New York: Penguin, 2008.

———. *The Radicalism of the American Revolution.* New York: Knopf, 1992.

———. *Revolutionary Characters: What Made the Founders Different.* New York: Penguin, 2006.

Wyatt-Brown, Bertram. *Southern Honor: Ethics and Behavior in the Old South.* New York: Oxford University Press, 1982.

Young, Bennett H. *History and Texts of the Three Constitutions of Kentucky.* Louisville, KY: Courier-Journal Job Printing, 1890.

INDEX

Banking, *continued*
57–59, 62–72, 145–47, 186, 264, 281*n*21,
282*n*24; national banking generally, 71, 112,
191, 227, 249, 252, 256; and Polk, 144, 188,
229, 314*n*11, 316*n*31; private banking, 169;
proliferation of state banks, 235, 238; state
bank in Kentucky, 69, 70, 146, 147, 186,
188, 234; state bank of Tennessee, 141–47,
158, 186, 188, 234; in Tennessee, 71, 131–35,
140–47, 158, 159, 169, 175–76, 186, 188, 264,
295*n*3, 296*n*10; and Van Buren, 220, 238,
240; and White, 132, 177, 188, 316*n*37. *See
also* Second Bank of the United States
Banks, Henry, 37–38
Baptists, 57
Bard, William, 271*n*15
Bardstown, Ky., 22–23, 34, 38, 53, 56–57, 74,
280*n*2
Bardstown Pleiades, 280*n*2, 291*n*5
Barrell, Samuel, 218–20, 223, 235, 311*n*9, 311–
12*nn*12–14
Barrow, M., 142
Barry, William T., 174, 184, 186, 202
Bass, John M.: Arkansas land owned by, 217,
222; as executor of FG's will, 260; FG's
business relationship with generally, 169;
and FG's dying, 260; and FG's land specu-
lation in Tennessee, 312*n*14; land owned by,
260; marriage of, 173; and Union Bank of
Tennessee, 234–35, 253
Bass, Peter, 173
Bayard, James, 111
Bell, John: and banking, 230; candidacy of,
for U.S. Senate (1832), 213; as Cumberland
College trustee, 299*n*26; election of, to
U.S. Congress (1827), 165, 171, 178; and Indian Removal Act, 185; Jackson's relationship with, 226; as lawyer, 171; Overton on,
178–79; as Speaker of the House, 229–30;
and Tennessee elections of 1837, 236, 237;
and Whig Party, 229–32, 248; and White
candidacy for presidency, 231
Bennett, Charles L., 123–24, 293*n*7
Benton, Thomas Hart: Clay's relationship
with, 285*n*13; and FG, 85, 88, 300*n*15; and

Force Bill, 205; and independent-Treasury
bill, 250; and Jackson's presidential candidacy, 160, 161, 299*n*8; and land policy, 192,
239; as lawyer, 86–87; as orator, 125, 191,
193; personality of, 191, 306*n*2; on slavery,
193; in U.S. Senate, 183, 190–91, 285*n*13;
and Webster's rejection of nullification, 193
Bergeron, Paul H., 308*n*36
Berrien, John, 202
Berry family, 18
Bibb, George: Clay's defeat of, for U.S. Senate, 72; Crittenden as law student of, 138;
death of, 263; and FG, 291*n*5, 302*n*15; and
Force Bill, 205; and internal improvements,
185; and Jefferson Day dinner (1830), 195; as
Kentucky Court of Appeals chief justice,
283*n*5; and Kentucky Insurance Company,
63–64; law practice of, 263; and relation-
ship between Calhoun and Jackson, 197; as
secretary of the treasury in Tyler adminis-
tration, 263; in U.S. Congress, 94, 183, 186,
263; and War of 1812, 288*n*26; Washington,
D.C. residence of, 93
Biddle, Charles, 310*n*11
Biddle, Nicholas, 187, 188, 226–28
Billiards, 280*n*3
Bird, Henry, 17
Blackburn, Rev. Gideon, 293*nn*17–18
Blacks. *See* Free blacks; Slavery
Blair, Francis, 196, 197, 200, 210, 237, 254
Blair, James, 278*n*8
Bledsoe, Jesse, 25, 74
Bledsoe, William, 45, 46, 277–78*n*18
Blount, William, 88, 286*n*3
Blount, Willie, 88
Blount faction, 88, 90, 131–32, 139–46, 159–63,
176, 214
Boone, Daniel, 281*n*16
Bowers, Claude G., 313*n*6
Boyce's Executors v. Grundy, 165–66, 301*n*2
Bradford, John O., 236
Bradley, William A., 218
Branch, John, 202
Breckinridge, John: as attorney general of
U.S., 67, 243; and banking privileges for